COVERT OPERATIONS UNVEILING ORGANIZED CRIME

New York Police Department "cop doc" Dr. Dan Rudofossi delves into what it meant to live as a deep-cover operative through narratives with Joe Pistone, the FBI agent who spent six years living as Donnie Brasco as a member of the Bonanno crime family. When Operation Donnie Brasco abruptly closed, it was the longest and most successful infiltration of a Mafia family. Dr. Rudofossi underscores Pistone's genius to survive daily challenges of infiltration by using innovations in the ecological niches of Mafia violence. Donnie Brasco's "mental toughness," resilience, and ingenuity are understood through Rudofossi's signature *Eco-Ethological Existential Analysis*. Mapping out why and how trauma shaped functional dissociation as unconscious adaptation, the author's experience as a police psychologist—that is, a "cop doc"—helps decode the bigger picture of conflict, resolution, and compromise in the disparate worlds of policing and organized crime. This unique look at the costs and successes of tracking, infiltrating, arresting, and convicting those involved in organized crime is a groundbreaking read for law enforcement personnel, criminal justice, homeland security, law students, police psychologists, as well as anyone fascinated by the world of organized crime.

Dr. Daniel M. Rudofossi, as licensed psychologist and police sergeant (NYPD Ret.), is an active police surgeon for Amtrak Police—FOP NY. Dr. Rudofossi's guides range from assessing and treating complex PTSD to terrorism's impact, to working with mentally ill persons on the street. Dr. Rudofossi's extensive experience as a professor and clinician segues into his professional forums on police and public safety complex PTSD, grief, and dissociative disorders, as his integrative therapeutic approach—the *Eco-Ethological Existential Analytic Method*—is gaining acceptance by universities, police departments, and clinicians. He is the only cop doc to open the vista he forged with FBI Special Agent Joe D. Pistone, which you have in your hands.

"July 27, 1981 – the FBI ended its six-year undercover operation against the American Mafia. The primary Undercover Agent was me, Special Agent Joseph D. Pistone. Seventeen trials in Federal Courts throughout the United States of America followed, with the results of the investigation: the beginning of the downfall of the American Mafia.

"For six years of my life, I spent each year as an Undercover Special Agent of Hoover's Federal Bureau of investigation. To the Mafia I was Donnie Brasco: to my peers, FBI Special Agent Pistone. After many hours and interviews speaking with Doctor Dan Rudofossi, I must say that he captured my thoughts, feelings and 'mind-set' perfectly. I can relate to Dr. Rudofossi as a Cop and Cop Doc: For me, our work on exploring my experience and mind-set through existential analysis is key to how and why I adapted my mental toughness and resilience using an Eco-Ethological Existential Analysis. My deepest appreciation for all you do to help our Brothers and Sisters in Blue as our True Blue Cop Doc Dan Rudofossi!"

—**Special Agent Joseph D. Pistone FBI**

"*Covert Operations Unveiling Organized Crime: Using Operation Donnie Brasco to Understand the Complex Trauma of Deep Cover* is an eye opener. The thing for me, as a first-grade detective, is it's not during the rush of the ring side fight, but it's when the boxing stops that all hell is let loose. It is in the prison of our 'mind-set' that gets many of us deep covers under and down for the count. Dr. Rudofossi has educated us to 'addiction to trauma' when the ceiling falls in on you and crushes your soul. That 'quantum psychic moment of trauma', as he calls it, is set in the ecological niche where the motivation of survival rides high in the saddle. Working on understanding this complexity, for me, is brought to life in the chapters that follow as Special Agent Pistone and Cop Dr. Rudofossi chart out their own Ecological-Ethological Existential Analysis. Unfreezing being stuck as the ability to help us who are traumatized with a difference made in some victim, witness, survivor and even as he boldly shares, some unique Wiseguy's life – redemption is possible."

—**NYPD First Grade Detective Tommy Dades,** *author of bestselling* **Friends of the Family: The inside story of the Mafia Cops Case**

COVERT OPERATIONS UNVEILING ORGANIZED CRIME

Using Operation Donnie Brasco to Understand the Complex Trauma of Deep Cover

Dr. Daniel M. Rudofossi, Psy.D., Ph.D.

NEW YORK AND LONDON

Cover image: © Getty Images

First published 2023
by Routledge
605 Third Avenue, New York, NY 10158

and by Routledge
4 Park Square, Milton Park, Abingdon, Oxon, OX14 4RN

Routledge is an imprint of the Taylor & Francis Group, an informa business

© 2023 Daniel M. Rudofossi

The right of Daniel M. Rudofossi to be identified as author of this work has been asserted in accordance with sections 77 and 78 of the Copyright, Designs and Patents Act 1988.

All rights reserved. No part of this book may be reprinted or reproduced or utilised in any form or by any electronic, mechanical, or other means, now known or hereafter invented, including photocopying and recording, or in any information storage or retrieval system, without permission in writing from the publishers.

Trademark notice: Product or corporate names may be trademarks or registered trademarks, and are used only for identification and explanation without intent to infringe.

ISBN: 978-1-032-20275-4 (hbk)
ISBN: 978-1-032-20273-0 (pbk)
ISBN: 978-1-032-20276-1 (ebk)

DOI: 10.4324/9781032202761

Typeset in Bembo
by codeMantra

CONTENTS

Foreword by Special Agent, FBI Ret. Joseph Dominick Pistone — *vii*
Foreword by 1st Grade Detective, NYPD, Tommy Dades — *ix*
Acknowledgments — *xiii*

    Introduction — 1

1 Toward Understanding Process, Ingenuity, and Stealth Under Deep Cover — 8

2 Genius in Motion: Becoming Donnie Brasco — 23

3 Patronizing—Police, Mafia, and Family: Eco-Ethological Triangulation — 50

4 Boundaries in Mafia Culture: Totem and Taboos — 72

5 Active Analysis and Adaptive Functional Dissociation: Intuitive Ingenuity — 100

6 Dialogue, Insight, and Discovery—A Canopy of Shadows and Hues — 120

7 Disenfranchised Losses and Complex PTSD—*Eco-Ethological Existential Analysis* — 151

    Epilogue—Future of No Illusions: Centurioncide (Complex Traumatic Loss and Dissociation) — 191

Index — *207*

FOREWORD BY SPECIAL AGENT, FBI RET. JOSEPH DOMINICK PISTONE

Former teacher, US Naval Intelligence Officer, author, and the most prolific and ingenious FBI special agent to master the organizational, intelligence, and operational domain of the world, cultural-anthropology, and psychology of the Mafia, as a special agent, Joe Dominick Pistone spent six years of doing deep cover under the created identity of Donnie Brasco. His experience was uniquely framed and cultivated by the ingenuity of Special Agent Pistone. Keep in mind Donnie Brasco was born in and under the leadership of FBI Director J. Edgar Hoover, which itself was a feat, most legendary in the context of his historic leadership of the FBI. History and narrative elucidate and capture in an artful way the scientific insights and lessons learned from Joseph Dominick Pistone that is sorely needed. For he is not only a genius who has created many constructive results, but in my opinion as a cop doc for three decades of my own life, I find Special Agent Pistone's life work is a national treasure. In a small part, bringing to fruition the results and insights of his own professional and personal dynamics to emulate is of critical importance. Further, writing this book in Joseph Dominick Pistone's lifetime is equally important. Credibility and affirmation of Joe Pistone as legendary is reflective of truth as expressed and supported in his own words, with veracity, ingenuity, and commitment as insights "unveiled."

July 27, 1981, the FBI ended its six-year undercover operation against the American Mafia. The primary undercover agent was me, Special Agent Joseph D. Pistone.

I had no idea Operation Donnie Brasco would propel me into the spotlight for years to come: seventeen trials in federal courts throughout the United States of America. The results of the investigation were the beginning of the downfall of the American Mafia.

For six years of my life, I spent each year as an undercover special agent of Hoover's Federal Bureau of Investigation. I was in the Mafia as Donnie Brasco and away from my family. My absences resulted in me missing my children's birthdays, graduations, and first Holy Communion. Resilience and my faith kept me intact as Doc Dan Rudofossi and I explore in our interviews and dialogue.

Many people ask me a poignant question, "how did the six years change me?" My answer is, "it" did not. I never lost my core values or beliefs. I attribute that to my mental toughness and the ability to stay focused on the task at hand.

After many hours speaking with Doctor Dan Rudofossi, I must say that he captured my thoughts, feelings, and "mindset" perfectly. Dr. Dan was a cop doc on the job after being a street cop with 200-plus collars before completing his two master's degrees and doctorate while on the job, and doing the job. I can relate to him as one of my brothers in blue and as a cop and cop doc. Doc, thank you for putting my ideas and thoughts to the printed page. Thank you again for describing my ***identity modes*** and not altered personality or simplistic notions as role plays and play-acting. Your framing my identity, which was not split but adaptative functional dissociation with identity mode shifts motivated within different niches of ecological demands and survival motivation, makes perfect sense and is helpful and respectful to deep-cover operatives.

For me, our work on exploring my experience and mindset through existential analysis is on point and covered the differences in the wiseguys as well, which is key toward how and why I adapted using my mental toughness and resilience with faith and belief in my ability to get the job done as it unfolded. You understand and present my mindset and feelings as only you could in your assessment using an *Eco-Ethological Existential Analysis*!

My deepest appreciation for all you do to help our brothers and sisters in blue and just being the cop doc: true blue cop doc Dan Rudofossi!

Yours in friendship always,

Special Agent Joseph D. Pistone, FBI

FOREWORD BY 1ST GRADE DETECTIVE, NYPD, TOMMY DADES

Detective 1st Grade, NYPD, Thomas Dades as pugilist/Golden Glove boxer, athlete, and brilliant investigator was legendary for many reasons, not the least his ability to punch his way out of bureaucratic tangles and open up on one hand the blue walls of silence within the NYPD, and the ruses, beguiling, and cached nature of the criminal syndicate. Obfuscated in all his roads to the truth being murder, and the murderers in cold cases left dormant was Det. Dades' hawkish eyes and third ear of detection. His ingenuity, pugnacity, and integrity to doggedly pursue corruption led to the arrest and conviction of two notorious wiseguys. These wiseguys hid undercover as they led double lives as NYPD detectives of note, and at the same time deep-sixed innocent and not-so-innocent associates, related to Casso's competing Mafia families. Det. Dades' heroism and dogged detective work speak volumes to his emotional and intellectual prowess, including calling on his colleague in the FBI, Special Agent Joseph D. Pistone, to share his expertise along with Michael Vecchione, Chief of Brooklyn DA, as a complex and successful prosecution of cold cases of murder where the hitman double-dipped in murder and betrayal of our shared gold shields. The doll of the city payroll palled behind Anthony Casso's payroll, as the conflict between shield of police and shielding Mafia captains was only semantic at best for Louie Ippolito and Steve Caracappa as NYPD detectives whose sham led to chagrin for all who don our shield. In connection with Det. Tommy Dades, it is in his inimitable words with Special Agent Joe D. Pistone that a striking existential realization is brought to light: "Louie Ippolito was born into a Mafia family and actually was able to become a police officer." Truth be told, perhaps if he did not slip backward into the cultural shield of his family, he likely would have become another bulwark in the shield against crime so many of us in the NYPD and FBI have lost our lives for. It is tragic that Ippolito and Caracappa chose the path they did. It is unforgettable that the courage, determination, and integrity of Det. Tommy Dades' ingenuity broke down all barriers and two of NYPD's worst were taken off the streets by one of NYPD's finest, bravest, brilliant, and best!

Author of Dades, T., Vecchione, M., & Fischer, D. (2009). Friends of the family: The inside story of the mafia cops' case. New York: Harper and Collins Publishers.

Foreword by 1st Grade Detective, NYPD, Tommy Dades

Covert Operations Unveiling Organized Crime will help the clueless who are not first responders understand the complexity of what even first responders don't fully understand. It is an eye-opener.

Pause as you consider patrol, investigations, and emergency police work—adrenaline rushes flood each division. For me as a 1st Grade detective who figured out Det. Louis Eppolito and Det. Stephen Caracappa were not the detective cop aces that captured and put wiseguys away, but the rogue cops with shields that worked as Mafia hitmen while donning their medals of honor, the rush and punch of it all felt like the rewinding of reverberations as a Golden Glove boxer at knock-out time, and I have felt what that is like many times. The thing is, for me, as a detective who has seen it all, it's not during the rush of the ring-side fight, but it's when the boxing stops all hell is let loose. It is in the prison of our "mindset" that gets many of us deep covers under and down for the count. Dr. Rudofossi has educated us to "addiction to trauma" when the ceiling falls in on you and crushes your soul. That "quantum psychic moment of trauma," as he calls it, is set in the ecological niche where the motivation of survival rides high in the saddle.

In my 20-plus years from a naive rookie beating the concrete to a peppered collaring 1st Grade detective in my dealing with wiseguys, I experienced what our cop doc calls "disenfranchised losses" that traumatize me and many others as detectives. Take the cold cases which remain unfinished business. Even when done well, some aspect of our victims and even perps remain as ghosts in psychological corridors in the trauma scars we hold in our memories. Dr. Rudofossi unravels and defines reality with the best detective alive today, Special Agent Joe Pistone. Personalities of wiseguys are seen as different as they really are, ranging from "almost being genteel men" born into the culture of "this thing of ours" who could have been great businessmen, yet on the other hand are seen as cold-blooded killers who whack you and say don't take "It" personal.

Professor Dr. Rudofossi's odyssey with Special Agent Joe Pistone aka Donnie Brasco captures a real understanding and education of what the real deal of detective work is. No fantasy yarn here, he offers an assessment and healing of what adaptation and maladaptation is and how it occurs under the covers of deep cover. Doc's book will help all first responders open up to understanding a world pumped up by way too many adrenaline rushes. For me on a personal level, at the time I found my never-give-up detective style to be a good feeling. A feeling that was similar to stepping into a boxing ring. I enjoyed it all. But when you no longer are in police work or a boxing ring and don't feel that rush, that is when that "trauma-drama" as Dr Rudofossi calls "It," emerges. "It" is the trauma as being framed in the ecological niches and with survival motivation that stirs you inside.

The working on understanding this complexity for me is brought to life in the chapters that follow as Special Agent Pistone and Cop Dr. Rudofossi chart out their own *Ecological-Ethological Existential Analysis*. It's real as your mind starts to wander sometimes in directions that aren't making you feel good, including the differences in dealing with wiseguys who in some ways, as he put it, are all too human. Some wiseguys, we discover, are born to be "bad guys," but others hatch in that ecology and survival motivation as ethological with their own existential losses left in the dark as I have come to understand. Long-time service and then an abrupt end is a loss which causes trauma when we stop doing detective work. Unfreezing being stuck is helped in the existential analysis Dr. Rudofossi has etched in as the ability to help us who are traumatized and leave our marks by making a difference in some victim, witness, survivor, and even, as he boldly shares, some unique wiseguy's life. Redemption is possible. As a first responder, as Cop Doc Rudofossi and Special Agent Joe Pistone know all too well, as do I, our calling and being "on the job" is unique. It is truly a spiritual calling, just like a long hitch in the armed forces.

When it's over, nothing can replace that feeling you had while in service of our city as a cop or our country as a soldier.

I keep in touch with a lot of the guys and gals I worked with in the NYPD, DEA, and FBI, as we are like-minded officers. We are all are on the same page nowadays that the lack of respect that the public feels toward law enforcement in general is offset by this book as Dr. Rudofossi educated me and many other officers that our humanity and compassion is sometimes hidden from us as much as the public. I love it and Cop Doc Rudofossi and Special Agent Joe Pistone for sharing this story with the world and taking away the unjust and distorted stereotypes of who we are, why we do what we do. That takes courage and, as Joe says it well, tough-mindedness!

If you never did it, you can't talk about "It." The missed holidays, the long hours, being super protective, it all takes a toll. But I wouldn't trade my time in it for anything. It brings out who you really are! I spent 20-plus years in the NYPD and retired a 1st Grade Detective, plus 4 years as an investigator with the Brooklyn District Attorney's Office. I worked for the Police Athletic League as a boxing coach. I saw redemption in the kids from the broken homes that came around in becoming boxers like me. I wouldn't trade those years for anything.

Joe Coffee said it best at his retirement, "Thank you for a front row seat to the greatest show on the earth." Open the real interviews of Special Agent Joseph Dominick Pistone and Cop Doc Dan Rudofossi as you see what it means to survive deep cover under the covers.

Thomas Dades, Detective 1st Grade, NYPD

ACKNOWLEDGMENTS

First, and in profound appreciation for my ability to have survived and grown in my faith in the highest being—the highest spiritual force, G–d!

I often reflect, as many greater folks than I have said, "There go I, but for the grace of G–d, go I!"

It has been my good fortune to have so many blessings that follow, but of all grace is my soulmate, my wife Brachah, and my kids, sisters, and extended family members. My patients and students, which include of course scores of police, special agents, and others in public and private service.

Thank you Ms. Ellen Boyne, Chief Acquisition Editor at Routledge, who stood by in making this possible in the first place! Much gratitude to Ms. Kate Taylor for guiding me in your inimitable and superb manner in my first book written for the United Kingdom branch, as my earlier books are on the other side in the United States. The joint collegial style of Ms. Boyne and Ms. Taylor was seamless and emboldening in allowing my own creative written expression peppered with a pinch of sanguinity.

In this book I will forgo the merit-worthy accolades of my mentors and many others who paved the way for wisdom and insight with responsibility. You all know my profound respect and valuing of each of you!

I honor and respect two inspiring souls that are now passed into the world of souls: my beloved mother, interior designer Sally Sarah, and beloved father as violinist/poet, Harry Julius, a combat veteran with four ribbons USN. Also my grandfather Morris, an infantryman in World War I, US Army, who fought under General Pershing and brought warmth and love in my life, and my grandmother, Alto Bella, whose beautiful soul was taken too early. I salute your courage, humanity, and friendship! Biala Rebbe, thank you for your timeless noetic wisdom!

In partnership with the finest officer-patients, I owe my education and wisdom I am still learning from, by each of you. Each journey hopefully enlightened your path as it did mine! To cop doc peers paving new roads without forgetting our own beaten paths! To my students at NYU, and St John's University, and NYPD the brightest and finest—the best alongside the DEA and FBI agents!

Special Agent Joseph Dominick Pistone, whose genius enlightened me and all the readers who have this wonderful account of discovery, inspiration, and indomitable courage, you shine on us all as a true-blue American hero! Salute Special Agent Joseph Dominick Pistone, brother in blue, always my respect and gratitude shines in each page of this tome for the courage and brilliance you've lived and I have had the privilege of being the clinician and cop doc to explore with you!

INTRODUCTION

Operation Donnie Brasco—Uncovering Resilience and Ingenuity Within Deep Cover

The book in your hand is written as a casebook. Through real narratives, a clinician as police forensic psychologist and a special agent of the Federal Bureau of Investigation (FBI) uncover myths, totems, and taboos within three worlds: the world of law enforcement, the world of the deep cover, and the world of the organized criminal enterprise. This was no easy task. My casebook outlines the mindset of a special agent who overcame formidable challenges by entering the culture of organized crime with remarkable success.

The casebook encapsulates a series of interviews, probing questions, and a willingness by both participants to sketch out a significant psychologically informative and criminological understanding that has not been done before.

Our narrative is recorded and transformed into seven chapters highlighting forensic and police psychology, criminology, and criminal justice issues. Coordinates map out the history of how Joe Pistone singularly achieved deep cover into the Mafia. His intelligence and operational success is a conduit within law enforcement and joint prosecutors' bridges that heralded and offers the promise of unheard-of success.

Students in the fields of criminal justice, law, homeland security, and criminal and forensic psychology will be able to gain from this learning experience. In my tenure as a cop doc in the New York Police Department (NYPD) and the Drug Enforcement Administration (DEA), I developed heuristic approaches to clinically assess, treat, and note the progress and regress of mental and behavioral health in officers and special agents. I have written clinician's guides, and in educating students I have written casebooks. One such successful casebook is *Cop Doc: The Police Psychologist's Casebook—Narratives from Police Psychology* (Routledge, 2017).

This casebook offers the student reader material to learn from and gain much ground for lessons about field police and investigative work. In learning motivation, a key to opening up students' minds is not only the historic and novel experiences that emerge in our interviews, but perspective. The subject matter of interest that coheres to what students and their professors have a burning interest in, without risk of being burned by that interest, is to understand the risks, the choices, and the consequences of real deep-cover work. Mindfulness is woven across the lattice of the culture of law enforcement, the distinct micro-culture within law enforcement of deep-cover operatives, and crossing into the subculture of the "gangsters." The concoction is a mix of the special agent doing deep cover in an ecological niche where culture and survival ethologically shape violence, and rules of the Mafia dominate. Doing deep cover requires fitting in. Fitting in to a Mafia-dominated culture is not a swing shift, a mood swing, and not a rotating tour—it is a 24 hour by 7 day a week task for the deep-cover agent.

Adaptation and survival cannot be taught in a textbook, but we will examine what can be gained in an academic setting that enlightens and bridges gaps in our understanding of deep cover.

The Mafia and police deep cover are all about setting up walls. The blue wall of silence in police circles is within the bond of loyalty of one's law enforcement unit. Omertà, as a wall of silence or face death in the Mafia, is a blood loyalty. Both ask the members to be willing to take a bullet for one another rather than be labeled and put in the bull's-eye of being a "rat."

Such boundaries are interesting studies in semantics, where a "rat" in police circles is a snitch who gives away the secrets of police inner circles. In the Mafia a "rat" is a snitch who talks to police and is an informer. In policing, an Internal Affairs undercover officer who "acts as if she is a member of the unit and gathers information on corruption, brutality, or sabotage of the integrity of the police department is also a snitch, aka a "rat."

The sociological, anthropological, and most pressing psychological costs to the individual officer/special agent is paralleled in looking into the impact on the boss or capo di tutti and underboss within each organized crime Mafia family. In practice, the mafioso family hierarchy at the time of Operation Donnie Brasco included the Bonannos, Colombos, Gambinos, Balistrieris, and Genoveses. In each respective family, larger cultural differences and demands shaped conflict and competition. In a way, this shaping primed ethological motivation and survival value on the streets and in the parlors, bars, and markets where business was done—including the infamous "sit-downs." Parallels in law enforcement exist as in the small and tighter units, such as organized crime units in city locations to larger field divisions.

Boundary setting is not apparent even to those who attempt to crack the atomic code of explicit rules for the wiseguy, the deep cover, and the overall societal rules where motivation is the most important ingredient of success or failure. Rules are crucial and must be learned in subtle ways. Deeper rules emerge as you read and learn from the narrative style Special Agent Joe Pistone and I work through. Complex and implicit laws and regulations in the Mafia, the police, and investigative operations are fleshed out in each chapter.

Centering deep cover directs attention to ignored emotional and ethologically shaped motivation. Ethological means motivation, where human beings are primed for survival within the context of biological, ecological, and animalistic niches. Using Goleman's construct, emotional intelligence for our purpose is redirected to grounding ability and skillful adaptation to fit into an emotional-ethological niche where life and death is caught in a furtive glance, a challenging frown, or a bellow beyond a belch. Boundaries are replete in doing deep cover. The boundaries set are invisible on one hand, with deception by camouflage, and fitting in by another "as-if" one is a "born killer." It is often called infiltration, but together with Special Agent Joe Pistone and Donnie Brasco, I will examine that word and the hypothetical construct that is implied.

After all, this book is not about repeating lessons already known by students and repetitively taught in the world of academic criminal justice. Yet the psychology of what is not apparent, and is even unconscious, to the officer and associates in the Mafia is amenable to an understanding in academia. A sorely needed infusion to keep you as students aligned and educated as to the real deep-cover world is bridged in and through assignments given in the casebook. Such assignments help your professor ask incisive questions, and in the ecological niche of the specific class can also be expanded upon into a novel dynamic for the readers and instructor to explore.

Questions Emerge

What is the impact on those who live by tracking, infiltrating, arresting, and convicting gangsters? In attempting to answer some of these questions, more will arise and some will remain unanswered and spur research for students with expert faculty to guide them.

The other side of the world of the gangsters is the world of the law enforcement officer uniquely walking the tightrope, not of assuming another identity, but living as the person they discover within their own style as the deep-cover identity. This is what will be offered in this casebook, along with my *Ecological-Ethological Existential Analytic Approach* to deep cover.

Readers, I address you as students having predilections for specialized information. Intelligence is seriously covered here and is useful and applicable, an example being how and why homicide investigations can be understood much better by gaining an understanding of the impact of witnessing violence in the extreme as a deep cover and surviving emotionally and mentally. Indeed, there are those who are specialists in investigations, homeland security and law enforcement, and law, as well as psychology/psychiatry and allied health fields interested in the applicability of a book on deep cover, not only for their own developing growth theoretically, but for application as an allied professional. Dialogue as interaction, and bonds transcending being a gangster and special agent/detective in real time are assessed and understood in a cultural, ecological, and ethological context for criminal justice students. Deals are made in the interest of breaking a case, and it benefits the law enforcement officer and the guy who is wise at times in ways that are untapped and undetected, save a pause and peek. Lessons and summaries are given context and importance within each chapter with key terms highlighted in boxes and descriptions of concepts for use in criminal justice and criminology classes.

The mission of an agent asked to break a case, as for the criminal who commits specific crimes, has one converging point unheard and unspoken: "It." Instead of leaving out entire contexts and the losses and biopsychosocial context of criminal behavior and dealing with "It" from the different worlds of law enforcement and prosecution, organized crime and defense attorneys, and the deep cover and Mafia associate, ecological ground in which survival is primed is given words, conceptual foundations, and understanding: paradigmatic shifts where classification and hypothetical constructs replace ignorance and enforced silence are presented.

Insight and responsibility replace indifference and bravado as education makes clearer inroads into the unspoken psychological experiences of all involved.

Presidents of the United States swaying from different poles of politics have all spoken of Donnie Brasco as the representative of effective detective skill and impact on crime, perhaps more so than any other law enforcement officer in the history of the Federal Bureau of Investigation. From the drab bank robber to the stealthy domestic terrorist, Donnie Brasco has been mentioned and is known.

But the real Special Agent Joseph Dominick Pistone, who is better known as a celebrity special agent of the elite Federal Bureau of Investigation unit, is who I am privileged to work with here. What is factual is that Special Agent Pistone's prowess and legendary success and true ability to successfully live as a wiseguy for six years within the toughest of all crime families of the Mafia, the Gambino and then Bonanno families of La Cosa Nostra, is not presented in this book as poetic or psychodramatic.

This casebook will assess and offer the criminal justice and forensic psychology student the real stalwart special agent of the FBI, whose extraordinary odyssey had no time out and debriefing sessions as he crafted a new identity across many fronts and impasses with success. Challenging beyond what most tenured combat veterans live through, Joe endured situations where life and death hung on a vendetta's sword. The slightest hint at being discovered was certain death.

Joe managed redirecting the framework in which he vitally changed directions to stave off certain death threats. Special Agent Pistone's "back-up" was his own ingenuity of coordinating his mind and body in a way that was not prescribed in any book or training manual. Joe initiated what he kept running on, which was his own "mental toughness." What "mental toughness" means is fleshed out in our dialogue throughout the book. Joe's "mental toughness" intersects with police ethics and psychology in dynamic and interesting motifs enlightening the anthropologically aware student. Behind the legend of Donnie Brasco, disposable and common myths are exposed for the student as unprofessional and wild speculation. For example, Donnie Brasco was not the greatest actor, playing a role. Donnie Brasco was Joe Pistone, and he lived with remarkable adaptation abilities and skills charted out in a biopsychosocial ecological-ethological context. My *Ecological-Ethological Existential Analysis* is presented in terms easily understood by students and taught by your professor. Examples come to life as we understand Joe Pistone's adaptations, shaped and responsive to ecological and cultural demands with a need to survive. Dissociation as an ingenious adaptation, used consciously and unconsciously by Joe Pistone as Donnie Brasco, is given much thought. That adaptation is framed in ecological niches as survival motivation. For example, understanding how Donnie Brasco existed and acted in Mafia circles is given a context biopsychologically as an adaptative functional dissociation. Joe's ability to adaptively functionally dissociate is not without many dangers, illustrated in the chapter covering this remarkable agility. "It" cannot be undone, and perhaps ever repeated again.

The ability Donnie Brasco arguably employed heuristically for six years was exactly the right synergy of performance at an active and engaged level of emotional, hard-wired, and dynamic intelligence. Educating criminal justice students of key dynamics and special sociological and anthropological issues summarized as dissociation is given context in these allied fields of clinical and forensic psychology. Biases and misunderstood aspects about Special Agent Joe Pistone's definitive work on technical aspects and operational effectiveness is redirected to the science of psychological analysis and criminal justice theory and practice.

Joe Pistone's legendary work as a deep-cover agent practitioner is transformed into clearer segues into the "why," "how," "when," and "where" to succeed doing the nuts and bolts of deep-cover operations. Arguably, Special Agent Joseph Pistone is an outlier in law enforcement operations and military intelligence. Outliers are well worth understanding. In reality, an outlier nowadays may be tested, and the bounds of restrictions and impositions that failed to challenge the threat of organized crime until Joe Pistone succeeded may be breached more often if lessons are learned. In the final chapter in the book, we discuss how the war on organized crime is much more sophisticated and complex nowadays. Lessons that are relevant, reliable, and most effective are brought to light for applied wisdom culled from Operation Donnie Brasco's success as a "tipping point."

In my own sphere of interaction with Joe Pistone, I lay out a navigational tool by looking at the culture, macro- and micro-level interactions, and dynamics that create interactions for effective law enforcement intervention, postvention, and later, looking back, suggestions for prevention of organized crime monopolies and takeovers. The taking away of lessons is within a conventional style of learning with students in each chapter. However, the distilling of each lesson is built on the flow of one lesson and chapter into the next. Operational definitions are offered as heuristic boundaries for the student of criminal justice and forensic psychology to observe and confirm and disconfirm, as fixed rules are too concrete from a case study and field observational layout.

The foundation given in this book to a formal student or one who is simply interested in this unique field, whether a new student or an advanced graduate student, provides ideas and lessons to be gained in plain prose and narrative discourse.

Conflict is identified and graphed within the subtler approaches of deep-cover resolution. Compromise formations are achieved by paying attention to and delineating how and why pauses were acted on. We trace and decipher the cognitive-emotive and behavioral map Joe Pistone innovated in his identity as a gangster in the Bonanno crime family. It is in the details of Joe's highly individualized work within law enforcement that a novel bridge between the world of policing and organized crime was established, with lawful and effective intervention. This success is a case study of Operation Donnie Brasco through the mindset of the special agent who did it. It is also a larger casebook of academic rigor focusing on applied investigative and intelligence operations that you as a student can and will learn from.

Looked at from a cultural-anthropologic paradigm in the tradition of Mead, Boas, and Joseph Campbell, the odyssey of Operation Donnie Brasco was achieved most remarkably by a pioneer with the tenacity and intellect to succeed. This is part of the contextual foundation woven into the narrative. As transformed in this way, a very different story is told of how Joe Pistone, with the rich historic and unique dynamics of becoming an observing-participant as participant observer, developed from a street-smart naval intelligence officer into a special agent in the FBI who fit in and shaped the longest successful infiltration into two of the five Mafia families. The bridges he created have not been disclosed, and our *Eco-Ethological Existential Analysis* is explored within the conceptual world of psychology and cultural anthropology from a biopsychosocial paradigm. Joseph Dominick Pistone, who became and survived as none other than Donnie Brasco, which was his own creation, is a study in itself in personality dynamics and identity consolidation and identity modes in adaptive functional and maladaptive functional dissociative processes. Entering into Little Italy's enclave and living "as if" he was a small-time thief and etching himself into and on the teetering edge of being "made" by the new soon-to-be capo of the Bonanno crime family, Sonny Black Napolitano, was a ritual of coming of age within the Mafia subculture itself. This developmental path with the dynamic complexity deserves understanding by students seeking to explore and become criminal justice students and practitioners. This is also framed in rich psychodynamic, existential, and anthropologically informed understanding for students to process and perhaps explore in other venues.

Special Agent Pistone as a pioneer was quite aware on a cognitive, behavioral, and emotive level that the boundaries allowable by law enforcement and law limited his scope of deep cover. Yet Special Agent Pistone brokered deals intuitively and ingeniously to merge disparate Mafia families and bridge gaps not achieved by the wiseguys themselves. This is not written about in the context of clinical, forensic, and police psychology and criminal justice. However, it is fitting to point out that definitive works on deep-cover experiences and infiltrating the Mafia exist, and both have been done by Joe Pistone himself. This is placed in contextual and paradigm development for students and practitioners seeking to better understand La Cosa Nostra as "this thing of ours" being punctured by Joe Pistone creating his own niche within the toughest of ecological spaces and with the fiercest of survival motivation ethologically. This is a scientific account via narrative analysis.

Joe Pistone's trust and his stalwart commitment toward this book educating criminal justice and criminology students about Mafia and police culture as he experienced it makes this casebook merit-worthy. From biopsychosocial developmental, psychological, and clinical perspectives, students are guided in placing policing ingenuity, integrity, and creativity in a historic, as well as scientific, perspective. Joe Pistone was and is a creative genius in the conceptual paradigm of my clinical and research experience. Finally, Joe Pistone's vision transcended his own cultural and ecological-ethological niche within his own unit of Organized Crime Counter Intelligence and Operations, the FBI, the larger law enforcement culture, the Mafia culture and rules, and the local syndicates pierced by his operation.

Punctuating the boundaries of practice is framed as an anomaly that was not accidental, but heuristically planned as it emerges in a Socratic-friendly but disciplined series of our interviews. Ingenious risks that were calculated for success were tried and refined in a sophisticated manner. Joe Pistone's contributions and successes and errors in Operation Donnie Brasco are still being evidenced today.

Credibility as Clinician Practitioner Researcher and Academic Professor

Who am I to dare break into this undisclosed information with Joseph Dominick Pistone? As a retired law enforcement officer nowadays, but quite active in the 1980s, I became a rookie NYPD police officer in 1987, and was initiated by gunfire to the brutality of drug peddling and violent crime. Crime was on the high-rise, with vicious drive-by assassinations of one gang mob leader by another. Police officers and special agents fell tragically, too young and way too fast, in the asphalt layers of dreams and illusions known as the Big Apple where, incidentally, Joe Pistone worked the Mafia and I the beats of New York streets.

Pausing, it would be a mistake to include the organized crime families as thugs tossed in with street gangs or terrorists. La Cosa Nostra is, and was, much more than disorganized drive-by shooter gangs, or even, for that matter, street thugs with order and a blueprint. It is true that violence and vengeance can be almost unparalleled when Mafia hits are made. But there is a difference!

The cultural nuances and history of each Mafia family is viewed as having its own ecological and ethological niche steeped in survival and adaptation. Survival in an ecology where murder rates were outdone in New York and particularly three of the five boroughs was fact in the late 1980s to early 1990s. Donnie Brasco had to survive with and part of six years under the threat of some of the infamous butchers as they were called by their peers. I was entrusted by Joseph Pistone to tell the psychological and biopsychosocial layout of his experiences with the goal of education and a realistic understanding to learn from for students desiring his accumulated wisdom. As a tenured clinician, my challenge was and is to present a trustworthy understanding of cumulative trauma, complex loss, and bereavement with ingenuity to survive by a law enforcement investigative special agent of the FBI, who learned and lived under the leadership of J. Edgar Hoover.

By looking at the psychology of murder and silence in an organized crime family, groundbreaking intelligence for police, clinical psychologists, psychiatrists, and criminal justice students and administrators to learn prevention and postvention is delivered. Opening up trauma and loss with the most successful deep-cover agent in the history of the FBI is growth and progress for recruits and students into the world of law enforcement. The tactical moves and strategic planning open new avenues of investigation as research students can gain in graduate work to follow.

The style of each chapter opens up with an introduction to the topic highlighted. Ongoing dialogue flows with discipline as Special Agent Joseph Dominick Pistone and Cop Doc Dan Rudofossi interact. Each chapter ends with a Forensic Psych Cop Doc Corner proffering insight by tackling unexplored problems, misperceived assumptions about motives and ingenuity, and other issues unknown and now explored as working hypotheses. All our conversations were reviewed by Joseph Pistone as veridical and respectful presentations. The balance of law enforcement on one hand, and the conservation of mental health in a criminal justice paradigm is consistently delivered.

Finally, this guide fits you if you are a forensic, police, general psychology, sociology, anthropology, homeland security/criminology student, professional, or, of course, professor.

Four cultures—undercover investigators, organized crime and American La Cosa Nostra, prosecutors and police, administrators and legislators impacting on law enforcement professionals—are given space in our narrative and layout, with a special sensitivity for you the reader as a student, whatever level you are at presently.

It is my goal to make this casebook relevant, useful, and broad enough to educate participants and observers impacted by policing and deep-cover operations, as well as my core audience as students as I mentioned above.

For professors, the following note is for you: this book demonstrates the applicability of using my *Eco-Ethological Existential Analysis* principles in clinically challenging situations that include different crime families within the Mafia, as extraordinarily unfamiliar to American and European readers, but poignant, as relevant as death, murder, and the psychological sequelae of such harsh trauma and loss emerge.

The transformation of the information in narrative form is done in a seamless manner for students to read in casebook format which segues and complements a textbook approach. The casebook can be a core requirement in academic courses for new students with one year of criminal justice core curriculum to advanced graduate students. Finally, as suggested, this could be adapted by small to huge police and public safety training academies in the US and UK with a potential for international use.

1

TOWARD UNDERSTANDING PROCESS, INGENUITY, AND STEALTH UNDER DEEP COVER

Introduction

This casebook offers a deeper psychological understanding of the behavior, passion, emotional investment, and mindset in doing undercover work. Forensic and police psychology as science serves as the foundation to understand the psychological context of what was known as Operation Donnie Brasco and carried out by Federal Bureau of Investigation Special Agent (FBI, SA) Joe Pistone.

This casebook will offer you as a student a better handle on the complexities, demands, and psychological, biosocial, and anthropological context of what an undercover investigator is, and is not. But let's first take a look at how this book is organized and how you can get the most out of the course you are taking. The layout in each chapter begins with an "**Introduction**" section, followed by some "**Questions to Guide You**" that serve as points of interest to guide your seeking answers in the text to follow. "**Key Terms**" are given to increase your knowledge and application of concepts fleshed out in the text as each new topic is covered and flows into another related topic. At the end of the chapter content area, you will be given a "**Summary**" that offers you a brief review of the major areas covered. In realizing that students need a special place to debrief, a "**Cop Doc Corner for Students Only**" will deliver an overview of what is to follow in the next chapter and some key psychological insights to place in your carry-bag as you travel in your own college campus. You will then be directed to a final section titled, "**Important Definitions and Concepts to Keep in Mind**," which gives you subtle additions to select definitions you've already been given within the chapter. The exciting part to come, in a section titled "**Conceptual and Writing Exercises for Student and Professor Only**," is you actually doing some research, including reviewing literature, magazine articles, and media presentations on related chapter topics designed to give you an edge in your understanding of deep-cover operations As with all good experiences, the end is a summary of citations used and is, of course, titled "**References**." I tend to use the references section as a means of offering further readings and ways to find out more information than this text offers. It is a great way to support your points of presentation, research, and development as a student. It is not required, but strongly advised that each student take an introductory course in forensic psychology and criminal justice before taking this advanced course on the psychology of deep-cover operations.

DOI: 10.4324/9781032202761-2

Returning to the contents of the casebook, you will note that the layout you are given is all about the fundamentals of learning about the acculturation and adaptation of a law enforcement officer into the world of deep cover. Deep cover is the ultimate in investigative operations. Most detectives who do outstanding police and investigative work will not make it into doing deep cover. But deep cover impacts on all levels of society that are "legitimate" and "illegitimate." You are aware this book focuses on the example and study of Operation Donnie Brasco. It is, as you already know, not a novel, not a history, not a yarn that captures the excitement and rush of what has already been done by Joe Pistone. I do not want to repeat what is original. I refer you, as a student, to read the books written by the ultimate observing participant and leader in understanding organized crime within the Mafia and La Cosa Nostra: the books written by Joseph Dominick Pistone will stand as definitive works of art, just as those by masters such as Pablo Picasso and Salvador Dali within the world of abstract art. Insofar as they are masterpieces, they cannot be imitated or replaced. Not now and not ever! Why? Because they transcended the *paradigms* in existence at the time their masterpieces were created. The work of Pistone and his wisdom also stand unique in the world of deep cover, espionage, and the education on the world of the gangster (Gardner, 1993; Goleman, 2005; May, 1994; Piaget, 2001).

My own motivation as a cop doc is that I care deeply for police and public safety officers' health and wellness (Orwell, 2005; Rudofossi, 1997, 2007, 2017). What I am offering is a unique vista as a cop doc, including a map of the mind and an understanding of the ingenuity of a quintessential gentleman and warrior.

Like all mortals, Pistone will move on, but his multidimensional complexity and ingenuity will be here on this journey of life for all who wear the shield. Further, this work will motivate you to pursue detective/investigative work as an undercover to deep cover, or for you to seek a different path for yourself.

Let's pause for a moment, and begin by looking at some questions as coordinates. These coordinates in each chapter, as in this first one, will guide our journey. If you accept my invitation to embark on "our odyssey" together, I proffer myself as your navigator.

So, kindly get ready to enter the cockpit as the pilot as we start filling our vessel of knowledge with our first case example to be traversed. As navigator, I will ask questions and you will ease into a pace that feels just right in finding the answers as you move forward. Let's move onward and forward as we begin exploring the following questions.

Questions to Guide You as Navigational Tools: Learning Objectives

1. What are "deep-cover operations" and how, if at all, are they different from "undercover operations" in the context of law enforcement and public safety culture?
2. What is a cop doc and what skills, education, and training are necessary to use this term as identifying oneself in the world of law enforcement?
3. Are there any parallels in the code of silence in the police world known as the "blue-wall" and the world of the organized crime members' code of silence?
4. What is meant by "compromise formation" in unconscious conflicts in the science of psychoanalytic science?
5. Can a committed law enforcement officer and an organized crime member both be influenced and impacted by unconscious drives and their resolution in "compromise formations"?
6. What is meant by tough-mindedness as a necessary way of doing deep cover in the world of infiltration of organized crime families, and who can this concept be attributed too?

Key Terms

Active listening
Adaptive functional dissociation
Compromise formation
Destrudo drive derivative
Eros drive derivative
Forensic assessment
Hypervigilance
Hypothetical constructs
Identity modes
Maladaptive functional dissociation
Noetic values
Paradigm

Hypothetical Constructs Framing the Foundation of Learning Deep Cover

Answering the above questions is best achieved by gaining an understanding of the major concepts and what psychologists, psychiatrists, other mental health professionals, and sociologists and criminologists use at times as *hypothetical constructs* (Kerlinger & Lee, 1999; Kitaeff, 2007). These constructs are the framework of theories, and for our purposes mean the less-known aspects of what becomes the driving force behind our understanding of events, people's behavior, cultural patterns, and personality within events, and the interactions that develop. Remember that, as scientists, it is important to observe and record in different ways what we observe by having a set of working definitions and ideally can measure in some way as we communicate with and among other scientists and folks that can use, and work with, our findings.

Hypothetical constructs are in part both the unconscious and conscious motivation underlying major processes we experience. As observers, we classify and define such major processes and seek to find what it is that gradually influences behavior, cognitions, and emotions as sharper and better-defined correlative factors. In the process of finding out the particular "how" and "what" that influence behavior, emotions, and cognitions, we also discern factors that motivate the answers as to the "why" of thoughts, behaviors, and emotional shifts and stability.

If we are able to prove with evidence repeatedly the sought after cause(s), or what is known as causality, then we have moved closer to defining and operationalizing the hypothetical constructs. With hypothetical constructs in mind, let's begin our understanding of deep cover within the context of Special Agent Pistone's experiences as a deep-cover FBI agent.

Deep Cover or Undercover Operations

Deep cover requires a police officer or special agent to fit in and become part of the group and subculture that is deviant from societal norms, mores, and customs they are asked to infiltrate. As you may imagine, this requires an unusually long period of time, energy, and resilience by the officer, who must work alone and without support during long duty periods. His/her own ability to deceive the group infiltrated is crucial. If his/her identity as a police officer/special agent is discovered, the consequence is highly likely being murdered in a special and excessively cruel manner. Deep cover is not a regular aspect of detective work; it is also not undercover investigative work.

Undercover investigative work is carried out routinely by police officers/special agents and public safety officers. The goal is to disguise their law enforcement identity while mingling in a crowd, group, or specific setting. *The task it to detect and arrest criminals, usually involved in brief acts of crime, and in a short, time-limited manner.* While undercover investigative work is dangerous and requires sophisticated skills, it is generally done in team approaches and is not nearly as dangerous as deep-cover operations (Conroy & Orthmann, 2014; Gilmartin, 2002).

Active Listening and Learning the Key Individual Differences from Special Agent Pistone

Pistone's becoming a member of a community that would murder (i.e., "whack") an associate for speaking too loosely with a law enforcement officer is not a single event of potential trauma and loss. It is the total of cumulative and divergent experiences of loss and trauma navigated without falling victim to the anhedonia most succumb to. Even those with constitutions as spartan as Joe's often do not have the Athenian diplomacy and sharp emotional and mental acuity he was born with and refined to the level of art wed to the science of being a sleuth. In trying to analyze what challenges Joe had to confront, one must first identify and adequately understand the fundamentals. Simplistic formulas that reduce masterpieces into a sketch or comparing Joe to an actor or an egregious wild card agent/detective amount to arrogance at best and mirror hateful stereotypes at worst.

Further, what Joe did was a masterpiece of multiple events and choices, each cascading with a tempo and alignment that could have been derailed with tragic death, not only Joe's, but of others involved. The term "infiltrating the mob" does not do justice to the challenges and adaptations that were necessary to undertake a creative endeavor such as Pistone accomplished in his day-to-day activities.

In the 1990s, operationalizing and analyzing my own method developed in the trenches of working with police and public safety officers, I developed what I called an *Eco-Ethological Existential Analysis* (Rudofossi, 1997, 2007). In my conversational interviews with Joe, I do what is critical and significant to Joe as a normal guy and a brother in blue, which is stop, pause, direct, and redirect as the navigator of the conversation as I empathically ensure accuracy in operationalizing the focal points as coordinated with my pilot as each chapter flows forward. My doctorates and master's degrees and experience of being a street cop myself gives me credibility to enter, respectfully, to learn and to express what is learned, but not to speculate.

My job is to examine, analyze, confirm, and disconfirm as far as conscious assessment allows me, and then to delve gently and collaboratively in reconstructing the gaps in the puzzle of doing an adequate job of uncovering the deep-cover agent/detective. In achieving much more than surviving for six years within the Bonanno, Gambino, Profaci, Gagliano, and Mangano families, which would be remarkable for a deep cover alone, what Donnie Brasco did can be seen through the lenses of forensic and police psychology.

Psychological Imagination, Outliers, and Anomaly as Markers in Operation Donnie Brasco

Ensuring the real Joseph Dominick Pistone is understood as a pioneer who crafted an innovation that was hitherto unknown and unexplored is crucial. The anomaly as outlier in his achievements is important in order to create a bridge of understanding to and from. As students, you will earn a grade if you complete this course well and adequately in your own competence. In the police department, if you are appointed as a detective, you can earn what is called grades: 1st signifies you achieved extraordinary status; 2nd is that you are an excellent investigator; and 3rd is you are rated as a can-do and good investigator. Pistone was a 1st Grade detective.

Throughout this book I will not hesitate to clarify and confront what is remarkable and inimitable in Joseph Dominick Pistone's willful and ever-resilient existential center. However, it has not been interpreted before as it will be using my approach: ecologically, ethologically, and dynamically rooted in derivatives of drives and schemas of cognitive awareness (Kagan, 2011, 2012, 2016). Making explicit some of those existential struggles hidden in what is called "noetic-values" in Joe's challenges is defined and made conscious (Frankl, 1979; Fromm, 1957; Lowry, 1979; May, 2009). Noetic values are those influences that are not external to the participant, but are intrinsically motivational; what is called a person's moral and ethical compass as soulful and undiscovered self (Jung, 1955, 2006).

I am not the only cop doc, although we are as rare as undercover agents, but I am the only one to ever attempt what is done here. Cop docs are law enforcement officers who have worked for at least 10 years of service, achieved a doctoral degree, for example MD or PhD, and are licensed as a mental/medical health professional who continues assessment, ambulatory interventions, and treatment with public safety officers.

I suggest that in very rare cases, phylogenic and phenotypic development is punctuated by the ingenuity of a novel thinker (Rudofossi, 2017). That is where genius can be viewed in an eco-ethological framework as changing the culture of police deep cover. For example, Special Agent Joe Pistone piqued cultural changes within the domain of law enforcement and evolving methods of investigations and infiltration. It is a responsibility and, in my view, a civic duty long overdue, that Pistone is given credit for the impact of his deep-cover operation that was uniquely ingenious. In looking at *"paradigms"* as ways in which we organize information and gather evidence to support or disconfirm our hypotheses between variables as theory is built, at times research and clinical scientists obtain unexpected results. At times, for example, forensic/police psychologists and criminologists obtain rare and unexpectable results. An unexpectable result is not answered by the paradigm in existence, and is known as an outlier, or anomaly. Anomaly as outlier can spur shifts in paradigmatic thinking about what is observed and that which scientists seek answers to (Kitaeff, 2019; Rudofossi, 2017). Pistone's undercover operation was, as we shall discover, replete with anomaly and outliers that need to be placed in a way that is made understandable once the successes, failures, and rare innovations Pistone strategized with purpose and effect in indictments and convictions of Mafia family syndicates are established. *Anomaly* as *outliers* using his psychological imagination centers an understanding and defining of his genius as extraordinary hidden vision made visible to scientific progress (Gardner, 1993; Goleman, 2005; May, 1994; Piaget, 2001; Sternberg, 2001; Taylor, 1983; Vygotsky, 1978).

Psychological Mindedness—Adaptive Functional Dissociation as Donnie Brasco

Special Agent Joseph Pistone was a can-do and with-it law enforcement officer who broke the mold of expectations. He did so under the leadership of the most exacting of bosses, that is, the famous FBI director, J. Edgar Hoover. Exacting and perfectionistic as J. Edgar Hoover was in his time as founder and director of the FBI, Joe Pistone excelled as a special agent. Joe was a street kid from Patterson, NJ, who, as a teacher for a short stint and a US Naval Intelligence professional, aspired to and achieved an unparalleled secure front in being able to maintain two identity modes—one as Joe Pistone, FBI special agent, and the other as Donnie Brasco, the aspiring wiseguy in the Mafia. As a doer, Joe's innovation was in creating himself as Donnie Brasco. His theory of mental toughness matches actual behavior.

Joseph Dominick Pistone revolutionized the perception of the capacity and expansion of the psychological imagination of investigation and survival through his use of multiple eco-ethological niches while doing investigative work. This fact is of great importance for the professions of law enforcement and police and forensic psychology/psychiatry, and useful for investigators willing to emulate his work with domestic and foreign organized crime syndicates.

Joe teaches us his meaning of tough-mindedness. As explored in our interviews, Joe used what I have defined as *adaptive functional dissociation* (Rudofossi, 1997, 2007). For now, adaptive functional dissociation is not looked at as a disorder but as an evolutionary mode of identity that officers shift into consciously and unconsciously (Kagan, 2011, 2012, 2016). These shifts will be understood on a more exacting level as we move forward chapter by chapter looking at Joe's experiences through the multiplicity and plasticity of his worlds.

Special Agent Joseph Pistone aka Donnie Brasco: Multiple Worlds and Identity Modes

Let's stop and pause for more than a fleeting moment. The choice to work undercover as a law enforcement officer is momentous and not just a knee-jerk response. Such a choice encompasses an entire universe that has been mystified nowadays. Such bemusement expresses projections of wishes hardly fulfilled through media presentations of the wiseguy.

Regardless of a killer's crafty trade in murder, mayhem, and violence, the parallel world of deep cover undulates with undercover codes that provoke illusion in many dimensions and layers. The looming question is "why" and "how" such darkness is alluring.

The world of the Mafia wiseguy includes sex, violence, and power unbridled and unmitigated in its power politics. Freud identified the drives that most agitate our unconscious motivation as the sexual and aggressive depths respectively known as Eros and Destrudo (Brenner, 1979, 2008). Holy alliances are what solidifies society and the nuclear family in societal growth. Yet, in a parallel universe, La Cosa Nostra has its compromises that impact on the collective unconscious and the individual unconscious compromises of sexual and aggressive tendencies. This is acted out in rituals and individual differences that emerge in the Mafia hierarchy.

My clinical supervisor in psychoanalytic ventures was Dr. Charles Brenner (Brenner, 1979) and as he modified Freud's drive theory (Brenner, 1979, 2008), he added the discovery of what is known as compromise formations (Brenner, 1979). The formations of sexual and aggressive drives which are unconscious, and hence unknown to the performer who unwittingly caches his/her drives for sexual and aggressive goals, become transformed into what is socially acceptable to lessen the problem with being anxious, paranoid, and depressively withdrawn from life and censure. Whacking the opposition may be more sanguine in both interpretations of that term than confronting the devil in the details of motivations. Viewed from a drive-oriented paradigm, an existential compromise formation is provoked when one's depth of conscience and integrity is challenged from different vantage points. Vision is reduced to nonsensical assumptions and wild speculations such as saying agents are great actors and role players that are sociopathic experts in order to do their job well. While a special agent must live, not act, in their world as a member as well as a participant in other worlds, he/she can never forget their self as they know and identify it in reality.

Deep-cover Survival and Adaptation in the Ecological Culture of Crime and Violence

Deep-cover operations, however fascinating to many, invite enterprising scientists, journalists, students of forensic psychology/psychiatry, criminal justice/criminology, and law as practiced for the defense and the prosecution looking for some definitive answer in an uncertain and, to a degree, chaotic world of law enforcement and organized crime syndicates.

Wiseguys keep all of the aforementioned in business and as "nothing personal" when they go about "doing their business." We law enforcement officers, as said so well, "on the job" we do "our job," leaving no one behind.

Undercover implies mystique and shadow and substance that is ever present and hardly seen in the public eyes except as portrayed in fictional presentations.

Discipline, tough-mindedness, and ingenuity are requisite when a law enforcement officer (LEO) dares to tread in the predatory underworld. Predators are ready to pounce in a moment's notice. Those who infiltrate are not given an easy death, and torture is the rule, not the exception.

Not only is the constant threat of violence an issue, but the hidden world of forces, including the bureaucratic pressure of LEO agencies, pull on the deep cover, who must be aware of where he/she treads to preserve the integrity of their mission and of course their own life.

Hypervigilance: In Law Enforcement Officers and Mafia Members

Treading in the world of the wiseguy requires hypervigilance that calls on the special agent, police detective, or intelligence officer to match tempo to the dances of crime and violence with finesse that hides their police habits and cultural mores. Hints of extraordinary pressure put on the agent are at times acknowledged under the assumption that this is playing of roles. This assumption is not accurate, but is believed by many to be true. Where does the deep cover go to when he/she believes the shit is really going to hit the fan of exposure? If a student of psychiatry/psychology would really like to gauge the bursting level of pressure, it is crucial to realize for a moment that the so-called average police professional doing patrol duties with no specialized detective skills is subject to random acts of violence and racism against police, which I titled "Centurioncide" (Rudofossi & Maloney, 2019), sudden shocks both natural and unnatural thrown at her/him without warning. It is intense, repetitive, and impactful.

Scarring that marks an officer can last for many years before "It" emerges in flashbacks, nightmares, and intrusions into both waking and sleeping life, without any recourse toward seeking help. Seeking help is often looked at as weaknesses and the exposure of one's vulnerable spot. Officers learn to use barbs and boundaries to protect our private lives and sensibility in what is touted as the blue wall of silence. But it is not always silent and not always withdrawn anger and depression—it is at times countered with aggression and addictions that are deadly to the officer him/herself. A colleague and friend of mine added a critical concept to the lexicon of the dense underbrush of ideas in the domain of trauma. Dr. Martin Gilmartin, retired police lieutenant, empathically and empirically supports what he called hypervigilance as a schema police use both consciously and unconsciously in surviving on the streets, and that certainly rotates around the hub of patrol (Gilmartin, 2002; Conroy & Orthmann, 2014).

Hypervigilance impacts on an officer's need to accurately perceive the world around them regarding who is the "bad guy" and who is the "good guy/good gal." In a heartbeat moment, a mistake can cost that officer his/her life. Hypervigilance and the blue wall of silence both shield the officer from sharing not only with civilians what is endured in the line of duty, but also his/her own family. Spouses, children, and parents are left far out of the realm of war stories except for the rare unavoidable spill-over in media reports (Gilmartin, 2002; Kitaeff, 2019).

This hypervigilance and blue wall prevent outsiders from knowing what is going on within the confines created to protect each officer from violations by those outside.

Guardedness includes being alert to holding in one's real feelings evoked in the line of duty as a police officer. There is a need to adapt and function at higher levels of police work, including being a detective or investigator, if one has the ability to deal with complex human interactions. The term "homicided" fits well in the "hood," where forceful street acquisitions have permanent outcomes, outcomes that are fatal or carry life sentences.

Doing deep cover is for the very rare, and there are few officers who can put up with what is far more than being dressed for the role assigned by the bureau, administration, or department. A deep-cover agent is a unique member of an elite corps of men and women in the blue culture.

Blue Blood: Loyalty in Police

Many have used the term "blue blood" when referring to officers (Conroy & Orthmann, 2014; Kitaeff, 2019; Rudofossi, 1997, 2007), meaning the heart and soul of the police culture is embedded in the patrol officers who do the grunt work, day in and night out. The holding glue of pride and power as an officer of the law is nowhere more cached than when that officer is given the task to embrace an identity that is oppositional to his/her core.

I have touched on the fact that I cannot summarize the complexities of patrol, specialized emergency units, and even plainclothes street-crime units as I have in other books. Much has been written about the trauma and grief officers endure and how, why, and when interventions are needed.

How, why, and when to stay on the fence is equally as impactful toward healing. More than ever, those who have no idea about the reality of police and the trauma officers experience are prompted to come out with a new gimmicky technique to cure the wounded warriors. At best they are harmless antidotes that don't work, and at worst they are iatrogenic and supplied by cult-like groupies that harm police and their families as no gatekeeper protects the finest from the worst snake-oil sellers and their panacea potions. Finally, keep in mind the fact that many levels of awesome police work exist, but are not covered here.

The cover we will segue into now is measured in the deep and almost unfathomable challenges that one of the smartest, intuitive, and strategic LEOs ever in the saddle of deep-cover work shares with me as a cop doc. Let me qualify that this book as not being written by that LEO or associates. It is based on our dialogues over a number of years.

It is with intention that I bring to each reader the wisdom and experience that is generated in the catalytic process of discovery of becoming Donnie Brasco in the real life of Joseph Dominick Pistone. Pistone would not say this about himself, but I share with you my unapologetic insistence that he is a genius. I do not use the term "genius" to flatter the creative and synergistic power of Joseph to be able to infiltrate one of the most powerful protective moats in organized crime (Gardner, 1993; Goleman, 2005; May, 1994; Piaget, 2001; Sternberg, 2001; Taylor, 1983; Vygotsky, 1978). Joe Pistone's genius is in his mindful understanding, which is not relegated to his acquisition of remarkable arrests and indictments followed by prosecutions, but in his six years of doing deep cover: Operation Donnie Brasco, as a whole, was in theory deemed impossible to achieve—but in fact surpassed any infiltration done at that point from a historic and operational perspective in law enforcement. In six years, Donnie Brasco was groomed to be a "made member" of the Bonanno family by the newly appointed capo di tutti, Sonny Black Napolitano. That achievement as a whole process was done with mindful strategy and is evidence of Joe Pistone's "genius" (Gardner, 1993; Goleman, 2005; May, 1994; Piaget, 2001; Rudofossi, 1997, 2007, 2017; Sternberg, 2001; Taylor, 1983; Vygotsky, 1978). In understanding Pistone's creative "genius," unexamined traumatic loss for both capo Sonny Black Napolitano and Special Agent Pistone is equally put in perspective and understood as tragic costs that are inexorable.

Deep-cover Operative: Indefatigable Commitment and Courage

Joseph Dominick Pistone has what Dr. Viktor Frankl, who survived Auschwitz death camp, called the "indefatigable human spirit" (Frankl, 1979; May, 1994; Rudofossi, 2007; Yalom, 1980).

This book is dedicated to educating others as to the depth and grasp of the honor and respect due him, as well as the invaluable lessons we can gain from his ingenuity and courage. In my classes taught at John Jay College, New York University, and at St. John's University, some students point out the tough, no-nonsense style of Joe Pistone as Donnie Brasco. It is the elegance behind the veneer that will yield to pause as we examine the mindful undercover strategy of Operation Donnie Brasco.

Omertà, The Blue Wall of Silence, the Power of Silence, the Hippocratic Oath to HIPPA

It was ingenious and necessary for what I have coined "adaptive functional dissociation" for Pistone to create a tough but sensitive persona for Donnie Brasco. In doing so, he saved more than one not-so-smart tough guy from almost certain death, which may have come from a 45-caliber slug, for example, by Captain Tony Mirra of the Bonanno family. Omertà (the code of silence) in the Mafia, although paralleling that of law enforcement, will also be viewed as a cultural adaptation that is not only smart but coded genetically as a phenotype for survival. The bridge of the blue wall of silence and omertà is not up for some outsider to judge without insight.

Surrendering information by paid informants to the police or FBI has been a deadly proposition for members of any gang and that includes organized crime. Until Pistone successfully infiltrated the Mafia, the most unreliable informants were the go-to intelligence people for investigators seeking to solve complex crimes.

As a classically trained clinician and police officer, I beckon to the wisdom of cultural anthropologists such as Franz Boas and his famous students Margaret Mead and Ruth Benedict, and the warning to not interfere with the culture in a head-on clash, thinking one could change what both cultural and psychological biopsychosocial evolution and eco-ethological niches have primed for individual and group survival. Rather, Pistone puts it well with his nursing his three mistresses, musing the rock of Gibraltar, the rock of Justice, and the rock of Wiseguys.

Hypervigilance and the blue wall of silence are the most pressing influences on officers. Influences need a destination point to gather momentum before being analyzed. In order to analyze any human endeavor, we must understand the definitions offered within a context that can be operationalized and measured to some degree.

Destination: Embarking Point Unknown

Like Socrates, most investigators and scientists, including forensic, police, and medical psychologists/psychiatrists, frame compelling questions to find answers. The answers give some information from which more questions are asked and more answers are sought. In order to build a case, one needs evidence and an agreement on what is acceptable as evidence. In order to understand the ingenuity of Special Agent Pistone, I share a trust and affinity for seeking the truth. Some aspects of truth from my training as a licensed psychologist are ferreted out on a level any good investigator could achieve, while others could only be understood by a trained psychologist/psychiatrist. In understanding the novel dynamics of Joseph Pistone's mind, I had to combine my own decades of being a police supervisor and investigator as well as a clinician without reducing the picture into a linear black-and-white image that casts purely good guys/gals against villainous bad guys/gals.

Undercover of Shadows to Recover: Questions and More Questions to Ask

A few questions to unravel will give you an understanding of what I mean to convey. The questions to think about follow:

1. What if a special agent as LEO cannot present himself as the real detective/special agent he/she is to the public?
2. What if that special agent as LEO cannot present himself as the real detective/special agent he/she is to his peers for support in a direct way?
3. What if that special agent as LEO cannot present himself to the criminals he must investigate and ethically deal with in his/her investigations?
4. What if that special agent as LEO cannot confide in his bosses fully who offer cover and protection almost always for other LEOs?
5. What if that special agent as LEO cannot confide in his best friend and wife as to his whereabouts and his threat to life and limb?
6. What if that special agent as LEO has no map in place as to what, where, when, and how he is to gain and secure the trust of men who vow to be adept at murder as diplomacy at any moment?
7. What if that special agent as LEO has to, in a moment's notice, survive his new bosses' (aka bad guys) sense of doing justice that is diametrically opposed to what his LEO agency demands of him?

Toward Answering Tough Questions About Doing Deep Cover

In asking some questions such as the ones above, I hope to cover the how, what, when, and where questions that Joseph had to encounter in reality. In order to grasp any answers, the fact is, how and why a special agent for the FBI can become unentangled with the wiseguys becomes tangible when we stop first and take a real pause.

Influencing the choices an agent must make is not based on meditative analysis but instead on razor-sharp and effective lifesaving decisions. Such influences couched in question form can be understood as building a context for the experiences of Special Agent Joseph Dominick Pistone's initiation into organized crime families.

Toward Cultural Competence in Learning How to Survive Violence in the Mafia Ecology

The culture of wiseguys includes what we might call a "red wall of silence," omertà. Red, as the color suggests blood, and blood flows fluently within the arteries of organized crime and the multiple networks that have been forged. In trying to gain an understanding, a method that pretends to be scientific cannot be slanted one way. In understanding a cultural phenomenon such as La Cosa Nostra, it is crucial to not get swept away into the entrancing aspects of what is sexy, as much as it is important to not wash away the cruel and cold dimensions of murder. Murder by caprice or by deliberate planning is unsavory and equivalent in impact and result for the victims and their families. If we pause, we can ask whether anyone is fully aware of the risks involved and the cost that is permanent. Divulging secret information for most people has consequences within the bounds of friendship and sacred relationships such as marriage.

Within most communities there are rituals and rites regarding consequences for those who violate rules regarding secrecy and loyalty, but none perhaps as severe as the violation of secrecy sworn to in being made within the organized crime family. For the Mafia associate, or made member, violating special information leads to being labelled a "rat." Likewise, within the law enforcement community and culture, being labelled a rat also results in some heavy consequences.

The penalty for being a rat and breaking silence in Mafia families entails death; for LEOs it entails ostracism, being abandoned by your fellow officers in a time of need. That abandonment in the line of duty for a police officer can result in death. Both omertà and the blue wall of silence have their consequences, which can range from death to apathy. Apathy is said to be worse than hatred. Apathy can be seen when a 20-year fellow mafioso says to his colleague in arms, it is nothing personal, just business, but after you enjoy this meal on the house we are going for a ride. That ride means to your own execution for violating a rule one is sworn to uphold in that Mafia family. In the world of LEOs, it is withdrawal and abandonment when you call for police assistance, and all responders are unavailable or silent when the bad guys are closing in.

This cultural competence of understanding shapes and influences ecologically the power of silence and how "It" impacts on LEOs and wiseguys.

The design of culture is never one direction, but tri-directional. The following is a guide of this tri-directional movement.

1. Culture impacts on the individual within his cultural circles of support or ostracism psychophysiologically. Complementarity means the individual can and does repeat the lessons learned within the rites, mores, and taboos of his/her cultural circle and his/her response to that culture.
2. Another direction is that as a member of that culture, as an individual one can accept and foreclose on his/her cultural heritage. As social psychologist Marcia points out, it is a done deal in foreclosed identity status formation (Marcia, 1966, 1967).
3. A member of a culture one is born into, can rebel. He/she can deal with the pressures of punishment and painful consequences by choosing to take a different course.
4. For example, as a law enforcement officer, the motivation at all times is triggered by holding the elusive pull of action and navigating one's own survival. Similarly, the wiseguy also must navigate within the maze of his/her culture or face death or very painful consequences.
5. Another direction is that the influence of culture is almost always strengthened and tested when there are breaks in what is expected and supported. For example, if an LEO could infiltrate a powerful organized crime family and succeed in penetrating the thicket of obstacles therein, the impact on the organized crime culture is deep shock waves, the impact on the law enforcement culture is success, and the impact overall to society is gained wisdom for public viewing.

If this sounds a bit complicated to grapple with—it is! It is also what I intend to unravel based on my interviews with my esteemed and expert sleuth Special Agent Joseph Dominick Pistone.

The wiseguys have said at times, "It is what it is," implying that the horrors and pains of "It" cannot be changed. It also means to accept reality, as if your fate is written in concrete.

This "It," as interpreted by the police officer, is of real interest to me. Why? That is a crucial question that needs to be asked in each case as a boundary to understand the importance given to this colloquial expression. As we move on in our exploration, I hope to enhance your investment in the workings of the mind and soul of the deep-cover agent Joseph Dominick Pistone. We will return to the semantics of meaning in the heaviest of police-related issues, that is, homicide.

From Homicide to Trauma and "Its" Impact

The term "trauma" nowadays is often used in out-of-place dramatized contexts such as when folks have lost an election and bemoan suffering from traumatized loss. This usage belittles the enormity of loss experienced by police. "It" is the trauma and grief of deep cover for all parties involved and the reality of what it exacts through one case study: the experiences of Special Agent Joseph Pistone. Pistone's creative and revolutionary method is one that requires a trained third ear analytically, and a cop's intuitive sensibility to unravel as we move forward by actively listening to important lessons in personality dynamics, criminology, and forensic psychology.

Summary

In this chapter we surveyed the field of deep cover by defining what our field of interest really encompasses. Deep cover works in an administrative modality; in a clinically applied domain it applies trauma and grief applications in the field of practice; and does not deny assessment and intervention in a military population. It is crucial to reread, and before moving on get the major concepts down as a foundation by reviewing all definitions and concepts given.

It is the beginning of our journey, but the wisdom may be the best that can be done. At times, the costliest to all parties involved is a cost exacted that pays a reward that transcends all conflict, which is compromise and insight for and toward meaning as life moves forward intractably. In life moving forward, tragically there are no survivors in its wake save the lessons learned well for posterity in the marathon of life which is for those that too transcend our time, relatively speaking—without being relativistic and reductionistic.

In the next chapter, narrative analysis will be achieved through interviews that are presented as dialogue between Special Agent Pistone and Dr. Rudofossi. The dialogue offers the student of criminal justice, police and forensic psychology, and homeland security a rich and sorely needed understanding as a framework. That lattice is one you can build on moving forward in your own career planning as a researcher, clinician trainee, or future law enforcement or law professional.

Cop Doc Corner for Students Only

Dialogue compels the reader to actively listen and empathically attune in a way in which all that may be gotten is much less likely to be forgotten and shelved. Shelving a book or record as past heroics and unclear records, for the record leaves the contemporary with much that has to be learned anew with all the pitfalls, and not everyone that falls into a snake pit emerges whole and even likely to survive. From the next chapter until the Epilogue, the process and flow of our conversation is charged with coordinates of meaning to assist you as a future leader in criminal justice and perhaps a criminal investigator.

The dialogue offers you as a student of criminal, police, and forensic psychology a rich and sorely needed understanding which will give you a context to build your own framework and insight into the process of the psychology of investigations. We will assess the heavy cost it wistfully contorts for all involved.

This said, most importantly, you are invited to a responsive, respectful narrative, and complex and perplexing dilemmas faced by the finest of the finest, who are able to master the crisscross boxes mused into infiltrations with every hitch imaginable. This thrust forward is done in the inimitable words of Special Agent Pistone via "mental toughness" woven into the adhesion of each chapter educating as we move on in our exploration of deep-cover operations.

Let's move forward and review concepts important to understand in this chapter.

Important Definitions and Concepts to Keep in Mind

Active listening

Active listening is the ability to suspend your own preconceived notions, opinions, and judgment of a situation or problem until you hear and absorb the full presentation of another's understanding and communication of a situation or problem. In our casebook this means you can try to tolerate a position, viewpoint, understanding a problem, situation, or issue that is very difficult to hear. Still, with patience and the attempt to gain an understanding, it is key to listen to all communication before interrupting with your own thinking (even if silently in your own mind) and answering the other communicator while he/she is expressing their own viewpoint.

Cop doc

A licensed doctoral-level clinician who also served as a law enforcement officer for at least ten years. The continuing assistance and support of fellow law enforcement officers and their family members dealing with mental and behavioral disorders is a requirement.

Deep-cover operations

Deep-cover operations are performed under the most secretive and covert planning within a law enforcement agency. It is crucial to consider this assignment requires the ability to function and innovate approaches with others with a higher level of emotional intelligence required to fit in and appear being with-it with other people who have oppositional and criminal goals in mind. The violent ecology and ethological motivation for survival is unusually difficult and is usually not considered to be a factor in doing the operative functions of deep cover.

Compromise formation

Compromise formation is a hypothetical construct in psychoanalytic theory. In assessment, intervention, and treatment conceptualized by Dr. Freud and refined by Dr. Charles Brenner, compromise formations are solutions that bridge drives that are biological, such as a craving for sexual intimacy, and a stimulation of aggressive tendencies in a patient or any person that is not accessible to awareness or mental retrieval processes (Brenner, 1979, 2008; Rudofossi, 2007). This conflict develops when strong emotional and mental representations of a wish, memory of a desire, or idea that is unacceptable in a societal way (remember societal includes cultural and ecological influences a person experiences in development) pushes for expression. That push is done by desires such as Eros (sexual) or Destrudo (aggressive) that are cached and censored from conscious awareness. Societal rules and mores or customs that are deemed unacceptable are not just suppressed, which is a semi-conscious awareness, but are also hidden by unconscious blind spots from being known by the person using such defenses himself. The cumulative impact of traumatic losses and adjustment creates compromise formations which we will also modify by including noetic values.

Noetic values

Noetic values are understood in the context of "heroic" actions that put one at grave risk to save others' lives. Explanations sought in psychosocial-, psychosexual-, or biopsychosocial-driven analysis leave much unanswered. Noetic values come from unreducible motivation that is beyond one's self-interest (Frankl, 1979; Lowry, 1979; Kagan, 2016; May, 1994; Yalom, 1980): Without considering the direct costs from a psychosocial-, psychosexual-, or biopsychosocial-driven cause, human actions and compassion appear to be a strength and insight well worth the consideration as we explore the actions and success of Operation Donnie Brasco.

Conceptual and Writing Exercises for Student and Professor Only

1. Find a paper published in an academic journal on deep cover using your chosen major as an area to do a literature search. For example, criminal justice, sociology, psychology, homeland security, forensic psychology, or forensic science. Obtain a copy of the paper and summarize your findings for the class in a presentation.
2. With permission of your professor and the university, do an informal interview where you can take notes and record "why" and "what" motivated the author of the paper or presentation above to engage in the research or write about deep cover.
3. In reviewing this chapter, list five reasons the author has presented as to why learning about deep cover is a worthy endeavor. Do this even if you never intend on becoming a forensic psychology major or cop doc.
4. Do a search of criminal justice, criminology, and law journals to see if you can obtain an article that covers the specific area of deep-cover operations and the historic case of Joe Pistone is used as illustrative of the process. How detailed is the case example and does it also cover the psychological underpinnings of doing deep cover in any meaningful manner? If not, using your own psychological imagination and investigative scientific mindset, why do you think the inclusion of this paradigm is avoided?
5. Find a case example of an alleged member of the Mafia who committed a number of newsworthy crimes, including murder. Seek out a legal summary of the defense attorney who differed in strong and influential ways from the prosecutor. Is there any unconscious defenses and inferiority schemas that were used in the trial as mitigating factors to consider? Try to find a case example from doing a search of reliable and valid sources such as Lexus or Sociological, Psychological Abstracts or with help from the librarian at your university.

References

Brenner, C. (1979). The components of psychic conflict and its consequence in mental life. *Psychoanalytic Quarterly*, 48(4), 547–567.
Brenner, C. (2008). Aspects of psychoanalytic theory: Drives, defense and the pleasure-unpleasure principle. *Psychoanalytic Quarterly*, 77(3), 707–717.
Conroy, D., & Orthmann, C. H. (2014). *Surviving a law enforcement career: A guide for cops and those who love them*. Rosemont, MN: Innovative Systems.

Frankl, V. (1979). *The unheard cry for meaning: Psychotherapy and humanism.* New York: Simon and Schuster.
Fromm, E. (1957). *The forgotten language: An introduction to the understanding of dreams, fairy tales, and myths.* New York: Grove.
Gardner, H. (1993). *Multiple intelligences: The theory in practice.* New York: Basic.
Gilmartin, K. (2002). *Emotional survival for law enforcement.* Arizona: E-S Press.
Goleman, D. (2005). *Emotional intelligence: Why it can matter more than IQ.* New York: Bantam.
Jung, C. G. (1955). *Modern man in search of soul.* San Diego, CA: Harcourt Brace.
Jung, C. G. (2006). *The undiscovered self.* New York: Berkley Press.
Kagan, J. (2011). *John Bowlby—From psychoanalysis to ethology.* Hoboken, NJ: Wiley Blackwell.
Kagan, J. (2012). *Psychology's ghosts: The crisis in the profession and the way back.* New Haven & London: Yale University Press.
Kagan, J. (2016). *On being human: Why mind matters.* New Haven & London: Yale University Press.
Kerlinger, F., & Lee, H. (1999). *Foundations of behavioral research* (4th ed.). Belmont, CA: Wadsworth.
Kitaeff, J. (2007). *Malingering, lies and junk science in the courtroom.* Amherst, NY: Cambria Press.
Kitaeff, J. (2019). *The handbook of police psychology* (2nd ed.). New York: Routledge.
Lowry, R. (1979). *The journals of Abraham Maslow.* Monterey, CA: Brooks/Coles.
Marcia, J. E. (1966). Development and validation of ego-identity status. *Journal of Personality and Social Psychology,* (3), 551–558.
Marcia, J. E. (1967). Ego-identity status: Relationship to change in self-esteem, general maladjustment, and authoritarianism. *Journal of Personality,* 35(1), 119–133.
May, R. (1994). *The courage to create.* New York: W.W. Norton.
May, R. (2009). *Man's search for himself.* New York: W.W. Norton.
Orwell, G. (2005). *Why I write.* New York: Penguin.
Piaget, J. (2001). *The psychology of intelligence.* New York & London: Routledge.
Rudofossi, D. M. (1997). *The impact of trauma and loss on affective differential profiles of police officers.* Bell Harbor, MI: Bell and Howell.
Rudofossi, D. M. (2007). *Working with traumatized police-officer patients: A clinician's guide to complex PTSD syndromes in public safety professionals.* New York: Routledge.
Rudofossi, D. M. (2017). *Cop doc. The police psychologist's casebook—Narratives from police psychology.* New York: Routledge.
Rudofossi, D., & Maloney, M. (2019). *Aborigine trail: Trails, travail, and triumph using psychology with Aborigine police.* Amherst, NY: Teneo Press.
Sternberg, R. J. (2001). *The evolution of intelligence.* New York: Psychology Press.
Taylor, E. (1983). *William James on exceptional mental states: The 1896 Lowell Lectures reconstructed.* New York: Scribner & Sons.
Vygotsky, L. S. (1978). *Mind in society: The development of higher psychological processes.* Cambridge, MA: Harvard University Press.
Yalom, I. D. (1980). *Existential psychotherapy.* New York: Basic.

2
GENIUS IN MOTION
Becoming Donnie Brasco

Introduction

After laying the foundations for understanding deep cover in Chapter 1, we now shift our attention toward understanding what it was like to endure the mental and physical training required to become an FBI special agent during the 1970s and specifically what this was like for Joe Dominick Pistone toward becoming Special Agent Pistone. Becoming a field agent is a tough and arduous road. Expectable performance standards are achieved in developing skills in different areas such as firearms, driving, arrest, and custody challenges in street situations, to name a few.

Becoming a police officer demands competence and expert acquisition of skills in steps that are gradual and yet, as in the FBI, field operations can shift to sudden emergencies with little time to strategize. The NYPD officer as FBI agent is given tasks to conquer during training that are as unexpectable as possible to introduce the law enforcement officer to the realities of street encounters.

The risk of being stalked and shot in the line of duty is a realistic event in police work and heightened in investigative work. This fact can arguably feel as if being stalked, shot at, and put at risk is routine for agents and officers, who must learn to deal with, as much as we all do, our eventual death. This mindset is far from reality based.

The reality of being shot at and actually injured, from severe to life threatening, is not an experience an officer can truly prepare for, but with training, it is true that chances of survival are increased. Being threatened and assaulted ought not ever be acceptable as routine (Rudofossi, 1997, 2007). Rather, understanding threats and violence targeting law enforcement officers is always nested in an ecology of trauma that distorts what is expectable and "normal" to experience.

Most standard training lies with a mental and behavioral skillset that helps afford a model that shapes an officer/special agent for challenges to safety and survival. An ecology of constant threats of violence targeting officers impacts on each officer's survival skill. The mindset of overcoming threats can be prepared for in some measure by education and role plays; the remainder must be learned in real situations as they develop in unpredictable and uncontrollable ways as they develop in the street encounters. In looking at becoming a deep-cover agent, keep in mind that the basics for any police and special agent demand adaptability, reasoning, and analytic skills, and some creativity in staying alive in hostile and threatening situations.

24   Genius in Motion: Becoming Donnie Brasco

One can say that being a police officer entails priming up for emotional and ethological intelligence to distinguish between real threats and less probable threats as one navigates in training and then in real testing experiences as officer development happens in field training.

This chapter covers the training and experiences of becoming a special agent in the Federal Bureau of Investigation.

The opening narrative between Special Agent Joe Pistone and Professor Cop Doc Dan allows a filtration of insight as to the hidden process of becoming an agent doing deep-cover operations: transitioning from field special agent to becoming Donnie Brasco in the world of the Mafia, Joe Pistone offers a world that has yet to be explored using the unique vista of police psychology. On one hand, Joe Pistone numbs certain emotions and feelings as adaptation at its best. On the other hand, functioning while acting as one identity is switched into another person's identity is draining over long periods of time.

Showing true states of emotion, such as warmth, compassion, sensitivity, and gentleness can eclipse being "tough enough" in the eyes of predators. Being taken and labeled as a "too easy going fellow" can lead to death. In an ecological niche of violence, where toughness is the meter of success, such as the Mafia ecology Joe Pistone entered as Donnie Brasco, being perceived as soft is weakness.

Joe Pistone's initiation rites were shaped in an ecology where toughness and violence demanded a new identity being forged, paradoxically without Joe losing who he was and becoming the wiseguy he was destined to become. Joe camouflaged his real identity as special agent LEO by camouflage. Camouflage offers one key in learning how adaptation takes place. In mimicking personality differences needed to successfully assimilate into a cultural and ecological niche at odds with the law enforcement culture, Joe's new identity modality and identity mode emerged. Keep in mind concrete intelligence, such as "book smarts" alone, may not offer the emotional flexibility and creativity needed to survive such stress and strain needed in becoming a deep-cover special agent.

Before exploring all these fascinating and dangerous adaptations, let's pause. In our pause, let's review some important questions you may be asking yourself already.

Questions to Guide You as Navigational Tools: Learning Objectives

1. What types of intelligence gathering facilitate a baseline to gain entry into the elite world of special agents doing deep cover?
2. What are three key focal dimensions of intelligence that are necessary for succeeding as a special agent doing covert intelligence?
3. Is there a specific intelligence suggested by Joe Pistone that can become a focus of further study and research for field practice applicable to doing detective work?
4. Knowing the three types of intelligence psychologists have discovered, can an agent become more attentive toward cultivating these intelligences to succeed as an agent?
5. In learning about the varying levels of intelligence, are they conscious goals to be pursued or is it wiser to allow articulation by a less structured and more natural process to develop?
6. What does Special Agent Joe Pistone think of concrete intelligence in distinction to the process of intrinsic tendencies emerging?
7. Is the process of doing deep cover amenable to field experiments?
8. Is doing deep cover comparable to naturally occurring field experiments?
9. In exploration of one's ecological niche as a special agent doing deep cover, does detection of subtle clues enhance survival, or is it a waste of precious time?
10. Is camouflage as understood in animal behavior a contextual process that lends remarkable insight to the process of survival in deep cover operatives, such as Joe Pistone?

Key Terms as Coordinate Postings

Adaptive functional dissociation in an Eco-Ethological Existential Model
Maladaptive dysfunctional dissociation
Camouflage as boundary building
Donnie Brasco identity mode
Standard operating procedures
Reductionistic caricatures of police officers

Camouflage as Boundary in Eco-Ethological Niches—Death and Prey

Let's start by viewing our last question as a segue to answering all the questions posed in our introduction to this chapter. How can an ecology primed for violence paradoxically ensure survival for the agent? If camouflaging fear and caution is crucial in doing undercover operations, the most compelling question is, "Why?"

Camouflage as cover from an ethological perspective demands that an animal in a situation of grave peril must fit in with the surrounding ecology or risk become prey to the predator.

In a similar vein an operative doing deep cover must act as if he/she fits in to the ecological ethological niche and rituals in order to survive. Doing camouflage is very challenging and demands enormous emotional control and strategic thinking. Yet with all the strategic planning, in reality it must seem as if one is not thinking at all, but rather fitting in with the rest of the predators. This is true in a pack of wolves and this is true in a pack of gangsters.

All the while the agent, without making it a conscious task, must keep all this in mind and quite conscious for self-survival. Ultimately, strategically surviving the ordeal of deep-cover operations means forgetting constantly be vigilant, but assimilating and accommodating to the demands of the specific ecological-ethological niche one must survive in by camouflaging their real identity and needs.

Camouflage is anchored in the ecological-ethological niche primed for survival in the haunts the deep cover must survive and emotionally adapt to. The deft transition to be endured must be purposive and existentially centered for the officer/agent in order to survive with purpose in a spiritually impoverished world (Rudofossi, 1997, 2007).

Thus far, camouflage occurs in an ecological niche with ethological (meaning survival value) that specializes (speciation, biologically speaking) in the deep cover in which one's identity can never be exposed, disclosed, or leak out unintentionally to others. By leaking out, what is meant is disclosing to others cues, rituals, or communicating one's real identity.

Emotional leakage can kill, so the right timing is almost always crucial, adding another complex piece to camouflage. Remember, emotional leakage is natural (Goffman, 1963; Kendon, 1990) in humans' interaction as much as animals such as *canine lupus* or animals such as wolves. The skillful caching of one's real and genuine angst, anger, and anguish is very difficult to do, but heightening such a task to deep-cover operations is excruciating painful in one's adaptation to impossible and unexplored tasks as Joe Pistone had to forge as a pioneer.

Camouflage as Boundary in Eco-Ethological Niches—Mobbing as Prey Mimics Predator

As an initiate into organized crime, it is important to consider that each family (organized crime dynasty) had its own unique written and unwritten rules that had commonalities with the other Mafia families. However, each Mafia family has its own rules, customs, and major boss or capo di tutti. The differences may be viewed as one would a different culture or an ecological niche that supports certain behaviors that lead toward acceptance and assimilation into that community, and other behaviors, communications, and emotions expressed that will lead to exposure to a higher level of exclusion, mistrust, and eventual expulsion. It is important to realize the unwritten laws and hidden language and hidden dimension of each family is not different than any subcultural group in a larger cultural equivalent (Hall, 1966, 1973). The need to assert a territorial imperative within that limitation of the family that ruled, and other families that cooperated or struggled to gain hegemony of space and competition, set the behavioral design for internal wars or bridges in each family and the fate of its members (Hall, 1966, 1973; Sommer, 1969, 1978).

It is in this context that a major component of camouflage Joe Pistone had to master was the hidden language and cultural sensitivity of the Mafia family he was an initiate in, for example, beginning as an associate within the Columbo family and later Bonanno family. The fact Joe was camouflaged so well and bridged lattices to other families prominent in the constellations of the region of organized crime families he was accepted into was anomalous for an outsider. By being able to create a reputation as being tough-minded which traversed the culture of the NY FBI field division and the culture of the NY Mafia families, Joe Pistone used a method similar to mobbing in ethology. Mobbing is when a prey animal turns on its predator and in an unusual manner pursues the predator as if it is going to attack and defeat it in a mock attack. The inflation of power is more impressive and jarring to the predator, inexplicably causing a chain reaction of retreat and flight.

In a way Joe Pistone forging a new identity modality of being a tough guy and tough-minded in two Mafia families offers us a context of the task at hand and the identity not played as in a role play, but lived through and with as Donnie Brasco.

Camouflage as Boundary in Eco-Ethological Niches—Inhibiting Violence-Piquing Integration

Understanding identity modes offers an understanding of how and why the agents' different adaptations are shaped by evolutionary and biological drives. These drives are unconscious, and existentially center who and how the agent remains his true self. This true self emerges within the complexities of each identity mode (Rudofossi, 1997).

An identity mode is *operationally shaped by motivation for survival* (ethological) in an ecological niche(s). An identity mode always presents itself as adaptive or maladaptive within dissociative states. Functional adaptation in each dissociative state is a defensive constellation that is dynamic in the context in which *it emerges and affords survival within the eco-ethological niche it develops in.*

Intuitive Sensibility: Knowing individual differences creates safety zones in different eco-ethological niches

Special Agent Joe Pistone, without MD or PhD, had the creative ability to understand the complexities of individual differences. Some questions emerge here. What did it take to become acclimated to a culture of violence and with different soldiers to bosses in each respective Mafia family? Did Joe Pistone accommodate his own genuine self in order for Donnie Brasco to emerge? The ideal of "integrity" needed to remain being FBI Agent Joseph Dominick Pistone had to be at odds with certain character traits Donnie Brasco lived and acted out with; how did Joe Pistone deal with this challenge? The collisions of cultures and collusion of politics over real-deal needs of the agent to do his job is highlighted at the conclusion of this chapter's dialogue with a fragment of a police officer's experience recounted by Joe Pistone. In this case the officer's self-defense is thrown under the bus of quick fixes and convenient band-aids over the truth of trauma in the gun battles. Retold by professor and instructor Joseph Pistone, who does his own peer support with colleagues of ours injured in the field of battle on the concrete streets of urban war zones, it will provide some answers and lead to further questions.

Dialogue as Narrative and Contextual Analysis Special Agent Pistone and Cop Doc Dan R.

Take heed as your lean forward and actively listen in pausing and hearing what is said in the interstitial spacing of meaningful words woven in the depth of process as dialogue unfolds between Special Agent Joseph Dominick Pistone and me. Comments here and in each chapter will be italicized to craft important educational points and to enhance your understanding as students of criminal justice, forensic psychology, and homeland security and law.

FBI AGENT JOSEPH DOMINICK PISTONE: "Hey, hey Doc I got you. What's up, how are you today?"

COP DR DAN RUDOFOSSI: "I'm fine, Special Agent Joe. Thanks for asking. You know, I am wondering if anything comes to mind from our last conversation regarding doing deep cover. If you recall, I had left off saying in my view the idea of role playing as you confirmed briefly has no reality as to what you did as a deep-cover special agent. In my view saying you were doing a role play is way too simple a judgment of the complex identity you lived with as Donnie Brasco. Do you think I have a point in iterating your point as a segue for students to gain perspective on your experiences as a deep-cover agent?"

FBI AGENT JOSEPH DOMINICK PISTONE: "I do agree it is important as to your point. Let me say, it is totally off base, as some reporters and even fellow law enforcement officers to believe that what I did in doing infiltration, *'was acting a role play and acting in general'*. Your choice to point this perspective, is point on, Doc. Reasserting this point is correct. Acting is not what I did for six years. Dealing with wiseguys and living in deep cover is much more than that. It is living as you really are, as it makes sense to me! Meaning not as an actor plays a role given to him/her but living it out as it actually happens in reality. Does that sound right to you?"

COP DR DAN RUDOFOSSI: "It does sound right to me Special Agent Joe Pistone. Your point resonates with my theory. When, I developed the *Eco-Ethological Existential Analytic Approach* to traumatic loss and dissociative states of consciousness among police officers and special agents as we discussed outside of these interviews, and you are familiar with my clinical books, I pointed out that being selected for 'deep-cover operations' necessitates that those who are appointed be well above average intelligence. In fact, let me specify that above average intelligence among all populations, and especially within the police population."

FBI AGENT JOSEPH DOMINICK PISTONE: "I agree Doc, but can you specify the type of intelligence you mean so as to synchronize our points together. Meaning do you mean street smarts or book smarts here as in academic smarts?"

COP DR DAN RUDOFOSSI: "Let me say in identifying the problems of adaptation to a maladaptive ecological niche of gangsters, the pressure to survive takes exquisite wisdom, craft, and intuition. A book smart both/and street smart. Let's pause and think about what is meant by book smarts by both of us is what may mean an almost eidetic memory, like a photo shot you can hold in your own memory with excellent retention. The street smarts being a fluid intelligence or one that is dynamic, meaning you can pinpoint new problems by identifying them and in a short time come up with some immediate and workable solutions without much preparation. That is a gifted level of intelligence I am speaking of. I would call that the colloquial 'bare-bone' minimum."

FBI AGENT JOSEPH DOMINICK PISTONE: "That makes sense to me. I like the combination, but I had the book-smart guy as the one whose head is in books day and night but not much experience on the street. I am thinking of your point. Go on, tell me more of what you have in mind and I will let you know if I agree."

COP DR DAN RUDOFOSSI: "From my experience what I am saying is worth fleshing out first. Police officers and special agents have above average intelligence on an emotional level and fluid level than most civilians I've encountered. Let me give an example, as to general intelligence in officers I will share with you anecdotally that a colleague in the medical profession critiqued my treatment title. As you know, **Eco** for ecology and ***Ethological*** which in our context means survival motivation for human and animals is too complicated for law enforcement professional to tackle. I retorted to my colleague that the belief that cops, cop docs, and agents are kind of 'low IQ dudes and dudettes' that cannot possibly understand four words most high school students could learn and apply after three classes *is not understanding real cops, but caricatures that are biased and reductionistic.* He demurred and actually realized his bias."

FBI AGENT JOSEPH DOMINICK PISTONE: "That is what I meant by book smarts as different from street smarts. You know you just illustrated that in your doctor colleague and friend who is not a cop doc and does not know our world as you do by living as a cop as I have. The idea I was acting can and role playing is assumed by those who are only book smart, but not street smart is my point."

COP DR DAN RUDOFOSSI: "Special Agent Joe P., let me suggest that in my view the idea deep-cover police and agents acting out fantasies and playing fantasy roles as role plays is a rotten fantasy of perhaps the voyeurs of what you do. A scientist, cop doc, or other professionals, including students who seek real understanding, will quickly understand that analogy is quite simplistic. The point of intelligence is to say it may be looked at as steps. First, ethological motivation for survival is shaped within a niche that is always ecologically based. Second that ecological niche supplies what is affordable within that environment. Third is, in any and every way the special agent/detective doing deep-cover operations and intel gathering can use what he/she finds affordable that agent can adapt to and manipulate, and that indicates creative intelligence as well, perhaps a book smarts that is useful and practical. The goal in mind regardless of other goals is gaining deep intelligence about that organized crime family. In that regard you are a scientist and researcher with or without portfolio. Does that make sense to you? In other words, does this layout of reality looked at another way from a forensic psychology professor and cop doc sound sensible to you?"

FBI AGENT JOSEPH DOMINICK PISTONE: "Yes, it absolutely makes sense to me Doc. Infiltrating a crime family is a form of undercover most can't do. Qualifying my thoughts, it's not because they're not good cops or agents. What it takes is, that extra mental toughness. By mental toughness I mean the ability to do the job. That is to focus to do the job as it happens spontaneously. Doing what needs to get done. Getting the job done, in fact, is a key to those who are rare enough to break into the world of the Mafia. Being able to become agents/detectives who can infiltrate the world of the gangster is not a one-time fantasy, it is a real immersion into their world, their culture, and their values. What you call their ecology and survival is key, ethological motivation."

"Doc, I think we are right on target with an assumption in academics. Many, not all, but a lot of administrators think that being an undercover is acting. They also assume most of us are not that bright and need to be educated by solely academic people who are book smart. Book smarts has its place but not on the streets or in doing infiltration of the Mafia. Lacking in street smarts can get an agent or detective killed."

COP DR DAN RUDOFOSSI: "Let me ask you, Special Agent Joe Pistone, since you infiltrated the Mafia for six years, and had at least five USA presidents quote 'that if they could "clone you" to figure out the operations of organized crime groups worldwide they could get a handle on it,' what can be done to educate those who may be more inclined toward 'book smarts' to improve their understanding of the reality you face as a 'deep-cover operative'?"

FBI AGENT JOSEPH DOMINICK PISTONE: "I find many book-smart administrators pass over a basic skill by which they get the point here is to respect the deep-cover agent, means learning to understand what we are doing as operatives or intel agents by observing first."

"I mean really doing what is necessary to learn directly from us as individuals. Learn from us by understanding teamwork is about listening to the less-educated field-experienced operative when it is all done. So, what I mean to illustrate is a case that let's say is folded in and closed. Yes, the academic can know some small aspect of deep cover by reading such and such a book."

"But book reading does not reach out and give the student what it really is like to be a deep cover. Being with the agent, that is, in person, and asking questions and learning from the operative the nuances as to why he did this and not that is basic to this education and experience for starts."

"That ability to fit in different situations with 'being-yourself' is very important, as I teach those I train. I show them and express to them in person what it is I want to teach him/her not just have them read the book. You can't only learn that from a book, no matter how well written, experience is the best teacher. Like you said in earlier conversations being in an identity mode to conduct operations is not reading about an identity mode as a teacher or instructor, it's doing it."

COP DR DAN RUDOFOSSI: "Can you give an example to educate the students?"

FBI AGENT JOSEPH DOMINICK PISTONE: "Yeah, the aspect of what you call 'identity modes' are the switches officers go through in developing into different modes of identity. An example is by being yourself, by knowing your own-self and your real values. So, even though you need to put on a front to gangsters and switch when you are with one like Tony Mirra, and not the same as when you are with Sonny Black Napolitano. I keep my awareness, I am the real me, whether under cover, or an FBI special agent, that is also what I mean by mental toughness, capish?"

COP DR DAN RUDOFOSSI: "Capito! I call such ability which is rare, quite a gift in those officers/agents/detectives who can skillfully use and adapt with their own emerging identity modes by understanding the process of dissociation many of us undergo during heavy situations, especially traumatic ones, such as dealing with Tony Mirra rather than Sonny Black Napolitano."

FBI AGENT JOSEPH DOMINICK PISTONE: "Yeah, it's a world of difference because Tony Mirra would as soon shoot you if you mess up by not nodding a certain way, while Sonny Black would get a cup of espresso and really talk to you like a regular guy."

COP DR DAN RUDOFOSSI: "As you put it earlier, if I got it right, your need to survive is crucial and in sync with my eco-ethological analysis. It is never role plays or acting a part as prepared for in Hollywood, and Broadway plays. Identity modes is not altering your complete personality and losing yourself identity, at least not fully. The motivation if I am getting it right, is putting our scientific focus on etching in ethologically, is survival in the ecological niche you find yourself in, and at times with little preparation."

FBI AGENT JOSEPH DOMINICK PISTONE: "Yeah, that's right. Because if you are in the wrong place, at the wrong time, and you are the wrong guy chosen to do deep cover, you have a slim to zero chance of coming out alive. You will likely be wrapped in an Indian throw rug and tossed out with the junk by a private san-man to the dumping grounds and ground up fertilizer. You will become an unknown and missing person who disappeared without a trace save the capo who had the hit on you for being revealed as a deep cover and now deep sixed."

COP DR DAN RUDOFOSSI: "It is interesting that studies on primates such as chimpanzees and lowland gorillas where mistakes can be deadly when a member of one family ventures into the territory of another (Ardrey, 1966; Mitani et al., 2012; Hunt, 2020; Morris, 1994) and is not repairable if perceived as an encroachment on another's territory by primatologists who study human and primate behavior and culture. Stay with me on this comparison for a moment, because primates ventures in their day-to-day life is as telling as to what you as an agent being placed in a subtle war zone as organized crime syndicates requires. Let me explain if I am being sensible in your experience. We know that chimpanzees are anything but stupid playthings as depicted in our own anthropomorphic versions. Chimpanzees have constant violent and deadly potential, *if they feel their territory is threatened by an impostor to their own clan*. While exceptions of humans living with chimpanzees and lowland gorillas that kept very cautious boundaries [very bright and empathic and acknowledged for their ingenuity and genius such as field scientists include Drs Fosse, Goodall, Morris, and Lorenz to name a few], chimpanzees and lowland gorillas as other primates expanded our knowledge ethologically and ecologically speaking."

FBI AGENT JOSEPH DOMINICK PISTONE: "Yeah, so what is the comparison here Doc. Are you asking me if I can connect with the chimpanzees and lowland gorillas as primitive as being able to live among gangsters?"

COP DR DAN RUDOFOSSI: "Kind of, let me further state, the scientists I mentioned not only lived but became intimately involved in the daily lives of primates and I don't think any real study ever fully captured the depth of that impact ethologically and ecologically speaking from an existential analysis. I am not suggesting we try to extrapolate about that, but the research suggests some very key findings about the violence and cooperation in such a culture as well as differences in primate eco-ethological niches which is key into my enquiry as to your own unique experiences."

FBI AGENT JOSEPH DOMINICK PISTONE: "Go on Doc, I'm listening to your line of thinking and where you are going with this."

COP DR DAN RUDOFOSSI: "Where I am going with this is seeking answers by narrowing down the findings and the comparison for future research and clinical value. Although Fosse and Goodall or Morris did not actually live among the chimpanzees as chimpanzees, or gorillas, they did not infiltrate the primate community and make camp within their hierarchy as another gorilla but as an outsider participant with clear kept boundaries—no easy feat and pioneering. The analogy is clear. Barring being politically correct, but honestly and scientifically making a comparison: Let's say you entered a gorilla's primate family which is well established and the alpha male gorilla realized you were challenging that primate's alpha status, or even encroaching on his territory, your skull would be crushed in, in short order."

"Let's pause and get very real as to your superb adaptation within the crime families. Is it not true, that if you crossed capo Toni Mirra or the likes of him, the same result for you could have occurred?" [Assent by Special Agent, Joe Pistone with "Uh, Hum."]

"The ingenuity of doing what you did is an incredibly complex adaptation in the community of organized crime families which is draped in violence, status, and territorial imperatives that if violated cause immediate death. An analogous, but not direct comparison, is unique eco-ethological niches that differ in primate eco-ethological niches. No less ingenious emotionally and strategically you had to feign being an actual initiate to associate and all the way through becoming a made member of the Bonanno crime family. By initiating contact and infiltrating the crime family of La Cosa Nostra when violence and death threatens you at one wrong territorial gesture, violation of rules as proxemics or space allowed verbally or physically you could get whacked as equivalent to a gorilla getting brained as a stray gorilla trying to initiate status in a new family of gorillas. My specific question for you Joe Pistone as initiate Donnie Brasco, is does this analogy resonate with you as realistic in the real threats you faced? Your ingenuity was remarkable if not ingenious as Jane Goodall entering the territory she did, but more intense because she did not become a gorilla mate but an observing participant [Rudofossi & Maloney, 2019], you became the associate successfully and I would say all but portfolio the made wiseguy, does that make sense to you, or am I totally off?"

FBI AGENT JOSEPH DOMINICK PISTONE: "Yes, what you said makes a lot of sense. You're on course. I like the analogy, although you used it and called it as it is. I didn't call myself ingenious, but as you're the cop doc, I won't argue that point. You are right as to the potential undercover having to realize, and more so the administration, that the undercover is operating in the world of the gangster. I would agree that world can be and is often as dangerous as the gorilla and chimpanzee at war within their family units and without as you've also shared with me."

COP DR DAN RUDOFOSSI: "In other words, as I have also gained from the beginning of our friendship and collegial relationship that you clearly related, the world of the gangster is not the world of the law enforcement administrator or politicization of the criminal justice world. I am adding that if I got it right, this is not a minor gloss over or expression but one that clinician-scientists and investigators, academicians, and practitioner's need to really understand at a deeper and more comprehensive level. Correct?"

FBI AGENT JOSEPH DOMINICK PISTONE: "Doc, you nailed it. In fact, your comparisons and eco-ethological approach adds another understanding to help communicate to the uninformed that the undercover is not operating in the world of law enforcement. And if he's made into a wiseguy as a made member of that particular family, all is given to him. His infiltration is successful, and he is accepted, he is no longer able to operate in the world of law enforcement, as he now has been accepted in that world of the gangster. The administrators, many academics only, and politicians and lawyers make a major mistake in thinking the undercover agent has to operate in the world of law enforcement officer versus the world of the gangsters he has to infiltrate. Somehow, he can maintain that law enforcement character while getting deeper and more wrapped up in becoming a gangster. That is farthest from the truth and the comparison with adaptation is really not adaptation as I said if the agent is discovered to be a law enforcement officer, he is cooked as the goose in the pot and will be sent down river."

"Being in that identity mode as the gangster includes knowing the unwritten rules only gangsters know and their real members and not going back and forth making an error by forgetting or doing it as if you are playing a role. If you do that you will get your head bashed in, just like that chimpanzee or gorilla you spoke about. So, in my opinion, what you said, and my own thoughts and what I am relating to your readers is on target, as far as I'm concerned. You either do it, or fail at doing it, and the result of being found out is simple as pie, 'You're Done!'"

COP DR DAN RUDOFOSSI: "Taking our understanding further along, in a way, if I am on track, then the identity mode of the gangster is more like what you became and being 'Donnie Brasco'? In my own desire and respect for your transformation and development into your other identity mode for six years and the after-impact and re-emergence of Joe Pistone as more wise and more adept in your expert knowledge as Donnie Brasco, let me ask you a question: By disseminating that rare knowledge and wisdom, to educate other chiefs, special agents in charge, clinicians, and students to learn from, I understand that your adaptation in an ethologically sense of survival as to the emotional and mental demands, cultural mores, rituals to survive in the crime family was no less in demands than in an ecology such as the primate example we used, and much more in depth as humans we can add the diplomacy and discernment of human community as much more sophisticated implicitly and soulfully. [Special Agent Pistone assents with "Yeah, I got you, go ahead."] Fitting into the Mafia hierarchy, as you did from an unknown initiate into the very seat of operations of the Bonanno family demanded mastery of the implicit rules to tie into ensuring on one hand your extraordinary success, and on the other primal primate-level survival!"

"In other words, accurate and real diplomacy undercover offers survival above the covers as each day passes. Does this sound like I am getting what you lived through with any sensibility, or am I getting off course?"

FBI AGENT JOSEPH DOMINICK PISTONE: "You're on course. The comparison you used fits. Like I said, the undercover has to satisfy the world of the gangster. The right thing is operating in that foreign world. Your comparison is good because a very violent and stone-cold killer is exactly like that world real gorillas. A wrong move into forbidden territory and violating a rule that is even unwritten but should be known spells Death."

"Gangsters are not interested in excuses like, 'Sorry, I didn't know Boss.' It is nothing personal to the gangster to whack you, it is doing business. You violate that rule, and you are done. Maybe now, maybe later, but you are in their scopes."

"Doing your homework by studying and knowing your territory and the bosses and players is key to survival. It is a good analogy with the qualifications you made as well. The burden is on the agent to satisfy all the needs of the wiseguy culture. That wiseguy culture is not all and the same also. Some general rules apply as I spell out in my book, *The Way of the Wiseguy*, as that ecology to survive in [Pistone, 2004]. It is very demanding to say the least. As you put it, it demands a high level of being spontaneous to adapt to the world of the gangster. That ecology is a constant life of unpredictability and danger even when things look fine, and on the level. Nothing is cookie-cutter neat and sweet, or predictable. I would say it is even like a chimpanzee walking into a den of gorillas and his cover is blown, we all know the result of that fiasco and the mess to follow."

COP DR DAN RUDOFOSSI: "That mess confirms the point. It is a messy business and clearly the one major point for the student and pro here is that the worlds of law enforcement and gangster are not parallel but perhaps reciprocal, parallel antitheses along the links that are common threads. That thread is never, ever making the mistake that when you enter infiltration or even consider investigation of organized crime you bring your law enforcement knapsack. Leave it in the precinct locker room and get a Borsellino wide-brim Panama fedora hat, an unlit Cuban cigar, with a rum and coke on the rocks in a coffee cup and enter the front door."

FBI AGENT JOSEPH DOMINICK PISTONE: "Yeah, the man in the white hat and Corfram shoes polished will get a hi and bye and clam-up response."

> **Lesson Learned Street Smarts and Book Smarts Count**
>
> The point here is that Special Agent Pistone and I are synchronizing the street-smart piece as a focal point to consider. The rules and regulations, the dress code, the protocol for assigning tours of duty and sign-in, as well as firearms and uniform are not valid in the world of the gangster. As a participant observer initiate learns very well and experiences as best as possible the mores, the dress codes, and the so-called irrelevant aspects of the culture you intend to understand by respectful imitation and practice fitting in as best you could. In this way the book smarts and street smarts converge. The lesson is to immerse yourself in both dimensions as thoroughly as possible.

COP DR DAN RUDOFOSSI: "Joe, let me run a concept by you for now. As you know, I have developed over two decades of clinical work and research in the area of complex trauma, complicated grief, and dissociative disorders with police and public safety professionals. The gist of an important survival mode all first responders get into is what I called *adaptive functional dissociation*. From a psychological point of view, at times of severe stress and trauma, adaptative can become *maladaptive dysfunctional dissociation*."

FBI AGENT JOSEPH DOMINICK PISTONE: "Explain to me what you mean by all first responders using this adaptative functional dissociation first before the maladaptive and dysfunctional dissociation?"

COP DR DAN RUDOFOSSI: "Sure, let me explain. First, the core aspects of adaptative functional dissociation is where an officer is functioning and for all purposes adapting to life at home, and at being a police officer is going as well as can be expected. The measure of going well as can be expected is what is called SOP or standard operating procedure. But for psychologists and psychiatrists this standard of functioning is defined with measurements that are reliable instruments used to measure feelings and thoughts about an event, say a shooting, kidnapping, or car accident an officer is involved in. It is all about thoughts and emotions one can consciously recall and disclose in self-report measures."

"In my first book [Rudofossi, 2007] I explained to clinicians and in my survivor's guide for officers and their families [Rudofossi, 2012] that as law enforcement officers we are taught to maintain command presence. You know better than most, that means one presents as strong and knowledgeable and gains control of the room, or the street, as we say in the NYPD. Polite at the same time, one must always be in authority and maintain control of self and others on the street. On the controlled streets most officers can appear well and healthy enough. Even after a shooting, multiple homicides, a train or truck wreck where emergency service unit or technical assistance unit is called when asked by the NYPD doc or cop doc, how are you doing? Would you like to join, or nowadays you will join such and such debriefing? The position taken is, 'Hey, my partner may use your help, or that cop from the other unit, or department, but in all honesty I am fine.' Deferring assistance from mental health professionals that are outside of the department holds even more stigma. But that ability to function adaptively is in all honesty, just that—the ability to function and at the same time to dissociate well enough to do what must be done and not cave in to full blown depression, angst, anxiety, mania or retreat and withdrawal."

> **Adaptive Functional Dissociation**
>
> Dissociation, in brief, is developed when an officer responds to different demands afforded in the ecological niche in which she/he must survive ethologically. It is within the adaptive function of dissociation and identity modes that officers become able to deal with the enormous variation in eco-ethological niches and the varieties of cumulative trauma and loss. Identity modes and adaptive functional dissociation are largely unconscious and need to be explored in order to gain an understanding and sensibility beyond labels and misappropriations of intentions due to the ecological niche and ethological motivation which incorporates cultural differences as well.

FBI AGENT JOSEPH DOMINICK PISTONE: "Doc, wasn't it a shrink like you that developed the whole way of coping we used to say, "The I'm okay, and you're okay stuff," the NYPD and FBI taught its agents may have been partially the mantra we all learnt to deal with staying out of the rubber room and keep doing our jobs. The adaptive functional dissociation is exactly the way cops cope with all the stuff that hits the fan on the streets. It makes sense and works."

COP DR DAN RUDOFOSSI: "That is so true and my point is it works well and is organic. But it also has a very toxic outcome in many cases if not most. Let me illustrate. Identity modes are the different aspects that shade our responses to trouble, danger, and even fear when doing our specific job."

> **Identity Modes**
>
> The identity modes that emerge are really defenses which assist the officer in managing to develop a personality structure around dealing with certain types of very demanding events that pull out the defenses necessitated. In time, similar events trigger these altered identity modes that emerge and become more crystallized within that officer's identity and in sync with his/her police personality style.

"For example, you may have to function and adapt as a first responder dealing with shifts toward survival when you confront a perpetrator who car-jacked an elderly couple's car and has shot at you. Whether special agent or police officer a *take down and collar identity mode is provoked eco-ethologically*. The perpetrator hits into some parked cars and your identity mode shifts as he sets his .45 caliber stolen Ruger downhill at you in the perfect 'M' of his sights. He is now in between cars as a police caravan has left you alone in a moment. That moment lasts forever in your own mind."

"Your thinking, emotional, mood, and temperament is now *an LEO warrior identity mode readying for spontaneous firefighting*. Within two minutes what feels like an eternity is heightened as his firearm jams and when you are ready to fire on him to stop his murderous rampage he flees and gets hit and pinned. Or you unload and hit him with a volley of shots and he is down and now you begin CPR."

"You suddenly once again have shifted into another very different, *compassionate mercy identity mode*. In this identity mode you are now focused mentally, physically, and tactically on doing rescue of the 'bad-guy.' Civilians cannot understand this easily. This bad guy as miscreant tried to hurt you minutes ago and you were on a crash course on survival—your own—and now you are mentally and emotionally in an identity mode of trying to keep our 'reformed perpetrator' alive. He didn't change but you have as your identity mode is triggered as it has been from your first similar experience and you are suddenly calling for a bus [ambulance] and you are desperately trying to keep him breathing. These identity modes are not conscious and are challenging to even the best of officers and drains your ability to adapt to strain and stress."

"Most of all it is occurring when you are adaptively functioning and dissociating while of course needing to function at a high level of competence. It is conceived as standard operating procedure; in real time and space it is anything but SOP."

> **Standard operating procedure (SOP)** is a short-hand communication among police and it means that the officer who has undergone whatever the challenge in the field is, it is all okay and quite normalized. The problem is that it is not normal, but it is accepted as such in order to be able to process the intensity and duration of the trauma endured in many circumstances beyond the officer's control. Standard operating procedure often goes hand in foot with adaptive functional dissociation as it occludes any real processing of the impact of each traumatic event and its accumulation over long periods of time.

"Saying it is SOP helps us as LEOs to cope with the stress and strain, but only temporary band-aiding the pain and the emotional weight of trauma. The trauma of being placed into the conflicting identity modes demanding our attention and focus is often put on hold and accumulates over a decade or two on the job, sometimes it is a decade or two after the job, but it catches up with all of us, one way and manifestation or another."

FBI AGENT JOSEPH DOMINICK PISTONE: "What makes a lot of sense to me is the adaptive functioning under fire and in all these different situations. It takes very strong mental toughness to maintain satisfying the different worlds and the bosses in each of these different worlds you call the eco-ethological niches. The different identity modes need to be managed as one person; I never lost being me although I agree I had to adapt with different modes of identity. I like the concept and that resonates with me. I was not abnormal or mentally ill, but I had to deal with as you say a lot of stress and strain and life-threatening situations as part of the world of the gangster."

COP DR DAN RUDOFOSSI: "I really appreciate your validating not only my theory of cumulative police trauma but the contextual analysis of the eco-ethological analysis and identity modes, standard operating procedure, and adaptive functional dissociation."

FBI AGENT JOSEPH DOMINICK PISTONE: "I know you said you were going to get to the toxic effect. How does this take place? Is it that some officers crack under the identity modes or can't adapt to the different demands of survival ethologically?"

COP DR DAN RUDOFOSSI: "That's a great question and let me open by repeating that in my world as a cop doc I see the majority of officers, special agents, and those on the front line to say nothing of officers and agents as you are very rare in what you achieved and endured to walk away unscathed by the scars and losses of scores of traumata we all lost count of keeping score on. Let me point out now, although we'll deal with 'It' later, the crucial part of my theory and treatment is the existential center of finding you and me in the whirlwind of the traumatic spiral and anchor meaning and purpose to replace 'Its' coordinates. For now, the impact on the heart and soul of the officer/special agent in dealing with the heaps of traumatic losses and returning to a healthier self after the dust and bones settle the scoring, calls for an *Eco-Ethological Existential Analysis* we will revisit later. The heart of the problem of maladaptive dysfunctional dissociation is when an officer is taken off their assignment, promoted, or even after retirement. It is at this point when that officer is 'far away' from the dis-stress of 'the job' and 'doing the job' as we in law enforcement like to call our particular job. It is when separation from the noise and the switching of identity modes that the trouble begins."

Maladaptive Dysfunctional Dissociation

Maladaptive dysfunctional dissociation is the dissembling and decompensation of defenses that shaped and modeled the different identity modes in the context of ongoing eco-ethological niches of trauma, violence, and loss. The derivatives of drives from aggression, sexual, biosocial, physiological, and cognitive all served to keep the officer acting as if all was normal in a world hardly healthy and balanced. Daily, officers deal with extraordinary events and civilians as well as colleagues and other professionals under the highest levels of stress and strain. The sudden disequilibrium of leaving the job, being injured on the job, being re-assigned, having the operation ended abruptly and before the agent or detective has closed the cases to his/her level of satisfaction and professional and personal best disrupts the entire interlocking process and all the conscious and unconscious dynamics. The assessment and treatment are very time consuming and cost much in empathy, reconstructing the injuries, and guiding the healing and recovery.

"The traumatic losses that have accumulated no longer have functional outlets in being active in the eco-ethological niches established; without outlets to function in, the identity modes spiral into dysfunctional identity issues as dissociative grief and trauma disorders converge. This brews at concentrated levels. The outlet to use 20-plus years of expressing standard operating procedure and command presence is abruptly absent with no command to safely hide in, and no job to functionally operate in anymore. Losses replace purposes in functioning, adaptation patterns learned become maladaptation, dysfunction, and severe dissociation in complex PTSD and complicated grief."

"The old line when you are dealing 'with it all' as a deep cover in this regard is parallel to the Blue Knight on patrol. Joseph Wambaugh called it straight in *The Blue Knight* [Wambaugh, 1973], in my own words we have all heard this, 'it's all routine in a cop's daily beat. Once you've been through your rookie years you've seen it all.' Do you relate to this?"

FBI AGENT JOSEPH DOMINICK PISTONE: "Yes, and it's true from the beat cop and detective it's all thought to be routine, I get your point, and let me tell you, as you know being a cop and having been a gold shield yourself, it's not routine. Police work can feel routine but you never know what is around the corner on patrol but in the world of infiltration multiply that many times over."

"It is living in the world of the wiseguy. Administrators think the undercover again operates in the world of law enforcement and must. I operated in the world of the gangster. Your concept and description of identity modes places the agent into many conflicts as to the different pressures demanding attention."

"When you ask an agent to adapt there is no guide you can turn to. Not boss to see you through step by step. You need to have the 'mental toughness' and immerse yourself into the world of the gangster".

"What they ask is simple and not realistic in expecting the agent to immerse into that gangster's world and identify with being and becoming the gangster by expecting the special agent to convince wiseguys that you really are one of them from A to Z. But then the administrator expects you to live in the world of prim and proper orderly law enforcement. It is truly a Disney and boy scout rodeo show, it is not doable."

"That is why all you've said so far and I have added to it, is to say, I agree with you. I really fully agree with you! You are a cop doc and to me, and other law enforcement officers, it means a lot. It means you had to be in the saddle and effect many collars and get really dirty on the streets—that is why you get it. You had to have gotten into it, or you too would have been capped or whacked on the streets of Brooklyn North in the late 1980s or 1990s. Doc, it's not a role as in a lot of these classes trainees say to me, even other law enforcement officers say to me, 'Joe, you must have been a hell of an actor. You played the Donnie Brasco perfectly.'"

"Well, it's not acting, Doc, it is being yourself. It's not a role play as you explained, and it's not acting as they in administration think it is. Again, it's being yourself. I was me, yes, even as Donnie Brasco. Your way as a psychologist explains my mindset so far, as it was and is. I didn't and don't ever have multiple personalities. There is one me and yes, Donnie Brasco was me as well, an identity mode makes sense. A split personality alters, or multiple personality disorder, does not to me."

COP DR DAN RUDOFOSSI: "Exactly, and well said! Thank you much. My point is that clinicians not psychopathologize your adaptation; in attempting to understand and learn from you, insight demands responsibility. As psychologists/psychiatrists we need to learn and adapt to patients' worlds and stop trying to make the world in our own linear model. Legislating right from wrong ways of being and becoming as psychologists/psychiatrists/physicians' altruism is more or less sophistry. When ingenuity and adaptation is reduced to psychiatric categorization it is certainly not science, but politicization. The short diversion here is worth the critical thinking as scientists and investigators we just indulged in. Getting back on track, Special Agent Joe Pistone, is there an analogy you can use to educate me and the readers as far as the world of the gangster and law enforcement as you lived your deep-cover identity mode as Donnie Brasco for six plus years?"

FBI AGENT JOSEPH DOMINICK PISTONE: "The undercover must satisfy, as I said, those three mistresses and to do the right thing. As I mentioned earlier, you need to know your enemy well."

"You have to get into it. It's beyond culture. You need to know your enemy and their own society. All these organized crime guys are in their own separate world. You need to keep your ethics as to who you are. That is why you got to know your enemy and their culture and how they operate within their society. All these organized crime families operate within their cultural and ecology with their own codes and customs and their own morals. It's not like normal society and the point of survival, as you say, ethological motivation, is on point. The context is that ecological niche you are thrust into. You are accepted, or you are thrown out."

"You are not dealing with law enforcement rules and regulations and you're also not dealing with normal society and culture as regular people. You are dealing with gangsters and their own world and rules which are different than anything normal."

"It is as violent as a society of gorillas. But they are smart, not brutes. As your approach suggests Doc, they have their own rules, families, or you can say, tribes, and eco-ethological niches."

"Do you remember in the movie, *Donnie Brasco*, when Lefty was proposing me for membership in the Bonanno family? When Sonny Black was told Lefty was going to propose me for membership in the Bonanno family, he gave me the thumbs up I was going to be inducted into the Bonanno family. One of the things Lefty told me was the deal was being made, and I was successful. I was establishing myself; I was well on my way to becoming made in the Bonanno family. So, I say to Lefty, 'I'm doing pretty good now, and so what's my advantage of being inducted into the family?'"

"Lefty, he's as serious as can be, he looks me straight in my eyes and says, 'Donnie you can lie. Yes, you can steal. You can cheat. Donnie Brasco you can even murder a guy, and it's all legit, it's all legitimate!'"

"I mean that's the mindset, you know. No time to even get off track as in deep cover when you start, you are on your own track. You make it, or you are broken by it and within it."

COP DR DAN RUDOFOSSI: "If I am getting it right, I may be getting it wrong. Please, correct me if I am wrong, or off course. Here, it goes, Joe, in the eco-ethological niche you were asked to infiltrate and therefore to survive, if I have heard it right, you successfully assimilated and accommodated as a member of the crime family as an acceptable member. You achieved becoming an 'associate.'"

"You had ingeniously and with extraordinary skill reached all but portfolio, as I conceptualize it, as a **made man**. As the 'made man,' that is, in the universe of the gangster, becoming a legit wiseguy, within the Bonanno crime family, is achieved by being a made man."

"You were on the cusp of doing so, and being the first to do so, as you had been the first to already reach the highest level you did within the Mafia. Amazingly, your personage as Donnie Brasco was an identity modality that was created by your own ingenuity for six years."

"The pressure cooker on you to achieve this even with full mental awareness and ingenious emotional and strategic genius is remarkable. On an existential level, others don't get the aspect that makes you who you are, a human being. No matter how we look at it, the ingenuity Donnie Brasco you not only created, but breathed and lived in for six years of life. Your own life is not an alter ego or altered identity as much as he is part of you and yet will always be a shadow of your real identity as Joseph Dominick Pistone. The identity mode of Donnie Brasco is truly a result of the tough-minded integrity in which you crafted consciously the defenses and the resilience to be Donnie. In another whole dimension of your existence as Donnie you shifted and danced in the shadows of hiding, crafting camouflage, and mimicking the gangsters until you excelled at their ways and meaning largely without conscious pursuit, but more so as unconscious allowance of letting go and letting identity as a gangster ensue."

FBI AGENT JOSEPH DOMINICK PISTONE: "Yeah, I agree with what you're saying. Being human is being yourself. The need to prove who you are is not done with words, or even on a conscious and intentional planned level. It is done by actually surviving and getting the job done well. Being thorough in your identity mode is matching up to the demands of the ecology you are, yes thrust into."

"I did do that with mental toughness, when you think about it that way. The distance of not knowing what deep cover and even police work is about is so far removed from many who speak as if they do know.

"Knowing is not by reading a book or trying to speculate about what is the right way to do. It is in doing it that you learn if you can actually survive and do it. Then you look at the media portrayal of law enforcement work as warped and distorted. How could understanding be achieved in this culture as to what I had achieved without portfolio as you said, Doc?"

COP DR DAN RUDOFOSSI: "That is a great point and question in our anti-police biased ecology. Outside of some very rare perps with a shield which we can discuss later if okay with you such as the Mafia cops, most cops are stalwart citizens and first responders that are disenfranchised. Others who have no street savvy and were born and bred in places where they cannot connect to the street is a real limitation. Those who have grown up and lived in the streets may also judge with harshness and without compassion as given to all other groups. It is clear from your point of view, that a high level of intelligence is requisite when you ask someone to enter the belly of the beast. He/she needs to live that identity, not act as if they are in play world and fantasia as we have established."

"It seems to me that in your reality, you more than anyone in our line of work has given more and done more than all of us. Yet although your identity modes change, you have maintained your own identity overall as Joseph Pistone throughout."

"Your survival in a concrete jungle mentality was similar but unlike a cultural anthropologist. To put it bluntly, as I do with my students, Joe, you needed to be tough and bounce with the wiseguys, or be rejected as a deep cover. You did that for six years."

"If you were rejected, you would have died. If you are discovered as a police detective or agent, at best you become a pawn as hostage."

"So, you put your life on the line. You did your job with courage and bravely, while others cannot forget what they never knew in the first place. I am aware as you educated me and all, those rules and regulations don't exist formally. As a deep cover you were asked to do what most of us mere mortals can't come close to do. That includes me!"

"At some level this knowledge, as well as the fact that you achieved the highest level for a deep cover and lived the life of a wiseguy for all of us, at times must suck dirt?"

FBI AGENT JOSEPH DOMINICK PISTONE: "Yeah, exactly right! You were a real cop and did the job. You are a cop doc who talks with other cops, you talk with deep-cover agents, and get the real deal stuff we deal with on in the same streets you also did street-crime collars. Many of these others get their ideal programs and their ideas by reading other people's books as I've shared."

"It is naive to think they really know about trauma and the real stuff we go through in deep cover without ever wearing a shield. The other part of disconnect is you've cared and stood by with us as you have, and do to this day. By thinking a book or a few courses will give students the experience of the street is naive at best, and deadly to a selected agent who has been coached in this and believes it is a truth to live by, as taught by an academic. Sorry Doc, that is the truth as I see it and I've shared why this truth to me is self-evident."

COP DR DAN RUDOFOSSI: "Can you give me an example of this experience you had with one of the academics that was particularly disturbing?"

FBI AGENT JOSEPH DOMINICK PISTONE: "Yes, I was doing training overseas to educate some potential agents in doing and learning about undercover work. In my lecture I was interrupted a number of times. I stopped and I looked at this guy and said, 'Hey, if you have something to say, say it to me at the end of the lecture. I'll listen to what it is you want to say, but don't interrupt me. and what I am saying.' He didn't talk after. He waited to the end of the lecture, because earlier he had interjected his comments. He was glib with his views up to that point. I waited. Well, when the lecture had ended, I asked him directly, have you ever done any deep-cover work yourself?"

"Have you interviewed any undercover agents yourself? Have you done any of this type of work as a psychologist, or psychiatrist by finding out information as a researcher or clinical doc? His answer was honestly, 'No!' Well, then I asked him, 'where did you get all this information about what deep-cover agents do, and how to assess them, or us, or for that matter, me?'"

"Well, Doc, he looks down. He says, 'You may have been Donnie Brasco, but I read so and so psychologist and psychiatrist. The leading authorities say to do this series of tests first and here you think you can judge the quality of these candidates on your street experience. It doesn't work that way in conducting real scientific-based judgments.'"

"I told him without missing a heartbeat, 'I don't care about your Dr. Shit man, the radical man. All you're doing is parroting someone else's work and applying it to making judgments in real life and situations where the agent is needed. That is someone like you who has never been out on the street.'"

"Doc, you know that's the problem. You know this is the real problem right here. This is the first undercover job this guy ever became associated with. Yet, he has every opinion to spout out about undercovers, but with no real knowledge."

"I kept this last part to myself and said at that point, 'Let me ask you, when you do sit down with undercovers, your approach is based on some thinking that you read from some other academic who had never been out on the street. You realize that right now, you're not listening at all, but speaking over real undercovers. Further, you're doing some selection after assessing the potential undercover agent for a position. In my view, having lived this deep cover for six years of my life, you have no idea what you actually are talking about as an agent.'"

"'Rather it is really some academic you've listened to that gives you your expertise. So, you did not listen at all to the most important man or woman to interview, the undercover himself. How could you bring yourself to believe you really understand any of this?' He couldn't answer and was silent after that education by me."

"Does that make sense to you Doc, as to this guy's nerve in doing so and the danger of misreading the needs of agents and what makes an agent who he/she is and how he can do his job well. You can't get this out of any book you know. [Rhetorically expressed.]

Humility and Respect of Expert Practitioners

This is truly a great lesson for students and instructors. The best learning is done by actively listening. If you are trying to speak over the other person rather than hear what he/she is expressing then you cannot learn. What many who teach forget is Special Agent Joe Pistone's point parallels Dr. Freud's, which is an analytic attitude in which the clinician learns by being silent and gaining information or intelligence without smug judgment. As a member of a class, please allow your professor to finish her/his line of thinking first before needing to show how smart you may be. Much wisdom is gained in silent witnessing and absorbing what is said first and responding later after you hear and confirm what you think you've heard was really said.

COP DR DAN RUDOFOSSI: [With empathy and connection.] "Joseph yes, superbly spoken, and it is hubris and umbrage both that replaces a speed loader and the rounds shots as duds."

"I am with you completely. Real scientists and effective professors frame hypotheses and work with humility and due diligence to become culturally competent."

"Without blowing smoke and condescending on some of my peers in academia, I also understand and respect and value you as the marathon runner. What I mean is that you ran a mental and emotional marathon as a deep cover. Who can run a marathon for six years in law enforcement and be as effective in academia? It is intellectual arrogance if not intellectual fascism to discount and dismiss your own ability and skill. The fact you were all but a made member of the Bonanno crime family, is in reality further than anyone ever went in an organized crime family. At the same time, you've educated the world of law enforcement and criminal justice about the real Mafia more than any other law enforcement officer, academic, or administrator has ever done. The fact that unlike the giants in applying and becoming participant observers such as Franz Boas, Margaret Mead, Edward Sapir, and Benjamin Lee Whorf, who respectively lived and learnt from Baffin Island Inuit, Samoans, Native American tribes, and the development of linguistic and cultural differences. The insight into being respectful and learning gently from the cultures one studied and not advocating, interfering, and dismissing cultural patterns which in the vast cases of doing so is as damaging as apathy. Further the interplay of language and culture and the importance of individual differences as in narrowing down relativity within cultural differences underlies the Sapir-Whorf hypothesis [Boas, 1911; Mead, 1975; Sapir, 1916; Sapir & Irvine, 2002]. I don't want to get academic, but the problem is it is not the book smarts that count but being a scholar and practicing as one which means your ego is left on the coat rack when you invite someone in to share collegially. If I become a stiff shirt and starched collar, please let me know?"

FBI AGENT JOSEPH DOMINICK PISTONE: "Exactly! You are no stiff shirt and show no stuffy starch in your collar. I am glad you pursued your line of questioning. A lot of administrators are not immersed in the undercover business. The administrators don't look at the undercover as a person with a lot of intelligence. To them, you're on a level two, and they are on a level ten. They talk and assume you are less than intelligent and need to be taught the A, B, Cs of the job. The reality is they never have been a deep cover and lived as one. So, you gotta pull them up to understand this reality as well. It would be good if they took heed of professors Boas, Mead, Sapir, and Whorf as it is clear they may have read them but did not absorb lessons from them."

"Let me give you an example, Doc. We were doing an undercover assessment and choosing who will make a good informant. With a number of administrators sitting in we also had contracted some other experts such as psychologists, psychiatrists. We all were sitting around. The psych docs start off by telling me that this guy is good, and this other guy is not going to be good as an informant. This is the time we were moving to close down the operation, Donnie Brasco. The assessment goal sought out, who would be an informant, and who would not?"

"Without missing a beat and with cocksure certainty, these shrinks and academics were pointing out who would be a 'good and reliable informant' and who would not be! With no room to even turn and look in my direction and say, 'Special Agent Joe Pistone, what do you think?'"

"They made their decisions. They and the administrators informed me as to why they made their decision. Again, no desire to hear my opinion as different than their own, they had made up their minds and closed off any other mindset opinion and that included my own."

"The result Doc, was they were completely off in their decision making. I told the psychologist and psychiatrist you are totally wrong. I told them straight out, and why. Their override was something like, 'this guy will do such and such because his personality traits are such and such. His mood and temperament are such that he will go along with the agents that move ahead with trying to flip these associates.' They explained why, or why not, in a very academic sense. This guy will turn from wiseguy over to informant. Well, again they were consistently wrong in their assessment. Consequentially, no one turned."

"So, you know here we go again, they were left wasting a lot of time and energy because they felt inside that this guy—meaning me—can't know as much as psychologists and psychiatrists about deep cover. You know what I mean?"

COP DR DAN RUDOFOSSI: "Yeah, I think I do, but I will pause and confirm if that's ok and describe what you shared with me from the lingo of a psychologist who was taught classically as a street cop, son of a dad who was USN all the way, and from classic analysts such as my mentor Dr. Charles Brenner, Dr. Albert Ellis, Dr. R. R. Ellis protégé of Dr. Carl Rodger, and Dr. Frankl via Drs A. Graber and B. Barnes."

"In regards to psychologists and psychiatrists, I was trained by the developers of cognitive-behavioral, psychoanalytic, client-centered, pastoral, and existential treatment and assessment. My wisdom is not to prescribe a one-style-and-fit treatment for all patients/clients but to stop, pause, and learn from each patient's unique background, training, and educational perspective first, then to consider one's approach that is responsive to what one must first identify, assess, and process as doable and not doable in this context. I must actively listen and learn to be able to assess, identify problems, and accommodate by expert acquisition of relative knowledge before trying to approach a sophisticated task asked of me, such a task would be using my skill-set as a licensed psychologist and cop doc to understand the needs of the FBI task force in selecting a specific agent to infiltrate a specific eco-ethological niche and his/her existential strength, and now that I am learning from you as a colleague with much more wisdom in deep cover operations, their level and adaptability in '**mental toughness development**.'"

Cop Doc Dan Rudofossi Lessons on Problem Identification and Solutions

First, being advocates of agendas is anathema to the entire tradition of assessment and treatment.

Second, actively listening means to first be silent and before formulating any diagnosis to contextualize the cultural and religious beliefs of one's patient/client as key.

Third, is in working with patients/clients, the clinician can help or if not then refer to another practitioner better suited to handle the issues, if one cannot assess or treat to the best of his/her ability and skills.

Fourth, is considering what is the best and healthiest outcome of the individual patient, selection, or appointment process by not abstracting, overidentifying with one's own social interpretation of utilitarianism, social, or political opinion toward others as a compass.

Fifth, paying attention to and respecting and valuing the patient/client's center of existence and purpose—supporting goals that are not harmful to him/her or others.

Sixth, is becoming reality based not fantasy based, reductionistic, or overly simplistic.

Seventh, all the six above rules require integrity to follow and conserve one's own traditions and skills by humbly learning of others' traditions, experience, and skills respectfully and admitting gaps in one's own limitations as the greatest strength. This humility will be a source of gaining respect and interaction that is truly decent and healthy, not arrogant and delimiting.

"When I review my own wisdom as these lessons and I cross-check myself, I then confirm my thoughts by asking without losing any sense of my own center, Hey, am I getting it right?" [Assent from Special Agent Joe D. Pistone I am on track I continue.]

"The intuitive and existential centering of you as an expert in my own thoughts is an eco-ethological niche where you went way beyond a purely academic approach. You were able to pick up on a deeper level what was critically important in this potential informant, for example, versus that guy in becoming a potential informant as far as who would hold the bag and not run with it was based on your wealth of experience. Meaning your experience and all you learned including studies and classes you took and your own education you used. But that judgment was not legislated but taken as real, relevant, and useful information—not 'fugazy' information. But information or intel that is simply conjecture without the groundwork can get a fellow LEO caught off-guard and 'homicided' as they say in the hood. That is, if you just went by some template some academic wrote, you may have been writing off your own wisdom which fortunately you never surrendered to following and conforming too. This is another hidden strength I am thinking of when I re-assess your own experiences with you. Does that point make sense? That is, you filtering out the worthy and useful education from the speculative stuff and using what is an effective fit for real-life applications?"

FBI AGENT JOSEPH DOMINICK PISTONE: "Yes, that makes sense and, in that vein, here is another issue. What would make a psychiatrist/psychologist suggest that sex equates with stress relief over trauma as recounted to me? Were I to choose to do so, it would be in a private sense and a sensitive topic to discuss. But that is something I can do myself. In other words, this is not a solution to dealing with a particularly difficult situation for me. Do I seriously need a doc to tell me to relieve my stress or another agent's stress by masturbating for example?!?"

COP DR DAN RUDOFOSSI: "Forgive my language, it's stayed with me as a street cop. To be clear, the psychologists and psychiatrists as is true of administration as you've educated me, was a 'hoot and howling inaccurate.' To try to assist you and other agents in dealing with stress, homework is necessary on the part of the clinician. Gaining accurate and useful information as to the human patient, suspect, witness, and potential informant you are interacting with is effective. Trying to understand the future likelihood of, for example, a candidate who desires becoming an informant is all an issue of probability. It is not a certainty. Knowing potential can be enhanced by a focused understanding of who he/she is as an individual. Not a large study that is perhaps of interest, but tells you and me nothing about his/her potential as an individual and future as a reliable informant. The academic, political, and administrative executive, while at times may be well meaning, may not get the amount of traumatic loss say agents and officers from deep cover to patrol go through within a week of surviving the asphalt streets. This trauma and loss also are framed around what is disenfranchised by those in charge administratively who ignore the wealth of useful and highly specialized wisdom and experience of tenured agents."

FBI AGENT JOSEPH DOMINICK PISTONE: "He or she is just giving general prescriptions to deal with a specific agent's problems which does not help the issue of dealing with the strain of the job itself. Masturbation exacerbates loneliness and self-indulgence, not intimacy as far as I can tell. There are others who have religious objections and did not say a word so as not to offend the psychiatrist, but they felt offended and also a bit taken aback."

COP DR DAN RUDOFOSSI: "I named my approach the *Eco-Ethological Existential Analytic Approach* to police and public safety complex trauma, grief, and dissociative disorders. My approach focuses on the issue of who are you are as an individual, what you are dealing with in your own experience of trauma and loss, and what and why this experience among the scores of others impacts on you the way it does? What is the level of not only stress, but one's existential belief and sensibility? Sensibility does not swing in one direction, but it depends on the agent and his/her center core beliefs including faith. Most LEOs, regardless of personal religious differences, do believe in a higher being as G–d."

FBI AGENT JOSEPH DOMINICK PISTONE: "You nailed it on the head of the problem. Any psychologist attempting to work with LEOs needs to understand the importance of respecting boundaries regardless of their own view or ideas about the world. An approach that focuses on responsibility of what is specific to that officer. I agree, Doc, the specifics that count for the psychologist doc is learning new stuff they don't know and can't know. Not getting defensive and I like your point, whether you meant exactly the experience of eating humility pie or not, the true world in which that officer moves in is crucial to beginning to open the closed door which is clammed shut if the agent or detective picks up that he/she is not respected as a real person with his own views and knowledge. I mean, I like your approach to getting the real gritty and dirty aspects of police work. With deep cover it is magnified and exponentially increased. Well, that's why cops hang around with cops. It's clear I want to talk with someone who has been on the streets and in the bag. Look, whenever there is a public newsworthy incident, who does the media go after, but police?"

"Think about it. The subject becomes secondary. It is always about the officer. For example, 'why didn't the officer shoot him twice, why did she shoot him seven times?' We don't shoot to wound, we shoot to stop, and shoot to lock down. How many guys in a gun battle are going to shoot the gun out of the guy's hand? That only happens in John Wayne movies. The media can ask me as an expert, or you to answer them. They have no idea. If they had an idea and understood the police culture, they would never ask such a ludicrous question. The amateur questions leave me with a big clue, how clueless are these fantasies about police and special agents. They want to be controversial so they can sell papers. I feel some reporters and news circuits want to make it as sensational and juicy goosy as possible."

"Let me give you an example, Doc, Okay?" [Cop Doc Dan R. gesticulates assent to Special Agent Joe Pistone.] "I give talks to homicide investigators all over the world. On one tour I was talking to one of the investigators during this international conference on homicide investigations. This investigator got shot and hit in the hip and had to get his hip replaced after the perp shot him during a routine car stop. Our officer is going down after he is shot in the hip. In choosing wisely, the officer shot the perp before he went out cold. He fortunately managed to deliver a shot to the perp before he would have killed that officer. That officer is innocent and was doing his job. Well, what's the first thing they do to our officer?" [Pause, waiting for my response.]

COP DR DAN RUDOFOSSI: "I believe, they first removed his firearm and gathered the shells spent, rounds unfired, and ferreted out all evidence within the inner and outer perimeter. They got all witnesses to investigate the shooting. Their primary bottom line was to see if the evidence bore out the shooting as kosher, or fugazy."

FBI AGENT JOSEPH DOMINICK PISTONE: "That's right from your experience as a sergeant. They did just that. They then brought the cop before the grand jury, they wanted the jury to confirm if it was a good shooting, or a bad shooting. The one cop this perp shot and paralyzed was done seven years ago. He got out of jail and went drinking pretty much within a few weeks. He was bragging as a cop hater that he had shot the other cop in the back in his earlier days. He said that was then, the cop survived. He added to the bar buddies that this time unlike earlier, 'I am going to kill me a cop tonight.'"

"The perp as recounted to me by the officer at the homicide conference was drunk when he got into his car. With alcohol which was noticeable he angled himself ready to shoot and kill the officer who would stop him with full intention to murder him. The guy was drunk and as he gets out of car, not listening to orders to stay put, he shot our officer point blank."

"Our officer falls down and he is able to before losing consciousness fire back and the perp trying to kill him, dies. This is identifiable as a perp who seven years ago shot a cop and served prison time for that felony. Now our officer is lying there. Remember, after a routine stop this officer is down for the count after being shot and in pure self-defense to avoid being killed, he defends himself and the perp is shot dead."

COP DR DAN RUDOFOSSI: "Justifiable and clear use of legit power to disempower illegitimate force against an intentional murder aimed at oneself."

FBI AGENT JOSEPH DOMINICK PISTONE: "What kind of a deal is it when the prosecutor treats this hero police officer shot after dealing with a perp who has tried to kill him? The reality is he is made to stand before a grand jury on a good shooting."

"This is even after IAB [Internal Affairs Bureau] determines our officer is good on all counts. The perp was intoxicated and shot him with no provocation and no incident. He was on record as a wannabe cop killer."

COP DR DAN RUDOFOSSI: "You put it very well Special Agent Joseph Pistone as to what kind of a deal it is. In the societal obligation to an officer who is doing his job so well and in great merit defended himself and other officers from being victimized by stopping the threat of a homicidal man who thinks killing cops is a pastime to be boastful about—no fair deal was done by having a victim of extreme violence go through a re-traumatization again."

"Losses such as his is cut with another poor label. Saying this is a critical incident does little justice and words count as does language within police culture. He endured a quantum psychic moment where multiple shocks including the apathy and lack of compassion for a law enforcement officer who will endure many aftershocks for a very long time. The cumulative cost of trauma and loss is almost beyond sensibility. The politicians and the administrators walk away, but what about the public safety officer's well-being mentally and psychologically?" [We will move on an explore this in our following chapters, we have begun to unravel some of the harsher realities and we will do so in the approach I developed with Joseph D. Pistone as my resident expert colleague respectfully and with both of my third and large ears connected to learn from and respond empathically to and with.]

Summary

In this chapter we had an eagle's-eye view of the panorama of deep cover by understanding some impasses for Joe Pistone as special agent identity mode when dealing with colleagues and administrators.

That is to say, we took a deeper and operational definition as a more measurable and identifiable hypothetical construct to explore in your class and outside of the university. Let's pause and review a fascinating confirmation of the *Eco-Ethological Existential Approach* which offers a cultural and contextual aspect to psychopathology as much as an individual differences approach when dealing with the process and the regression and fixation in what is called dissociative disorders.

Remember the traditional assessment and diagnostic approach offers a personality disorder and clinical disorder known as multiple personality disorder, and now is called dissociative identity disorder. The root of this disorder is that multiple alters of personality emerge in the patient who is suffering from this disorder. In Rudofossi's approach, the dissociative process is also identical but the alters are called identity modes and result as defenses that emerge and crystalize almost always in an ecological niche and with the motivation for survival known as ethological dimensions.

46   Genius in Motion: Becoming Donnie Brasco

Thus, ethological is not just analogized in this chapter with primates and their behavioral patterns but with their cognitive patterns and schemas. That is not to reduce human complexity but to illustrate the derivatives of drives which are sexual, social and cultural, and aggressive and territorial. In addition, we touched on the existential dimension which, to return to the noetic dimension, is the part that emerges in eco-ethological-laden motivation and shapes and is influenced by one's own integrity and hardiness spiritually.

In enduring the murders, the corruption, the violence, and rites and ritual taboos and mores within the eco-ethological niches of the Mafia families respectfully as in the law enforcement families, it is imperative to become participant observers.

Returning to the identity modes of being operational LEO deep-cover identity mode, Donnie Brasco identity mode as Bonanno family associate, it is not the host personality alter but Joe Dominick Pistone that rides the fault-line of these major identity modes and the others we touched on. Joe D. Pistone adds to our analysis by educating you and me about what he defines as his mental toughness and resiliency as part of his own emotional genius. This is no easy feat as I move in heuristic and Socratic links responsively with him at this pace.

We will move beyond our advancing knowledge and traverse complementary explorations of anthropology, clinical psychology as personality and biology within ecological and ethological dimensions as our picture is not reduced, but expanded together in the following chapter.

Cop Doc Corner for Students Only—Debriefing

The unique emotional intelligence of Joseph Pistone was extant before such knowledge as emotional intelligence was identified: empathy and active listening as a hidden dimension of the deep cover not spoken of in many law enforcement circles, is made visible here. It is painful and enlightening for Special Agent Pistone and me as Cop Doc Dan R. to become aware of the dimensions of book smarts and street smarts and how and why both matter. Words matter and so does understanding the enormity of forgetting lessons worth conserving in scientists of anthropology as is true of psychology; some of the giants in the field have been looked at in some measure in this chapter and the first one. Some popular ideas that have become mantras on campus may fall to the sides as fads resurrected and politicized without much evidence in sweeping legislation that will not stand the test of time and science.

One of these is the idea that one can be free of bias based on exclusion or inclusion of factors that are biological. Dr. Franz Boas challenged eugenics and biological determinism as politicization of the scientific evidence and victoried. Labeling based on race, religion, and creed is not based on real evidence and science. This is true of all groups, races, and other social groupings. Theories, no matter how well packaged, are bound up with faulty premises, and conclusions as non sequiturs when forcing one's own view without listening to others is the decline of the individual scholar and the collective ability to grow intellectually and practically as book smart and street-smart scholars.

By using some sources brought up in this chapter as a burgeoning student of forensic psychology, homeland security, law, and anthropology, you may gain much knowledge that has been forgotten. It is now ripe for insight and the match of responsibility to stand up to the challenge and the large reward to follow. Backing into a corner of conformity is obscurity. Saying it is what it is and not thinking constructively in a critical manner is not helpful toward growth and expansion in mindfulness.

'Its' absence in becoming a wiseguy is noticeable. It is never what 'It' purports to be. If 'It' is what it is, then all loss, all trauma, all maladaptive experiences, and emotional weights to negative experiences could be forgotten and put away in some dark corner and never reopened again. In this chapter we started to get raw and see a sensitive and responsive movement toward and away from some very heavy and light topics. Popular dramatized versions of trauma wiseguys assert match what police alike use as a way of coping with heavy trauma. The 'It' is exactly what is identified as we have opened the wonder and the challenges to psychology and anthropology as sciences and clinical fields that when applied are so much more than 'book smarts,' but that does not take away the ingenuity and street smarts and experiences of a learned and wise tenured colleague who is assisting me identify some 'Its' as Joe Pistone bravely details his experiences.

We leave our second chapter as a launching pad. Keep in mind what will follow as we explore Special Agent Joseph Pistone's odyssey in navigating the inner workings of the belly of the beast. We will experience compound losses far beyond the experiences of most complex trauma and cumulative losses. Imagine, as I dared to do with Special Agent Joe Pistone, what is it like to really awake every day for 2,190 days, that is for six years duration, and deal with all the insults to your own sensibility—day in and night out, and by your lone-self!

If you as the student of criminal justice dare to imagine as you stop, pause, and now think about this reality: Agent Joe Pistone's nights last in perpetuity with the potential of all the cumulative trauma—rebounding in a crushing wave. This has not happened in Joseph. But it does in many others and that is of great interest to me, and you. The reason that has not happened is perhaps understandable and we may decipher, in part, by actively listening and formulating questions and getting some answers to use and apply.

A tsunami of trauma folds in on itself as its relentless path and death can deluge one's own back yard when the action stops. The real genuine Joseph Pistone under the covers of sleuthing has just been touched on at this point. Who is Joseph Dominick Pistone as a real-life human being as compared to the hero and ingenious sleuth he is by deed and result? In the next chapter we will move backward to the beginning in an approach that respectfully seeks truth and justice for one of America's real-deal deep-cover sleuths and master teachers of the craft.

Important Definitions and Concepts to Keep in Mind

Adaptive functional dissociation in an eco-ethological existential model

Adaptative functional dissociation has been explained in this chapter as a healthier assimilation and accommodation in an eco-ethological niche. Remember, an eco-ethological niche is not limited to only a violent, survival-primed environment. Eco-ethological niches includes all types and varieties of environments. Shaping, speciation, and scaffolding to novel behaviors and bridges to established patterns of schema-related motivation is always motivated by survival and in the *Eco-Ethological Existential Analytic Model*—the center of one's purpose and meaning is not excluded. The purpose of the officer for our purposes that specializes in doing undercover operations or intelligence work as Special Agent Joe Pistone has asserted strongly is not acting, nor role playing. The adaptive functional dissociation model bridges the gaps in clinical and practical applied models as to how an agent, investigator, detective, intelligence analyst, and diversion investigator, to name a few, can seem so highly adaptive and resilient and still dissociating into different identity modes that may synchronize smoothly and some that collide and clash in a cacophonous bellow.

Standard operating procedure

Standard operating procedure was described in this chapter in a succinct highlight box. In conceptualizing the importance of officers and other professionals including military officers and soldiers, the reality is SOP communicates a conformity and relinquishing of individual responsibility and insight individually. When an officer has acted out of the norm for officers, for example, she/he has acted extra-punitively, the result is a court martial, or for the LEO, a departmental trial room. In these airings out of consequences and sentencing, it is often that one hears the age-old excuse, I was only following orders and I obeyed. It is realizing that while SOP may be protocol, it is not free, and the actions must be deemed judgeable or the result is an abjuring of all culpability and responsibility as an autonomous police or military officer.

Reductionistic caricatures of police officers

Here the officer is grossly misrepresented as an unusually angelic or demonic personage and with little resemblance as the fallible and imperfect human being he/she is in reality. The assumption here is biased and also caricatures that often are offensive toward officers simply because they are police or special agents. The caricatures of officers can be done in the guise of lumping officers together in a stereotypical manner. Reducing the exquisite and unique aspects of differential impact on development in biological, psychological, and social growth and stagnation is part of this caricaturing process. Officers' individual differences when minimized or denied expression contribute to the caricature and reductionism of police officers.

Conceptual and Writing Exercises for Student and Professor Only

1. Look up any of the sources on primatology and target a literature search on aggression and territoriality among different primate families. Be sure to look for identical members of that specific primate not similar simians. Summarize two journal articles done in comparative psychology or biology and focus on another biography of a law enforcement officer/public safety officer who does plainclothes assignments and write a paper as a criminal justice, sociology, psychology, homeland security, forensic psychology, or forensic science student on how that aggression was dealt with by the plainclothes officer, agent. Obtain a copy of the paper and summarize your findings for the class in a presentation.
2. With permission of your professor and the university, do an informal interview where you can take notes and record "why" and "what" motivated a primatologist if you cannot obtain biographical material explaining what motivated him/her to become a primatologist. Did you find commonalities among students in the class you are taking as to why those who are in, or have chosen law enforcement, are planning a career in this area?
3. Get an article or book on multiple personality disorder and see if you can analyze serious problems this disorder presents in the case example. One place you can look is in the library and in books on psychopathology or abnormal psychology. In my first clinical book in 2007 or 2009, look up the topic of dissociative identity disorder and compare my approach to the standard paradigm dealing with dissociative identity disorder under identity modes and adaptive functional dissociation. Which view do you resonate on as being more comprehensive in understanding dissociative disorders? Second which theory and approach do you believe is more effective?
4. In your library visit enlist your librarian or professor of librarian science and try to locate an original article by Franz Boas, Margret Mead, Ruth Benedict, Edward Sapir, or Gregory Bateson. After you get hold of any of these generative and timeless research pieces, summarize the findings in terms of lessons learned for you about critically thinking about research and sensitivity against advocating one's own point of view. Now pause and take a deeper look at one textbook, guide you've read, articles assigned for a class that covers

some new social theory in anthropology, psychology, psychiatry, sociology, and police science. Answer the following questions: Do you see any striking contradictions in assertions wildly made about entire groups on race, religion, inclusion, or exclusion without any real evidence scientifically? Do you have an issue with these assertions, but fear expressing your own unique view based on social, psychological-psychiatric views, or police science paradigms that are popular?

References

Ardrey, R. (1966). *The territorial imperative: The personal investigation into the animal origins of property and nations.* New York: Atheneum.
Boas, F. (1911). *The mind of primitive man.* New York: Macmillan.
Goffman, E. (1963). *Stigma: Notes on the management of spoiled identity.* New York: Prentice Hall.
Hall, T. E. (1966). *The hidden dimension.* New York: Doubleday.
Hall, T. E. (1973). *The silent language.* New York: Anchor.
Hunt, K. (2020). *Chimpanzee: Lessons learnt from our sister species.* Cambridge: Cambridge University Press.
Kendon, A. (1990). *Conducting interaction.* London: Cambridge University Press.
Mead, M. (1975). *Growing up in New Guinea.* Harper Collins.
Mitani, J., Call, J., Kappeller, P., Palombit, R., & Silk, J. (2012). *The evolution of primate societies.* Chicago: University of Chicago Press.
Morris, D. (1994). *The naked ape trilogy: Naked Ape, Human Zoo, Intimate Behavior.* London: Jonathan Cape.
Pistone, J. D. (2004). *The way of the wiseguy.* Philadelphia: Running Press.
Rudofossi, D. M. (1997). *The impact of trauma and loss on affective differential profiles of police officers.* Bell Harbor, MI: Bell and Howell.
Rudofossi, D. M. (2007). *Working with traumatized police-officer patients: A clinician's guide to complex PTSD syndromes in public safety professionals.* New York & London: Routledge.
Rudofossi, D. M. (2012). *A street survival guide for public safety officers: The cop doc's strategies for surviving trauma, loss, and terrorism.* New York & London: Routledge.
Rudofossi, D., & Maloney, M. (2019). *Aborigine trail: Trails, travail, and triumph using psychology with Aborigine police.* Amherst, NY: Teneo Press.
Sapir, E. (1916). *Time perspective in Aboriginal American culture, A study in method.* Ottawa, Canada: Government Printing Press.
Sapir, E., & Irvine, J. (2002). *The psychology of culture: A course of lectures.* Berlin: Walter de Gruyter.
Sommer, R. (1969). *Personal space: The behavioral basis of design.* New Jersey: Prentice Hall.
Sommer, R. (1978). *The mind's eye: Imagery in everyday life.* New York: Delta.
Wambaugh, J. (1973). *The blue knight.* London: First Sphere.

3
PATRONIZING—POLICE, MAFIA, AND FAMILY

Eco-Ethological Triangulation

Introduction

In the first two chapters you gained a glimpse into the complexity, ingenuity, stress, and strain endured and repositioned as Special Agent Joe Pistone parlayed into the shadows: the shadow is actually his identity mode as Donnie Brasco. Let's pause as we move forward and appreciate how Dr. Professor Jung introduced all psychologists, as he was wont, with Dr. Charles Brenner, to call doctoral-level psychiatrists and psychologists—psychologists such as Professor Dr. Sigmund Freud called himself. Dr. Charles Brenner, who was a torchbearer and in his own right a revisionist in the classic psychoanalytic tradition of clinical case supervision with the author (Brenner, 1973, 1979; Freud, 1990, 2019), informed me he was a *psychologist*, as was I as a '*doctor of the mind.*' As psychologists, both psychoanalysis and existential analysis offer insight into the responsibleness of our understanding the shadow as a double in all human beings. Not a literal double, but another identity mode as we build our understanding of the impact of the development of defensive conscious and largely unconscious ways we process adaptation and maladaptation to trauma, loss, and territorial violence. This constellation of defenses is never considered without understanding the impact of ecological niches as different. The differences of each ecological niche afford different vantage points for the active participant. Notwithstanding keeping in mind that each operative agent is in an unpredictable ecological milieu: hostile and built to neutralize, his/her ability to assimilate and accommodate are enormous obstacles to overcome. In overcoming these obstacles, keep in mind the development of some defenses is nested in the most primary of psychological drives to survive rather than to withdraw. All these defenses (conscious and unconscious), the ecological and ethological motivating dimensions, and the built-in defensive constellations of organized criminal enterprises, challenge not just the skill, physical and police persona, but the emotional and mental intelligence and resilience requisite to deal with it all and not dissociate maladaptively and dysfunctionally.

It is to the existential hub of existence that we must search and ferret out the personality dynamics without dismantling the working process of deep cover as being ever surreptitious and cached. In achieving this objective, we traverse the different eco-ethological niches of Special Agent Joe Pistone's identity mode and Donnie Brasco's identity mode. In doing so we will revisit Dr. Brenner's conceptualization of compromise formation, Dr. Viktor Frankl's noetic dimension, Professor Solevetchik's soul-sickness, Dr. Otto Kernberg's projective identification, and Dr. Masterson's closet narcissism and exhibitionistic narcissism to enlighten our paths.

Crossing the cultural and ecological niches shaped by survival motivation in viewing triangulation in this chapter is crucial as a cornerstone in our understanding of deep cover within the lenses of a cognitive behavioral, psychoanalytic, and the author's *Eco-Ethological Existential Analytic* paradigm.

Parenthetically, alienists framed early abnormal psychology, or as it is sometimes called, psychopathology: abnormal psychology requires research and assessment of reliable and valid instruments to guide the clinician who will ultimately make his/her diagnosis. That diagnosis indicates the range from mild to severe as to the quality, duration, and intensity of mental illness, and the path toward health at different focal points, as measured in treatment.

The hypothetical construct of doubleganger, the double, and multiple personalities from the metaphysical and physical perspective, in part emerged with the cultural trappings of revolutions and upheaval and within an eco-ethological framework (Carr, 2006; Rudofossi, 2017). The idea of a parallel human being living a parallel existence is beyond the scope of this guide, but it is certainly not beyond the analysis of our knowledge of quantum physics and individuation from the collective unconscious, which is relevant to viewing the cultural and individuation of becoming a 'special agent operative' and 'wiseguy' in parallel and oppositional world views.

As we move on in the chapter, we will use these concepts as strong cornerstones to guide what is not etched out in visible boundaries, but in the navigation through the many streams of survival and defenses used to integrate one's personality development as individuation in the shifts into different eco-ethological niches. Our focus must turn to Joe Pistone as he carries on living the duality, double identity mode, which is not kept as a shadow but becomes his primary identity for six years, and in this context his own metaphor of satisfying the three mistresses that proffer dancing with his identity as both Donnie Brasco and Joe Pistone.

But if you for a moment, kindly stop, pause, and redirect to a critical point and pay attention, Joe Pistone created Donnie Brasco. That is, Joe Pistone developed Donnie Brasco's identity step by step and within his own steps. Donnie's identity developed within a context in which no script was ever written. Donnie Brasco had life because Joe Pistone had life and was potentially present, but unlived before Joe Pistone took the leap of ingenuity and mental toughness to find him, nurture his identity mode, and, like the "Golem," deconstruct his identity as an operational shadow and yet very real wiseguy among wiseguys.

FBI elite agent Joseph Pistone stepped out of his FBI Corfram shoes and refitted into a retro "rookie-wiseguy." Black-and-white loafers and mafiosi loafers are as dichotomous as it comes when following the cultural rules of do and don'ts in the ecological niche of the Mafia.

Stop for more than a moment; let's reflect on the enormity of his mission. How intense is it when we pause, where split-second rage by a notorious made gangster could leave you dead before you even realize you've been shot and hit the ground?

An ecological niche is biological, and within that sphere lie other spheres including behaviors afforded in each particular situation that emerge within walls that act as insular boundaries within that layout. In all ecological niches in the Mafia, as is true in policing, ethological motivation as a concept may be understood as surviving, as we explored earlier in a primate ecology. Dr Abraham Maslow's prodigious research supported the hierarchical nature of our existential needs which correlate with the biopsychosocial motivations for ethological survival within the groups we live in (Maslow, 1973). The need for security is essential and primary. Ethology, as operationally defined here, emphasizes the reality of '*survival-motivation*'—*as the motivation to survive* (Becker, 1997; Brenner, 2008; Campbell, 2008; Frankl, 1979; Fromm, 1957; Jung, 1969, 2009; Rank, 2004; Rudofossi, 2012; Shatz et al., 2004; Solovetchik, 1992).

My framework helps understanding a part of the depth of deep cover from a scientific perspective; in this chapter and the fourth, "identity modes," as operationally defined within the context of an ecological and ethological approach, will become real as a razor's slice and the boundaries carved out of experience (Rudofossi, 2007). Identity modes emerge in eco-ethological niches, and this crucial bit of wisdom will help toward understanding the challenges of creating identity from scratch for Joe Pistone as Donnie Brasco.

As cops, the idea of modes is nothing new, as almost all cops know, as do their loved ones, what is meant when a cop says, "I'm in the mode." I'm in the mode is the same as saying I am in an altered state of mind and body where all distraction melts away, and I am not only focused on the task at hand, but what is asked of me in the moment of my task is to become who I already am, but at such a heightened level of awareness that it is an altered state of consciousness and extant unconscious state as well. The shadow is always constructed in light of reality, although the shadow only refracts the essence of what it really is at its essential center. In asking an agent to become his shadow, only a true artist and scientifically minded human being can dance in both worlds and double as agent and as wiseguy without a split in heart, soul, and mind. This is what Joe Pistone will explain and educate us all about throughout our narrative exploration, for he brings to flesh the forgotten language of daring to dream, the healthy and resilient fulcrum of tolerating anxiety within the wells and depth of being individually minded in a sense of becoming as he did in Donnie Brasco, as much as his re-adjustment post-deep cover as Joe Pistone.

Questions to Guide You as Navigational Tools: Learning Objectives

1. Through the dynamic interplay of variables, is it possible to define and classify key units of distress, eu-stress, adaptive dissociation, maladaptive dissociation, and resilient diplomacy from the interactions and training Joe Pistone underwent?
2. Do deep-cover functions require intelligence gathering, then analyzing what intel is gathered and sieved in the field as useful in dry runs by agents unconsciously for operational effectiveness?
3. Is it true that individual differences in personality are crucial in making choices as to who can be a special agent and dealing with the complexities of the interactions faced?
4. Is it possible that any agent with the desire and commitment toward becoming a deep cover can succeed?
5. Is success as an undercover operative as simple as the common-sense aphorism of 90 percent perspiration and perseverance and only 10 percent innate ability?
6. Is it elitist and narrow to suggest only a few law enforcement officers can become effective and facile as special agents of the FBI or DEA, and even rarer the ability to become and skill to survive as a special agent?
7. Are there literally three mistresses as suggested by Special Agent Joe Pistone that an FBI operative has to satisfy, and what is really meant by his colloquialism applied to deep cover?
8. What connection did the Bonanno family have with the Trafficante family and both with the Balistrieri family in Milwaukee?

Key Terms

Encounter
Quantum psychic moment of trauma
Noetic dimension
Sit-down
Colliding eco-ethological niches and world views
Third ear

Joe, unlike myself, is gifted in being on point, succinct to the point of alacrity, and yet superbly "tough-minded." I am sanguine and take pauses, as is the malady of being a psychologist. But almost all psychologists never take for granted the conscious expression such as "tough-mindedness" as being what it pretends to be on face value. So, no apology on either my front, or Joe's cover. We will both explore and understand Joe Pistone's vision as it unfolds in new creases and corners. Let's dive in toward gaining new ground in our understanding of deep cover.

FBI AGENT JOSEPH DOMINICK PISTONE: "It's been a while Doc, how are you?"

COP DR DAN RUDOFOSSI: "I'm doing fine thank you, Special Agent Joe P." [We exchange niceties. On a personal note, Joe is never short in tone, rude, or too busy to answer a call. I consider our relationship one of brothers in blue and always collegial.] "You?" [All is well as can be.] "I look forward to looking deeper into what you crafted and mastered as 'mental toughness.' In understanding what you call 'mental toughness,' what comes to mind?"

FBI AGENT JOSEPH DOMINICK PISTONE: "It's living not only among 'gangsters,' for me it was being 'Donnie Brasco,' a law enforcement officer, special agent, FBI, and a family man. You know, you don't get more intimate than life and death situations colliding when you're infiltrating the Mafia. One moment all is smooth and, well, the next all can be upside down."

COP DR DAN RUDOFOSSI: "In a blink of an eye, and a flutter of a heartbeat loose lips sink ships in doing work where disclosure causes death [Rudofossi, 2013]. In law enforcement, sketching out the character development of real perps is crucial to survive in the world of the gangster. I was thinking of the Sopranos to the well-oiled detective and special agent quip, 'It is what It is' in response to some horror crime scene. The 'It' signals an all-out cue. That cue gives us a clue, **adaptive functional dissociation** at some later point will become **maladaptive dysfunctional dissociation**. A hitman slicing life out of someone recused for being a 'rat,' being diced up like a slice of pineapple, is not a simple slice to witness and process. Seeing death, loss, and extreme violence is not a one-time task. What was so keen in the law enforcement-minded officer can switch in a heartbeat as dissociation shifts identities that worked, and suddenly it all ends abruptly. You know what I mean?"

FBI AGENT JOSEPH DOMINICK PISTONE: "Yeah, I got you Doc. Hey, 'It' took me six years of survival. Purpose. Not falling off track. It's not like I went home and at the end of a 9 to 5 I had a cold beer and dinner waiting for me. I could hardly kick back and relax. I had to satisfy three mistresses." [Subtle and almost inaudible grin and exhalation.] "Hum …, not all three at the same time," [serious tone] "but I had to satisfy all three mistresses. All of them and I am dead serious about that."

COP DR DAN RUDOFOSSI: "I don't know why, but, Frank Ol' Blue Eyes Sinatra singing, 'Strangers in the Night' comes to my own mind."

FBI AGENT JOSEPH DOMINICK PISTONE: "It was like that. Sinatra's interesting tune and words, 'Strangers in the Night.' Doc it was an *encounter in the gangster's world*, a dark and shadowy world and not a world of normal human beings you like to use for us who have more feelings and not hard-core, stone-cold-blooded killers. It's not the law enforcement world, or the knight on the white horse. You know, it's not family-life oriented."

COP DR DAN RUDOFOSSI: "*Encounter*' may just be the right word that holds, not just expresses what you actually accomplished. In keeping it together for six years, as you're educating me, it is clear 'encounter' hides the psychologically minded metaphor for what is called by psychoanalysts one's '*third-ear*' [Reik, 1953, 1956]. You are, in other words, listening with an attitude of attention that grasps unwritten, informal, emotive fragments others convey, and hook into what is potentially valuable and move with it to further discovery and usefulness."

"As an existential analyst, if I am getting it right, you not only encountered wiseguys, you encountered by tilting your third ear, to actively listen to 'the police brass,' the 'legal-eagle prosecutors,' and 'hostile defense attorneys.'"

"Most important is on an intuitive level, you encountered your peers when in a gangster identity mode, and on the street, cops, detectives, and special agents in detective identity mode. The last mistress was none other than your wife and family you encountered in your identity mode as family man. I do not imply anything contrived or planned, but shifting identities as you've placed the three mistresses as analogy, and roundly as metaphor."

FBI AGENT JOSEPH DOMINICK PISTONE: "That's good, real good, Doc. That sounds right. That is what I meant by the three mistresses for starters. It is also the colliding of different worlds too, what you call the ecological niche and survival is an issue that does not go away. It cannot be filed in a lily-white envelope and sealed with a signature slapped on the lips of the flaps closed. It is not fitting in the world of the law enforcement world, or family mode identity."

COP DR DAN RUDOFOSSI: "Thank you, Professor Joe Pistone. Your word, *colliding* as in collisions of worlds, here is draped in viewpoints and meaning. Worlds that link motivations, even if oppositional. If I am getting the picture right, prosecution and anti-prosecution, disclosure and non-disclosure, infiltration and invitation, sit-downs and massacres—they all distance each world from the other. It seems your worlds shift patronizing, reducing fiction to genuine knowledge. Accurate knowledge leads to wisdom. Your distinct and different identity modes, without occluding one for the other, are separate realities, separate demands, articulated differences in defense against you becoming vulnerable. To ethologically survive in your eco-ethological worlds you didn't patronize all three of your mistresses, each vied for your attention, you had to function and hide your identity modes. The flow, ebbs, and tides of dancing in your tryst of identity modes in the murky shadows of identity and integrity pushed and pulled you, Joseph D. Pistone?"

FBI AGENT JOSEPH DOMINICK PISTONE: "Hidden identity or as you say identity modes cannot be learned in any book or guide; it must be natural. It comes to you as a real person with your own personality. You got the basics, or you don't. That's not a judgment, or put down, but reality. Again, this idea some psychiatrists and psychologists have about play-acting to learn. Pretending, as in acting, just doesn't work and can get the undercover agent killed. So yeah, if you are asking me to confirm your hypothesis, it is a confirmation. Not an academic thumbs-up, but avoiding a sit-down with gangsters as a thumbs-down."

COP DR DAN RUDOFOSSI: "So, demanding on you lightning speed and adaptation shifts oscillating all three identity modes, as gangster Donnie Brasco identity mode; special agent LEO identity mode; and integrity as family man, community leader, Joseph Dominick Pistone identity mode. It is listening with your third ear, or sixth sense as to what is intuitive, and may not ever be reducible in doing operations as in deep cover. It makes superb sense in adaptation that works. It also costs much in strain and stress to the mind and body."

FBI AGENT JOSEPH DOMINICK PISTONE: "Yeah, that sixth sense is grounded in real street smarts. Doc, you can't reduce this stuff into a neat package. If you conform to administrators and their directives, you become a spoke in the wheel but never create a difference that counts. That is the point. But it is much more than that. I'll tell you what Doc, splattered blood, mud, guts, and pain just doesn't fit well with the white starched shirts and Corfram gloss shoes of the FBI. J. E. Hoover was all spirit and fight. He was tough alright, but he knew the importance of what needed to be tried with no guarantee. J. E. Hoover as FBI director let me do it and supported Operation Donnie Brasco. In that way he was a stand-up and good boss."

COP DR DAN RUDOFOSSI: "If I got it right, in your estimation, taking away discretion and the messy and real skill of discernment is a formula for disaster. Discretion cannot be corrected, nor prescribed, according to the wisdom of both J. E. Hoover, FBI founder and director, and Special Agent Joseph Dominick Pistone aka Donnie Brasco, right?"

FBI AGENT JOSEPH DOMINICK PISTONE: "Of course, you're right on point here, Doc. I am not one for political correctness. That is why I am successful, and you are in what you do as a cop doc. Look, remember, when I was Donnie Brasco, J. E. Hoover, as I shared with you, did not accept the nonsense of excuses for everything. Nowadays, all kinds of bad behavior is acceptable, because, and why as excuses. He was not a tyrant; Hoover allowed mistakes, but ones that were fixable. If you screwed up, especially intentionally, you paid a price."

"I had what you describe, psychologists and psychiatrists call a 'third ear.' So did J. E. Hoover. He understood broad and important issues. He took smart risks for the safety and security of America. People forget, but it was J. Edgar Hoover who founded and crafted the FBI. We did a good job considering the attempts at sabotage and terrorism, here and abroad."

"Still, J. E. Hoover was fair, not overhanded or unfair. In my opinion and experience, that is the way to run the FBI. The right way to support cops and prosecutors. In fact, the other side respect you when you do what is called for. You don't try to fit everyone into the same cookie-cutter mold. Life doesn't work that way. It never did work that way and never will."

"Truth be told, no formula for one-fits-all. The bureaucrats think that formula needs to be politically correct and fit everyone in, but that is the formula for failing. Not everyone is cut out to be a special agent and not every special agent is cut out to do undercover, and certainly only a very few tough-minded and committed with natural ability can do infiltration. Here, in deep cover, failure means a gruesome death by stone-cold killers."

COP DR DAN RUDOFOSSI: "I hear you loud and clear. Dr. Reik's 'third ear' [1953, 1956] suggests listening and using discernment by proscribing any pre-set formula as to 'what,' 'when,' 'where,' 'why,' and 'how' to say 'It'."

"You also are correct, as you know, I say in my clinical guides [Rudofossi, 2007, 2009] allowing yourself to pause and actively listen to the intuitive sense internally to guide your own wisdom makes sense and supports survival. I have affirmed your words to clinicians to pause and not prescribe formulaic applications of treatment, as one treatment cannot be set in a mold for each patient, officer or civilian, voluntarily or mandatory, and average or gifted. Most of what we hear is not spoken out loud. We intuit a lot of information and select unconsciously what is stored for later."

"Joe, we have not really spoken about, or read about, the *'deeper aspect of motivation' in doing and self-selection for achieving deep cover*. If I could ask you again, about your deepest motivation to do deep-cover work. As a cop doc, I am very interested in the question of 'why?' in terms of your own motivation. What motivated you to actually do and become a deep-cover agent for six plus years of your life?"

FBI AGENT JOSEPH DOMINICK PISTONE: "Well, Doc Dan, I have been asked about that by a few different journalists and shrinks. They were looking for some deep philosophical answer. But I will tell you, the simple answer was I was an FBI agent, I was tasked to do a job, and I did it!"

"With you Doc, let me go more deeper. I happen to be good at undercover work. I started doing undercover work in Naval Intelligence. I gathered intel in the Navy. I was just good at it. My assignments were not the same as later in infiltrating the mob, but I was able to do what I had to do well. I completed my missions effectively. I took my objectives seriously, and my goal was to fulfill my goals without wasting time and risking more than necessary. Remember, I grew up in Patterson, New Jersey. I knew the streets from being a kid in a tough section. I was a street-smart kid from Patterson, New Jersey."

"I chose going to college and I got my degree in anthropology. I did a stint as a teacher for one way and I knew how to teach and learn. I had the basics down pat."

"I recommend knowing the personalities of the people you're going to deal with. Knowing who you're going to mingle with and that includes their strengths and weaknesses. I always studied what I needed to know, including the basics of jewelry when I began as Donnie Brasco and a petty thief. I was able to gain my basics as a law enforcement officer in the Navy. I was given Naval Intelligence and with a college degree in anthropology."

"Remember, when I began as an agent, I gradually put my skill on knowing how to drive eighteen-wheelers into practice in the hijack unit of the FBI. Being Sicilian, I was a good fit to attempt to infiltrate the Mafia which requires being Sicilian to gain entry to being made."

"As far as ingratiating myself with the bad guys, the wiseguys, or other people for that matter, to me it was covert. I was assigned a task—I did that task well. It was a special task and I took it on, as I always do. Hey, if I was assigned a task to investigate a bank robbery, I would do that to the best of my ability. It just so happened that I had that knack."

[Pausing for moment of reflection.] "Let me share with you as a cop doc. Not everybody can work undercover. *You gotta have that extra bit of mental toughness, and also that sense, a little extra sense of how and what to do.* But I also did it for another reason, I did it because of my love of being on the job, love of being an FBI agent. You know, being assigned a task to conduct an investigation, and do it well, was enough motivation for me. That's it. I didn't do it to go against Italians, meaning you are Italian and you want to take down the mob as Italian American mafiosos. I didn't do it to take on and wipe out all drug gangs. I did it because I wanted to take down the mob. Not because they were Italian. It was my job. It was a sense of duty to the FBI, myself, and my country as a patriot. You follow what I'm saying, does this make sense to you?"

COP DR DAN RUDOFOSSI: "Yes, it does make sense. It makes sense to me, big time! 'Being on the job,' that shield you heroically choose to carry makes all the sense to me as a good cop doc. Parenthetically, knowing what you faced is stunning to me. As a street cop with over 200 collars, and no violations in the last years of the 80s in Bed Stuy and Fort Greene and the early 90s, I know how much the job means to us both. Different jobs, but the same goal in policing, stopping criminal behavior and perps. You and I are cops, I get it! But, your '*encounters*' are one path. A path no one else has traveled as you have, and that is why motivation is key to our psychological understanding, including, perhaps, some insights we can explore together from associations that emerge, if that is sensible to you?"

FBI AGENT JOSEPH DOMINICK PISTONE: "Yeah, yeah, I got you Doc. Well, it was my motivation from a sense of duty, a sense of duty to the FBI, to the country, and to myself as I said. You know it was a way of getting bad guys off the street."

"It sounds simple, and it was simple. There was no deep philosophical thinking behind it all. This was my job. I was committed to it. Whatever undercover task I was given, I went at it with all my best."

COP DR DAN RUDOFOSSI: "You know, as you were talking about it, it seems like in your gut you became compelled in a way to do what you knew was right. But like you said, you had a knack for it. To be frank, a skill most of us could not get past first base. As you said, if I heard you right, you got a taste for it through Naval Intelligence, in the United States Navy?" [Nod assenting.]

"If I got you right, on a deeper level you used your street-smart thinking, Joseph. You knew or intuited with your street smarts as a Jersey street-kid survivalist, if I remember correctly." [Joe nods assent again.] "So, your skill to navigate through and learn a system that most of us, and I include myself as a street cop, would not have a clue to achieve, as only you could, as you uniquely, did. This was heavy-duty stuff. Getting into the Bonanno crime family, then superbly convincing each member that ran with you that Donnie Brasco was a real guy, and one that was a rising star in organized crime."

FBI AGENT JOSEPH DOMINICK PISTONE: "The world of the gangster is very different than ours in law enforcement. It is different than Naval intel and the Navy period. It is different than community affairs and representatives. We are talking about gangsters who can break bread with their own brother, or in-law and turn outlaw in a drop of a glance by whacking him instantly. No problems and no issues are the ways of the gangster. You are guilty and not proven innocent. Think about that world. It is very different than our own world. Our values and our needs. It is a world on its own axis."

COP DR DAN RUDOFOSSI: "Joe, the axis of evil." [A giggle.] "When I ask you about motivation, I have something different in mind. Let me explain. A simple question can only provoke a simple response. The motivational question I have focused on, what you describe as your 'mental toughness' and what you alluded to, that is something more than even your conscious sense of being tough-minded. I don't want to open others to misperceive the depth of your experiences and your own unique meaning. So, if we look at motivation as a calling card, it's a bit different. A calling card for you doing a job you intuited doing, and successfully dared to imagine as a vista, before you even embarked on your first step, is what I am getting at. Does that make sense to you in our fleshing out the context of trying to wrestle out the underlying motivation to do the undercover job as it evolved, and to redirect our attention to the process in your skill and sensitivities as a special agent?"

FBI AGENT JOSEPH DOMINICK PISTONE: "Absolutely! You see you got me thinking about a very important point. That point of departure is what is left out. What is left out, and how you can see incorporating it into your book, are facts as to what I actually did during my six years in becoming a wiseguy. What is left out of a lot of interviews, and what is asked of me, misses the reality."

"That reality is that a lot of people don't realize that during my investigation I married the Bonanno family with two other crime families. Two Mafia families actually had a sit-down and were readying to go into illegal business together with each other. The full picture includes the fact that these two different Mafia families are from different parts of the country."

"If someone knows anything about the Mafia, you know what a task that was for me to set up. One slip-up and you take a visit to the capo. He answers and ushers you in. You stand up, salute, and sit down in the express trip to the Gemini Bar-Club. You then sip your last espresso to the concrete graveyard under the blue sea. The deep blue sea of the Canarsie Pier."

Gemini Club and Murder Inc.

When a bad guy or gal has a 9mm semi-automatic pistol pointed in your back and telling you to take a ride, the ethological motivation to survive is riding high in your adrenaline belt, or you're already dead. As Donnie Brasco knew well, the Gemini Lounge in Flatlands Avenue was a gangster hangout, where not all who came in for a drink of sambuca with the capo left in luxury. Plenty of wannabes and even made guys left in concrete shoes crafted to sink deeply along Shore Parkway.

COP DR DAN RUDOFOSSI: "The ingenuity you employed at so many different angles was a work of genius. If I got it right, you not only broke the molds of law enforcement, but with deft skill and diplomacy clinically, if I can use the term, you brokered the icy edges and allied the vying interests toward allegiance. In a way it was an incredible intervention. At the same time, an insight is fleshing out just how far your ingenuity and effectiveness aided your own creation of the shadow figure of yourself as wiseguy, which not only emerged successfully, but innovatively as a maverick within the wiseguy culture and families themselves!"

FBI AGENT JOSEPH DOMINICK PISTONE: "If you look at it realistically, two Mafia families going in business was unheard of. This is especially true as most of the time it is a made guy who can even attempt to do what I did. But, yeah, if you look at it the way it happened in reality, the prompting of an associate to negotiate this marriage was really unheard of and pretty much impossible."

"Engineering the Bonanno family to meet with and to liaison with and merge with the Balistrieri family was a feat. You know, engineering the Bonanno to visit with Santos Trafficante was even more of a job to undertake, and I did it."

"I mean it's lost on a lot of people who don't know how the mob operates. Some of these people in journalism and history dabble in a superficial understanding of organized crime."

"That task of undercover operations in which any FBI agent would even attempt making this bridge would be rare, but here it was me, Doc."

"I infiltrated the Bonanno family and then went into interstate business with the Balistrieri family from Milwaukee. This was a feat undone. This was not the end of the tasks at hand for the opportunity opened and the Miami mob boss Santos Trafficante joining in with the Balistrieri and Bonanno family was a colossal feat."

"A colossal feat as ever undertaken in undercover operations [passionate and with emphasis]. It just doesn't happen, period, and when the success is an undercover operation and it is very rare, it is missed on most who have read my books and viewed the movies as to what was done here! Where Johnny Depp acts as me, and Pacino plays Lefty Ben Ruggiero."

COP DR DAN RUDOFOSSI: "I have a question here as well, Joe, did you evolve with your strategic plan in a fully conscious way to get into the Bonanno family and then craft the wedding of all three families uniting? What I mean is, did you use your deft diplomacy and dancing with and among all three families as far as you remember more unconsciously, that is, spontaneously as openings availed itself?"

FBI AGENT JOSEPH DOMINICK PISTONE: "The answer is both. As in my book, I will share with you another aspect of my work to add some understanding as to my wedding of all three families. That aspect of my work is that they [FBI] had an undercover operation in Milwaukee. That operation was going nowhere. In light of my success in the New York family, they asked me if I could bring in the Bonannos. You just don't go to Benjamin Ruggiero and Capo Mike Sabella and say you got a friend in Milwaukee. Look Doc, there is only one person that saves your life. That is, you! You know what I am saying, [pause] in that business?" [I assent and actively listen.]

Emotional Intelligence, Pragmatic Intelligence, and Creative Genius

It is more than passing interest to understand the contradictory and violent ecological niches of each of the different major families and the eco-ethological niches as variations that differ from one another. Not only are they working in liaison with one another at all times, there is a potential family all-out war under the surface of perceived duplicity, infidelity, or breach in omertà. Joe maneuvered each capo and underboss who is the operational chief officer to realize what was potential into actual fertile ground to close the deals made. For law enforcement, this goldmine brought the intelligence gaps and criminality into full microscopic vision and dissemination. It illustrated what could be pragmatically applied. If Joe Pistone was a wiseguy, he would be ingenious in his statesmanship if this criminal enterprise was legitimate. It of course was not. The fact it was not is only supplemented by Donnie Brasco as Joe Pistone's creative mindset. As Donnie Brasco faced multiple events of potentially deadly encounters with Mafia members, his unconscious adaptive functional dissociation emerged. Remembering the survival of Joe Pistone depended on Donnie Brasco fitting in and innovating his identity under the myriad challenges of the varieties of Mafia cultures he developed his identity in, was not only a Herculean marathon but required an ingenious mindset. The evidence of Joe Pistone's genius is in the remarkable adaptation of Donnie Brasco as a member of the Bonanno crime family entrusted as a liaison to the others while functioning as a deep-cover special agent of the FBI. The fact his innate intelligence and skill forged such liaison and success furthers the masterpiece of his genius on a practical, analytic, and creative level (Gardner, 1983, 1999; Sternberg, 1981, 1997, 1999). It is crucial to perceive that the analytic, creative dimensions of intelligence as multi-modal synchronize only by the skill to adroitly place one's innate ability with well-placed and precise effect in a way that his Mafia colleagues accepted as genuine—well placed and timed with exactitude. Joe Pistone did this with remarkable ability in each move done convincingly or he would have been killed. This is an uncomfortable truth, well known in the Mafia and police circles alike.

COP DR DAN RUDOFOSSI: "The ethological motivation to save your life is an ongoing fulcrum to shape and direct your creative and analytic mind. In my ongoing education of your personality style and ingenuity, if I am not reaching too far, does colliding eco-ethological niches and world views make sense to you? Before you answer, what I mean is that, for me, it appears both consciously, and more so unconsciously, you danced within the shifting ecological niches you were hurled into. The varieties of individual differences in each capo's personality and their entourage could make or break you. It's amazing you handled all this information and with exquisite skill and balance. Not only did you need to shift in your identity modes, but you shifted in radically changing ecological niches of survival and personality differences of warring factions in the Bonanno family and outside the family."

FBI AGENT JOSEPH DOMINICK PISTONE: "You need to cultivate this possibility of shifting and dancing with the different entourage; it is not academic or at the level of skill that is intentional, or planned, but it is saving life. I mean, saving your own life. Still, simultaneously I was very intentionally attempting to marry these three families to one another and avert a bloodbath and also to gain intelligence. I had to work hard at laying down the framework of what I am planning on doing first."

"As I said, you, nor does anyone, dare to go to Mike Sabella who was our captain, or for that matter, as I said earlier, and speak to Lefty Ruggiero and tell them what to do. [Laugh of serious import.] It's clear Doc, in my situation [eco-ethological niche] where one is in the Motion Club, the HRT Navy Seals are not there to save the operation, and not there to save your ass as well if something goes wrong. You get my meaning?" [My "Uhm" suffices, I get it alright—all too well.]

"There is only one person who can save the operation. You know who that is right? [Rhetorically posed.] That is you! No one is there when they pull the trigger, you are alone. You could die alone! Just like that, murdered. You can get wrapped up in a large carpet like a hotdog. Taken out to some depot, and put in for recycling."

"Ninety-five percent of the time it was me, and me alone. No cover, and no back-up. Remember, I had no one to cover me with the bad guys. No one covering me at all, in fact, for most of the time I was alone, doing deep cover."

"There is no one riding in on a white horse to save you. No team of other cops to back you up. You were there, alone—by your lone-self. It is colliding and collisions that can occur, like when Lefty asked about the Abscam boat, named *Left Hand*. He was trying to see if I had set him up by using that same boat to hold a party with Trafficante. It took a lot of maneuvering and convincing to get over the fact our party boat was the boat used in Abscam. I was on the tightrope. It is that kind of out-of-nowhere hit which almost makes its deadly mark if I slipped and Lefty figured it all out. He almost did, but didn't. It was a hairsbreadth away, but it remained hidden. Take that risk and that makes it even harder to imagine the colossal feat of negotiating the marriages among these three families. I'm speaking out loud with you, Doc. You know what I mean?"

COP DR DAN RUDOFOSSI: "Special Agent Joe Pistone, if I am getting it right, and I may not be getting it right, so please correct me if I am off: I envision your multifaceted tasks as most similar to a CIA operative in a foreign land doing intelligence gathering. If you get caught and your goose is caught, you are cooked. You are stuck in what I call a quantum psychic moment of trauma. You and I know you'd have to deal with a death almost unimaginable. Your own murder! That is by human standards having your hands and arms cut off and debauched as horrific and happened to Sonny Black Napolitano." [Silence painfully felt and held, between us two.] "Joe P., I remember seeing the results on the streets as a cop and sergeant at bad deals between drug dealers. It doesn't take much to get one of the drug dealers to feel threatened. If they feel you're a credible threat or a 'rat,' they'll drop you and me in the time a quarter drops and knocks off an espresso cup atop a cappuccino maker. A human being can shatter into bits on the floor in a bloody mess, correct?"

FBI AGENT JOSEPH DOMINICK PISTONE: "Exactly! Doc, you got it, yes, exactly. Remember 95 percent of the time, I had no cover team. It was me and the bad guys. No one was there to cover my back. No one to support my cover during operations."

"Attempting to marry these families, you must first lay the groundwork, drop hints, and persuade the Bonannos. You must cover your ass. You need to know who you're dealing with. I'll use the term caution. But it is much more than that. Not being aware some of the time, but all the time. In reality, you got to be fully alert and aware—all the time. I drove 18-wheel rigs. When you drive heavy hardware like that you cannot drift off. Not a moment of being hazy, lazy, or slack off. In the world of wiseguys there is no cooping [cooping is a term used by cops to take a break like going up to a roof landing in public housing and smoking a cigarette or taking some coffee and looking at the skyline]. You can find yourself in a world of major headaches and trouble if you are not fully present and aware. To repeat, you cannot afford a slip-up. Because even though I knew the undercovers who attempted to assist and orchestrate the deals, I needed to let the Bonannos believe it was their deal. It was theirs at all times, no confusion, not an iota. It was not mine to own. I allowed them to create and own their work as they brokered their own deals. The reason I did that was to avoid that quantum moment of shock if they ever found out my real identity as an FBI agent. So, if things turned sour, I redirected the bosses to the fact it was their ideas and their ownership, not my own. I would tell Lefty Ruggiero, 'I told you about this guy but you brought this guy in. If it doesn't work out, it was not me, boss, it was your decision.' In other words it was them who brought this deal into reality and not me. 'It was you who brought this deal into reality and put it away.' This was another demand of the situation. It also could in that quantum moment cause death—my own."

COP DR DAN RUDOFOSSI: "The risk of the quantum psychic moment of traumatic loss was always teetering around you and your identity modes in the eco-ethological niches you danced in. It is exactly your intuitive reasoning and analytic mind that prompted you to rise at the right time, grasp key moments to persuade, and then move in when closing the deals among the Bonanno family, with the Trafficante family. Then add to all this, it's not only the Trafficante family, but also the Balistrieri family in Milwaukee? This was not preplanned, if I got it right; you had to simultaneously tactically apply different diplomatic skills as your own identity modes shifted to accommodate each ecological cultural and survival demands."

FBI AGENT JOSEPH DOMINICK PISTONE: "It was not preplanned. Yes, I moved with the situation as it developed. But I knew who I was dealing with and when I was dealing with whom, individually. I felt the situation and moved with it. It became reality, not with clarity but with my own ability to adapt in these different situations, ecological niches. I had to choose. Risky, but calculated and well-planned choices to take risks that were not accidental, I made each choice in bridging these gaps. I didn't think of it then. But now thinking about it, Doc, if we put it all together and think back. It was gargantuan, as I said at first."

"It was the difference of the Bonanno family here in New York and the Trafficante family in Miami and the Balistrieri family in Milwaukee. It was the constant jealousy of who I was an apprentice of, Mirra, Ruggiero, or Napolitano. It was the decisions as to when and how long to stay with the wiseguys and when I needed to get a break. I had to always figure out how much and when to put my foot down and where to do it."

COP DR DAN RUDOFOSSI: "Psychologically speaking Joe, your intellectual ability to remember all these facts and individuals at the same time as you became ever aware of danger and survival required a remarkable memory. I know you said that of Lefty Ruggiero, but along with dynamic fluidity in your own intelligence, it seems like yours was the Fountain of Deleon. What I mean is, your concrete short-term memory and dynamic long-term memory worked at exceptional levels of functioning and interaction for your own working identities to adapt without disclosure. This, as we figured, was achieved as your identity modes functionally dissociated, and yet you maintained mindful awareness at all times. I am tempted to say your motivation was in part, hypervigilance, but it is not that easy to reduce or describe. It appears you were **hyper-intuitive** to all these different dimensions. It was overtaxing and demanding attention to strategize your approach at all times and places, and yet you did this without major fatigue and breakdown when you were in the saddle."

FBI AGENT JOSEPH DOMINICK PISTONE: "I think your hyper-intuitive piece adds to what I went through because, as you suggest, I had to always be aware, too, not only different wiseguy sensitivities, but their pain and what ticked off each family associate and boss. Although, remember, I didn't always avoid confrontation at all times and at all costs. That is not wise and will help the agent look weak. I proved a point and stood my ground to impress on some of the lieutenants I was my own man. I could be relied on by not watering down my opinion or stance intelligently with the right boss and never with the wrong boss."

COP DR DAN RUDOFOSSI: "Like in your deft crafting of the tripartite alliance as your own ingenuity. You discerned the needs and demands of the three families so well as to broker a deal that promised to merge three disconnected families by focusing on their potential for business. You made a novel connection with alliances that were not possible in the real gangster world, that is before Operation Donnie Brasco. As a law enforcement agent with enormous handicaps, you never capitulated to stagnation, panic, withdrawal, or crippling anxiety."

"From a psychiatric perspective as a cop doc, you were able to embrace a forgotten language and anxiety for motivation rather than withdraw. Evident for clinicians and administrators to witness as much as you and I, that your unique gift is the power of your ingenuity to change the history of law enforcement. The success of your infiltration must include understanding the reality of your accomplishments to break the mold of what was done up to you stepping up to the batter's plate, was you hit a homerun with bases loaded."

"Matching and balancing the three families is not fitting in, it is fitting each family and setting each one up for a major deal you brokered. You provide evidence of doing what was hitherto impossible. Genius in part is gaining an understanding of what you actually achieved in law enforcement deep cover and infiltration and placing this novel event and its wisdom on the learning table to scaffold benefits for future and present agents in the field of espionage and deep cover."

FBI AGENT JOSEPH DOMINICK PISTONE: "Interesting Doc, I didn't think of my work this way, but I think what you are saying is tapping into the psychological truth of what happened. It is a lot to process, and I didn't ever do this academically, but it is definitely highly mental, and I used psychology and anthropology as I majored in a long, long time ago. Go on please."

COP DR DAN RUDOFOSSI: "If I really got it right and have used my third ear correctly, when you were in Milwaukee you never used a role you played. To repeat a very important point you and I are bringing out here, adapting and functionally dissociating as Donnie Brasco to infiltrate to the highest level of being a wiseguy strategist without the need to get the title and to tug with your fishing line as to hooking all three wiseguy heads into the leader that wouldn't snap is part of the colossal success as well. But added to this complexity is your discerning differences in self, others, environment as ecological niches, and the potential for violence and attacks on yourself. Another part of your own dynamic intelligence is your intuitive sense of who you were dealing with, each gangster's sensitivities and proclivities as gangsters, is extraordinary. If we can pause for a moment here, you put it very well in your own words."

"For example, Lefty Ruggiero vying for your attention and control from Brooklyn had entrusted you as is true of Mike Sabella and the legendary Don Trafficante who created a president and allegedly took him down when he didn't play fair ball. JFK was a stupendous feat, indeed. Santos Trafficante, who reached into Cuba and back to Miami, connected to Carlos Marcella of New Orleans, and around to Washington DC via the Kennedys was nothing short of being brilliant. Although on the other side of the law, he was a Machiavellian strategist, who felt betrayed by the Kennedys but maneuvered around them with the skill of a statesman behind the scenes. I say this because the depth of your savvy to navigate in the politics and statesmanship of wiseguys like these was to me colossal in your emotional and diplomatic ingenuity. Further of note is the lack of putting these pieces together, which I am doing piecemeal now, is to iterate at the core of your synergy is genius. That is your own genius, Joe Dominick Pistone. This is not to flatter you! I hope my point does not remain at the top of the intellectual canopy in criminal justice, but at the ground level with humility where we feel most comfortable."

"This is nothing to say of your finesse and courage connecting to Balistrieri in Milwaukee. The danger and the scintillation had to be awesome as much as overwhelming, even if you had a full-time cop doc and team behind you. But you didn't have any such support. You did all this on your own. If I can say, this is a new dimension. A new dimension where your statesmanship in negotiating a deal with the elite, the brilliant masters of deception, on one level of analysis, was forged."

"On another level of analysis, the different families being criminals does not negate their intellectual prowess and humanity, as you encountered each from an existential perspective as you broke through to gain their trust and confidence. Some of the wiseguys had humanity; although unconventional and murderous of other wiseguys, there was some redeemable center to be targeted."

"In your intellectual fieldwork, you remarkably persuaded the different heads of Mafia families to merge. Besides your purpose of gaining intelligence on their operations as not only unparalleled, but moving into unchartered territory without any real cover."

"You without any real fire-power outside of the firearms you were given by the Mafia via Lefty aka Benjamin Ruggiero, you sidestepped and engaged with very different men who were capable of extreme violence. Your own facile assuaging of their violent potential not only with you, with the likes of Tony Mirra as capo whose blood thirst was notorious even among La Cosa Nostra. No one less than a law enforcement officer working deep cover for the Federal Bureau of Investigation as Donnie Brasco, an associate within the Bonanno crime family for six years, is exceptional. Does that make sense to you as a perspective when we look at this feat psychologically as genius by creative achievement from multiple levels of assessment? Or am I off into La La Land, Special Agent Joe Dominick Pistone?"

FBI AGENT JOSEPH DOMINICK PISTONE: "You're on track Dr. Dan Rudofossi. Let me add to your knowing my mindset. What else is important to consider is as you've asked and suggested, is how I had to work off of knowing each member's personality quirks and idiosynchronicity."

"My answer is, I had to play them according to their personality. For example, if I am close to Lefty Ruggiero, and Tony Mirra even more so, I have to be wary of any offensive comment, intentional or not."

"When Sonny Black, for example, took a liking to me, it made Lefty Ruggiero jealous. That was so because, as you remember, he vouched for me being a good potential wiseguy from the beginning. I was his guy. Lefty was big into the wiseguy persona and he took it dead serious."

"If I am in conversation with Sonny and he tells me something, I have to, when Lefty calls, relay and play it all off to Lefty. In other words, I needed to relay to Lefty exactly what Sonny said, and with quite a bit of persuading make sure I am not overstepping his authority and sidestepping in with Sonny Black Napolitano."

"One of things was I had the contract on Bruno as the son of Sonny Red Indelicato. It was my responsibility to kill Bruno period, no ifs, ands, or buts."

"Remember, it was part of doing business at that time. For me it's like you're thinking, I can't get anyone to do it for me and kill Bruno. I can't say, 'gee whiz good fellow, I am an FBI agent and it's all over.' I wish but can't tell the authorities or Sonny Red's kid, 'Bruno, you're under arrest.'"

"I am stuck although I am solicited to kill Bruno the son of Sonny Red because Sonny Black told me to do so. I have no identification on me as an FBI agent. I have no back-up. If I am told to go for a ride and do my job, I have to do as I am ordered if I can't get away in that quantum psychic moment."

"Meaning I am told to whack Bruno. If I hesitate or worse delay going along with them to do the hit: This is real! I mean they're going to kill me, if I don't kill Bruno. You have to make a decision and I am not going to die for a gangster, as there is no glory in dying for a gangster."

"I would have to do what I had to do. Get it? I had to preserve my life. I was not going to die for a gangster. Bruno Indelicato was a gangster. I would then have to deal with the aftermath. That's one of the problems with undercover operations. If the supervisor is not an undercover in his/her life, these split-second decisions you have to make is not understood."

"It's as if you've never been there and they cannot understand the pressure and the demands to survive yourself are not negotiable. Not negotiable for a gangster: either you deliver the fatal bullet and get made as a member of the family, or you get one and get whacked if you don't. No rocket science to this stuff. If you are to take the bullet, you are dead. If you are forced to deliver that fatal bullet, you are no good dead!"

"To be a good undercover it is a guy who is a little bit of a thinker and can handle a situation in the moment and don't need a committee to make a choice. I agree with what you said and your interpretation as it makes me think and those in power as administrators to get off the high horses and ivory towers. You need to do what you have to do in order to see the next day. It is hard and not enviable, but you know what Doc, this is what being deep cover is all about, period. So, boom, I knew intuitively as you hammered it on the head, I can handle it where mental toughness comes in and works. It is not knuckle-dragging into deep cover, it is slipping under cover and doing what needs to be done to survive and get your objectives done."

COP DR DAN RUDOFOSSI: "In order for you to get each wiseguy to connect with you demands, in one of my own worlds, which is the world of psychology/psychiatry, your executive strategic mindset-frontal lobes and cerebral hemispheres demanded synchrony with your highest level of emotional intelligence—I suggest an existential awareness that is remarkably active and empathic. Let me point out what I am asking by contextualizing my question with Lefty. Benjamin Lefty Ruggiero could go off and turn on a dime if he felt you betrayed him, didn't show enough respect, didn't tolerate his incessant rants. Lefty had a no-nonsense steel-trap memory, which is amazing in the light of his drinking and smoking. But take, for instance, his self-centered smoking in cars with the windows rolled up, if I recall correctly." [Joe Pistone gives me his aha, hum.] "Tolerating and not triggering Lefty's lack of empathy in this regard, not others, is ingratiating and also obnoxious. This is to say nothing of Captain Tony Mirra and his hot-coal temper."

"I remember your recalled for me your own off-the-cuff intervention when some poor mouthy guy in the bar would be Swiss cheese with hot-lead holes over smoke and shadows for disparaging Tony as an Italian American?"

"Or someone like Kuklinski as a hitman for Mirra. Mirra who you broke bread with and made deals with. Richard Kuklinski killed a poor fellow needing to take a pee who stepped ahead of him as he stalked him before strangulation, as he put it a unique way."

"The fact you could dance with these wiseguys and some of the extreme murderers they had tagging along without stepping on their 'unique toes' is clearly emotional ingenuity. It is nonstop hyper-intuitive emotional and mental mentation that breaks the charts of emotional IQ. You had to have a strategist's mind, be a master of ceremony, a wiseguy who is always tough enough, and a street cop's instincts to keep you always one head in front of the wiseguy next to you. He can turn on you, without you realizing if you don't keep your proverbial antennas up and on focus at all times. You always had to be wary enough to survive within the particular family's mores and taboos as well as the general culture of the mob at once."

FBI AGENT JOSEPH DOMINICK PISTONE: "Yeah that is absolutely correct. Where Lefty was volatile and you had to be very leery of his reactions all the time, Sonny Black Napolitano was not. Sonny was not as volatile and could converse at times in a normal way."

"But with Lefty you never could show weakness. Never! I knew you could go ten feet, but I couldn't go that eleventh one with Lefty Ruggiero. You know what I mean?" [Rhetorical.]

"But going the ten feet he knew I wasn't a push-over, but an inch over the eleventh foot I knew he would blow up at me and all over the place as a punk that was disrespecting or worse challenging his authority as a made wiseguy."

"As an undercover you got to know your enemy, and you got to know your subject. Doc, if you don't know your enemy, you wouldn't defeat them. You need to know their personality. Each one is quite different. In the end, as you know, I saved Lefty's life, but you couldn't save Sonny Black Napolitano. In a way I guess a relationship develops after all this time you break bread and converse about even inane stuff and more so about things you have in common with one another."

COP DR DAN RUDOFOSSI: "Could you elaborate for me?"

FBI AGENT JOSEPH DOMINICK PISTONE: "You don't spend time, 16 to17 hours a day, with even miserable people that you don't develop a relationship with. For me I did develop relationships as I said with that person. I gather evidence and hopefully convict you and send you to jail if you are a wiseguy or perp. But, at times, you feel sometime like you've hit a brick wall."

"Look, I work with a lot of undercover agents and they can't hit that wall. What I mean is, you gotta put away the conversations and shared dinners and entertainment and say that I am going to put you in jail."

"Maybe the hardest part for the deep-cover special agent is that for many, that bond and relationship get blurry to them. The agent or detective caves in to emotional ties they develop. It is that understanding that is crucial as to why there are a very few who could actually do the work as an undercover. It is not because you are cold and unfeeling, but you must be tough-minded and do your job as a deep cover and not ever forget what you set out to do and why you're doing it is to protect the citizens from criminal enterprises taking over their communities. It's not that they are not good agents or detectives, but this level of deep cover is very strenuous and draining, only a rare few have what it takes in mental toughness to complete the job they started!"

COP DR DAN RUDOFOSSI: "If I got you right, Joe, it is because they get too hooked into the emotional transference in the relationship that develops. Let me give a brief bridge to what I mean. It reminds me of what is called the analytic attitude in treatment [Brenner, 1973]. A very few clinicians can consistently stay within a classic analytic attitude, that is, without getting hooked into what is transferred from one's own earlier relationships into the current relationship that exists between the therapist and the patient."

"What a patient brings to therapy is *transference* and derives from relationships with his/her parents and authority figures, including defenses and unconscious desires and fears of getting caught."

"Counter-transference occurs when the clinician misinterprets or acts on their own needs and not their patient's, mainly unconsciously. It aids the clinician and the patient alike when this is brought out and analyzed. Mental toughness can be interpreted as a boundary similar to an analytic attitude."

"Psychoanalysts try to not get entangled with their own personal needs and wishes when working with a patient. In your description your mental toughness is a boundary that protects you from being vulnerable and open to being compromised. While you need to be real, you can't get hooked and caught up off guard as is true of the psychoanalyst or he/she loses touch with treatment and effectiveness."

"If I am correct, the FBI asks you, as in the NYPD, to resist with tough-mindedness and infiltrate by becoming a member of that crime family for example, but you and I know regardless of how diligent you are, at least some leakage occurs without support."

"You have to be given leeway and a cop doc to talk to when you can. My hope is that you are not asked insensitive or downright stupid questions, and worse given prescriptions to masturbate your stress away instead of respectful solutions that fit well enough with your own reality."

FBI AGENT JOSEPH DOMINICK PISTONE: "That is correct, Doc! When I was in Quantico my partner who is a doc, a psychologist like yourself, does training with other law enforcement officers with me."

"We spoke to agents overseas and their number-one gripe was lack of support from administrators, and often their own police supervisors. There has to be something to these complaints because it can't be a consistent gripe with no basis to it."

"It's tough to explain to a lot of them that the bosses don't get it. When agents and cops do detective work, the bosses still have the picture that all you are is flash with the leather jacket, and 'you all drive fancy cars' and don't have normal police tours and hours."

"You are, in other words, a great actor and role player and not a real cop for the streets. It still prevails today. That is this false myth about us as deep covers and even street plainclothes cops. This false myth is still going on, even on the inside, you know?"

COP DR DAN RUDOFOSSI: "I know too well as the chief police psychologist with Human Health Service Group of Drug Enforcement Administration EAP nationwide. Unlike the special operations men and women of today and yesteryear, you had to work on your own from A to Z again in uncharted waters. Parallel to what I heard in the NYPD as the director of Clinical Services of Member Assistance Program city-wide from 1996–2000, as its first cop doc and predecessor to POPPA [Police Organization Providing Peer Assistance]."

FBI AGENT JOSEPH DOMINICK PISTONE: "Yeah, special ops work with a plan to strategically take down operationally who they practice and rehearse with as a team approach like FAST [Foreign-deployed Advisory Support Teams, which are Drug Enforcement Administration units who receive training from Special Operations Command] operatives. The team have their targets as the bad guys they know, they have studied long and hard—before taking action. As a team, each member is fully supported. But that does not exist when you are deep cover."

"Here is another little thing I want to bring out as I do in my own classes in this regard as lack of support for the deep cover. The undercover has to satisfy three mistresses as we discussed."

"I let agents know your first mistress is your organization. It is the job itself as the first mistress is the law enforcement community itself. But for the undercover I include your bosses will not and cannot know the full ramifications of what a deep cover must really undergo and forgo."

"The second mistress you gotta satisfy is the bad guys. The ones you are infiltrating must feel you are serving them well. You need to ensure they feel good about what you are doing. You need to definitely convince them that you are real. You need to know their world as wiseguys and their rules, or else you will be whacked. Of course, in reality, you are not one of them. So, satisfying them is extremely challenging, as they live in a different world with different and contradictory rules than normal human beings."

"The third mistress you gotta satisfy is your family and ensure your homelife is okay. You need to know they're doing well, but you are pulled by the first two mistresses every which way. The first two mistresses are all distracting and negative influences to a stable and normal homelife."

"The establishment does not see the truths of the three mistresses to this very day. Yes, although programs exist and you hear whispers about the truth of what we deal with, whispers are really only whispers. The establishment of bosses and bureaucrats don't get the meaning of the three mistresses as the job, whether police department or bureau; the second one as the wiseguy or criminal family you are infiltrating and the fact their demands and what they need from you to bring in such as money etc.; and your own family itself to satisfy your spouse as your partner and help her/him feel secure and relate to you as a spouse is often destroyed. The balls you have to juggle is a feat in itself. You get the picture and know it well, I am sure."

COP DR DAN RUDOFOSSI: "I got it, right, as we all have had those mistresses as cops to a degree on a continuum, but none are like what beckons different needs, she demands from you as reciprocal for responsiveness you need to ask of each mistress."

"The first mistress asks of you to go to choir practice after the job is over and still remain squeaky clean and pure as the driven snow when you are on the job, or home. The first mistress includes the police department, bureau or administration, and prosecutors as well."

"The second mistress wants you to be the dark prince, and get down and dirty as you can with her. If you follow the wiseguy rules, mistress one and two will clash as expected. Both demand full loyalty and neither is capable of fully understanding you need to be loyal to both. While you stoke one in a respectful but satisfying manner, separate and distinctly, the other mistress is spying through the back door. You keep it as business as usual until you close the deal."

"The third mistress is your family. Especially your wife or mate, and you don't talk to your wife the way you do either of the first mistresses. Your wife is your ultimate and real partner."

"The other two mistresses are real, that is, as long you're under the covers, with each one. The first mistress is always very demanding as well. In the long run, if you keep your wife and kids happy, you succeed by not letting the shit waves of a puritan hose you down as the first mistress."

"The other mistress is the wild card; she can ruin your world with one messy outcome after the other."

"One reality is the third mistress is the real deal for the long running in this odyssey we call life. Does that capture the reality while forgiving my rough sketch, Special Agent Joe Pistone, aka Donnie Brasco?"

68 Police, Mafia, and Family

FBI AGENT JOSEPH DOMINICK PISTONE: "That's a good metaphor and it does work for me Doc. It is a well, good sketch of what it is like managing the triangle of the three mistresses and not letting the good one, the bad one, and the ugly one ever get confused in our minds, and as you say confusing fact from fiction. Ciao!"

Summary

In this chapter the metaphor describing the three mistresses is truly the metaphor of Special Agent Joseph Dominick Pistone. Culling out Joe Pistone's perspicuity to seal the deal of an alliance among three vying families can be seen as a metaphor for three tribes striving to gain water and food. Joe Pistone succeeded almost perfectly. As an outsider of three vying Mafia families, Donnie Brasco tilted the scale of internal Mafia bellicosity to a tame tempo. His success was the tipping point that succeeded where even genuine Mafia associates and made wiseguys failed.

One of the two potential tipping points were out of his control when Special Agent Joe Pistone's wife had a near fatal accident on her way to meet him on his way home from his meeting in the Midwest. This accident and the conflict over mistresses were keen competition for the deep cover. Joe wanted desperately to stay with his wife for her hospital stay. He also wanted to continue under pressure of the job needing completion in arranging the deal with the capo of the Balistrieri family. This conflict was jarring and could have melted down the entire operation.

The second glitch was the other FBI special agent attempting to break into the Balistrieri family caught blue-handed in the carmine bloody jar of organized crime. In this regard the breaking through of barriers was made even more extraordinary. Joe Pistone managed to keep him alive by feigning he was to be given a harsher outcome by Donnie Brasco himself.

The mistress of law-and-order agents and police require starched Oxford collars and color-coordinated ties matching dress gloves for fine dinner attire and court appearances. Neatly parsed words and expression must mollify the need for picture perfection along with the white horse one rides in on. This mistress had to be given her due.

The other mistress was wiseguy families demanding from Joe the rouge of heated tarantellas as amusement. All this was to be achieved in his shadow identity as liaison and broker of deals behind smoking screens and darkened windowpanes. The other side of the second mistress is that her Spartan demands call for nothing less than business attitude. Spelled out in each ecological niche of each family and the survival rules of each boss in each family demanding full loyalty, nothing less is accepted, and anything less spells death.

Cop Doc Corner for Students Only—Debriefing

The independence of mindfulness and individuality of Special Agent Joe Pistone is crucial in seeking any agent or officer to be a candidate for deep cover. The gift of Joe Pistone's genius is not replicable, and certainly not in its fulgence and spectrum as he broke so many molds. Special Agent Joe's inimitable combination succeeded in overcoming impossible odds (Becker, 1997).

In the assignment section to follow, take the opportunity to ferret out how the impossible is possible, even if largely improbable, by tackling one of the difficult questions for yourself and presenting it to the group. In gaining tough-mindedness, remember that seeking out challenges is not to be avoided but will lasso in your own unique voice and test your own ability to think on your toes.

Expanding the law enforcement capacity and ability of what Homeland Security can expand to within a forensic police psychologist's imagination is spread from the vistas of a future agent who will learn from the legendary success and wisdom of Special Agent Joseph Dominick Pistone. Or an agent or detective who may be highly gifted and courageous by offering a stepping-stone onto a ladder which can add to the challenge of tackling organized crime and its evolution in the world of mobsters, criminals, and gangsters.

Important Definitions and Concepts to Keep in Mind

Encounter

Encounter as described in detail and fleshed out in dialogue with Special Agent Joe Pistone and me entailed genuine experiences that challenged his core beliefs and depths of what counts in life, from the standpoint of being and becoming a wiseguy while remaining a member of the elite law enforcement bureau—the FBI. It is the peak moments from an existential vantage point as to what is purposeful and Joe was responsive to in his own real self away from the identity modes as Donnie Brasco, special agent, and even family man, but as his real heartful and soulful choices made in the span of his life and the precious moments he made such choices in.

Quantum intra-psychic moment of trauma

Quantum intra-psychic moment of trauma is a hypothetical construct I presented in 2007 (Rudofossi, 2007) as a way of assessment and intervention in ambulatory complex trauma experiences police endure. It is not a tipping point, but the impact of a novel experience of traumatic loss that disrupts the prior coping defenses (consciously and unconsciously) experienced by police officers and agents in the field. It is an unusual experience as the shock may be felt but unprocessed for a length of not only months but years, and in some cases I had telescoping of traumatic losses return after decades of being repressed unconsciously in patients. It is not assimilated or accommodated in Piaget's construct of intelligence and problem solving.

Noetic dimension

Noetic dimension is the spiritual and soulful transcendence by which all human beings transcend the physical, mental, soma, or bodily influences that impinge and subdue the will to live and encounter meaning and purpose. This ability to transcend the physical, mental, and environmental influences by drawing from the wells within that are not reducible is what provokes courage, tenacity, and ingenuity, such as Joe Pistone enduring six years of living among and within the Mafia families, and the demands that would fatigue, depress, and trigger dissembling and decompensation in otherwise healthy police and special agents.

Sit-down

Sit-down is the moment when the boss or underboss in a crime family calls you in to discuss a matter of grave importance. It is often literally grave as it becomes life or death in a judgment that hardly resembles any legal proceeding and involves violent means of setting an example of someone who is an associate to even a full made member of that particular crime family deserving due to a violation of protocol from a beating to execution-style slaying.

It is not always that somber and can be a sit-down for an appointment, assignment, and promotion. It is most often used in the cultural nuances of the Mafia as a negative and violent sentencing of the violator of the Mafia family rules.

Conceptual and Writing Exercises for Student and Professor Only

1. A ladder to aspire toward in our war on terror as a psychological war first and foremost begins with organized criminal enterprises. Unlike the Italian mafiosi that have not dealt with foreign enemies to the United States, United Kingdom, and European Union, others have. Look up Operation Underworld to see the alliance forged between the Department of War and an Italian organized crime syndicate family to protect the banks of America from axis invasion during World War II.
2. In the attempt to close down money laundering, which fuels the use of human trafficking ranging from illegal use of immigrants to gain ground by subterfuge and infiltration of legitimate businesses, rogues, including officers who are corrupt and betray their shield, have rarely been implicated. What, if anything, do plainclothes officers acting as civilians do to help deter such illegal practices? How does this chapter or earlier ones assist you in thinking of a solution? In presenting your summary, be prepared to discuss pitfalls and challenges of fair work practices and disclosures to all employees.
3. Choose one incident that Joseph Dominick Pistone endured in his six years of undercover as presented in this chapter. Stop, and take a long pause and note the entire incident. As you commit the incident to a separate piece of paper, with your professor's assistance choose one recorder to note the emotions and thoughts each student in the group has as you recall the event Special Agent Joe Pistone experienced as you imagine he felt. You are to imagine being in his shoes so to speak. Let's use one example: imagine if you were the real special agent of the FBI, Joseph Dominick Pistone, and Benjamin Lefty Ruggiero, who is armed with a high-powered pistol in his lap, shows you the photo of the Abscam incident and questions you about your possible involvement in that incident. Remember, in reality, Donnie Brasco is Joseph Dominick Pistone the FBI agent. I may say I felt the emotion of shock and I was frightened with the thought of what if Lefty knows I am an FBI agent. How will he kill me? This is a beginning. Assess with your professor as to how much trauma and loss he faces as he is challenged. In doing this project as small groups, select one leader student to gain intelligence which is accessible from reliable criminal justice, homeland security, and law authorities in realistically appraising the harm and violence Benjamin Lefty Ruggiero was capable of inflicting on Donnie Brasco to appreciate the real risks our heroic agent endured in just this one unidentified event he experienced.
4. In this project, please make a list of your own exquisite strengths and some weaknesses in your desire to enter law enforcement. How do you think you can use the concept of mental toughness to overcome some limitations? What can you do if you were asked to do a plainclothes assignment in your chosen area of law enforcement/public safety work? Do you think you may be one of the few officers who has the inner strength and conviction as well as fortitude to become a candidate of the FBI? If you were asked, and your professor may ask you, what did you learn in this chapter in regard to taking on the identity you may be asked to survive in and as? What might you do, for example, in learning, as Joseph Dominick Pistone did, to infiltrate the Mafia as a petty jewel thief?

References

Becker, E. (1997). *The denial of death.* New York: Simon & Schuster.
Brenner, C. (1973). *An elementary textbook of psychoanalysis.* New York & London: Anchor Books, Doubleday.
Brenner, C. (1979). The components of psychic conflict and its consequence in mental life. *Psychoanalytic Quarterly,* 48(4), 547–567.

Brenner, C. (2008). Aspects of psychoanalytic theory: Drives, defense and the pleasure-unpleasure principle. *Psychoanalytic Quarterly*, 3, 707–717.
Carr, C. (2006). *The alienist*. New York: Random House.
Campbell, J. (2008). *The hero with a thousand faces*. Novato, CA: New World Library.
Freud, S. (1990). *Beyond the pleasure principle*. New York & London: W.W. Norton.
Freud, S. (2019). *The ego and the id*. New York: Clydesdale.
Frankl, V. (1979). *The unheard cry for meaning: Psychotherapy and humanism*. New York: Simon and Schuster.
Fromm, E. (1957). *The forgotten language: An introduction to the understanding of dreams, fairy tales, and myths*. New York: Grove.
Gardner, H. (1983). *Frames of mind: The theory of multiple intelligences*. New York: Basic Books.
Gardner, H. (1999). *Intelligence reframed: Multiple intelligences for the 21st century*. New York: Basic Books.
Jung, G. C. (1969). *The archetypes and the collective unconscious*. Princeton, NJ: Princeton University Press.
Jung, G. C. (2009). *The red book: Liber novus*. New York & London: W.W. Norton.
Maslow, A. (1973). *The farther reaches of human nature*. London: Penguin.
Rank, O. (2004). *The myth of the birth of the hero: A psychological interpretation of the myth*. Baltimore, MD: John Hopkins University Press.
Reik, T. (1953). *The secret self: Psychoanalytic experiences in life and literature*. New York: Farrar, Straus, and Young.
Reik, T. (1956). *Listening with the third ear*. New York: Grove Press.
Rudofossi, D. M. (2007). *Working with traumatized police-officer patients: A clinician's guide to complex PTSD syndromes in public safety professionals*. New York & London: Routledge.
Rudofossi, D. M. (2009). *A cop doc's guide to public safety complex trauma syndrome: Using five police personality styles*. Amityville, NY: Baywood.
Rudofossi, D. M. (2012). *A street survival guide for public safety officers: The cop doc's strategies for surviving trauma, loss, and terrorism*. New York & London: Routledge.
Rudofossi, D. M. (2013). *A cop doc's guide to understanding terrorism as human evil: Healing from complex trauma syndromes for military, police, and public safety officers and their families*. Amityville, NY: Baywood.
Rudofossi, D. M. (2017). *Cop doc: The police psychologists' casebook—narratives from police psychology*. New York and London: Routledge.
Shatz, D., Wowelsky, B. J., & Ziegler, R. (2004). *Essays from Professor Joseph Solevetchik, Out of the whirlwind: Essays on mourning, suffering and the human condition*. Hoboken, NJ: Ktav.
Solevetchik, J. (1992). *The lonely man of faith*. New York: Doubleday.
Sternberg, J. R. (1981). Intelligence and non-entrenchment. *Journal of Educational Psychology* 73, 1–16.
Sternberg, J. R. (1997). *Successful intelligence*. New York: Plume.
Sternberg, J. R. (1999). The theory of successful intelligence. *Review of General Psychology*, 3, 292–316.

4
BOUNDARIES IN MAFIA CULTURE
Totem and Taboos

Introduction

Cultural importance gives behaviors, thoughts, and emotions a context that demands attention from each participant. What one ought to do, and not do, takes experience and the willingness to learn what is expected of him/her. This is poignant in doing any type of detective work in a cultural context. In even thinking of doing undercover and, more so, deep cover, it is essential for survival and adaptation ethologically speaking.

The dos and don'ts in Mafia culture contextualize rules as acts of commission or omission. All cultural rules lay out what is to be considered valued, less cherished, negative, outright destructive, less destructive, and neutral if such a value exists. It is what clinicians and researchers call a Likert scale on a continuum if we are to use an analogy to help us understand that cultural motifs are not linear (Skaggs, 2022). Cultural rules can be seen as lying on a continuum. Notwithstanding the range on a continuum, any move beyond certain boundaries, including rules within a Mafia family, can mean death for even a perceived violation. Based on the importance given the violation, one may say that anyone who violates that boundary is deserving of death in that culture and family structure. Culture is born in ecological contexts.

An ecological context is the overall arch of any cultural context. Survival of the culture is given the most important value for the individual participant within that culture, and in the expanding circles outside of each circle. Circles of ecological and cultural meaning cohere survival for all members as participants.

Conceptualizing that circular nature as potentially expanding in concentric and widening circles into infinite space is exciting to ponder. For our purpose, we will look into the reciprocal contractions as a center circle reduces its own space—inexplicable and perhaps in a transcendent means beyond its own conscious capacity to control such contraction.

Keep in mind it is concentric circles that are linked in space over time as the most valuable circles of rules and coordinates useful in surviving and for survival itself. Considering each circle in concentric circles is presented by our key witness, participant, and educator—Joe Dominick Pistone, who centered himself as Donnie Brasco and survived in contracting and expanding contextual space ecologically and ethologically and is a springboard to learn from.

For example, as his law enforcement identity mode, Joe D. Pistone complemented his identity mode as Donnie Brasco. *He was loyal in his identity mode as Special Agent Joe Pistone, and loyal*

DOI: 10.4324/9781032202761-5

to both his identity mode as Donnie Brasco and his identity mode as special agent in this compelling chapter.

Let's peer inside by beginning with the most important criterion for being a wiseguy initiate culturally and ecologically in the ethological niche as a law enforcement deep-cover undercover of camouflage. Acts of perceived disloyalty are considered betrayal within the ecological edges that surround each Mafia family. In achieving survival within the Mafia Bonanno family, a don't do means don't act in a certain way or you've betrayed trust. For example, as we are educating, flirting with another made member of the Mafia family's mate, or ex-mate, is likely to result in being executed. Such an act as snitching to police, or law enforcement as an act of commission—for example, breaching omertà, which is the rule to keep silence to others outside of one's Mafia family—results in death by murder (Pistone & Woodley, 1989; Pistone, 2004; Pistone & Brandt, 2007).

But acts that are omissions, such as do not neglect ensuring all profits as agreed to your boss as payments earned is indeed paid to him, is considered unforgivable capital theft and deserves capital punishment in the Mafia family. But let's say it's the holidays and the associate in the Mafia family awards himself a hidden tip of $500, squirreling away $500 from your immediate boss is also not a clever one-over trick, it is a one-way ticket to capital punishment (Pistone & Woodley, 1989; Pistone, 2004; Pistone & Brandt, 2007).

In mathematics, as in psychological-anthropological science, we call these acts of omission rules—coordinates in one's spatial adaptations and limitations to growth. These rules and the process of initiation in the Mafia family are best looked at as mores that stitch together the foundations of that culture.

Mores include hidden and unwritten, but well-known and learned, rituals that create trust or distance for any member within that Mafia family.

Explicit Rules: Ecological Boundaries and Ethological Survival Motivation

There are explicit and well-known rules of a particular culture that define an ecological space that one cannot cross. In not crossing that line for our purposes and understanding, remember that, as we have clarified in earlier chapters, ethological motivation is unwritten, mainly unconscious, and implicit aspects of learned mores. Violations of Mafia family mores are deadly. Remember, in earlier chapters ethological motivation is a shorthand for survival motivation, which covers life and death struggles within cultural and territorial imperatives. How so?

In answering this question and others in the chapter we will look into the subtle and explicit mores—etching purpose within the world of Mafia families through the lenses of microcultural eco-ethological niches. These eco-ethological niches are hidden from, and yet function within, a larger macro-cultural society.

As in all cultures, boundaries withhold differences made noticeable by outsiders whose attempts to intrude are answered by aggression on a continuum. Common borders within cultures bring together similar groups to the host macro-culture. Violations of such borders can bring aggression and even death.

Multi-cultural Boundaries: Exclusion is Maintenance by Default in Mafia Family Systems

Please stop, pause, and redirect your attention to a critical point. Forceful attempts to correct cultural differences by forcing another culture to fit the host culture, bypassing real differences including its sacred cultural mores, results in a Procrustean method. The Procrustean method is a forceful attempt to alter the naturally unfolding and heuristic nature of real-life events and culture within an eco-ethological framework prior to exploration into the host culture. Respecting boundaries and not pushing the edges is a way of being different and tolerant. Being indifferent to the reality of any culture as experienced within that culture itself is Procrustean force. It is not only dangerous ethologically, but also indignant toward reality, and, frankly speaking, arrogant to the differences within that culture. Why?

Boundaries in cultural and religious groups are the totems and taboos of how each cultural and religious group expresses what is right and wrong behaviors. In answering "why" and "how" to conduct such behaviors and even in what manner to think of such practices, it is key for the investigator as scientist as much as LEO to learn and enjoin the mores as practiced. This is rare nowadays and yet is a key toward success in infiltration.

Without that reality check, Special Agent Joe D. Pistone would not have fit in to the Mafia families as he did. Rather, Joe Pistone understood what tenured scientists and clinicians in the "know-how" and "with-it" have figured out. Indeed, effective scientists who become successful become expert and adept within a different ecological cultural context with little notice of entry, by not forcing any change but assimilation and accommodation to that cultural milieu.

With the facts we have affirmed at this point, looking back to earlier chapters, we viewed the three mistresses as coordinates Special Agent Joe Pistone, in doing deep cover, actually did.

Stepping back, let me re-emphasize that "mistresses" is an metaphor. Such metaphors emerged from the creative ingenuity and mindset of Special Agent Joe Pistone.

Effective cultural anthropologists, clinicians, and researchers respect the cultural mores and metaphors as we will do in viewing the Mafia family and our participating expert, Special Agent Joe Pistone. Joe Pistone as Donnie Brasco was, and is, a success. In my position as navigator, I pitch in, if only to keep the integrity of the witness's words and attention to details as crucial within the motif Special Agent Joe Pistone educates us about.

In this fourth chapter, Special Agent Joseph Pistone in our ongoing dialogue illustrates with newer and novel insights as to the psychology of what becoming an undercover operative really means. Again, notwithstanding that as law enforcement officers we (including myself as a cop doc) cannot abide, condone, or ever excuse away what is stone-cold killing of others. Notwithstanding the revolting aspects of murder and violence in the Mafia families on the other hand, a larger panorama as vista is to be understood, as it is, in reality, not in fiction, or by fictionalizing or forcing corrections to amend his, or my, text, or our dynamic dialogue. In fact, survival as eco-ethological influences that are shaped by and shape survival motivation are created by existentially unconscious and conscious derivatives of drives such as social, cultural, sexual, aggressive, and creative impulses and tendencies in all of us, commonalities we share in awareness and in shadows.

Common ground is stretched when we view mores, rituals, and shared life skills between the rough and tumble acculturation of the distinct Mafia families and some extended police and military families. It also may make sense in some ways toward understanding the complex bridges formed in others that defy gravity and cookie-cutter legal drafts as stratagems.

The strategy used by Joe Pistone is one that all teachers and professors who are beloved educators intuitively know.

Ant-Lion and Ant: The Lure of Haste

The well-kept hidden strategy used by the ant-lion is the one used by the snapping alligator turtle that sets traps in the sweet allure of its own tongue as bait to catch the unsuspecting fish. By humbling oneself and allowing the suspect to set him/herself up for detection is part of the strategy in a controlled and strategic manner. The Mafia family is not naive as to the danger of infiltration by law enforcement agents. In the case of Donnie Brasco, the variables and the eco-ethological niches were variable as much as the personalities and character strengths and limits that each captain as boss in each respective Mafia family was. Special Agent Joe Pistone's ingenuity to not only ensure acts of commission fit, but as he moved the movers to negotiations and innovations, while not rattling the shakers to move against him, as acts of omission, subtly applied, are as valuable as the ant that learns how to strategically surpass the lure of the ant-lion. Further, although Mafia families' paths are all the more different than Joe Pistone's path, the perfidy within the families toward one another was akin to vying ant-lions. Joe's tough-minded commitment was to stay loyal to a vision that needed disclosure to understand the models of La Cosa Nostra and the single-mindedness to infiltrate the blind spots and to scaffold a link toward discovery for police, unknown before Donnie Brasco emerged. It is this genius to survive that is most valuable and least understood by law enforcement administrators.

Success was not only set and marked by outcomes alone, but in the process of what happened. The ingenuity lay in Joe leading the bosses of the families into connections never imagined before.

Let's move from the context I have laid out for you in this chapter to evidence that frames my assertion by asking some poignant questions.

Questions to Guide You as Navigational Tools: Learning Objectives

1. In understanding mores as navigational markings in the Mafia family, how did Special Agent Joe Pistone learn the subtle nuances of how to fit in, when to act, or omit acting on choices left to his intuitive perceptions and burgeoning knowledge of each Mafia family?
2. What dangers did Joe Pistone have to veer away from as he moved deeper in his identity mode as Donnie Brasco?
3. When confronted with such stark vacillations that shifted from genteel meetings to abrupt threats of execution with little warning, how did Donnie Brasco respond—behaviorally, mentally, and emotionally?
4. While skills were acquired by Special Agent Joe Pistone in quantum moments of trauma and adaptation, did threats of leakage and disclosure come close to jeopardizing Operation Donnie Brasco?
5. What are hypothetical constructs underlying the processes of assimilation and accommodation by Special Agent Joe Pistone into his identity mode as Donnie Brasco that can be better understood through the lenses of psychology, anthropology, and clinical psychology and psychiatry?
6. How is understanding the process of dos and don'ts from an *Ecological Ethological Existential Analysis Approach* a way of not reducing the actual operational effectiveness of Operation Donnie Brasco into a formula, and still gaining much useful wisdom for police and law enforcement officers?
7. Does evidence of hidden resilience emerge collaboratively with Dr. Rudofossi and Special Agent Joe Pistone as their *Eco-Ethological Existential Analysis* seeks to understand Donnie Brasco as an observing participant who is at once a member of the Mafia and simultaneously a member of the FBI?

Key Terms

De-individuation as a process for the special agent
Made man
Markings
Shadow and doubles
Sit-downs

From learning the in-depth meaning of coordinate postings above, let's mark Joe Dominick Pistone's novel insights and learn as we segue into my narrative with Donnie Brasco. Markings, as suggested earlier, are more than a literal footnote or marks highlighted on pages under scrutiny, as United Nations Secretary General Dag Hammarskjold educated us (Hammarskjold, 1966). Masterfully parsing out all leads until elimination yields the choicest effective narrow strait toward the rivulet of truth takes discipline and discernment; it takes a mental toughness to reject poor fits. Of all forensic psychologists and detectives I have worked with and known, including placing me in this mélange as a street cop to gold shield with 200-plus collars and sergeant in the NYPD, I know of no other detective, detective sergeant plus, who matches the strategic or analytic ingenuity of Joe Dominick Pistone. The most astute forensic/police psychologists and street-wise NYPD detectives, solely, or even in a team effort, could not could match the check-mating Joe did in the tic-tac-toeing of the girth and berth of La Cosa Nostra.

Put another way, the Ockham's razor of diplomacy is one in which the other side can still awaken with dignity. Dignity is genuinely offered after defeat: Joe Pistone did what was needed to mollify the three families that could have triggered a triathlon of blood vendettas—he instead, paradoxically, in his own inimitable style, broke bread and mollified savagery into a sanguine genteel merger of the three different families, as we open our dialogue on a quaint summer afternoon.

COP DR DAN RUDOFOSSI: "Good afternoon Special Agent Joe Pistone. I wanted to run some thoughts by you if that's okay?"

FBI AGENT JOSEPH DOMINICK PISTONE: "Sure Doc, go ahead. How are you doing today?"

COP DR DAN RUDOFOSSI: "All is well, thanks, and much appreciated. So, let me start by saying I was thinking a lot about what I learned from our last dialogue. Boundaries, boundaries, and boundaries we say when we implement clinical intervention and treatment goals when working with patients with certain personality disorders. But boundaries, while the norm to ensure proper compliance with staying on track with treatment, serve as a secondary membrane that protects us from harm and invasion. For example, rules of officer spacing and distancing shield each patient and doc from transmission of COVID-19, but also from meddlesome snoops trying to get the cover on what is above, and below cover of treatment. Analogously, trying to achieve a deeper understanding of the world of the gangster, you have asserted to me that the world of the gangster is not the world of the law enforcement officer and prosecutor! Their worlds are different from the larger societies' world views as we've been educated by you in earlier discussions. You've discussed these boundaries as clear norms that must not be stepped on, or over by the agent trying to gain a handle on some of the underworld reckonings and customs. Correct?"

FBI AGENT JOSEPH DOMINICK PISTONE: "Yeah, that sums it up nicely. Doc, as I said, it is not the world that the lily-white knighted horse rides in on that is the world of the gangster where stone-cold killers live by an entirely different code of dos and don'ts. Capish?"

COP DR DAN RUDOFOSSI: "Capito. If I got it right, and I may have it wrong, it is boundaries etched in dos and don'ts as marks that distinguish in-posts and out-posts along the way of survival. Therefore, wisdom and knowledge are redefined in the ecological value of ethological motivation to survive in a violent environment." [Joe Pistone, assents.] "So, fleshing out some flesh of defining boundaries, a concept from a diplomat and the first UN Secretary General Dag Hammarskjold called 'markings' lays a foundation for a path to cross over and into [Hammarskjold, 1966]. Markings, as General Hammarskjold wove it, is akin to synchronizations that fold into our collective unconscious. Each 'marking' is worth pausing for a moment to operationally define. In his poetic diary in which he articulates what he auscultates as a diplomat—fleshing out boundaries of self and others in larger-than-life cultures, such as American or Italian society, helped keep his soul centered while crossing into dangerous territory of warring factions in the Congo and elsewhere [Hammarskjold, 1966]. We looked into primatology earlier as well. It makes sense in adding an element often ignored for political convenience and which limits our scientific and reality understanding of what a special agent of your caliber really endures for the sake of the police agency and for all of society."

FBI AGENT JOSEPH DOMINICK PISTONE: "That makes a great deal of sense in realistically understanding that the administrators and top brass of law enforcement agencies are not in touch and in tune with the reality of the markings that real deep cover requires. It in a way is simple as being able to do the job. As you suggest, it is good to reflect on the many steps you may not spend the time on thinking about. Pausing and reflection is important after doing the job. I agree this is very important. I am hearing for the first time how these basic steps are not really discussed and given a name. You know, it is critical for those in administration and the law to understand these realities we agents not only face but must create and re-create each time we do a job and interact with gangsters, new bridges and footing as we move along."

COP DR DAN RUDOFOSSI: "Your feedback is crucial. Without your confirmation, or disconfirmation, in gathering evidence, I am at a loss. I know I am moving in the right direction by your lead and assent of my interpretation. In furthering our exploring of operationalizing boundaries, Dr. R. D. Laing, as an existential analyst, peered beyond obtuse walls by using the keys to unlock alleged closed worlds of those suffering through schizophrenia by language as a bridge. He called the existential experience from patients' accounts as schizos-phrenos [broken minded and hearted]. By contextualizing their experiences, we can better understand their 'schizoid withdrawal' from the sane society—or as he hints to his readers, perhaps, 'our not-so sane society'—to understand their perspective while maintaining our own boundaries. In differentiation of personality, Dr. Laing operationalizes *the divided self* by asserting healing begins by **de-individuation** of one's *self from Others* [Laing, 1970, 1972]. Dr. Laing sums up insensitivities toward mental illness by society at large. In discussing healthier adaptation, and less healthy maladaptation, mental illness in many ways rigidly defines the maladies of the population under analysis by dismissing the scrutiny of labels these patients are cast into. It may be valuable, as Dr. Laing points out, but the necessity of society to survive and maintain its own sense of wellness is also crucial."

"Deviancy may be understandable as a rebelling against overwhelming conformity, but it also is destructive to the overall societal wellness if, as it often happens too much of the time, rebellion tips the scales of one injustice into another. In this way one type of injustice articulated in a different eco-ethological context surpasses the earlier injustice. Reversal of damaging behaviors never legitimizes their damaging in the first place. Boundaries enliven reality."

"Boundaries in the clinical science of medicine, whether of mental or physical health, entail a **sensitivity** and **specificity** of approach that navigates respectfully societal impasses of permeable and impermeable circles as boundaries. Boundaries on one hand can be circles that lead to unending growth, but in other ways may lead to encircling the mind in endless chains of circuitous thinking. Without the aid of another, as in doctor and patient, professor and student, author and editor, special agent and Federal Bureau of Investigation, cop doc and special agent, actively listening and valuing the wisdom each imparts to one another in unequal but creative interactions, rule-less and endless floods of opinions and ideas collide. Dos and don'ts are the boundaries of elasticity and creative ingenuity and at the same time as concrete as a leaded weight on one deemed a rat in a police circle or La Cosa Nostra family at the heart of the matter. No such boundary or dos and don'ts can be fully written or prescribed, but they are as real as the day ushering in night and night lit up by the new dawn on the horizon of a shifting vista."

FBI AGENT JOSEPH DOMINICK PISTONE: "Doc, I gotta say you use million-dollar words, but when it fits, it fits, and it does. I like the definitions, and the complexity is interesting as I never have thought of this process as we are now. But it makes sense, and it does capture reality which is very hard when you are living with wiseguys and become one of them for over six years of my life."

COP DR DAN RUDOFOSSI: "In the six years and more of your own life, your artistic sketching with me of our psychological scientific boundaries perhaps can etch markings that permeate the blue walls of police silence. Perhaps in some ways also open the carmine-blushed Mafia folklore of omertà with insights and understanding that splice open such walls with sensibility at some level. Boundaries can become milestones that mark different spaces in general for the different worlds shaping the 'markings of each of the different families of the Mafia'—different venues of survival. Perhaps it is, on one hand, sensible to look at *boundaries as adaptations within an ecological niche that demand boundaries for each member daring to enjoin each family with its own unique and distinct mores and taboos.* In some ways, it is true the Mafia family is not so different than most other families, and within a culture that includes Sicilian culture. Not making excuses for stone-cold killers, the fact is, invasion by foreign conquerors generated a superb adaptation where invasion became an inviolate frame of life itself. Devolving, as time and experience moves on, maladaptation became in most societies, whether major or minor, illegitimate behaviors made legitimate: put another way, 'legit' behavior expressive of the mores that glued together each Mafia family with unqualifiedly illegitimate business cached as legitimate."

FBI AGENT JOSEPH DOMINICK PISTONE: "Doc, go on fully, and your conclusion here, is?"

COP DR DAN RUDOFOSSI: "Not a conclusion but a start of some new markings we are forging together. The mores and totems of what is acceptable, not acceptable, admirable, or to be held in contempt is crucial knowledge of what to do, and what not to do as prohibitions for associates to full members within each Mafia family's hierarchy. For example, being accepted throughout the major families was imploding when the territorial imperative of solid boundaries and the markings were threatened by various rebellious capos. Such boundary shifts and the capos that determined each shift in 'sit-downs' set the tempo of their own continuing life or death!"

FBI AGENT JOSEPH DOMINICK PISTONE: "If that is a question, you hit the target point on! As we discussed, it is the opposite of legit business to pay your boss in order to rise up the ranks from grunt to capo. But if you have the right pedigrees, as a Sicilian American you can do just that in the Mafia. In fact, that is the only way to go up the ranks and be successful, by paying it upward and in more bills."

COP DR DAN RUDOFOSSI: "If I got it correctly, the five families as a whole operate as an inverted pyramid. Meaning, an inverse mirror reflection when compared to the legality of larger society's function and parallel image exists as a gateway. In your own fitting in, you transcended rules while acting with integrity in your developing eco-ethological niche of Mafia culture. As Dr. Laing pointed out, individuation is crucial in being who one is as distinguished from others; something you bring to our attention is you intentionally were resistant to not being lulled into de-individuation. If you had conformed to protocol without that flash of action mediated by bold action when the moment was ripe to act and innovate, you would have been marked as an outsider although you would have been judged by law enforcement peers as an insider. This is not a judgment, but factual for now as a working hypothesis."

FBI AGENT JOSEPH DOMINICK PISTONE: "Yeah, your working hypothesis is a correct equation and is accurate."

COP DR DAN RUDOFOSSI: "In that equation, if we can now turn back the clock, is it accurate to say **y**ou were 35 years old when you got deeply involved in actually becoming Donnie Brasco? That is, Donnie Brasco which you created as you navigated the many pathways of experiences that came your way. I was wondering if you could share your history on what it is like, first in becoming an initiate into the FBI world for you."

FBI AGENT JOSEPH DOMINICK PISTONE: "Yeah, sure. I mean when I went through the academy times were very different than now. I entered the FBI when the original director was none other than Mr. J. Edgar Hoover."

"There was not any academy at Quantico as there is now. In fact, all your training was done at the Old Post Office in Washington DC. It was split between the Old Post Office and the Department of Justice."

"Although most of the training as an FBI agent recruit was done in the Old Post Office, that was part of the whole picture. For example, as an FBI recruit you would go to Quantico, Virginia, and you'd stay in one of the Marine barracks for your firearms and defensive tactics training. After, you would go there for around a week at a time. Afterwards you would then go back to Washington DC for a couple of weeks, and then shift back to Quantico Marine Base."

"That is, you'd stay in one of the United States Marine barracks while you were there. You also had to get housing arranged when you were in Washington DC as well. Yourself and on your own initiative."

"What was good about it is that they had certain apartments they had vetted. Meaning they said here is five different apartments. So although it cost money, you went in with two other guys and you shared the apartment for what I recall was 14 weeks."

"Back then, prior to the recruits of 1972 when they opened the FBI Academy, where everyone suddenly was pushed together and housed together, you chiseled out your own living space. The times when I was a recruit, like I said to you, meant we had to find living quarters on our own in Washington DC. Nobody felt entitled and you had to do your own thing and make your own way."

"When I came on, you had to wear a suit and tie every day. Our dress code included you went to class on time and on your own initiative as being quite significant. Except for when you were assigned to Quantico US Marine Corp Base, you had grays. What I mean by grays, is you had to wear the grey pants and grey shirts; they were your grays that you wore in Quantico. That's it, you know …"

COP DR DAN RUDOFOSSI: "I think so, as when I came on in the 1980s we had a uniform pants, but a powder blue shirt and Corfram shoes and you had better get your shirts starched and align your clip-on tie with a horizontal line to your Sam Browne belt buckle. But as I relate to your own experience with mine, I imagine you segue to the details here, are quite important—for a reason. Perhaps it afforded you the insight to existentially start being, and later becoming, Joe Dominick Pistone identity mode as special agent. I mean your identity mode as intel and operative agent."

FBI AGENT JOSEPH DOMINICK PISTONE: "Yeah, in that identity mode as intel and operative there was no babying you when you were on board, and if you fell overboard, you needed to figure on how to upright yourself, or get help from peers—or drown."

"You know, Doc, look—as I started to say, I worked under Mr. Hoover from 1969 until he died. I had no problems working under Hoover as the boss. There were rules, and everybody was subject to the same rules. It was clear that all of us were subject to Hoover's FBI and his rules."

"It was clear as day. You knew well, if you broke the rules, you would get a letter of censure, you would be on the bricks, or a week suspended without pay, or transferred someplace."

"But again, and serious as I can be, it is clear, you knew that the consequences were unambiguous in Hoover's FBI. Because you knew the rules, it was fair."

"For me, I had no problem with following the rules. It didn't matter who you were. That was it. In class, in training, there was an empty seat. Literally, an empty seat that meant something deeper than a space that remained unfilled. Let me fill you in on my meaning. You may come in one day and see the guy that sat next to you, suddenly, he is not there anymore. So, you start thinking silently to yourself. You start to solve the mystery. Well, it means he probably failed the test. If you didn't pass the exam, you were gone. So if you didn't pass the firearms test and training module, you were gone."

"There was no second, third, and fourth chances. No babying the candidates. You either had the merit and mental toughness I am speaking of throughout our conversations and sessions or you don't. It's not about being the nice guy and with smileys that cuts in doing the job of a cop and FBI special agent; it is down to the bare bones and wire—survival and street smarts that was getting a pass, or a failure and exit door."

COP DR DAN RUDOFOSSI: "If I'm getting it right, Special Agent Joe Pistone, to clarify, you needed to not only know the boundaries of the 'rules,' but to discipline yourself as a disciple of tough training, and embrace the organization of clarity in uncharted areas as well as goal setting in becoming an agent for you and your peers, at the time of Edgar Hoover. With all the support given, still and yet, you had to carve it as your own chart and identity as the agent you were to become. Initiative and motivation as much as learning and accepting the hurdles and challenge was part of the law enforcement attitude of Hoover's FBI."

FBI AGENT JOSEPH DOMINICK PISTONE: "That is on point. I don't mean to get off point but stay on point. But I meant to say look at the stuff that goes on today!"

"In days past, the type of stuff that has become acceptable within departments nowadays, was not! No way would the stuff that goes on with allegations founded to any degree and done by an FBI agent be acceptable for an agent that was sworn into J. E. Hoover's FBI."

"Let me tell you, Doc, in the old days they would be fired, or at least suspended, and then most of these agents that did some of the stuff they do nowadays would be gone. Do you know what I mean?"

COP DR DAN RUDOFOSSI: "I think so. But I want to clarify if I am correct, or off base here. You know me, Joe. So, in respecting your perspective as distinct, I'd like to check if I am on the right track with conveying to the reader your way of looking at policing and detective work."

"So, summarizing your points, there are a certain set of rules for the big brass nowadays which are allowed leeway above the other set of police and agents. This set of rules for the grunts and first-line cops who are police officers, detectives, and sergeants along with special agents and group supervisors in police, sheriff departments, and federal LEO's have the ground hard-core set rules that offer a violator no wiggle room."

"Further, the set of nuances and loopholes for the big brass allows all kind of apologies and excusable malfeasance nowadays which is hardly palpable for the big brass. Correct?"

FBI AGENT JOSEPH DOMINICK PISTONE: "On the money, Doc! Let me give you an example. I have a friend who became an Assistant Special Agent in Charge [ASAC] for one day. Why? He worked for one day and Hoover broke him down to the level of a street agent for trying to stretch muscles he didn't have authority to stretch."

"The point is, law enforcement is our military and there are rules as in all uniformed services. There is no bottom line for the military or law enforcement. Let me say, under J. E. Hoover, it was not IBM, nor an FBI that was politicized and money driven."

"IT IS IMPORTANT TO HAVE A UNIFORM SET OF RULES: The dos and don'ts must equally apply for all law enforcement, so as to keep morale intact and respectable. The fact is, that what is acceptable now—is, and was not acceptable, back then. For example, Doc, I know you were a street cop in Bed Stuy and Red Hook on the midnight crew in the late 80s. Tell me that you knew the dos and don'ts too as a cop and street cop/sergeant count in real time toward saving lives, including fellow officers and if need be, that included me and other special agents in the field! I'm correct, am I not?"

COP DR DAN RUDOFOSSI: "You are fully correct! Very true, yes, very true indeed. I got that down pat and that was my lifesaver and my peers' as well, of course you included. I like your point, that the rules and the dos and don'ts provide a lifesaver to the agent who takes the time to actively listen and intuit what he needs to understand."

"She/he needs to learn the ecological niche he is to work in and the *angles of ethological affordances* to survive in. In times of crisis, and to avert crisis, the rules serve your purpose by grounding stability and *marking* safety as the order of discipline and self-sacrifice in serving the citizens of the community we service without ever excluding our own fellow officers as the tightest first circle of community."

"If it makes sense to you, one thing in the dos and don'ts is for you it was a challenge much more than the average 'Joe'—no pun intended. Frankly, thinking about you and the rules of dos and don'ts, another challenge not spoken about by psychologists who study the trauma and dissociative aspects of doing deep cover is rather than interpreting for you what you may have experienced is to pause a while between gentle questions. It is you alone who achieved for six-plus years what others did not achieve. It is you alone that can only be understood by me for example, asking 'you' if I am on target or not—by clarifying conjecture of what I think you may have been thinking of about your own experiences. That does not preclude my own hypotheses drawn from my clinical reservoir and experience as a cop doc or detective sergeant. Only when I have the humility of knowing I don't know! At this origin of humility can I even begin to know you better. At knowing you better after these years, only then can I venture forth to interpret with your wisdom your own experience as you lived it and processed 'It.' So, moving with you toward understanding, am I beating the head of a dead horse, again no pun intended?"

"Special Agent Joseph Dominick Pistone, since I don't have the wisdom or intuitive sense to read directly into your mind, I was thinking to segue back to the dos and don'ts but inclusive of the three different worlds you lived in. Each world containing a distinct mistress as metaphor. Doing so, I remember Frank Sinatra's ownership of the way he 'wore his hat' in the blockbuster hit song he created to his bold individuality of being himself, I can't help but think that is your way Joe as well. Doing it your way—my own way!"

FBI AGENT JOSEPH DOMINICK PISTONE: "It is an interesting analogy and yeah, when you say it that way, by being yourself—you are doing what is necessary for a good cop and agent in being effective. Yes, I had shared with you earlier and other times in our dialogue that it is by being yourself that one embraces their own hat, infiltration, and being in the world of the gangster is not the world of the law enforcement officer, nor the world of homelife, and being a homebody. It is building up a case so that you must do what is necessary, and not being someone you are not."

COP DR DAN RUDOFOSSI: "To me the fact that you were able to navigate in many different worlds and with very distinct boundaries of ecology. Ecological niches with the pressure of survival as you've shared and I totally agree your own survival is not marginal—that is not reality. You did not agree to be a special agent so as to become a sacrificial sheep of some crime family or truth be told to follow a guidebook by administrators out of touch with reality."

FBI AGENT JOSEPH DOMINICK PISTONE: "Exactly and well placed as a metaphor, Doc, using my three mistresses as an illustration. Like, don't do this, it is not becoming a special agent. Yes, not as a norm, but in the mores of organized crime families and specifically the Bonanno crime family such as don't hesitate when you are ordered by the boss to carry out an order—mostly illegal—or you get whacked within the wiseguy world. Who do you follow?"

"Alternatively, don't knock a guy out while doing deep cover unless your life depends on it. The likelihood of daily incident reports and a mountain of paperwork not only leads to an avalanche of paperwork, but also emotional overload."

"Last, but not least, is happy wife equals happy life. That world means you are home to assist in the real-life mundane chores of domestic world life or welcome to the law enforcement world of strife. I had to exist for years as being a sojourner in the domestic world of my wife and kids as a heavy cost doing undercover and there is not an easy way around that hemisphere, nor circumference as it stands—that world is round and revolves around one hubby and wife and the kids!"

COP DR DAN RUDOFOSSI: "Your interpretation is eloquent and on point for me, although I can't add depth to your worlds as a gift in your illustration. Pausing, it is my understanding as well, as it strikes me that you made your own unique niche successfully at the same time you were working and thriving in the FBI heydays of J. E. Hoover."

"You had the ingenuity and strength of character for you to do that job. The adaptation and strategic process would strain a Guggenheim Fellows think tank. You created your own identity from an orphan who worked his way in the hood and Italian American ghetto from petty jewel thief making a pitch to join the most closed and feared La Cosa Nostra. In essence, it appears to me, that to becoming a made man without any documented portfolio in the final hours of operation as Donnie Brasco was a victory for law enforcement. If this makes sense to your own mindset, can you move in to help me out here with your own wisdom as toward understanding. By a process of what psychologists like me who are trained in psychoanalytic psychotherapy call 'free-association.' Free association is the method of allowing any thoughts that come to mind to be expressed. As my own mentor and training analyst Dr. Charles Brenner educated me, although we call this process 'free-association,' it is anything but free [Brenner, 1973, 1979]. Does that work for you?"

FBI AGENT JOSEPH DOMINICK PISTONE: "Yeah, I am going to tell you things as they come to mind. I am not trying to sort through them in perfect order, but as they are remembered. You know this has to do with being an undercover. I got this apartment at Ruppert Towers, at 92nd and 3rd Avenue in the city. You know, it's where they used to have a real brewery. You know once I infiltrated, most of the guys in the mob had lived around or in Knickerbocker Village."

"Keep in mind, so once I infiltrated into the family, Mirra and Lefty trusted me at that point. They said why don't you move down here. They confided in what I knew to be true, 'we know the rental agency and we can get you in without a hitch. Donnie, you can get an apartment and you don't have to go downtown and get a crazy costly apartment, or anything.'"

"I am not saying this to tell you I am smarter than any other undercover agent, or anything like that Doc. My thinking is, why do I want to be with them 48 hours a day, rather than 24 hours a day as it is already? You know, why increase my chances for even more criminal activity. If you are that close by to the bosses, guess what—you got it! You know what I am saying?"

COP DR DAN RUDOFOSSI: "Yeah, I do. Well, how did you handle that problem that emerged?"
FBI AGENT JOSEPH DOMINICK PISTONE: "I told them I like it up there in the upper east side of Manhattan. I have a nice apartment. Hey, it's clean and doable. They were up there to visit me. I said straight out, I don't see any need to move. No thanks."

"The fact as it stands, ten to one, another undercover, in fact most, would jump at the chance to relocate where the wiseguys lived. The undercover in those cases believed, hey if I am riding with them, I can see their every move. By not doing that, the other side not thought of, is I become immediate accessible and cheaper. By making my subtle but tough stand as to my living arrangement I become, and I am a real person to them. A real person to them, that is Lefty and Mirra."

"I have moved toward becoming real in their eyes. You following me as to why I did this and my motivation which the job couldn't understand [FBI/LE organization]?"

COP DR DAN RUDOFOSSI: "I think I am, so let me try to offer a hypothesis to you. It is by doing this counter-intuitive approach that you are not perceived as a wannabe, or buff."

"You are seen by making a tough and subtle choice which is part of a deeper intuitive strategy to get transformed into a real-deal wiseguy initiate. I then began with that move which is serious, toward being yourself by being able to carve out a reputation as a thinker, and not an automatic follower. Ironically, viewed from an existential point of view, you were not a conformist. By changing you for their dominant wishes to move within the Knickerbocker area, you and your identity mode—your attitude and street-smarts—within La Cosa Nostra would have come to a dead end. But it was your own tough-mindedness, you did not act in accord with wanting to fit in the mold as they had in mind for you. It is your other ingenuity we identified as tough-mindedness that enabled you to move beyond the law enforcement culture and myths. In establishing your own mold of Donnie Brasco, with your own mystique, your own character and personality, the strategy which was hidden and looked resistant worked. If you followed their game of tag and follow the leader blindly, you would have become the gel they could mold, and discard equally as well—as just another wiseguy wannabe. By setting your vistas on becoming separate and distinct from other agents as you improvised, you were shaping 'Donnie Brasco.' You seized the moments as they availed themselves to you. In your own ingenuity you eventually changed what law enforcement big brass and administrators delimited you to."

"But you also changed the mold remarkably and simultaneously within the mold that the wiseguy world view set up for you in forging your own identity as Donnie Brasco. Finally, you kept the card of your own real involvement at home life as opaque as you could. You did so honorably to protect your wife and certainly your kids from knowing the full range of your mission as you were charting that as well with great autonomy within the Mafia world."

FBI AGENT JOSEPH DOMINICK PISTONE: "Yes, that's right. Again, you know in dealing with physical situations and the way it was going at first, I told Jilly no disrespect, but I can't be with these guys anymore. The hardcore violent and criminal-type soldiers."

"You know. Again, what does it do to assert yourself in a way that lets the wiseguy know this is who you are? You are putting up the don'ts in a way they can understand and either accept or not. It makes your personality stand out as another person than they expected at first. For that matter, a person they thought you were."

"The wiseguy then is in for a change of mind. Lefty and Mirra, as you know, both went through their own adjustment with me. I think you are grasping with me what I mean here. That is what I am trying to get across. But that's the way it is when you are dealing with the mob as a deep cover for me. It's all about very subtle changes and stands you have to make as you become who you are as a wiseguy, in my own operation as Donnie Brasco."

COP DR DAN RUDOFOSSI: "I like that point Special Agent Joe P. If I am correct, in part you were establishing yourself first into the Columbo family as a guy who could be counted on. With tough-mindedness you gradually provided enough evidence to illustrate you were smart enough to learn the rules. But at the same time, you were courageous enough to untangle the ropes of the family when called upon 'to do' with creative zeal by avoiding doing too much and navigating from doing too little as a new associate. Shifting persuasively into the Bonanno family with Tony Mirra's mentoring, and Benjamin Ruggiero competing for you as his guy and major associate—the target was becoming a made man: made man as an implicit objective for you, while explicitly dancing among and with the mob bosses of the day. After initiation with Jilly, you held your own no different than an initiate within each family does in reality. Each Mafia family is woven with its own unique ecological niches and codes of dos and don'ts of survival ethologically speaking."

"Existentially, your mastery of arching these deft negotiations with each boss and underboss having their own personalities is quite interesting for us to traverse together as follows. In your own developing personality, it cannot be forgotten Donnie Brasco came into existence, *ex nihilo* as Winston Churchill would say, by the grace of G–d, and born *sui generis* by your own skillful craft consciously and artful unconscious—genius as a rare gift, cannot be denied as resonating in your infiltration as a masterpiece of sleuthing, espionage, and counter-espionage."

"Special Agent Joseph Dominick Pistone, in my clinician's and cop doc's mind's eye, you are not saying you are a genius, I am."

"While you and I can simplistically reduce your adaptations as an alter ego that acted well based on a shield, your acting skill, and support teams—in therapy as a cop doc I would show you that was not the real case. It would not only cheat you as Donnie Brasco as a real identity mode, it would cheat the Mafia bosses who accepted you in the families. It would foolishly steal the truth from ever being the template toward understanding the potential for wisdom and change you forged within the craft and courage of being a deep-cover special agent. Further, it doesn't cut the score you made on the streets and social club diplomacy by 'becoming' the wiseguy 'Donnie Brasco' from an existential center of life and living."

FBI AGENT JOSEPH DOMINICK PISTONE: "Donnie Brasco developed into existence as you suggest, Doc. I kept my hidden inner view of that real mirror as FBI Special Agent Joe Pistone. I had to learn how to gain the respect and understand *the markings* along the way of becoming Donnie and not falling off track as new challenges and obstacles got in the way. I overcame each one and some were very risky."

COP DR DAN RUDOFOSSI: "Pausing and not getting swept away in the undertide of the mystique and culture of organized crime as deadly and hard-core violence in which survival eco-ethologically speaking was achieved by you becoming Donnie Brasco. Ambitious, cautiously optimistic, and yet tough-minded sobriety as the brake pad you imprinted on his own unique strengths and identity was really your own."

"Strength was achieved by you identifying what was affordable in an ecology of survival. That included always being wary of the bosses you had to not only please, but persuade not to whack you as rat, incompetent, weak, dumb, or simply disposable, by being adaptive enough in your dissociative functioning of Donnie Brasco's identity modes. You also kept them respectful of who you were, who you were becoming within the family itself, and as a made man to be."

"Am I right in what I have suggested? In other words, in adaptive functioning, you dissociatively had to live as Donnie Brasco without forfeiting the true essential Joseph Dominick Pistone. Walking your dialectical tightrope, you were aware that the shadow was not the essence of you. Yet, at that time, if you ever allowed the shadow to fade into the light of detection, you would endanger Joseph Dominick Pistone as much as Donnie Brasco. You had to carry your informant as an identity you created. Hence it is quite a poor analogy to suggest you had fallen victim of the Stockholm Syndrome and 'identified with the aggressors.'"

"If I got your process and journey right, your adaptive and maladaptive moments as Donnie Brasco were without doubt done with the mindfulness of becoming a wiseguy informant who was an FBI agent at the same time. The doubling in the context of survival [ethologically motivated] was ingeniously colored and shaped as spontaneous at times [unconsciously] and methodically more of the times [consciously] within a very knowledge of the ecological niches and the personality dynamics you needed to become. Not theoretically, but in all the rough tumble and dirtiness of the street and club life!"

FBI AGENT JOSEPH DOMINICK PISTONE: "Yes! That is a way I have not exactly spelled out before. I never thought of this context of interpreting my experience psychologically and psychiatrically speaking, but your method respects my experience and my skill. You do that in a way, Doc, that doesn't point out my losing it under pressure, but the sensibility and adaptive necessities of my challenges better than other psychologists and psychiatrists have said. The point as my personality was on one hand, me, and yet I was developing that self-image and persona that was Donnie who came from being myself. Me staying tough with my decisions once made. I chose to say no and hold my ground when I needed to do just that. That is the first point of departure. You gave a correct understanding because I became real as Donnie Brasco, and I never lost being me, Joe Dominick Pistone, FBI agent, and also as a family man."

COP DR DAN RUDOFOSSI: "If I could, let me flesh this out with you." [Nod of assent.] "I can remember the feeling I had when you were asked to go to the back with Pat. That is, to the back of the social club when they were getting someone to vouch for you as legit. I could almost pee in my pants for you in that context. I felt in that moment with you as I did on the 14th floor of a housing project when faced with a potential riot of 100 rowdies at 2am, some sauced up on drug cocktails as we would call the speedball of coke and dope and some speed laced in with alcohol and others mellow yellow. We were the police—trying to maintain the peace."

"The edge here was we called for back-up calmly while the world felt like it would pop on fire in a heartbeat. You were a lone brother as a uniform member without one other brother or sister LEO to bail you out."

"You becoming real and forging your identity in one eco-ethological niche of survival after another, your center of identity as Donnie Brasco sensitively and emotionally expanded with each success you forged."

Being and Not Being: Becoming and Facticity

It is more than Shakespeare who pondered over the existentially laden question of to be or not to be in the face of life and death itself and the thousand shocks flesh is heir too. It is also Professor Martin Heidegger the philosopher, as is true of his lover Professor Hannah Arendt, who would ponder over the facticity of being hurled into the existential space one occupies in ecological reality and ethological survival for better or worse. Is the reduction of stimulus-response radical behaviorism a worthy concept for choices and consequent responsibleness in the heyday of one's greatest existential challenges? It is hard to steer clear of such powerful and evocative challenges to one's core being and becoming when life and death is the measure of the person who is doing deep cover. Normal mores and judgment must enter the picture in order to not lose one's essential self. Yet, the reality of dealing with one's own mortality and judgment of one's behaviors, thoughts, and emotions is not a relative and fixed question. The equilibrating concept that is extant here is an answer not reducible to a textbook answer. It is the challenge of being human in the most inhuman of conditions, circumstances, and tests that cannot be prescribed. The proscription demands the agent not be unhinged as a deep cover and yet not buckle under pressure to become a passive instrument of criminality within the world of the gangster. Such was the life of Joe Pistone on a daily basis as Donnie Brasco, where he was the shadow willingly of his own front. Genius perhaps is as enlightened as poetry suspending and contemplating its own motion—without overly emotionalizing.

"The boundaries of an object define its permeability, or lack of it. In an animal as in humans, our expansion occurs as we absorb more and more wisdom as survival increases, so does potential and risk-taking provide stepping-stones toward further mastery. That is what your genius provided in the perfect storm as only you could inform me and yourself as we analyze way beyond the surface of what appears as what we in the cop culture say 'as simple as that.' But nothing is simple as that, and what is that but what we remove from our own sensibility and sensitivity. Like you, I get the point of personality Joe Pistone as Donnie Brasco is not acting but being and becoming or we would not be conversing now, but I would know you as a tragic hero dropped by a wiseguy bullet. Yes?"

FBI AGENT JOSEPH DOMINICK PISTONE: "Yeah, that is absolutely correct, as these guys were different, all would drop me if they had known my identity as FBI agent while I was in the mix with them as Donnie Brasco at that time. Let me give you an example with some of the bosses and their own unique dos and don'ts. No reasoning with Tony Mirra."

"With Lefty you couldn't win an argument with him, but he wouldn't just get violent with you for having some disagreement with him."

"With Mirra it was a totally different story. Mirra's rules of engagement meant you knew that you had to be an arm's length away from him at all times. You needed to be aware he had a hair-trigger temper, without letting him know you knew."

"So, in response, without any formal training or rules to be learned, I knew by my own mind that I was creating a wall so he couldn't simply reach out to me in a violent caprice when he was in a 'shitty' mood and fight me to the death. He would win of course, eventually. I knew how to avoid or move around slighting him as he would imagine if I made a gesture or behavior by accident."

"More so, and I am saying it as it was, you could not back down. It's all about respect, as you know being a cop on the street; it's the same within wiseguy culture of not backing down when challenged."

"It's establishing your personality while working within their own ways. That is, their dos and don'ts in general is what you need to know as it is and was. But more important as the individual boss each was in his reality and world, you always were in his own world and rules and dos and don'ts too!"

"You can't teach this to deep-cover wannabes, it is something that comes up from the area you were raised in and the struggles you had to get through and conquer. The ability you're born with is part of the ability. It is also the ability to learn quickly and correctly and sort through what works and does not work intuitively. As I have said, it does not mean you're better as a cop, but truly a difference in your personality as to what you can and cannot do makes all the difference in the world as to your success and survival as well."

"The bosses are similar as well, and so as Donnie Brasco I had to survive by knowing very well what I learned in the field with each of these bosses as personalities were very different. You are on the money in your *Eco-Ethological Existential Analysis* because it makes sense clearly to me as to what I needed to do. But like you know what I said, and a lot of this stuff is second nature bred in you."

"How you grow up, how you know in your own neighborhood that is the way it is, like an athlete there are basketball players, and then there is Michael Jordan."

COP DR DAN RUDOFOSSI: "And there are FBI and DEA agents, and then there is Special Agent, Joseph Dominick Pistone. Going back for a moment Joe, you intuited that the one boss, capo Tony Mirra, could kill you within a moment's notice of a caprice, without even shutting an eyelid and lash."

"But with Benjamin Ruggiero, aka Lefty, it was very different, he loved the wiseguy classic culture and he would not fathom doing any killing unless he thought you were a rat or violated a sacred rule."

"With Sonny Black Napolitano, outside of his being a La Cosa Nostra capo, as an individual he at times at least could be human, interesting, have a sense of humor as Mirra and even Ruggiero could not—they didn't have it in them from the gut to the brain."

"Further, Sonny Black Napolitano had an above-average intelligence, and if not a member of the Bonanno crime family he may have turned on to a different profession, lifestyle, and outcome. I imagine we can say Sonny Black Napolitano's life was tragic insofar as he had potential to be a bona fide restaurateur and real diplomat with others as an expansive entrepreneur."

"But as capo, and almost head of the entire Bonanno family, he was almost at the top of his game and you were soon to follow, becoming a made man, formally."

So, if I got it right, it was brain science insofar as you used your mind and soulfully seemed to naturally develop an affinity of sorts for Mr. Sonny Black Napolitano. After all, in your own identity mode as wiseguy Donnie Brasco, who became part of your identity, even if a shadow, so to speak, was more than a ghost that disappears. You and Sonny Black Napolitano shared many a conversation on a personal, and if we stretch the fat slightly a bit wider, a collegial and decent manner. You both communicated in a down-to-earth way, as pals would at a deeper level."

FBI AGENT JOSEPH DOMINICK PISTONE: "As we discussed, it's second nature. It's the neighborhood and it's something you can't teach. It's not brain surgery: you first off either have that ability or you don't. Which you can't create if it is not within you as an agent as much as you can't create an Olympic athlete if he/she doesn't have the ability within to achieve a gold or bronze medal. This is Reality 101, if you get my point. I had the mental toughness to do my job and do it well. I knew who these guys were as stone-cold killers as well. I didn't make them that way and I provided the best way out for all of them as well."

COP DR DAN RUDOFOSSI: "Well, if I could for a moment pause and we can redirect, as it seems it's not rocket science, it seems like it's not brain science, but if we take a hard look at what you achieved, Joe Pistone as Donnie Brasco, it is quite a feat, and beside your innate facility and ability to move with each of these gangsters is that you were able to keep together what would break apart most men, most women, and most human beings faced with even remotely challenging situations for a transient day as in buy and busts and street-crime decoys tracking a serial rapist, armed robber, or even killer. It is time-referenced and also with a large support unit and mobile army with each unit decoy. It is an odyssey and reminds me of what Joseph Campbell called the victory of the hero after he is challenged and returns to his homelife a changed man because he now knows the secrets mere mortals seek to know, and due to lack of this odyssey cannot, except by the oracle of your gracious narrative retold with the doctor of the soul. An odyssey of the hero as very real. The ability to move around needs to highlight your ingenuity in dissociating in a way that was kept conscious as a survivor of cumulative and hard-core trauma. You were able to keep together what would break apart most LEOs. You became a hero not as fabricated but real as you are Joe. The journey could make any human being and LEO shaken and regressed to only emerge with a unique wisdom I have sought out here as another gift unspoken and to not be forgotten in your lifetime and beyond and mine included. You rescued them from themselves. To be returned to, it is remarkable as to your efforts to save Sonny Black Napolitano. These guys, as bad as they were, they had courage and, in some ways, held their position even if it was negative and harmful on one hand and on another there was a humanness to Sonny Black and at some level, as tough as you are, there was some connection that was very human in your connection to him."

FBI AGENT JOSEPH DOMINICK PISTONE: "It's hard to put it into words and explain. I don't know Doc, it's hard to express. A lot of these guys, at least some of them, are not complete knuckle-draggers, sought things out, he had common sense and in a real life he would have done better. I wouldn't say he would be a bank president, but he would get along like everyone else, so, yeah, if he had the opportunity to really choose and not be part of this family and culture, he may have been very different as a real guy. He would be a decent guy and have a real family life and contribute in many ways as a law-abiding and decent human being. But say if you look at Tony Mirra, he had the calling of being a wiseguy and would not be anyone different at all; even with all the opportunity he could be afforded he would be violent and a stone-cold murderer. He wasn't wired to be normal. How could you be wired to be normal if you're told to kill a guy you know from when you're ten years old and you are ready to do it, and actually do it, when you override your own decency to act that way. When your society tells you to do something you know is downright wrong and you do it, what is the hardwiring that allows you to do it. By society I mean the Mafia society."

"Not true of Sonny Black. How could you be wired right if you could do it without any afterthought of murdering a friend and family member for years with no problem? Sonny was not a hair-trigger killer looking to destroy another person simply because he had the authority within the family to do so. It is different. Although they were both mafiosi." [Pause]

COP DR DAN RUDOFOSSI: "Yes, this brings us back to a remarkably important question for personality studies or personology as it is called. That question is the 'why' underlying individual differences as of key importance and doing hostage negotiations as much as infiltration of any criminal enterprise which society must do in order to keep one inch ahead of the bosses on the other side of the blue vistas. The shadow is complementary on both sides of the fence and that is what we must wrestle with as Jacob's angel and ladder that in being honest goes as far uphill as it slides downhill."

FBI AGENT JOSEPH DOMINICK PISTONE: "That is on point! It is the shadow that remains with you, but as an agent you can't forget that you are always you. That is tough-mindedness as I mean it, do you get my meaning?"

COP DR DAN RUDOFOSSI: "I think I do, as you had to do the tarantellas most of the time with the capos but not with all of them and sometimes it was more like a waltz, and other times a street hop, skip, and jump forward and backward in which a hard-knuckle sandwich made an impression and in another it was a dialogue with meditation." [Joe nods an assent.]

FBI AGENT JOSEPH DOMINICK PISTONE: "Here's an interesting point Doc, that just came to my mind. I mean these guys that have five or six hits under their belts. You know, are they considered serial killers, and if not why not?"

COP DR DAN RUDOFOSSI: "In asking that question, I get you on this. It is not a culture question if I am correct; in other words, if John or Jane Doe set out to kill six individuals based on some prototype in his/her head and did it, we would say we have a serial killer on our hands."

FBI AGENT JOSEPH DOMINICK PISTONE: "I don't even know if we can say the Mafia is a real culture but, for example, if Tony Mirra does six hits as a wiseguy in a six-month period and covers his tracks to not get caught, of course why don't we say he is a serial killer?"

COP DR DAN RUDOFOSSI: "Yes, acting normal under an abnormal subcultural group and doing what the mores, ritual provide for, whacking a guy or gal for violating one of the major don'ts of that organized crime family is considered cultural competence. From an existential perspective and a real truthful one, it is murder, and if one commits murder multiple times it does provide a definition of being a serial killer and perhaps one can add a hitman/woman. But the truthful meaning is important to not mince as meat. All meat comes from a body and that body is slaughtered humanely or inhumanely but nonetheless is slaughter. So not calling it a serial killing is kind of white-washing away serial murder and making 'It legitimate' as much as saying like Tony Soprano 'It is what It is.' But you are on the psychological cutting edge existentially in asking that question and you and I contextualizing what you are actually asking so as to open up why we as a society of clinicians and also attorneys legitimize the very illegitimate murder incorporated without questioning not only the murderers but our capacity to accept what is illegitimate as legitimate."

FBI AGENT JOSEPH DOMINICK PISTONE: "Yes, and also who says this is a culture outright even though the Mafia as many things are looked at as if it is a culture?"

COP DR DAN RUDOFOSSI: "I like the way you are using the Socratic questioning, as I am to enhance the insight from a deep-cover and psychological clinical perspective. The outliers of culture overall include the unique world of the mafioso. Opening up your point as to saying any group has a cultural belonging is a complex question and one needing an answer. Anthropologically, it is fair to say these are subcultural, but due to the impact on our overall culture, including the impoverished myths that leave the door open to the mystique and allure of the underworld of the mob, intimate its perpetuity for ever and evermore."

FBI AGENT JOSEPH DOMINICK PISTONE: "In order to do what one does as a hitman, as I said, and we agree you need to be hardcore and hardwired to do that type of murder for the mob. It is a serial killer-like mentality to do one hit after another."

COP DR DAN RUDOFOSSI: "In my book, *A Cop Doc's Guide to Terrorism as Human Evil* [Rudofossi, 2013], I had the privilege of Professor Lt. Col. Dave Grossman US Army Rangers and Colonel Danny McKnight writing the Forward and Preface respectively. In my book, one of the cornerstones is the hypothesis predicating that political correctness and extreme pacificism is the fulcrum toward the rise in terror attacks. In a whisper of a confluence of two of the best minds, Albert Einstein and Sigmund Freud, analyzing war and destruction, the bottom line was the *pax Romana* and the fact both as pacifists were not lame ducks. They felt that a drive toward Destrudo and Thanatos littered all civilization and, in fact, in Freud's pivotal work *Beyond the Ego* he posited that in all of us in an unconscious conflict with our mature unconscious defenses lay the death instinct, or better put by my own training analysts and supervisor Dr. Charles Brenner, drive derivatives that are visible levels of darkness that betray the desire we all have to wreak destruction and death to our enemies. This is in distinction to our drive derivatives such as Eros and sublimation toward creative works and expression. Cutting off one's hands as symbols of not engaging in handshakes with fugazy unproven associates who may be LEOs is one side of the conscious interpretation, while the shadow side is the castration via blinding shots to the eyes and hand's ability to create torn off the informant and rat and the boss who has given the secrets to the law enforcement community unwittingly. I am not alluding to those like Joseph M. Valachi and, if I can say, Sammy the Bull Gravano as underboss to John Gotti who stepped up to the plate of testifying as to their own misgivings as well as their bosses. Here we are talking about errors and the deep-rooted fear of castration and its concomitant anxiety as fear to tread very carefully and silently within the chambers of the family's heart."

FBI AGENT JOSEPH DOMINICK PISTONE: "I mean from Kuklinski, he was insane, mentally disordered, but I don't think Lefty, Sonny, and Mirra had a mental disorder. Mirra was a cold killer and Ruggiero a notch better and Sonny Black was a notch better. You take Mirra, and when I was hanging out with him, he took care of his mother and the complexity of these guys is remarkable. Sonny had a heart; he had a dark side and yet he had a light heart. Lefty would get jealous over Sonny. I think Lefty, he kind of looked at me as possibly a father-son relationship as his son was a junkie and I was a street-smart gangster in the making which was more in line with Lefty and his way of thinking and being in life. I didn't bring my intelligence down to their level to infiltrate. I didn't make my intelligence as parallel to a street thug. It was something he caught on to. I dummied down myself to a degree to fit into his world, but not overdoing it."

COP DR DAN RUDOFOSSI: "It seems in your identity which was becoming stronger methodically and with artistic relish as a realist you carved your personality as Donnie Brasco as wise within the mores and totemic values of the Bonanno family by slow and mindful insertions of what you heuristically wanted to accomplish and in synchronicity with each capo's goals. If I got it right Joe, it was also your executive thinking at the core center of who you are and how you did cache your intellect by letting all the major capos believe and take credit for themselves in order to claim their ingenuity—which in reality was truly your own."

"From New York to Milwaukee, all the bosses and their soldiers, for all that time interacting with you, never realized who you really were as Special Agent Joe Pistone. Further, you were mollifying each according to their own peculiarities of personality and eliminating their doubt as you tested the febrile ground of each of their fears and compensatory behaviors, they used to overcome those fears by you reassuring them of their superior intellect and creativity, while it is clear to me and all listening now with their third ears it was your creative genius that worked so well. I remember when Dr. Charles Brenner was teaching me to listen with my third ear with the most difficult patients, including police and special agents, and the key was allowing their associations and their own interpretations to be woven into my own to maximize ownership absent my ego but without relinquishing our joint task, and hence the patient walked away feeling brilliant at her/his insight even though the interpretative ground was broken heuristically with my testing the nerve endings gently and ever so lightly as not to be reproached as another psychoanalyzing shrink. It never failed as a clinician and police supervisor investigator, professor, and expert, but I had all the leverage of convenience as my life was not endangered, but yours was. I was trained and supported and over a decade of graduate education and internships and you did this by yourself. Without giving you a formal IQ and EQ test, I will estimate your intellect quotient around 160 which is the high end of exceptional intelligence and clearly a deka-nominal equivalent higher than a genius."

FBI AGENT JOSEPH DOMINICK PISTONE: "Doc, I wouldn't argue with you as you are the psych doc and cop doc here. For me, I don't disagree with the way you very artfully put my intelligence out there as a deck of cards for all to see. I will take your word on your way of assessing my intelligence and that certainly is nice and does not offend me as some others' assumptions and comments. But, let me say I had to satisfy each of the three mistresses. I then did a walk on a taut tightrope to keep Lefty Ruggiero happy."

"Whenever Sonny Black would tell me stuff, I would cut Lefty into the loop. I knew if Lefty found out I had a separate conversation with Sonny and he was not informed as to the particulars he would be thrown off. What I mean is, Lefty would go into a rage and frenzy almost immediately. So, I had to tell Lefty about what Sonny and I discussed and then at the same time not letting Sonny know I had informed Lefty about what we just talked about. You following me, Doc?"

COP DR DAN RUDOFOSSI: "If I got it right, it is like the chain of command and hierarchy we have in the police department, which is you go to your boss first and not his boss to disclose any information to avoid embarrassment and the feeling you dropped a dime behind your boss's back by letting him know before you shared it with your direct supervisor."

FBI AGENT JOSEPH DOMINICK PISTONE: "Yeah, correct. It was a tightrope for six years. Walking across the Niagara Falls as you're pointing out for your analysis means dealing with the characters as I've explained so far. Each does have a different personality and need here."

COP DR DAN RUDOFOSSI: "I am wondering Special Agent Joe Pistone, if in leafing through your experience this was possible due to your faith in the Almighty. As we both agreed and you laughed with that deep laugh, I've come to know with you that signals the profundity of realization most cops have after the fact of gee whiz I made it through. How and why? Like me and you in our many discussions and dialogue realizing part of that transcends the identification of each variable with a glue that is invisible and is the soul of all creativity—faith in a power we call G–d larger than the sum of mortality?

FBI AGENT JOSEPH DOMINICK PISTONE: "Yeah, absolutely it was faith that carried me through these six years while I was walking a tightrope and my purpose of what I was doing all this work for was not for myself. The higher authority is going to look after you. My outlook was whatever is going to happen will happen and I am going to do my job. I know I am looked out for and by my higher authority."

COP DR DAN RUDOFOSSI: "Even in extremis, if there is a purpose to your life and this critically important mission you do not pursue blindly and fanatically, but allowed Donnie Brasco to ensue, your success helped you make almost any challenge tolerable vis-à-vis your faith in G–d. You were challenged many times and you never lost your sense of decency and moral compass. Some of this story of your odyssey has been romanticized and some stupefied by reducing your ingenuity to only a survival- and instinctual-driven story. Dr. Viktor Frankl called this the indefatigable spirit of meaning and logos we all pursue, not as a drive, but as an existential center that can be reached and stoked in the most adverse of situations, as he lived through Auschwitz and never succumbed to suicide or withdrawing from being a human being as is true of you Joseph Dominick Pistone."

"So, in our dialogue my interpretation includes letting your support group of clinicians and students of investigation understand your strength also lay in the fact you are truly a man of faith. By holding onto your own moral compass by choice, and yet at times you let go when you couldn't control what challenged your life and limb directly. Without surrendering your will to live and your purpose in actualizing your potential, the life preserver that kept you afloat was as you said, your higher authority."

"G–d was not, and will never be any human being, including J. Edgar Hoover, FBI Director Hoover, who also was there by the grace of G–d to do his job as well as he could—regardless of some of the mistakes he made like every fallible human being, in your experience was pretty well done."

"Existentially, Joseph Dominick Pistone, by allowing your own ability to flow and not trying to trap and freeze it by being someone else's character made for you to follow, your own personality and integrity by the grace of your tough-minded faith and belief transcended your own sphere of being in a physical and earthly fear which, while natural, was redirected. In redirecting in your pause, you indeed successfully allowed Donnie Brasco to live as shadow of the real Joseph Dominick Pistone, as the light of this duality and doppelgänger we all have intrinsically within our own unique psyches but few ever touch this odyssey of self-introspection existentially as his essential self and center. Does this make sense in a world of sensuality that has been reduced to sensitivity that is not on target, or am I off color and off base here in understanding and coloring in an aspect of your soulful existence that helped you survive the ecological niche of Mafia wars and divisions and unity in the vistas of survival motivation ethologically?"

FBI AGENT JOSEPH DOMINICK PISTONE: "Yes Doc, it makes sense, as I shared with you. I knew myself well and my own beliefs and yes, my faith in the higher being I believe in, which includes knowing what you're doing and being tough-minded in not losing track of your goal here in dealing with the cold-stone killers as they are. As I shared and agree your understanding is in sync with mine as each character is different and you need to understand how to approach each differently without being weak or giving the impression ever that you are not able to do what is required, as when Sonny Red Indelicato was whacked and the contract was out for his son Bruno. If I was called to do what I had to do, I would have done what was called for or die and was not willing to die for Bruno who also was a stone-cold killer if Sonny Black Napolitano had called me and I had to do it. That is as tough-minded as you can get. But that does not mean Donnie Brasco was an acting role and I was the master actor. Your concept and definition of what I did, if I got your interpretation as cop doc, makes sense to me because I was always me and not some split personality in Donnie Brasco. I was also Donnie Brasco, and being myself but with intention and not with preplanning but allowing what happened and my responses to guide me as the operation moved on toward me becoming a made man in the Bonanno family. Donnie became a wiseguy and yes, he was my creation and also me authentically as he was not out of control. I did survive and I had to move in an ecology of gangsters, and I was motivated to gain intelligence that would bring down organized crime as my job and operation. The only way to achieve my goal was if Donnie was cultivated as he became a part of me, as you said, a shadow while I was the light. He was also put to rest before I felt it was best, but I had no real choice here because my bosses at the time felt we couldn't sustain the dangers and pressures this operation cost and inflicted."

COP DR DAN RUDOFOSSI: "Your interpretation is on point as even in my theory the fact is the unconscious does not mean mindless, but the emphasis and the underlying motivation of darkness has lost its visibility but is indivisible and ever present even though you can't see it. As is true of the many losses and also the myths that are disposable about you which sting with assumptions which I aspire we are putting to rest as in being the law enforcement blue bloods we are able to do without mincing words or playing political hand-miming of reality. The shadow is as real as the stalwart man that produces the projected image consciously shown against a brilliant wall of retrospective as much as the hazy silhouette relentlessly pursued in a fog that occludes real images under smoking screens. Like Edgar Hoover and the Grays you've educated me and our readers about here, the myths constructed around figures that are larger than life usually are the projections of distortion and reduction of fear that characterizes the real essence of the individuals behind other screens. Such screen images as the Italian American stereotype and the gangster and hero alike as all that is superhuman, or subhuman, are distortions projected onto the screens we construct in our fantasies. Also as human as the constrictions that are the product of space on our time here."

FBI AGENT JOSEPH DOMINICK PISTONE: "The reality, as you put it, is the projections put on me is in some ways the projections put on police officers as well. True, it's on a different scale of experience, but essentials are parallel and circular. The fact is that very few officers can do the job of being a deep cover, or doing undercover work, period."

"Cops deal with many situations most civilians cannot endure with. It is because we speak the same language and culture that we understand one another, Doc. In that way the screen has been set and the drapes are open for others to see what the reality is. It is now, perhaps, less distorted than before we have had our conversations. By now the readers ought to know they are not looking at Hollywood, Bollywood, or any fiction to give them the truth of what was done, can be done as a deep cover, and will be done in the future. Not losing the fact that our dialogues frankly spoke about part of my life I've lived, and lived well. My tough-mindedness you've fleshed out and that is useful for others who may be considering this line of work. It is really doing the job that was and had become the key for me doing what I do best. As you quote him often and I do too Doc, we have heard Churchill say, and I know it carried me, 'there go I, but for the Grace of G–d, go I.'"

Summary

In this chapter it is clear that in Joe Pistone's thousands of hours living as an observing participant among mafiosi he gained their respect and trust. He developed from a novice to an expert in understanding just whom to approach, when to approach him/her, how to approach him/her, and what to do in the multiple nuances of mores, boundaries, and implicit and explicit rules of decorum within the culture of organized criminal enterprises. Intuitive hunches need to be correct.

Wrong hunches can lead to death, whether intentional or done by mistake. Analytic and pragmatic thinking that is uncannily accurate is not a norm to go by. So exceptional speed at processing threats and veridical appraisals on an intellectual level must suffice. For example, as a lone tiger boss (or underboss) that kills using a trigger sprung on a hair-splitting impulsive spring of anger, as Tony Mirra did when Donnie Brasco was marked as his wiseguy associate, called for being fully aware of how to avoid being put in situations where he would be called on to murder another associate.

Remember, taking a victim as someone who was considered trite or an average fellow was a possibility with such a made man.

Looking at it from a perspective that respects the ecological niche, a made man such as Benjamin Lefty Ruggiero is looking into the fact moments of being non-plussed, and then compulsively trying to ferret out an error in memory, ideals, or loyalty in Donnie Brasco was reality with Lefty for Joe. Lefty Ruggiero seemingly presented as a has-been nostalgic Mafia hitman, affable and friendly as could be: At other times he could flip and zealously guard the territory of an almost made associate such as Donnie Brasco from getting made if a minor disrespect piqued his endogenous agitation and pierced his rigid obsessive-compulsive border.

The threat of attacking and shooting Joe Pistone if his identity was ever compromised reached a tipping point more than once.

It was not as apparent, but essentially Lefty Ruggiero was more unpredictable than the turgid bellicosity of Tony Mirra. Tony Mirra could have suffered more from intermittent explosive disorder and borderline personality style if not disorder, but was unlikely to ever step into a therapist's office as his anti-social personality traits and narcissistic features made it nigh on impossible to ever admit any flaws to a shrink or, for that matter, an existential analyst at a stretch.

Third in our line-up of capos with personality differences, within ecological niches and the motivation for survival being tendentious at best with the real traditions of the Mafia was cached in the down-to-earth capo, Sonny Black Napolitano. He presented as elegant as a restaurateur and yet as esoteric as a pigeon collector enthusiast. In the identity mode of Donnie Brasco, Sonny Black was adroit and calculating in wiping out four competing Mafia captains simultaneously with one Machiavellian vendetta. He made no room for error in himself and others he perceived as perfidious. In finding out gangster Donnie Pistone was sterling special agent FBI, Joe Pistone, he did not prevaricate in his willfulness and rigidity and allowed himself to be an oblation as a Pyrrhic victory in his being vanquished as fitting an honorable hero who failed his legion.

This is not romantic notions, it is not honorable in law enforcement culture, but in staying clear of pejoration in the Mafia culture and ecological niches and ethological motivation for Sonny Black, this was a fitting end that was honorable.

We will revisit this from Joe Pistone's identity mode in a later chapter from the vista of complex trauma and grief. Pausing, the main point as students of deep cover to keep in mind is that capo Sonny Black was as unmistakably deadly as Tony Mirra and Lefty Ruggiero combined. Why and how is this legitimately articulated? In one bite swallowing the opposition in a pre-emptive strike when betrayal was felt is not unusual as fantasy.

Sonny Black Napolitano, in fact, choreographed his invidious execution with draconian alacrity brilliantly as bloodlust for power and vengeance when threats of his own territory emerged by the other four capos, as we now know.

On the other hand, his execution was no less than allowing his own demise to clear his name for allowing Donnie Brasco into the midst of the Bonanno crime family—in which we also want to footnote in all suicide lay the unconscious script for homicide of the object of affection—disaffected by being who he was not and not being who he claimed he was. All in a day of being an undercover in the deep cover of espionage and infiltration as Joe Pistone had to be. Sonny Black knew this in his own way as a gangster and cold-stone killer who regardless had the virtue of taking a bullet for Donnie Brasco and hence pardoning some of the heat off of Special Agent Joe Pistone.

Let's move into the flux and dynamic equilibrium of Special Agent Joe Pistone and Doc Dan R. as we make footnotes into 'markings' along the way of crocodiles on one side and hammer head/bull sharks on the other side. Sammy Bull Gravano is a tempting informant, as is Joe Valachi, his predecessor, to compare in some way the ingenuity of Joe Pistone. Both remain cold-stone killers and yet, regardless, the mark of courage to be as they are, in part, mark their paths as well.

Cop Doc Corner for Students Only—Debriefing

It ought to be clear as crystal and, paradoxically, as beautiful as crystal could be, no corner is left unexplored heuristically and with serendipity. From Freud to Einstein, there is no accident for the paths laid out in the trials, travails, and tribulations of Special Agent Joseph Pistone as he has gone into the real belly of the wiseguy world and came out the hero with his shadow intact and therefore his sanity.

The tragic optimism written about in the exquisite courage of Dr. Viktor Frankl is relevant and to be a cornerstone here as Special Agent Joe Pistone is exceptional as a survivor and one who touched on the slippery slope of madness he dwelled in and the violence, loss, and trauma all gangsters go through and usually to a grievous endpoint. This is the other side of Eden exposed, and not with venom, but with empathy in a tough-minded manner unique to Joe which bespeaks volumes of heart and soul. The fact that Dr. Frankl never succumbed to being less then human and humane in his being soulful is to me parallel in ways with the soulfulness of Joe Pistone as educator and the best detective I have ever interviewed and mutually can call a true-blue friend. The evidence is, after all the trauma and losses Dr. Frankl endured, he developed and refined the logotherapy and existential analysis that helped thousands including police and others. Dr. Frankl's genius lay in his ability to transcend Purgatory and Hell for six years on earth and to remain indubitably human. His example is what led to his credibility.

Although I am simplifying and using analogous predators, you can imagine that to be able to negotiate effectively—gather useful knowledge in a field of psychological check-mate and counter check-mate is no accident. Survival becomes masterpiecing compromise formations.

In gaining trust and leading mergers, Joe is the brain behind the veil of check-mating, crisscrossed without pushing his victory in their face and without them even realizing they were led to the Elysian fields of illusion.

Third is the footnotes of this chapter in my narrative of interviews with Joe Pistone will certainly capture cultural taboos of criminals who organize their dos and don'ts around the fringe of detection by law enforcement, and defection from the families when they violate such taboos. Not getting whacked and identifying with the aggressor (Freud) is not explanatory for the deep-cover side of Joe Pistone. Being and becoming a wiseguy via adaptive functional dissociation, including the identity modes from an ethological survival motivation within a war-zone ecological niche, and hidden experimental traumatic neurosis is the way one can become different identity modes without letting on and without falling apart.

Joe Dominick Pistone, after six years of a concoction of Purgatory and Hell, never left his humanity. His contributions unique in the world of law enforcement and the potential in being not one of the best detectives, but the best detective, can teach us all that at the end of the day, there go I, but for the Grace of G–d, go I. His faith is what fueled his tough-mindedness and helped him make it through the extremis of Hell to Purgatory and now on the right side where the angels dare to tread. Joe stands unique and special as an agent we in the world of mental health as much as law enforcement can salute as our hero!

Important Definitions and Concepts to Keep in Mind

Adaptive functional dissociation in an eco-ethological existential model

In understanding the complexity of functional dissociation that occurs only within the process of idiographic assimilation and ethological accommodation of survival motivation for the individual to the variations in threats and creaseless entry into ecological niches as a member of that eco-ethological niche, much compromise is endured. The complexity to be understood goes beyond the dynamics of narrative and must include a study of the geographic and biopsychosocial variations laden with ethological motivation. This is still quite limiting in the challenge to the serious clinician and researcher, as it is imperative to realize only through an analytic attitude in the most classic and traditional of discipline psychoanalytically and existentially can mundane realism be achieved by the observing participant and clinician-practitioner and scientist attempting to gain a veridical understanding of the deep-cover agent. Veridical or reality-based knowledge accounts for the censoring intentionally and involuntarily as unconscious. In looking at Lefty Ruggiero as a stalwart traditionalist and John Gotti in a different context and power relationship, the parallels are striking, as personality traits contextualized express an inability to transcend the limitations of their ideals of what being and living as a wiseguy means, say in comparison to Sammy the Bull Gravano as an underboss willing to cross the world into the law enforcement Rubicon, if we can take an *Eco-Ethological Existential Analytic* approach to his disclosure as confession and abreaction regardless of conscious censoring or denial. Perhaps it gives special agent administration some useful wisdom in navigating through wiseguy eco-ethological niches and bridging the rare insights Joe Pistone and Donnie Brasco affords our ignorance in being and becoming more educated. This in no way eclipses a fundamental for all students at your own level of development, as undergraduate, graduate, and even postgraduate, to succor the reality of economics and insight that drapes practical and applied wisdom as partial understanding that are momentous. In other words, momentous impact on the clinician cop doc and undercover agent in working through traumatic loss for the healthier agent who has not maladaptively dissociated is still effective and impactful intervention toward resilience and development.

Angles of ethological affordances to survive in

What is afforded in an ecology is the numerous and ingenious adaptations and limitations overcome without conscious awareness in the agent him/herself that is thrust into such chaotic and inchoate bits of knowledge laden with mines of misinformation and traps to expose the outsider as intruder. This makes superb sense from the wiseguy world view and paradigm, as a covert agent means the entire criminal enterprise is built on a house of cards in which one wrong pull of the joker means one has been infiltrated and the infiltrator, once labeled, is in grave danger. From the paradigm of law enforcement, this threat is often allowed in the desire to gain knowledge of the unknown variables and their interconnections as practiced. As the analogy goes, it is also literal, as no agent can push aside the need for extraordinary intuition, emotional intelligence, and concrete memory encoding of unknown and developing paradigmatic and fluid intelligence to stop or slow down the criminal enterprise under analysis, or if preferred, investigation. This is telling as it becomes clear that an agent who is successful must be a clinical-minded researcher, as well as a quite street-smart and savvy pioneer in the sense of all these dimensions. Keep in mind this work is a casebook meant to educate students, while not so hidden it serves as a springboard for research and theory development to supplement the understanding of the idiographic wisdom and to a degree the nomothetic wisdom

De-individuation mimicry to individuation as a process for the special agent

In an interesting presentation of a model to incorporate the classic Darley and Latané social distance model and diffusion of responsibility (Darley & Latané, 1968; Latané & Darley, 1969), evidence to bolster the firm foundation of de-individuation as conformity that pressures the individual to give up his own identity for fitting in a collective social identity is to a degree challenged by Joe Pistone's need to maintain the desirability of fitting in socially and disinhibiting boundaries that prevent mob mentality and ethological aggression as outlets with no consequential and reality-based limitations. In an agent entering deep cover as Joe Pistone did and becoming gangster Donnie Brasco identity mode by mimicking deindividuation into the Mafia family while staying balanced and with integrity, individuating as operations special agent identity mode as always being existentially superordinate. Mental toughness may seem a simple term but again revisited in this context couples moral integrity and altruism over and beyond the operationalized complexity of being in the shadow and duality of Donnie Brasco. It is not reducible to simple measurement, but as a work of art done with exacting scientific and unconscious exactitude, the product becomes evidence itself of the artist's genius. This is anchored in the achievement of the process and assertion of such success in this chapter owed to Joe Pistone's genius and charitable nature in sharing with all of us such extraordinary mindedness. It is more than a footnote for students interested in the enormity of peer pressure which in deep cover is double folded over because the culture of infiltration is one being learned and one that must be transcended by the agent's moral development, choices, and growth as a human being (Kohlberg, 1981). In this regard, Joe Pistone kept an integrity level that was uncompromising and at the highest level of moral development.

Sensitivity

The hypothetical construct of **sensitivity**, used in a research and scientific context, implies the pick-up of information, definitions of that information if novel, and attempts to understand such information without compromising the integrity of the exploration of what is being observed and categorized. This is true whether or not it is operational definitions or qualitative descriptions that are being explored for the first time. It is also used in a clinical sense in this chapter and book as we tackle subtle mores and even nuances that become rich with symbolic meaning once those behaviors, customs, and rites and rituals are contextualized and given a label.

Specificity and individuation

This is the underscoring of detecting and measuring what is critical in doing assessment and clinical intervention as to not only the hypothetical construct at hand through the lenses of overall cultural and nomothetic context as the distributions measured across large populations and the larger culture, but a different outlook. Let's take the examples given in this book and the elusive complexity of what Joe Pistone and Donnie Brasco meant by saying mental toughness is necessary to do deep cover with the fact that the world of the gangster is not the world of the law enforcement or normal people. It can be completely taken out of context and in asserting the respectful insights into reality as it is, not as it desired, Joe Pistone as educator is asserting idiographic and what Dr. Bornstein asserts as the specificity principle (Bornstein & Lerner,

2021). As discussed earlier, this crucial context is to be understood on an individual definition and interpretation that resists the forceful acceptance of national and cultural boundaries for the specific ability to describe, better understand, analyze and predict, and even boldly not advocate but subtly craft responses and responsiveness toward change in the most intemperate and even aggressive of ecological and ethological niches as I suggest, as possibilities to play with in the light of the enormity of Joe Pistone's wisdom ideographically which can help in an overall hopeful attempt to alter the larger cultural motif constructed nomothetically.

Sit-downs

Sit-downs are very serious rites of judgment and deliberation in which the presiding capo, who is a senatorial representative of the capo di tutti or the presiding father of the Mafia family(s), passes a sentence on the associate or made member that violates a do or don't. The sit-down can be a change in status and a promotion also, but in the parlance of its use, it is usually a very serious infraction of a rule where a sentence and its execution are carried out in swift succession. No appeals, and no adversarial process is done formally and no due process takes place. It is a ritual without any real sense of justice as larger society requires but is considered a ritual with substantive significance and done with all the trappings of a historic and aged rite of passage. I would say it is almost pharaonic in origin as entombing the staff of the Pharoah and by proxy and extension the emperor as it is written in cold sentence so it is done. Some violations are breaches in omertà, disloyalty to a capo or made member of the family, and breaches in overextending boundaries that are explicit or implicitly ought to be known. As in criminal law and jurisprudence, as in Mafia practice—ignorance of the law is no excuse for its breach. Unlike criminal law and jurisprudence, prosecution and sentencing is swift as a razor's slice and defense and appeal is pleading but hardly any clemency is found and as rare as a 10-carat diamond.

Conceptual and Writing Exercises for Student and Professor Only

1. Imagine for a moment being asked to try to be Joe Dominick Pistone for a day as deep cover. Doing so will take imagination and courage to review this chapter and to close your eyes and record when you open them as to how anxious, fearful, and agitated you may feel in at least five situations you can flesh out with at least one other student. Try to record how intense, how frequent, and how long the experience of anxiety, fear, and agitation, as well as hyperarousal, lasts for you. Now do the same with the partner student you are working with on this experiential project. Prepare to present to students in your class and to your professor.
2. Do you feel and can you imagine, after doing the above experiential exercise, ever pursuing becoming an FBI, DEA, NSA, ATF, Secret Service, or Elite Police Unit member and doing undercover assignments in counter terrorism operations? List five reasons that motivate you to continue on as a student aspiring to join such elite units?
3. Please summarize what you as a student were able to establish as three reasons you found exciting in listening to the experiences of Joe Pistone as an FBI special agent. What is the most important motivation you can disclose that complements your own desires for personal achievement? What is the other most important motivation that is aligned with the desire to serve others? Open your motivations to a larger conversation in which your professor will highlight truer approximations of real motivating factors which may synchronize with your own interpretation, and which factors are uniquely your own. Discuss.

4. Finally, take the time when alone to existentially and meaningfully ask yourself if first a law enforcement officer career path is really for you? Ask yourself, and without censoring yourself, seek why it may not be right for you? Now next on your list, why is it right for you? In retrospect, you may keep some of your results private knowledge and self-awareness and self-knowledge to enlighten your own existential insights and growth. With other findings you may bravely move on to share this with other students as well and your professor.

5. Highlighting your own cultural and eco-ethological existential niche as you experience life now, take some time to consider if you would consider some of the implicit mores and taboos in your own family, larger cultural circles, and society as you experience it. Now juxtapose your own perceptions of your own experiences culturally and add, as a unique individual, what varies as your personal likes and dislikes from the cultural hub of your life experiences. After you do that, compare your own likes and dislikes to the eco-ethological niche you experience most often—how much of your own life experiences are in sync with your own existential values and list the other experiences you must tolerate that are not. After you do this exercise, list some of the hardships in adjustment you have undergone to fit in. Now imagine and discuss how challenging it must have been on a spiritual and existential level for our educator Special Agent Joseph Dominick Pistone to have dealt with the dos and don'ts in the world of the wiseguys. Allow yourself to imagine if you think you could dare to try to be a special agent and if so, could you imagine boldly becoming a deep-cover agent? Why, or why not?

References

Brenner, C. (1973). *An elementary textbook of psychoanalysis.* New York and London: Anchor Books, Doubleday.

Brenner, C. (1979). The components of psychic conflict and its consequence in mental life. *Psychoanalytic Quarterly*, 48(4), 547–567.

Bornstein, H. M., & Lerner, M. R. (2021). Contributions of the specificity principle to theory, research, and application in the study of human development: A view of the issues. *Journal of Applied Developmental Psychology*, 75(July–August), 101294.

Darley, M. J., & Latané, B. (1968). Bystander intervention in emergencies: Diffusion of responsibility. *Journal of Personality and Social Psychology*, 8, 377–381.

Hammarskjold., D. (1966). *Markings.* New York: Knopf Press. Translated from the Swedish language by L. Sjoberg & W. H. Auden. Foreword by W. H. Auden.

Kohlberg, L. (1981). *Essays on moral development: The philosophy of moral development.* Volume 1. New York: Harper and Row.

Laing, R. D. (1970). *The divided self: An existential study in sanity and madness.* New York: Random House.

Laing, R. D. (1972). *Self and others.* London: Penguin.

Latané, B., & Darley, M. J. (1969). Bystander "apathy". *American Scientist*, 57(2), 244–268.

Pistone, J. D., & Woodley, R. (1989). *Donnie Brasco: My undercover life in the Mafia.* New York and London: Penguin.

Pistone, J. D. (2004). *The way of the wiseguy—Donnie Brasco aka Joseph D. Pistone.* Philadelphia and London: Running Press.

Pistone, J. D., & Brandt, C. (2007). *Unfinished business.* Philadelphia and London: Running Press.

Rudofossi, D. M. (2013). *A cop doc's guide to understanding terrorism as human evil: Healing from complex trauma syndromes for military, police, and public safety officers and their families.* Amityville, NY: Baywood.

Skaggs, E. G. (2022). *Test development and validation.* Thousand Oaks, London and New Delhi: Sage.

5
ACTIVE ANALYSIS AND ADAPTIVE FUNCTIONAL DISSOCIATION

Intuitive Ingenuity

Introduction

Our understanding of markings, mores, and cultural dos and don'ts have become understood as influenced within an ecological-ethological niche, but still much is left to explore. One new marking is what scientists do to explore and chart new maps (cartography) of regions, patterns, and associations to help others who wish to navigate in uncharted waters with at least a rough draft.

But what of a region unmapped and unexplored by law enforcement officers and agents? Special Agent Joe Pistone piloted and navigated without a map to chart out the bogs, miasma, and pitfalls for reconnaissance with the dos and don'ts we garnered in our markings of the last chapter. Stop, and pause first, as we contemplate empathically that Special Agent Joe Pistone navigated and piloted unexplored and uncharted territory.

As a psychologist-scientist, I ask you to redirect your attention with me. Let's understand the concept of **heuristic exploration**. As a scientist and clinician, testing one's prediction of the relationships that may exist among different factors under examination is not fleshing out all the factors that assist in understanding. One tests his/her hypothesis that underscores and targets a predictable outcome that is likely to be better understood.

In classes I've taught in police forums to detectives, special agents, or police officers as much as students of psychology and psychiatry, I share what is proscribed first, not prescribed. In other words, the lesson learned is by putting up your limitations as challenges first, you create a higher likelihood toward effective and veridical outcomes (Gardner, 1993; Gilmartin, 2002; Goleman, 2005; Rudofossi, 2017).

This is true for the law enforcement officer, the student of mental and medical health, and perhaps in any venture we attempt to do by studying and trying to predict the outcome of our behaviors during an event. Keep in mind, while not completely reducible to human relationships, many events do take place within the context of human interaction and relationships held firmly together. The ability to create and limit behaviors determines whether smooth, colliding, oscillating, or dynamic evolutions of effective solutions or wisdom to do whatever objective is sought can in fact be achieved.

Joe Pistone heuristically navigated through mazes unknown, unexplored, and even unidentified as they emerged. Charting out isles, lagoons, and rivulets all leading to the river of quelled

DOI: 10.4324/9781032202761-6

dreams and sharpened quills can sting, rip, and excoriate the unaware traveler eager to please and loud to argue, without a clue as to what urban jungle of concrete and shard glass one is navigating in and through.

In our joint venture of exploration, fundamental understanding of Joseph's wisdom emerges as fragments and are woven together here. Knowledge can be the bundle of information even a simple-minded person can learn eventually; wisdom is another horizon to behold. Wisdom is the use of knowledge that works and benefits others in a way that is productive and effective for other humans—wisdom becomes humane and purposive humanity.

Using a heuristic approach is a captain's portal to wisdom in glimpsing into Joseph Pistone's approach. As we already identified, stealth and hidden identity in the doppelgänger as a major sensible adaptation fleshed out earlier, we will now move into the physiology of the bare bones as we will fill in missing flesh to understand what was remarkable success in Operation Donnie Brasco. Six years within La Cosa Nostra as a man ready to be made is evidence of wisdom. Pause and relate the fact that being culturally competent when there is no guide save one's diplomacy and heuristic approach to sieve through interference and turbulent static was what kept Joe alive and also accepted, as Donnie Brasco moved in as luminary and Joe Pistone receded into the shadow of his operative.

This can be brought to light by an ingenious psychoanalyst and investigator of the mind, active analysis in the work of Dr. Sandor Ferenczi (Ferenczi, 1988). Ferenczi reversed identity modes as we have identified earlier, and had the patient become the analyst and the analyst the patient to assist understanding the roots of hidden and cached conflict. He coined this surreptitious method *active analysis*.

Active analysis was remarkably successful in some cases, and not in others. In dealing with trauma and police it is one technique I reserve when it is plausible due to all the dynamics present in the patient and my rapport as well as the resilience and creative bridge to sustain such an analysis. Keep this in mind as we explore briefly the healing aspect of investigative legal jurisprudence when the attorney (I have suggested adding police investigator and forensic clinician), while laying out a defense, and one may add even a prosecution, may open a window toward healing of the suspect, forensic defendant, or incarcerated felon. The term Professor Perlin coined was *therapeutic jurisprudence*.

Indeed, change for the betterment of the defendant is one dimension articulated by Professor Michael Perlin as a jurist of the first order in mental health and law in reviewing the propinquity of the insanity defense (Kitaeff, 2019; Perlin, 1994). These great minds and thinkers can be understood in the context of Dr. Viktor Frankl, the creator of logotherapy and existential analysis (Frankl, 1979). His method includes paradoxical intention, which in the 1970s was relegated to a wisdom only a select group of clinicians and practitioners of psychiatry and psychology could infuse in patients who had given up on life, living, and motivation to fight the good fight to recover from serious mental illness. By asking the patient to confront and do what he/she feared most, paradoxically often one would take the wind out of the sails fueling angst, anxiety, rage, and depression. Often the clinician would, and to this day will still, create an intervention which, by suggesting and supporting the opposite of withdrawing from one's fear, one finds he/she has conquered that very fear and root of suppression.

In our dialogue, I Socratically and dare I say therapeutically with Joe and his permission, share with the reader his wisdom which here more strikingly and convincingly is done unconsciously.

Dynamic, Oscillating, and Static Equilibrium: Ergonomic Flow of Deep Cover

In dynamic equilibrium, Donnie Brasco must follow the lead of Joseph Dominick Pistone, which at a level of threat and defense unconsciously and consciously threatened oscillating equilibrium from a dynamic equilibrium. If Joe Pistone remained passive to the changes and tried hard to fit in as an associate, a static equilibrium would occur and not only would no gains be made as he achieved, but his real identity as a deep cover would emerge as a parallel window to being to stuck in his world as a law enforcement officer not in his identity mode as a gangster Donnie Brasco.

It is here I introduce with Joe to you the concept Viktor Frankl wrote about only hintingly in his last work, the transcendental unconscious. The transcendental unconscious speaks volumes of the unconscious G–d as Frankl suggested (Frankl, 1979). This is not a theological work, but what I am suggesting here with evidence is that the unconscious dimension existentially is the depth of wisdom that is intuitive (Conroy & Orthmann, 2014; Rudofossi, 2007). It is made visible by actions and success, not always immediately tangible and measurable. Heuristically and with cultural competence, it is quite sound to state declaratively that Joe D. Pistone's success was a measure of fluid genius, spliced in sum of his emotional intelligence and cognate intellect coupled with a remarkable memory.

Operation Donnie Brasco demanded much of Joe Pistone as architect of the operation—no less than the operator who had to do the on-ground deep cover under the identity mode of someone he was not but became over time. If this sounds confusing, we are on the right track. Deep cover is hardly for all law enforcement officers and may always belong in a unique and extraordinary service goal for the very few and talented. Joe D. Pistone had to serve within a law enforcement paradigm by accommodating to the demands of being the intelligence agent, an operations agent, and executive front-line administrator through each and every component of Operation Donnie Brasco. In analysis of the various identity modes faced by Special Agent Joe D. Pistone, it is crucial for our own perspective to clearly organize our own questions. Questions that follow will help you plummet through and understand the process of becoming Donnie Brasco for Joe D. Pistone.

Questions to Guide You as Navigational Tools: Learning Objectives

1. How did being a Naval Intelligence Officer assist Special Agent Joe Dominick Pistone to segue into becoming a master sleuth as deep-cover operative?
2. Is intelligence gathering a major part of deep cover?
3. If intelligence gathering is so important in getting a handle on organized crime via informants, why is there is a need to infiltrate a crime syndicate such as a powerful Mafia family—where an agent is put at great risk of life and limb?
4. Isn't it easier to get paid informants to get an edge on the hidden happenings without taking on the risk of losing life and limb of the special agent?
5. Did being Italian American stymie Joe Dominick Pistone or was it a key to unraveling the tight network of organized crime?
6. Is there a reason that the famed Lt. Joseph Petrosino, who was a brilliant organized crime investigator, became a victim of treachery and perfidy and Joe Dominick Pistone survived?
7. Did Joe Pistone get the name and much more importantly the persona of Donnie Brasco from his FBI administrators and J. E. Hoover himself?
8. How did Donnie Brasco become the trade name of doing great detective deep cover as Joe Pistone succeeded in doing and in the naming of his infiltration Operation Donnie Brasco?

Key Terms

Heuristic exploration
Active analysis

Phylogenic development—ontogenetic charismatic genius
'Regressed toward the mean'—capitulation to original deviancy
Abysmal low frustration tolerance—aggression
High frustration tolerance—infiltration propensities
Addictive personality traits

No Practice Drills for Special Agent Undercover—Deeply Covered

COP DR DAN RUDOFOSSI: "Taking off from our last interview, I had a question that may be very basic but is important to understand. I am assuming, and I may be wrong, but it appears each experience as Donnie Brasco demanded *your toleration of frustration and spontaneous interruptions* that were undetermined as your infiltration skills grew with your burgeoning intel gathering."

FBI AGENT JOSEPH DOMINICK PISTONE: "Doc, patience is a virtue for those as yourself as a doc, for me patience is a survival mechanism psychologically. Timing is everything in doing deep cover and infiltration. There is a time to speak up and hold your ground and other times where silence and acting as if you don't have a clue and need guidance is another time. You need to know the clear difference and learn to act on the flip of a dime as the expression goes."

COP DR DAN RUDOFOSSI: "That helps a lot. Coloring your picture, it is not the knock-out and take-down tactics in law enforcement that, while necessary at times, takes the shadow of the more subtle diplomacy and exact timing you maneuvered. The spontaneity of working the right moment into the exact timing to be decisive to assert your own unique view could be decisive in getting yourself murdered if you speak out of place. Is there any education that can enrich that choice by future agents reading texts or pamphlets on tactics or strategy?"

FBI AGENT JOSEPH DOMINICK PISTONE: "Education that lasts is what works. The beginning of doing deep cover is all academic as the end point is application in the real world. The real-world application is always profoundly unpredictable!"

COP DR DAN RUDOFOSSI: "Special Agent Joe P., this is truly enigmatic, because ultimately education relies on academic theory and the dissemination of knowledge through media which includes books nowadays undone in 'e-books' and aids to the books, which dummy down the dummy guides. On the other hand, agents as well as police officers do need a foundation of college-level education to even begin and I imagine it is well worthwhile."

FBI AGENT JOSEPH DOMINICK PISTONE: "Yes, it is well worthwhile to get a college education at a college that offers a wide variety of coursework and specialization for a career in law enforcement and definitely that includes being an intel analyst to special agent operative. It is a basic foundation. It is not a foundation for doing deep cover if you get my drift. Again, the unpredictability of it all, and it is definitely not predictable, is almost impossible to educate a future agent in."

COP DR DAN RUDOFOSSI: "Prediction of success, I imagine, is impinged on by determining in all means available the best prediction in each situation as possible. If I am right, and we return to the point that tolerating frustration at very high levels helps the agent because you can't turn to a guide or training to solve the most challenging of compromises faced, is that the best we have?"

FBI AGENT JOSEPH DOMINICK PISTONE: "Wisdom is learned through experience and the agent's own method of strategy to pilot through the heavy turbulence. No conveniently nice-packaged guide can deliver the agent. It is as messy as the different characters of the gangsters you must deal with. Like it or not, the gangster's personality is what comes out and you got to deal with him."

COP DR DAN RUDOFOSSI: "So, it is your own heuristic approach with markings as coordinates that is in a sense intuitive, or I guess in my language as a scientist-practitioner, is heuristic. That is, on one hand it is grounded in many years of education, but each patient I work with is new and different. More so, each session is an opportunity to encounter genuinely and connect, or disconnect and be viewed as disingenuous and lose contact. I need to also tolerate the ambiguity and moods and swings of acceptance and endearment that move into rejection of treatment and cooperation as well. This toleration in therapy and education is a great learning curve. Without it the patient is lost in the therapist's ego if he/she loses toleration of frustration. On the other hand, some patients opt out without toleration of frustration as to the rules of engagement."

FBI AGENT JOSEPH DOMINICK PISTONE: "I think the analogy is good in that you get my point that in doing deep cover there is no definite outcome known and like you lose your patient at worst, you realize I lose my life at worst. Most of the times it may be all is stagnant and no movement is gained as in the beginning of operation Donnie Brasco. That demands a lot of patience and dealing with your ability to tolerate the unknowns, including the gangsters and the situations that just crop up unexpectedly and with no time to prep or call for any back-up. Kind of like being a cop doc in the field and not knowing what the officer you are seeing has been through, who he/she is, and how unearthed and fugazy or clear-minded he is."

COP DR DAN RUDOFOSSI: "Exactly, and in forensic and clinical work we call these individual differences recognition and rapport skills. Traits and features are consistent markings that help knowing from a practical and applied perspective. For example, whether we take an analogy from the world of biochemistry as much as the science of human psychology, there are three types of balancing acts. One is called *static equilibrium*, which can stop all progress to a standstill—the creative stream of thought is damned up. Or another equilibrium is *oscillating equilibrium*, which is equivalent to the flip-flop of an entire smooth operation such as chemical reactions that become a cacophony of noise and smoke with no control. Finally, a *dynamic equilibrium* is achieved with a fluency whereby different cultural mores, rituals, and customs configure in the right sequences: the fit is 'just right.' That 'just right fit' is what I as a clinician seek. If I am right, what you as a deep cover ideally seek is even more so, a 'just right fit.' The just right fit sets a dynamic and flowing equilibrium as ideal. But, if I am getting you right in educating me and my students, it is here that the analogy ends. Ends abruptly!"

FBI AGENT JOSEPH DOMINICK PISTONE: "Perfect synchrony with me, Doc. Understanding includes understanding individual gangsters and their personalities, and each one's differences in the constellation of their own Mafia families. This is complicated by the culture of Italian American culture and some people thinking you betrayed being Italian American or picking on the culture of gangsters who are Italian American, and this notion is as wrong and ignorant as is the law enforcement culture thinking anyone can do this work and following rules and regs as the way to success as an FBI special agent. Creativity is crucial and being tough-minded by knowing who you are, the objective you have in mind and need to make into reality."

COP DR DAN RUDOFOSSI: "Thank you kindly for your assessment of my own assessment; it helps. To review, you had to shadow your own doubleganger from a newbie wannabe wiseguy to becoming the established wiseguy Donnie Brasco. At the same time, as Joe D. Pistone you had to use all your street-wise skills and natural abilities combined to becoming the Italian American wannabe gangster gaining entry as a street-level grunt into La Cosa Nostra. You knew from the onset they will test you and try you every which way but loose. No free lunch. From your beginning as a petty jewel thief to the moment Operation Donnie Brasco closed down, six years you had to orchestrate anything but noise. You used cultural competence toward being the 'made wiseguy' without full portfolio."

FBI AGENT JOSEPH DOMINICK PISTONE: "Yes, again you are on point with me. I made it to wiseguy without full portfolio. I was accepted and although not officially made, I had crossed over into that identity. In your words, identity mode."

COP DR DAN RUDOFOSSI: "Joseph Dominick Pistone, you achieved what only the best of international spies achieved. If you were not Italian, did not know the culture well, you would not succeed as you did. You fit in because 'it was not acting' as you've vehemently and honestly shared. You connected the dots and moved as a genuine member of La Cosa Nostra with your identity established as Donnie Brasco. While it has not ever been articulated, forgive me for boldly asserting it needs to be understood, as I suggested earlier to you, that Donnie Brasco was created *ex nihilo* and *sui generis*. In plain English, this means that Donnie Brasco as a made wiseguy in the Bonanno Mafia family was born and nurtured from nothing. You, Joseph Dominick Pistone, by the grace of G–d in your own gift of ingenuity and imagination."

FBI AGENT JOSEPH DOMINICK PISTONE: "I now thank you as cop doc, you get it and maybe more than other cops and docs. You know, Doc, after Operation Donnie Brasco ended and we had indictments done and prosecution was launched, Lefty Benjamin Ruggiero denied in spite of all the evidence that I was FBI Agent Joseph Dominick Pistone. He could not wrap his mind that the double of Donnie Brasco was actually me. Special Agent Joseph Dominick Pistone, FBI."

COP DR DAN RUDOFOSSI: "I can imagine carrying around your existence as anything but light, insofar as you repeatedly had to prove and create credibility as a shadow of yourself, all the while keeping the integrity of your own identity. If this was not hard enough in different ecological niches surviving and behaving as a wiseguy when you are not one, stimulated your unique mind and brain to create solutions to problems hardly identified. If as a clinical and developmental psychologist I aspire to measure the ingenuity necessitated, I must add into the assessment the fact that each event with traumatic potential and actual impact adds more complexity to the learning curve you achieved. Just understanding this complexity for the readers alone will offer an education they have not had as of yet. Add to this the isolation of you as a special agent of the FBI into the mix who must rely on his own ingenuity, notwithstanding some auxiliary assistance, it is a remarkable repeat tactical achievement of survival where the odds are against you. The cognitive task is weighted with emotional skill to not lose track that for over six years your assignment and center of existence was developing Donnie Brasco."

FBI AGENT JOSEPH DOMINICK PISTONE: "How do you measure that, Doc; I mean all you just said? Can you really figure that out like a formula for students and even for myself to understand?"

COP DR DAN RUDOFOSSI: "To be totally frank, as a scientist who aspires to be honest and fully frank, quantifying such tasks would diminish and reduce the success of your infiltration and your legendary existence as both Joe Pistone and as Donnie Brasco. I would like to integrate your wisdom and ingenuity as a punctuation and pause to delve further with your help and generosity to explore your gift in the creative, practical, and analytic strategy you developed together. If we can redirect our attention to the becoming wiser by listening to you. In a way like Heinz ketchup, 'so slow and yet so good' as I used to hear, and watch my dad use on mom's spaghetti while my mom would animatedly point out for heaven's sake ketchup is not my marinara. It's all commercial."

FBI AGENT JOSEPH DOMINICK PISTONE: "That's good Doc, it's funny. I can imagine that conversation between your mom and dad. Like the undiscovered country lit up like a keg of dynamite stuck a fuse in one hot tomato. Your mom is right, Heinz ketchup is not marinara! But sticking up for your dad, although Heinz ketchup is not marinara, it sometimes can touch the right taste buds and tastes just right. Preferences is what wins, rather than rue the day." [Both of us laugh as we reminisce about the best generation ever, as our parents' cohorts are called.]

COP DR DAN RUDOFOSSI: "Special Agent Joe Pistone, I have an analogy that sounds kind of strange, and knowing me as you do, I will use any analogy, metaphor, or story to illustrate how and why an association works. So, my playful use of metaphor is as dead serious as the reality of the gum that is stuck on the Corfram shoes of those wanting to metamorph into detectives. Detectives and street cops alike will snicker. Some may grin, that are open to wit and analogy and who have some historic background in reading what I will propose. The point is getting smart folks to think. In attempting to give light to the enormity of your rescue interventions and the impact of your work in this country of ours, and others who are our allies, in my view you've saved not only civilian lives but have offered an education to other law enforcement officers as to staying alive in precarious situations where disclosure of identity will lead to certain death. Again, with your permission I would like to take a risk without minimizing, nor exaggerating, your contributions using an analogy that I think will shed light to readers. If I must cut, add, embolden, and underscore the truth of not only your ingenuity but existentially place your *noetic dimension* in perspective, to help others realize the ingenuity and beating the odds in surviving infiltration that you truly made happen."

FBI AGENT JOSEPH DOMINICK PISTONE: "I'm listening to this, although as I said I did not do what I did with any grand notion save motivation to do the right thing as a special agent and to give it my best which is what I did as I shared earlier, and you did get some subtle and important points in understanding that most don't and miss the big picture on as a cop doc, which is why you get me in the first place, because you've carried the shield as an LEO as well. So, shoot Doc."

COP DR DAN RUDOFOSSI: "So, here it goes. Although we are going to contextualize the unique Italian American connection and street smarts, guts, and mental toughness in being and arguably becoming you to sleuthing and deep-cover work, for now I will assert you saved countless future lives and arguably some of the lives of those who would have been dusted within contracts set up while you were wiseguy Donnie Brasco. Simultaneously with hiding the outer shine of Joe Pistone special agent, you intentionally and unconsciously at times shifted modes of identity Donnie developed within the fold of the other major identity you kept all along by being you as you focused on survival and also extending that safety net to multiple others from getting dusted. In my mind at least, someone comparable to you in this very overwhelming challenge for most of us is the inimitable gentleman who adored ladies and his Jewish adopted family while playing Nazi, Oskar Schindler. Schindler saved roughly 1,100 innocent Jews who committed no crime save being born Jewish in the Nazi madness that took over the Eastern European world. He had no identity to offer but one he had to catalyze living among and by the favor of the most unsavory types of criminals organized, the National Socialist Party of Germany. Oskar Schindler was no born savior of the Jews. However, Oskar Schindler was to become one. Schindler realized his unique potential for ingenuity and diplomatic skills could broker a deal when deals that included rescuing Jews was at a loss with a penalty of immediate death. Schindler made and blew millions of dollars burnt in pyres of lost bets, broads, and booze: But he saved worlds—innocent men, women, and children threatened by death at any moment were spared for timeless and countless fertile children and grandchildren and great-grandchildren. Oskar Schindler's true intentions would be understood after he was buried under a sea of debts incurred. He made deals with products that were paper missiles in the sand of diplomacy while negotiating lives for money, which is not so far from the contracts and stone-cold killings you navigated through without compromising you as the shield behind the shadow. Like you, he brought light into darkness, not light to disperse the dark shadows, and that is a major difference between ketchup and marinara."

FBI AGENT JOSEPH DOMINICK PISTONE: "Doc, that is a helluva comparison. I get your point that Oskar Schindler was a singular-minded and even tough-minded impostor if you want to look at him that way. That is poignant as a measure of his mettle when he rescued his hostages which were Jewish men, women, and children. That is as far as it goes, as I knew who I was, I never lost touch with me and who and what I was and doing. I recall he stayed straight in trying to rescue 'his Jews.' But as far as the complimentary analogy, I didn't save a thousand-plus innocent lives as he did. I saved a handful as you put it. I can agree with that point you make, and that does make sense Doc, in a way he did hide his true intention while he was doing. It's not an issue of ego, do you call it ego? I think it is self-confidence, you know. You dissociate yourself from being what can be looked at as a split personality as we discussed before. I don't know if that is the right term to use. I had to be myself, and you can't doubt how you are and what you intend to do. So, in comparison, I do agree the enormity of Schindler's work in that time may be over the top of my arena in that he was not hiding his identity, although he had probably more than his share of mistresses in being his true self."

COP DR DAN RUDOFOSSI: "The comparison between your work and Schindler needs qualifying, so let me try with one as best as I can. That comparison is between the quality of Heinz ketchup and real marinara. My dad used to love spaghetti with Heinz ketchup and, in confidence, so did I, but Mom would work up her magic marinara and only the Almighty could help me survive if I chose ketchup over marinara. But the analogy is left here. I will leave the reader to understand the meaning here as to which of you both is the ketchup, and who the real marinara. If someone does not know the difference, then you may want to put this book away and return when you're rested or, better yet, give it to a friend who may be better suited to reading this type of book. But what is telling to me is Israel, not Germany, honored this man first, and Oskar Schindler is one of very few among the Righteous People among the Nations. He was a hero rescuing victims from certain death during the Holocaust."

"You were at times erroneously told that you had something to pick with Italian Americans, but the truth is you belong in the Honor Legion of Italian American heroes."

"You are in the sphere of Lt. Joe Petrosino and surpassed his interventions as a sleuth, although his contributions were enormous. I use this analogy not to compare La Cosa Nostra to the Nazis because that is an impoverished, if not blatantly ignorant comparison. It is to make a point of insight responsibly. That point is that some La Cosa Nostra capos buttressed the waterfronts to protect the borders and boundaries of our country against the tyranny of fascism."

"So, my point in comparing your feats to Oskar Schindler is it to highlight the complexity of how and why what you achieved as a special agent is not lost on your ingenuity of how you operated on multidimensional levels of integrity and rescue. After all, the rise of the organized crime families and the desire to do well with one's fellows is not lost if the context is fleshed out. As Schindler infiltrated the National Socialists for six years, you infiltrated La Cosa Nostra for six years and closed down murder for a while as did Schindler. Ingenuity, surreptitious caching identity, and motivation coalesced in Gideon's sword in Schindler as it did with you."

FBI AGENT JOSEPH DOMINICK PISTONE: "It is an interesting analogy, Doc; I appreciate it considering your own background and your ability to see what others miss at times. Definitely hiding your motivation and identity is crucial as it was with Schindler. To be successful as a deep cover you're told or asked to take on a bad-guy personality, but how do you know what a bad-guy personality is? Being a wiseguy in the real world does not change if as a civilian or even LEO you don't have the balls to stand up to what you know is the right thing."

"What you believe in is crucial as to what you can do and certainly will not be able to do in the world of the undercover, as an undercover agent. You have to be yourself in real-life situations, when someone calls you out. In other words, you would do the same thing in undercover life as you would in a real situation that was not undercover."

"So, if you're not going to stand up for yourself in real life, you will certainly not stand up for yourself in a situation you are called out on as an undercover to do what needs to be done to stay alive and keep others alive. Again, that goes for standing up for your real beliefs in real life as well. That is the cut for self-selection into this world of deep-cover work. Before choosing yourself as even thinking of doing undercover, know the parameters of what cuts the grade and if you have the inner strength and mental toughness to do it. Know yourself first."

COP DR DAN RUDOFOSSI: "I like that point you're making! If I got you right, as I have gotten to know you Joe Pistone the gentleman, Special Agent Joseph Pistone, and Donnie Brasco the wiseguy who virtually was a made member of the Bonanno family without portfolio, is the fact you saved agents and other law enforcement officers from fates they never even knew they would experience, but very well could have, and likely would have if your intervention did not thwart, close down some gangsters and their associates."

"Many good cops, special agents, and detectives who are tough-minded and with inner strength may not pass the litmus test if being called out as you were. Of course, being called out is the test wiseguys use to test you in terms of loyalty. Those men and women who cannot take the pressure and heat of being called out without leaking out their identity as an LEO need to think twice and maybe three times before attempting to get into this specialized operational identity mode(s). You bailed yourself out and no doubt some of those in similar shoes."

"Whether doing deep cover or plainclothes work with your wisdom and stand-by-fellow-officers 'with-it' attitude. Such as Detective 1st Grade Tommy Dades, who heroically took on two detectives whose mistress got the best of them and they turned from undercover to not covering their own [Dades & Fischer, 2009]. Standing straight when called out, you stood by him too. Having lived through it all yourself you did what you had to do before they got hit by the wiseguys and others."

"On the other hand, I posit some wiseguys who would have perished without you taking them in when you did, and survived by your key intervention as a law enforcement officer in arresting them before they were classically whacked. You couldn't save them all, but you saved those who heard the bleating of slaughter and escaped the butcher's hatchet."

FBI AGENT JOSEPH DOMINICK PISTONE: "Yeah, look Doc, if you're not going to stand up for your own beliefs and yourself in the non-job-related real-life situations, then you're not going to stand up for yourself in deep-cover operations where real threat and death is thrown your way. I would agree that I did stand by my beliefs and that, as you set the record straight, did save lives if you think of what I did that way. I would agree with that. Does that make sense to you?"

COP DR DAN RUDOFOSSI: "Factually it does make superb sense to me. In fact, I know some law enforcement officers working for Joint District Attorney-PD offices, State Attorney General-PD offices, US Attorney offices, and State Police Criminal Investigative Units with backgrounds of family that were in La Cosa Nostra. Such officers 'regressed toward the mean' as we psychologists/psychiatrists would say, but most did not, thankfully."

"That regression means that most mere mortals return to being who they are by falling back in step and formation with where they came from in terms of family, culture, and religion. The ones I know went on to standing tough as outstanding investigators, even though the pull to return and regress at times was knocking on their memories and their path. They had it in them to model after heroes outside of their circle of birth and to embrace special agents as yourself to transcend their 'fate' as foreclosed. Choosing to be law enforcement officers instead was a real mental toughness, even when their assignments was OCCB [Organized Crime Control Bureau] to patrol officers. Integrity is a line that transcends types of assignments and details."

"In continuing from my other line of understanding your ingenuity and integrity in balancing all three identity modes as part of you as a whole person and special agent, it appears your point of being you included the fact that you were able to dance the tarantella with the wiseguys, the Charleston with the job of policing and law enforcement, and the waltz as a family man when you were allowed to return home over six years is unprecedented and therapeutic as in healing and saving lives as did Oskar Schindler no less who was deep cover and undercover. Save your personal integrity even as a private gentleman was never lost in the driven waves of temptation that inevitably also drew in many a great warrior. That is not a judgement on others, but again a remarkable achievement in a noetic dimension of being and becoming existentially centering your victory. It is a victory of heart and soul and also your example to transcend what becomes healing for others in this day and age when police and public safety are losing their moral compass and their sense of mental toughness to follow what they know is right in distinction to what is clearly wrong and not to be compromised. It was Abraham Lincoln who said, and I quote, 'Important principles may, and must be inflexible.'"

FBI AGENT JOSEPH DOMINICK PISTONE: "That is a good quote Dr Dan and conserves values and also tackles the demoralizing state good officers and special agents have to deal with when they are pushed under the bus of persuasion by media pundits and political considerations instead of setting the record straight. It is no accident nor pun that those who have chosen to move with the tide of coercion politically have fallen backwards and shot themselves in their own feet. Turning down the wrong path leads to being trapped. I hope my example keeps them straight in some ways, knowing as you are detailing and laying out as coordinates psychologically and existentially that which is possible in my history being told."

COP DR DAN RUDOFOSSI: "I think if we get others to understand your challenges in doing your operations with the integrity and sophistication you did and do with justice to you. The broad range of modeling is scaffolding and fluid for other unseemly and unlikely beneficiaries. Let me explain what I mean. Joe, for those you've arrested and even debriefed and worked up as potential informants as a credible expert, beyond reproach in my clinical view, was 'therapeutic.' By achieving the outcome of life, rather than getting whacked for wiseguys and some associates."

"In your masterpiece of unfinished business, assessment and credit unspoken about when you thwarted potentially young guys from becoming gangsters who would have joined up in the various families, but did not join up and is written and expressed between the lines. How many young potentials for wiseguy associates will think twice, and did and do as your example illustrated—crime does not pay in the long run, or even fast sprint."

"Your identity and heroism as viewed in the movie *Donnie Brasco* gave some guys who would have turned into eventual stone-cold killers some inspiration and a model from becoming disciplined and street-savvy cops. That tendency was there to do the right thing, but their own noetic dimension dimly lit. Every small flame holds a great light to set afire with passion as its fuel and reason as its sustenance. Your torch set young blue-blooded potential on fire with your way out of the wiseguy potential into a true-blue brother and sisterhood, in 'Its' place."

FBI AGENT JOSEPH DOMINICK PISTONE: "I did what I had to do, and I agree that led to some potential LEO's their ticket into a world of law enforcement rather than choosing what a life of crime would give them two slugs to the eyes and a lost hand and foot in concrete. I like the word 'therapeutic' in this context, for it is better than not to choose the LEO route, than the DOA slab."

COP DR DAN RUDOFOSSI: "As I gave the readers some background earlier in this interview when we discussed professor of law Michael Perlin posits therapeutic jurisprudence is when legal assessment to intervention can engender a healthier effect on the defendant's defense staff as much as the prosecution side—when knowledge and professionalism is applied to working up a case in a very humane manner as you did in educating those after the dust settled as best as you could humanely and with as much respect as could be afforded under the rubric of defense and prosecution jousting."

"Finally, you slowed the wheels of organized crime, single-handedly effecting cessation of hits and whack jobs from becoming reality for many potential victims in the wrong place and at the wrong time."

"In that way FBI Special Agent Joseph Pistone, as much as Donnie Brasco, you are pure marinara as you transformed your doubles as identity modes without transforming your deeper core sense of who you are with both insight and responsibility. In your case, the adaptive functional dissociation was used in your service here of rescue identity mode, as well Schindler who never became Jewish. In your case, you had to live the other identity of Donnie Brasco with the real Joseph Pistone in the shadows of the gangster identity mode, but you never lost touch with the inner core of in your words 'mental toughness' as the conscious and unconscious noetic dimension within you."

"Does that make sense to you, as my goal is to clarify my sense of your meaning of 'mental toughness' and 'wisdom' in a way that offers an interpretation that is sensible to you as well?"

FBI AGENT JOSEPH DOMINICK PISTONE: "Yeah, it is plausible. This is your clarification of reality as you see it Doc. It is not me that will argue with your interpretation. In fact, I think your clarification and interpretations uphold the integrity and tough-minded consistent approach I lived, not acted on, in Operation Donnie Brasco. But I did not pursue the goal of being any hero and especially not under the pressures Oskar Schindler had to endure by living in Nazi Germany."

COP DR DAN RUDOFOSSI: "You are the real-deal hero in Italian America society by some, but of course not all, as breaking the mold is always going to be criticized by those who dare not tread where you did and do, but make a living of criticizing others. I think transcending Italian American culture, for all law-abiding civilians, uniform members, and all human beings your heroism includes your ability to cultivate the wisdom of La Cosa Nostra without disrespecting the foundations of dos and don'ts and succeeding in keeping your moral compass as your navigational coordinates throughout the Donnie Brasco operation."

"I think of what we've worked on including you throwing a punch at a wannabe tough guy to save his life. Or you taking one or two punches for civilians so they would not endure the indignities and smarting countless hurts you did. In doing so, you calmed the beast in some notoriously hair-trigger rageful wiseguy such as Tony Mirra, who would without doubt have attacked and killed innocent family out-of-towners for crossing his lines with their own. That is out-of-towners who simply committed the crime of 'being on a phone too damn long' for the Don Mirra to tolerate in his abysmally low frustration tolerance."

"Many more examples could be sought. The fact you did what you could to break down the killing via civil wars that were about to rage. You gave intelligence a new meaning never known before in law enforcement circles as unique and life-saving. It is not you that ever was a rat, but it was you who actually ferreted out the rats within the families. Meaning the hardest-hit mafioso had clearly violated their own culture boundaries and strictures. That violation of the inviolate within their world meant death."

FBI AGENT JOSEPH DOMINICK PISTONE: "It is an interesting way of suggesting what could have been and would have been if the world was different than it was by suggesting my insertion saved lives. It is your background as a cop who is also a doc that does make sense that being undercover may have been a therapeutic intervention to some wiseguys and some potential bad guys by viewing my mental toughness as a stop-gap method. I even can smile at your hypotheses that saving a bad guy by having them redirect from being whacked by following my lead toward becoming witness protected and even imprisoned inmates."

"Interesting, very interesting. Again, you are saying that Doc, not me. But I do agree it makes sense of the nonsense said about me being the best actor by some other LEOs, or media pundits suggested in the past. It also gives some meaning I can agree with and even take comfort in as I am not as young as I was when this occurred a few decades ago."

COP DR DAN RUDOFOSSI: "The aging process is a hard pill to swallow for all of us, but dealing with the misunderstandings those assumptions and less-than-honest reviews of your challenges and your successes is one pill that this book promises to make palatable if I am doing right by you. Who you are has not changed in essence and your values are as timeless and as real as you were and will always be. What you did and resonates as done transcends the markings of time. Heroism to transcend one's rumors, slander as one's soul triumphs from vanquished to victor."

FBI AGENT JOSEPH DOMINICK PISTONE: "Yes, exactly, as the reducing of the truth is the fodder in which the unjust vanquish what is sensible, and will their way of thinking as if it is real while watching the values fought for as vanquished. I broke into the crime families and learned the way of the wiseguys to undo the hold on business and vices as the fuel to economize their will to power. The part not to be forgotten is each family member I worked with and broke bread with were human for many years. Being human does not disqualify one important fact I always kept in mind was that they were stone-cold killers as well. I did my job as best I could and with skill I learned as I moved along in my journey. Again, I had it inside me to do this job and I knew it."

COP DR DAN RUDOFOSSI: "If I am not off track, it was an inoculation you sought and you proffered to the law enforcement community the right dosages for infusion of the antidote you learned to titrate to the perfect level. That is captured in the formula you provided which is similar in depth and dimensionality to my assessment and intervention in complex trauma and complicated grief and dissociative disorders. I have stood by my own stance which is to proscribe definitive prescriptions to ensure treatments are retitrated to each ecological-ethological niche of survival motivation under the umbrella of real meaning and purpose, which can only be understood with one patient at a time. That does not mean general guidelines are not used, but without the differences each patient brings and what changes we are only grasping through a fog and hoping to hit an exact nerve that needs to be unhinged with deft precision."

FBI AGENT JOSEPH DOMINICK PISTONE: "I was an agent and I was good at it. I had done investigative work before in the United States Navy and I was good at it. I had moved from doing plainclothes investigations to doing deep cover. I was able to ingratiate myself with the wiseguys. When I was assigned a task to investigate a bank robbery, I did it to the very best of my ability and it just so happened I was asked to investigate the wiseguys. Not everyone has that knack to work undercover. You have to have that extra mental toughness and that extra bit of sense as we came to look at as police intuition, and I had that intuition; some just don't have and most don't in doing this job. I did it as I would any job I was given as a special agent. I did it for my love of being an FBI agent. I didn't do it because I wanted to take down drug gangs and I didn't do it because I wanted to take down Italians. Did you do it because you wanted to take down the mob? No. Let me qualify, I didn't want to take down the Italian mob. I wanted to take down the mob period due to the impact it had on innocent people. I am a law enforcement officer as you are and others who wear the shield."

COP DR DAN RUDOFOSSI: "You put it very well, not all can do the job you did as we worked on earlier in our interviews, and the fact is you had much to still do. Your masterpiece on deep cover, your book aptly titled *Unfinished Business*, for me includes the fact Lefty Ruggiero, if I got it right, was controlling and rigid in being the première type of old-school gangster who had another side which was his gambling or addictive personality trait. What we as psychologists would capture loosely here as a penchant for being obsessive compulsive in traits and also at the same time so tightly wired that when his penchant was sprung, he could spring forward as a recoiled wire—unwired and undaunted by reality's sting and recoil. Your ingenuity was as the musician and craftsman insofar as you allowed him to play his Rossini's *Barber of Seville* and also tightened his strings with just enough bounce to let him score his tune but not enough to let him let him sing as a canary and get swallowed by the fat tom-cats on the fence waiting to swipe on him?"

FBI AGENT JOSEPH DOMINICK PISTONE: "I'm not sure this has ever been covered anywhere and with us before, unsure if this goes along with your thought process on what we are analyzing. But I never disclosed the Milwaukee discovery to the Bonanno capos that Conte was found out to be a special agent by Balistrieri as the capo of that family. I knew that if the shit hit the fan I didn't want to be blamed for that exposure within the family as allowing that leak. I didn't want to be blamed; it was their decision, that it was Lefty and Mike's decision, not mine but theirs. When the bureau was informed, I was very tough in my decision-process-making choices here, and I was not going to risk the entire operation with a guy I didn't know well enough such as Conte and also to take the decision-making away from Lefty and Mike as to how to engineer this alliance, but as you pointed out correctly, it was my blueprint to achieve this alliance as I was in 1,000 percent to get this operation Donnie Brasco achieved. I did know Conte and so I dropped a call to Lefty and told him I know a guy from ten years ago and he's okay and no comment, so I plant a seed and that this guy I know from ten years ago reached out to me. I laid another seed, the guy I know from ten years ago called me again and told me he had a good business going and Lefty tells me he can't do a vending business, Donnie, as they'll blow him up [Special Agent Conte]. So, Lefty, hearing the area of Milwaukee, perks up and to full attention as I pick up his interest. I tell him he's trying to open up a vending business and it's stretched over a month and he's got some trucks, he got some machines, and he got his office, and he can't put machines in because he knows and told me the mob will blow him up. Lefty then asks me does he have any money; you know, real money with him. Did you ask him, Donnie? I said no, Lefty, I didn't push it and ask him. Lefty then says to me, well ask him and let me know. I get back to Lefty a few days later and I let him know when he asks again, he does have money, he says he has 100,000 in the bank at this time besides the machines and trucks and office. He says to me go out there and meet with him [Conte]. I do and I come back and again he questions me and I let him know, yeah Boss, he has the office, two trucks, and the machines to put out there. Lefty then says, okay let's go out there to Milwaukee and we meet with the boss, Mike Sabella, and Lefty lets him know now all I know and found out for Lefty. Then Lefty and I go out there to Milwaukee with Mike Sabella giving us the go on the trip. We come back and let Mike Sabella know that Conte has ten years of working with the Bonanno family, an associate of the Bonanno family. You know I did the same thing with the family from Florida with Don Trafficante himself. I let them do the prodding and pushing after I sowed one slow seed at a time to see if I was correct, and after I planted my seed it sprouted, but it was on their time for if it went south, it was not me that did it but my bosses that did it, and I did their bidding for them and their own ideas, it was not mine. I again insulated myself as much as I could by having ten years of not seeing Conte so if they were to take any risks it would be their dish being served hot or cold as they preferred to move forward, backward, or gently explore—but under all possibilities and circumstances it was their own choice and not mine"

COP DR DAN RUDOFOSSI: "If I have it right, Joe, in our speaking frankly here, you were able to lay down and engineer a lattice of protection for you and full accountability for the different capos you bridged as an alliance. The point is since they made these decisions so far after you could vouch for Conte that if any mishap happened and it did alas, it was Balistrieri as the Milwaukee boss and Mike Sabella and Lefty Ruggiero that has a sit-down and meeting so to speak and therefore, they were fucked if the deal was fugazy. But they were fucked twice over if it didn't work because you ensured they knew well in advance how precarious this waltz was potentially as a disguised tarantella. You Socratically did this to them and paradoxically you coasted their reality and placed in their own heads within their personal schemas. You got them to believe it was his own ideas and schemas as Sabella was the Bonanno captain here, and Sonny was the capo in the Florida angle. It was the layout as a template that worked so well in developing the outcome and plan in laying it all out. The effectiveness is the mettle of success as you were spared when Conte was identified and surreptitiously was closed down without the repercussions which if less well planned and integrated in the actual operation as you masterfully did would include you and your boss here and in Milwaukee and Florida not being with us today?"

FBI AGENT JOSEPH DOMINICK PISTONE: "Yes, Doc Dan, if I had vouched for this guy and said he is good and you can trust with him with a handshake and proverbial kiss to the boss and sealed the deal, I would have been killed and taken out for that mistake of saying he is not fugazy and hundred percent okay to work with."

COP DR DAN RUDOFOSSI: "You had to navigate through the minefields of these wiseguys, and if I got it right, what happened to Sonny Black Napolitano for extending his trust to you would have ironically, in a cruel twist, could have happened to you. Point blank exit. The real firing pin clicking if they discovered it was you who set this up as the fall guy. You would have for sure without room for doubt have taken the fall. [G–d forbid a million times.] Your mental toughness and realistic appraisal were on point to counter-point, reclaiming your own identity and life purpose."

FBI AGENT JOSEPH DOMINICK PISTONE: "Right, exactly Doc. As I said, 'mental toughness' is surviving in the ecology of the wiseguy culture. The fact you can be whacked in a heartbeat never took away from accepting your job is doing it with integrity as I always did."

Summary

The one area sadly unexplored in police psychology and criminology alike is the impact of individual genius to create a punctuation in counter-terrorism and counter-intelligence professionals. Joe Pistone's genius lay hidden under the layers of his groundbreaking work. His intuitive empathic synchronization within the varied Mafia families was not spontaneous. Joe Pistone was challenged on many fronts, not just one: personality differences, ecological-ethological niche diversity, and dos and don'ts that shift in the melee of variations. It was not just the Bonanno family but the other families Joe Pistone had to survive within, but impacted throughout in varying and important ways as beneficent.

On one hand, Joe's creative edge was surfeited by constant strain for survival by using toughness or resilience, piqued and proactive toward adaptation on his own. There is no class for Creativity 101 for agents. As we will learn again with Joe, his own ingenuity to survive and adapt helped him achieve insight into assimilation and accommodation to many unknowns.

Intelligence as a Triangular Cap—Uncorked: Psyche, Poesies, and Pragmatic Creativity

The circle of intelligence, best expressed by former American Psychological President Robert Sternberg (Sternberg, 2013), is captured by Frank Sinatra's, how 'I wear my cap' with the acronym of CAP.

C for Creativity for solving problems
A for Analytic problem identification
P for Pragmatic field and strategic adaptations

William James's pioneering work on exceptional intelligence as being a product of individuals and their own creative ingenuity as a cause to revolutions in thinking may be complemented by modifying Ernest Haeckel's theorem as a biologist and professor, as I have in an introductory textbook in forensic and police psychology, as follows.

Professor Rudofossi's "Aphorism about ingenuity in science: Human evolution 'ontogeny recapitulates phylogeny,' " taught by the evolutionary biologist Professor Ernest Haeckel, remains poignant. What is meant by Dr. Haeckel is that any individual member of a species develops along certain ecological (nurturing) and ethological (survival niches) shaped by the factors unique to his/her individual experiences. Professor Dr. Rudofossi posits a complementary hypothesis as follows (Rudofossi, 2017; Rudofossi & Maloney, 2019): phylogenic development is radically altered by ontogenetic charismatic genius. Pause and reflect on an anomaly as ingenuity and being a rare break with normative development. "Genius" applied and used well is anomalous. Individual genius (ontogeny) that is charismatic may alter a society by a quantum jump that punctuates human evolution. It does this by influencing ecological and ethological development in ways that over time alters cultural paths. The example of psychoanalysis suffices to illustrate the point that the influence of original (genius) and his/her seminal ideas coupled with the biography of a charismatic intense genius qualitatively presents evidence of changing society's perception and even outcomes on global levels of development. (Ontogeny as anomalous genius arguably can devolve a society in paths tried and failed with devastating results, as in Hitler's fascism, Goebbels' propaganda, and Goering's egomania.) Ontogeny can assist evolving society by eco-ethologically altering the trajectory of how societies treat the mentally ill and mentally disabled humanely by conservation of wisdom using, for example, existential analysis in novel approaches.

With this modification of Haeckel's theorem for phylogenic evolution came a recapitulation of phylogenic development; predictably the anomaly of Joe Pistone is the foundation for the pulls and pushes where culture, personality, and one's place in deep cover created a craft worthy of change and insight responsibly. Joe Pistone's averting collisions that could derail success was by understanding three mistresses' unique and competitive rivalry as the dos and don'ts of crime, crime stopping, and private and public sensibility. The forceful political and subcultural motif being directly torpedoed was averting collusion by sacrificing his values and the core of wisdom. The power of Joe Pistone's diplomatic wisdom was used against the force of the tides of different cultures by mastering the confluence of each with one another and his centering as the conduit. If we look at it, his confluence of navigating the needs of the different worlds is the opposite of a cacophony. Punctuating static convalescence of not going further into the belly of the underground crime syndicate was Special Agent Joe Pistone's novel approach as wisdom catalytically igniting a hidden revolution in the art, craft, and, arguably, science behind the psychology of counter-espionage.

Seeking wisdom in places such as organized crime helped navigate coordinates to unravel its secrets and to effectively dismantle its impact. Operation Donnie Brasco did just that as the novel emergence of the craft of ingenuity that shadowed Joseph Pistone.

Cop Doc Corner for Students Only—Debriefing

It is important, and I did explain in a collegial and educational manner not pedagogical, that Special Agent Joe Pistone understood the concept of "cognitive dissonance" and "motivational interviewing" before it was introduced to the public forum. Harry Stack Sullivan's method of interviewing and assessment without any prior learning was used to bridge the contradictions and polemics which could yield an equation of death for disrespecting some of the notorious cold-blooded killers including Tony Mirra if that fluid emotional and cognate transcendental unconscious was not piqued in the shield of what Agent Pistone has shared as "tough mindedness" in his boundary setting from the onset. This is again more evidence I am not shy of drawing and characterizing as genius, the mirroring of Joe's inner world as expressed to me over our drawn and unveiled sessions and interviews. For those of you who remember the television show *Columbo*, this ace detective supervisor was a bumbling type of intellectual who with full intention pretending to be less astute than he was, would allow the vulnerability of his quarry which were criminal predators to be identified. Lt. Columbo's discrimination skills as to who was the prey and predator, in a hidden manner identified and targeted the predator while saving the prey where possible in the nick of time that brief window allowed. Lt. Columbo's success is being always present but hardly noticeable as a threat, hence he was invited deeper and without boundaries until his case was woven. Like Socrates questioning modestly and gently, he opened the most rigid, cloistered, and closed shut doors. It is not dummying it down perhaps, as much as allowing the other side to open up. The armor we all wear whether wiseguy or a guy with wisdom is sensible, and ethologically makes superb sense. Why then do we not disclose our truest thoughts and motivations to others?

Only a fool would weave the thread of their truth without knowing the other party truly is invested in one's own interest too, for otherwise, what would stop him from sidestepping you and me if it benefited him or her?

We are talking about organized crime here, and although this is not a terrorist organization, it is crucial to realize that the fabric of all criminal activity and terrorism is at some level organized crime. Any organization that is criminal needs to protect itself in the steel wires of secrecy and stealth. To break through by tactics of forward physical entry into criminal organizations, although they offer temporary salves and dramatic solutions for a public desiring quick fixes, the answers are not permanent. The solution to organized crime in such tactics holds little solvency and almost no understanding. It is this piece that Joe Pistone educated us so well in this chapter, with a gentle tugging and interpretation that creates a window into a process that transcends the dynamics of his case and his intervention. I never felt or do feel as if my being a cop doc or professor offers more wisdom than Joseph Dominick Pistone, but more so, as two colleagues and he being the pilot. I learn and hopefully disseminate Joe Pistone's mind as field and map to navigate as metaphor and tangible markings for the brave agents who embark on such ventures as he did and to fellow students of the mind and doctors of the mind as well.

It is clear to me that the wisest of all academic universes will have some dean stop, pause, and award Joseph Dominick Pistone an honorary doctorate in criminology and forensic psychology as warranted here. But that is up to some chair and dean with the wisdom to deliver soon—for time whisks by as a tyrant—taking hold of each of us too fast and swiftly—save Joe Pistone's and my own favorite counter-point, there go I, but for the Grace of G-d, go I."

Important Definitions and Concepts to Keep in Mind

Heuristic exploration

Heuristic exploration, as applied in this chapter and book, is the decision to observe, note, and try to understand an event, an ecological niche, survival motivation, and nuance of culture that is unknown. In doing so, working hypotheses as a means of gaining intelligence softens the tendency to cover over one's mistakes by glossing them, rather than redirecting. As a deep cover, this humility in Donnie Brasco and Joe Pistone was a lifesaving approach. Due to unknown variables in doing an operation as complex as infiltration, heuristic approaches must be the measure of approach. The least dangerous and more controllable aspect of approach is always the best option. An applied police wisdom to the uninitiated is it's better to get to the emergency job in one piece, rather than never to get there in pieces as haste translates into chaos at best and death in the worst scenario.

Active analysis

Active analysis as presaged and used in its earliest form was the doctor of the mind as psychoanalyst framing the therapy and assessment in the context of reversal of identities. This was accomplished by Dr. Sandor Ferenczi's ingenious method of having the patient become the doctor and the doctor to free associate his/her clinical problems which, of course, was the patient repositioned as the therapist (Ferenczi, 1988). From here the patient was in a way provoked into formulating solutions clinically to assist his/her doctor and alleviating the censoring and stigma of being stuck in a patient identity mode. Invariably, this method helped and was further refined by other creative and generative clinicians over the century to follow.

Phylogenic development—ontogenetic charismatic genius

In Haeckel's formulation, the idea is that all species' development and growth is gradual. Dr. Haeckel suggested that the evolution of a species, or even a cultural group, is impacted by the individual's development. The individual development is cast in the mold of the majority of participants in that society; variations are of course accounted for, and slowly and gradually shift more novel changes that are rewarding and reinforced as productive into the societal structure and function. In the author's account, the genius of one individual unfolding creates and generatively offers a major shift as potentialities that become actualized as time moves forward. It is this author's opinion that Joseph Dominick Pistone has punctuated the work of deep cover, infiltration, intelligence gathering, and potentialities to a greater depth and breadth than prior to his entering and actively applying his genius to the myriad problems and solutions as identified as a special agent of the FBI.

Regressed toward the mean—capitulation to original deviancy

Here, and in an applied manner, it is nice to believe that deep cover will continue to grow by exponential leaps and bounds. The reality is that such growth is rare and is gradually covered over by the mundane leg and muscle work of daily undercover and intel gathering as achieved by the cadres of LEOs in the field of plainclothes and uniformed officers. The original deviancy here is meant the usual violence and territorial aggression in the militia and police eco-ethological niches. The weight of average and mundane performance has a natural pull toward the mean in regard to probability and clinical insight and will eventually give in to the deviancy from excellence and exceptional performance as regression and capitulation.

Abysmal low frustration tolerance—aggression

Low frustration tolerance is the resistance against frustration as intolerable. The irrational premises from a cognitive thought process and behavioral level of action by self-appraisal of a situation being intolerable lead to withdrawal from the situations that can provoke and promote growth in that very individual. Emotional and consequential factors of low frustration tolerance include the experience of raised levels of depression, aggression, anxiety, and addictive behaviors. These dysfunctional thoughts, behaviors, and emotional results all lead to further decline on a mental and physical health dimensional scale. In cases as described with Tony Mirra, the abysmal low frustration tolerance led to extreme aggression against innocent people that he ran into by intent or accident that disagreed with him on a personal or profession level as a gangster capo.

High frustration tolerance—infiltration propensities

In the case of Special Agent Joseph Dominick Pistone, I discovered with him that his high frustration tolerance is also another hidden dimension in his quintessential cohesive gestalt wholeness and wellness as an LEO to be able to handle the immense and enormous overload of stress and strain to become Donnie Brasco wannabe wiseguy to made wiseguy in the Bonanno crime family. It is the persistent high level of frustration tolerance during six long years of infiltration as endogenous and propensities within, not intermittent tolerance of frustration, that yielded such impressive operational and legal results for prosecutors: Joe Pistone's infiltration did and remains a legacy of Special Agent Pistone's infiltration propensities; among such unique propensities are his extraordinarily high frustration tolerance.

Addictive personality traits

Addictive personality traits include the tendency to form habits in the areas of overindulgence and the biopsychosocial pull toward alcoholism, drug addiction, and violence. Social process addictions include gambling, flirty to sexual compulsive behaviors, pornography, and even ritualization of death and destructive derivatives of Destrudo or destructive drives. Such addictive traits as smoking, gambling, and violence were replete in Benjamin Lefty Ruggiero. It undergirds some clinical disorders such as obsessive-compulsive disorder, alcohol use disorder, and intermittent anger explosive disorder to name a few. Note addictions are unusually difficult to extinguish completely and are prolific in LEOs and organized crime members.

Conceptual and Writing Exercises for Student and Professor Only

1. In reviewing the film and book *Schindler's List*, please compare the risks and the gain in doing deep cover for Schindler. Although Pistone's deep cover is different, do compare the risks and gains in doing deep cover for Pistone. Discuss the implications and importance of heroism and sacrifice for the sake of innocent others, and where the heart of deep cover converges and diverges.
2. Peter Blatty, a brilliant and polemical artist and author, incorporated what we have worked on as active analysis as conceptualized by Dr. Sandor Ferenczi in which the clinician becomes the patient and patient becomes the clinician (Ferenczi, 1988). In his original work, in which he explores Father Karis as a resistant exorcist who, in the real case, deals with a possession in a young boy, he is ultimately placed in the crossroad of exchanging his life for the boy's to ensure his congregant's life. In his next work, which is perhaps his most creative and less known, he integrates active analysis in what he called *The Ninth Configuration*. The protagonist is a cached identity and his psychiatrist who sets out to heal him of overwhelming trauma and acting out that has become hidden under layers of his deepest levels of existential unconscious repression. Gaining access to the film and book will take initiative. The challenge is to seek the conflict that the colonel/doctor has to overcome in treating a number of recalcitrant and very resistant patients. Is this process explained as role playing and understood as identity dissociative disorder, or is it understood much better and with sensibility via dissociative processes as identity modes and an *Eco-Ethological Existential Analysis*? Explain how and why. Use Rudofossi's model and in doing so use references in Kitaeff (2019), Rudofossi & Maloney (2019), and Rudofossi (1997, 2007, 2017).

References

Conroy, D., & Orthmann, C. H. (2014). *Surviving a law enforcement career: A guide for cops and those who love them*. Rosemont, MN: Innovative Systems.

Dades, T., & Fischer, D. (2009). *Friends of the family: The inside story of the mafia cops*. New York: Harper and Collins.

Ferenczi, S. (1988). *The clinical diary of Sandor Ferenczi*. Edited by Judith Dupont. Cambridge, MA: Harvard University Press.
Frankl, V. (1979). *The unheard cry for meaning: Psychotherapy and humanism*. New York: Simon and Schuster.
Gardner, H. (1993). *Multiple intelligences: The theory in practice*. New York: Basic Books.
Gilmartin, K. (2002). *Emotional survival for law enforcement*. Arizona: E-S Press.
Goleman, D. (2005). *Emotional intelligence: Why it can matter more than IQ*. New York: Bantam.
Kitaeff, J. (2019). *The handbook of police psychology* (2nd ed.). New York: Routledge.
Perlin, M. L. (1994). *The jurisprudence of the insanity defense*. Durham, NC: University of North Carolina Press.
Rudofossi, D. M. (1997). *The impact of trauma and loss on affective differential profiles of police officers*. Bell Harbor, MI: Bell and Howell.
Rudofossi, D. M. (2007). *Working with traumatized police-officer patients: A clinician's guide to complex PTSD syndromes in public safety officers*. New York & London: Routledge.
Rudofossi, D. M. (2017). *Cop doc: The police psychologist's casebook—narratives from police psychology*. New York & London: Routledge.
Rudofossi, D. M., & Maloney, M. (2019). *Aborigine trail: Trails, travail, and triumph using psychology with Aborigine police*. Amherst, NY: Teneo Press.
Sternberg, R. J. (2013). *The evolution of intelligence*. New York: Psychology Press.

6
DIALOGUE, INSIGHT, AND DISCOVERY—A CANOPY OF SHADOWS AND HUES

"Understanding depends only on the making of distinctions."
Attributed to Professor Moses C. Luzzatto

Introduction

Discernment is a key that facilitates success with tasks that range from fully articulated to almost unformed. What distinguishes success is knowing the right path to walk in. To distinguish such paths as the right path, one must know the wrong path to avoid. While gray is a wonderful analog to dimensionality on multiple levels, it can be an austere and an insipid color. Black and white distinctions are sometimes not only preferable but necessitated in the most human causes from start to finish. Chiaroscuro was the use of black and white for clear abstract art in the first of such type of art, as Pissarro well knew. Color can be condensed and contracted with more punch with exacting small attention to detail rather than larger looming vistas alone. As we will note, both the larger vista and the exacting minutiae may build the soundest foundations in distinct ways.

The ability to use discernment and even discrimination is not a negative pejorative quality but one in which choices determine outcome based on the best option among many that becomes deliberate and mindfully chosen. Professor Luzzatto keys in on this fact in applying the quality of limits to make real gains and succor success in real risky situations such as deep cover in which a strong declaration of limitations and options creates effective solutions and ultimately the best solution. For example, nowadays, as a pandemic such as SARS-CoV-2 (COVID-19) breaks out in novel manners as a terror cell gone viral—no pun intended—as scientists sifted through multiple hypotheses heuristically in proposing an antidote, not one but multiple possibilities led to a discriminating eye to select the best choice of many antidotes deemed possible. Not all antidotes prove effective. Some antidotes are discarded as junk science, some are avoided as worse—such as pernicious and deadly antidotes that are iatrogenic. The key of discernment is we need a vaccine and treatment with alacrity. Life and death hang in the balance of the scales between *discernment* as *distinguishing which* direction, path to take, with *what style* of intensity and *how much* effort is necessary.

DOI: 10.4324/9781032202761-7

Pause and take a deep breath for a moment now. You got the point well. Life and death are in the balance for all of us. But what does this have to do with the ingenuity of a legendary sleuth and his antidotes to organized crime?

It has everything to do with Professor Pistone. Professor Pistone is a good title since he teaches colleagues with a minimum of a college-level education in how to do detective work at its best. Agent Pistone's inimitable understanding of the culture of the Mafia, his day-to-day sleuthing and intelligence gathering, and the ecological niche where survival motivation was tested to the hilt while he maintained his "mental toughness" in all its dimensions is given in a distilled dialogue and elixir to follow!

Professor Pistone's educating you as the reader had begun chapters ago, with our narrative analysis. Through dialogue you were brought in as a witness to view Joseph Pistone's discernment: his choices between good and bad, what worked and didn't work, ranging from near misses to near-perfect results. No step-by-step guide existed to shape the impact of desirable goals and outcome. But it is the outcome and the durability of outcomes that remain the true judge of the worthiness of choices one makes. The tyranny of time is the judge and jury as to what impact an operation has. Time tests an operation's durability and reliability. The impact on organized crime and infiltration by Special Agent Joseph Dominick Pistone remains unapparelled in innovation, courage to test the limits of infiltration, and lasting success. This is no easy task. It is the insight and discovery of the very human being under the cover of law enforcement and, surprisingly, even wiseguy culture. To the tenured street cop, detective, and ranking member of law enforcement, it is not a surprise that under the wiseguy's toughest exterior lay some wisdom, and even qualities that offer hope in the tragic layers of our lives, and ultimate death.

Questions to Guide You as Navigational Tools: Learning Objectives

1. In the shadows of deep cover and law enforcement, agents/police doing their infiltration which leads to street crime units by whatever new name they are called—who and why are those with no experience in the real mores, totems, and taboos of the crime syndicate making judgments on how and when to interdict to break down hubs of major crimes against civilians and citizens who are innocent?
2. Does the overcontrolling of language, culture, and nuances lead to more violence and black markets underground by supporting some drug lords and organized crime figures while vanquishing others unwittingly due to not being able to modernize and cache their criminal activity?
3. If the oversight administratively of operations such as Donnie Brasco was curtailed and never allowed to fit into overly naive restrictions due to civil rights of criminal suspects, what is afforded in beneficence to those qualified and competent to fight crime by infiltration and gathering effective intelligence to fuel and guide the very operations that curtail freedom, to say nothing of the health and wellness of frontline law enforcement officers who risk life and limb and suffer the greatest violation of civil rights which is death by crime syndicate bosses?
4. Is the insight and discovery that the antidote for the worst societal strains and cultural challenges includes realizing it is not in legislating morality but in living with the fallibility of errors, messy outcomes, and lessons derived in each operation from the onset to its conclusion?
5. Is it worthwhile gaining as much learning via experience and wisdom by looking at sources of intelligence as coming from agents, detectives to counter-offensives in ecological-ethological niches at a more refined level?

6. Do the aspects of discernment, including the ability to discriminate between one method and another, one approach in distinction from another, lead to greater success than trying to correct each approach to fit a preformulated methodology rather than a heuristic exploration from the field research which is what has yielded the greatest success as scientists and practitioners from Aristotle forward?

Key Terms

Map as metaphor
Quantum psychic moment of trauma

Uncertainty Principle and Experimenter Effect

In moving forward to meet Joe Dominick Pistone as the FBI special agent to infiltrate the Mafia Bonanno family, we will work on chaining his fierce ability to discriminate on a number of levels from the dross of chimeras presented as real dragons from the tigers that play as if they are paper mâché and have teeth and fangs that can excoriate flesh and blood from bones. We will flesh out the bare bones that fit together and generate the hidden skeletal structure of Agent Pistone's eco-ethological mastery. The flesh, sinew, and process are held together by the vistas of what is the interstitial process of the existential analysis. Looking at the full picture, or *gestalt*, we will embark on an *Eco-Ethological Existential Analysis* of Pistone's deep cover where structure and function as an analog to anatomy and physiology of his unique craft is responsively sketched. We continue exploring the initiation rites toward being and becoming *Donnie Brasco wiseguy identity mode* as part of his *adaptive functional dissociative process*.

FBI AGENT JOE DOMINICK PISTONE: "Doc, as a special agent using what you have identified as my gangster identity mode, I had to become a petty jewel thief. I learned as I apprenticed to Jilly of the Columbo family. I proved myself. Remember that punk of a gangster was bartering for a fugazy [fake] to Lefty Benjie Ruggiero. He was taken aback by my ability to figure out the real deal from the fake veneer as the dude was playing him a fool. In my move in and timed well, I was able to alter Lefty's view of me. Lefty had an extraordinary memory and it stuck within his mind's bank that I was a capable. Most important, it initiated Lefty knowing I was loyal to him as a future wiseguy associate under his watch, so to speak."

COP DR DAN RUDOFOSSI: "It is beyond interesting as to how you learned to discern the fugazy from the real diamond. The chutzpah to confront the fugazy issue with Lefty as a made guy in the Bonanno family is to me worth pausing on and about. It reminds me of the business dealer who learns his blue diamond resembles the Wittelsbach diamond. But, distinguishing between a blue diamond and the Wittelsbach diamond as the proffered article succors his confidence and trust at the same time. Your expertise is doubly important because his security assurance expert must discriminate between fraudulent illusion in the product being sold in distinction to the authentic diamond being sought. Your detection, unlike the security assurance expert, was done in the boiler room of the city bars and under the intense scrutiny of a hypervigilant boss as Lefty was and in the context of the whole business affair being messy, uncontrolled, and chaotic as a crime scene. Equanimity and balance were maintained, as I understand, by you discerning what was a snow flake in the Mojavi desert. To me, you not being an expert or experienced in this field of gemology is extraordinary. You learned the field you were engineering in simultaneously with the field of espionage you were adaptively functioning in: bull's-eye on target! Does that make sense to you?"

FBI AGENT JOE DOMINICK PISTONE: "That makes sense as the bull's-eye focuses on the center of survival motivation. What I mean is, what works as the most effective measure. The ability to distinguish what is hidden from most other observers depends on the field as the ecological piece in this puzzle. Paying attention to the clues, the cues, and dynamics in your own area where you are infiltrating forces you to understand the specific symbols, signals, and hints that are clear and those not so clear and unnoticed. That discrimination between one and the other is crucial. So, knowing the difference is anything but chance and luck when dealing with a two-bit punk trying to scam Lefty Benjie Ruggiero."

COP DR DAN RUDOFOSSI: "Confronting the 'two-bit punk' in his culture was a choice. Your choice, if I am getting it right, that that could have ended in a homicide of this dude. This dude that crossed the line with Lefty by defrauding a made wiseguy in the Bonanno family!"

"But, if I am on point here, save your deft appreciation and discriminatory skills in truly understanding and salving Lefty's criminally violent vendetta side, the dude took a mild beating to prevent him being homicided by Lefty's five .38 slugs. Pausing as each subsequent choice you made consciously weighted down with unconscious dynamics lent themselves toward keying in on your own gangster identity mode known as Donnie Brasco, surviving ethologically in Lefty's ecological niche in his own unique world. That world had to become part of yours."

FBI AGENT JOE DOMINICK PISTONE: "It is totally on point. Detective work is not acting in the role as we established but living the identity you must live as a gangster if you are to succeed as a deep cover. Simply another notch on Lefty's belt is the two-bit punk's life. This never deters the pinheads who call police wrongly and target labels they project onto us. Hey, we are the good guys and gals with experience and that experience counts. I got the sense streetwise and moved forward as you said, heuristically, with a strong foundation but still in uncharted waters. I always kept in mind the risks, but took them not as a risk taker, but when I had too. Sensibly."

"But it gets to me that those with no experience as cops, or cop docs try to rewrite our culture. They get their wisdom from a penned quote. Yeah, it sounds right, but it is usually dead wrong. For example, suppose I didn't drop the two-bit punk a few pushes and a good punch or two, he would have been laid out for a wake and the end was imminent. So, for me Doc, as for you. The answer is, some wise street cops and I imagine wiseguys would agree on is, a pinhead ought to stay out of heady decision-making and have the humility to understand that fine point I am making. Quote radical man the rad man and let agents and police be the judges of their own work so civilians stay safe and well and never have to deal with the evil and messes they make and we clean up quietly and efficiently!"

COP DR DAN RUDOFOSSI: "Your point is well made! Your point of real definition, discrimination between real-deal police service and incompetence, as much as between junk science and real science and insight! 'Why' is an important question, and as investigators of crime and doctors of the mind and soul we are required to do so! Make sense in persistent and dogged pursuit of the why, whether unconscious or conscious, for even in partial answers we are left wiser and can apply wisdom rather than drift into our own illusions about how things should be. Let's find out why, and then figure out the best way to effect change!"

FBI AGENT JOE DOMINICK PISTONE: "I'll tell you why! I will repeat 'why?' a hundred and one times until it is understood by those who chose to rough it out with me. Integrity is carved out of loads of bull's leftovers that confuse, distort, and subvert reality as it truly is."

COP DR DAN RUDOFOSSI: "Agree, completely! How can my students, peers, and others learn if we do not give them the real doses they need to think critically about, the real-deal work done and the cost it tallies at the end of the tour of duty? It is your ability to hold on to your own values. The moral map you got in your head where no established map offers the proper path. The hints that help you look at the picture before it is ever sketched."

FBI AGENT JOE DOMINICK PISTONE: "Yeah. You see in all the years since I've finished my work, not only do they not seek my experience to select informants at times—these questions you're asking and we are working at answering are long buried and done. But these are very important questions, the 'why?' for administrators and legislators who snap judgments at law enforcement. They judge often too fast and incorrectly without getting the information necessary and knowing who did what and, as you emphasize, why. Hopefully the administrators will learn to have the humility to read this book too. In my mind, many are students as they don't have the experience, but as some students without wisdom, they too can be so cocky and not admit they are students too! You reminded me in the questions about why that there was no map pledged to paper, none for me to follow." [Undercurrent of grin emerging and relief shared.] "Hey, Doc, answer me, how can a pin-map coordinate the next move, except by acting like a pinhead?"

COP DR DAN RUDOFOSSI: "Forgive me, Special Agent Joe Pistone. Your analogy deserves another complementary one. Mine asks of the doe and stag alike, discernment divorced from politics and anthropomorphic assessment—like field police tactics—is what creates messy outcomes, can create life once you get down to what counts and what doesn't. Just as nature allows for all the varied expressions and rituals that sensibly perpetuate a species, so we may want to slow down and listen to the wisdom you gradually offer rather than reduce and simplify what is complex into rigid and turgid formulas as far as what I am learning. I am learning from you as the expert agent guiding and educating me as to what works and does not, is the grasp of not being a pinhead, with a pin-map—pinned down! You are creating the map as metaphor and not the metaphor as a map with linear algorithms of do a, b, and c, but rather let's see the seventy-plus-one way to explore the c, b, a's and leave each as potential not boxed-in maps with one option and one rigid guide."

FBI AGENT JOE DOMINICK PISTONE: "My strategy was to learn and survive in emerging ecologies and niches using your way of thinking and capturing the unknowns. My survival needs depended on knowing the individual soldiers and bosses from non-associates to associates and family wiseguy members. In some cases, as you know from my books and our talks, I was forced to gain intimacy with. What I mean is, I prefer to do a thousand other things than sit in my bathing suit with wiseguys and sip drinks and smell cigarette smoke all day and night. To be honest, they were not my preference, but I had a job to do and you learn to do as you must. I had to discriminate between what I wanted to do and I did to get the job done right."

COP DR DAN RUDOFOSSI: "Your point is subtle, but again discerning in wisdom. Discrimination is not bias, as we have worked out in the context in which you are suggesting. It is a good point and it is not downgrading or condescending toward another person. Discrimination is choosing quality over uncommonly bad sense."

FBI AGENT JOE DOMINICK PISTONE: "Let me give you an example of how doing things that work is a necessity at times and not a preference as well. So, making money for one's bosses is nothing new. But, taking one's self-earned cash and paying your boss's salary from your own earnings is different and is not strange to the Mafia world. It is new to most who learn of this habit of the syndicate! To me who joined up as an associate it was learning and moving in the ropes made as boundaries. That is discriminating between what I may prefer and what I learned as absolutely necessary in that culture outside of liking it, or not. Capish?"

COP DR DAN RUDOFOSSI: "Capito! I understand and I appreciate the education myself without changing your perspective and ingenuity in saying it as it was and is! That is in the Mafia culture as an ecological niche in which adaptation ethologically counts and here the survival affordance is appreciating the subtle changes in economics if I got it right?"

FBI AGENT JOE DOMINICK PISTONE: "Correct, economics is part of the skills I learned in the Mafia families. Not only one, but especially the Bonanno family. One major measure of success in the Mafia is earning money, take the money earned, and move it upwards in La Cosa Nostra to one's immediate boss. Secondly, and subtly, you then move along and gain momentum by rank and hierarchy as cash and tangible power moves forward and up the ranks. Third is you as an associate move up to the degree you can as well. If you are Sicilian then even more so. Understanding that set of rules and hierarchical set-up may be discrimination, but as you put it, it's not a bad word and in science it gives us a vantage point of understanding as well."

COP DR DAN RUDOFOSSI: "I think from an adaptive point of view the Mafia world and its logic defies the logic of the world at large and collides with the micro-management style of our world as law enforcement officers. That experience at first is counter-intuitive and discomforting."

FBI AGENT JOE DOMINICK PISTONE: "Well put Professor Rudofossi, but such upward flow of money earned and then taking off a percentage as agreed and paying your boss and him not paying you is the beginning. Your boss is expecting higher, and better pay-offs as a natural progression marks the realistic appraisal of the criminal syndicate's way of surviving. You express this as the ecological-ethological niche as an agent you will infiltrate. In doing so then you learn to do all this in order to survive and move up the ranks in their world, the world of the gangster."

"It is in their eco-ethological niche of the gangster and their world that you must survive and gain ground to get ahead. Being able to discriminate means not falling through the web of demands and services required. It is not on your timeline and convenience, but on their demands and call to do what it is they expect you to do. So, to repeat, discrimination is crucial as none of the ways of the wiseguy are even remotely like the regular normal world and people outside the syndicate. Most different is the world of law enforcement and law enforcement officers."

COP DR DAN RUDOFOSSI: "Regular people and the normal world is not the gangster world as I knew vaguely, and you've enriched my knowledge fully. It makes me think of what Professor Abraham Maslow called 'potentiality' [Maslow, 1971]. In sum, potentiality is a rich term and perhaps a bridge to use and help understand your experiences. Potentiality means the success is intuited and risk taken as possibility, not definite results. Probable positive results occur where success can be measured in outcomes in the field of experience."

"Field wisdom can only move without a prescription set in formulas like algorithms. Wisdom that is practical and emotionally 'with-it' lays the path for others in law enforcement to apply what is culled out from an eclectic psychological imagination. I think your own hyper-intuitive style of police personality is what we are in part talking about. The wisdom you have in emotional intelligence synergies, your hard-core memory, and more solid knowledge stored prodigiously based on the ethological needs and piqued into long-term memory systems."

"Existential analysis which targets what is the heart of the matter, and that is what counts. Even in the worst storm and the toughest battle, what resonates with all of us at the center of our existence and passion is the reason we do the work we do, such as the heroic work you do. It is your own life and the great risks you have taken. I say hyper-intuitive as part of your own genius because you did not stop, second guess, and contemplate all that you did—your having done it was successful on all fronts. The perfect fit for your own police personality style as hyper-intuitive [Rudofossi & Ellis, 1999; Rudofossi, 2007, 2009, 2012, 2013, 2015, 2017]. Parenthetically looking afterwards at the process when it slows down to reflection in the past corridors now open to enquiry in the grey regions of our minds and the lightness in our souls, it is now that you can really understand, place your own genius in its proper places as we move along. We are not analyzing you as a whole person but gaining insight into the dynamic stretch of your long experience and mindset, if I may express my own enthusiasm and respect for our journey into your experiences as Donnie Brasco and Joe Dominick Pistone."

FBI AGENT JOE DOMINICK PISTONE: "I'm with you and I think you got my mindset well thus far, Doc. The beginning of quality to me was the realization I was sifting through a maze of political acrobatics and applying as I shared my 'tough-mindedness.' The cold-blooded murdering gangsters, as I said, does not take away the real facts we discussed and you wrote about in your book on terrorism as human evil [Rudofossi, 2013]. I am referring to, at great risk of life, it was the wiseguys who volunteered to help set up a mission aligned with the Defense of America. I am referring to your pointing out Operation Underworld as a bulwark to protect US ports during World War II from sabotage by the Axis forces. The FBI of J. E. Hoover was complicit in it and diehard patriotism existed in our ranks and oddly with the wiseguys in this war effort. Compliments of the underworld, Department of War gangsters transformed into patriotic shadows in the rear of presentable intelligence fronts. Delegitimatized to the normal world remained illegitimate publicly but had become legitimate as victory became the motto in the undercurrents of the war against the Axis forces and world domination. Looking at the truth as it happened, Lucky Luciano of the Gambino family, the capo di tutti, and his ingenious accountant, Meyer Lansky, accomplished their goal. The bays and coastline were protected by the longshoremen of La Cosa Nostra until the war was won. They served as patriots and stone-cold killers in the same breath with a mission accomplished. We won the war and World War II ended with our becoming the victors."

COP DR DAN RUDOFOSSI: "I think in my desire to be an active listener as a clinician in attempting to capture your meaning to convey your wisdom, and even some of my own with you, reflects on the subtle and potent quality of discrimination. In the world of police investigations, letting the media know step-by-step transparency is not a good thing. Discrimination is not reducible always and in all contexts as a 'bad word.' In some contexts, discrimination is marginalizing and a negative approach to others, such as employment opportunity. But as scientists and investigators, discriminating skills help discernment between best to worst case scenarios and competent from incompetent professionals. Refreshingly, in the example of Operation Underworld, the odd coupling of gangster patriots guarding our national security interests during World War II was made all legit, no pun intended here. That was the right thing to do."

FBI AGENT JOE DOMINICK PISTONE: "True, Doc, but post-World War II, the legit became illegit again. Conflict re-emerged with the Cuban Missile Crisis, and the subsequent Bay of Pigs insurrection which was not successful. The Cuban Missile Crisis laid out the level of power brokers [legit and illegit] hashing out assassinations of foreign tyrants, such as Castro."

COP DR DAN RUDOFOSSI: "Pyrrhic victories of unfulfilled wishes left the devil known as better than the one unknown with Cuban tyranny in place as Castro celebrated his tenure. Unlike Castro's tenure on the Florida side of the Atlantic Ocean—Mafia boss of bosses, Santo Trafficante, Jr. connected, respected, and forged a novel relationship with you as Donnie Brasco. As a wiseguy associate, that balance of power you held, I think is unexplored and not understood. Let me share my view to see if I got it right. The first observation is that your ingenuity to persuade and existentially embrace Trafficante, Jr., is no less than becoming a master diplomat without portfolio. Secondly is, as Donnie Brasco you brokered high and low ranges of radar and detecting you as an FBI deep-cover agent with the mafioso successfully. Third is, Trafficante, Jr., besides his mafioso kingdom, influenced international and national political struggles that shadowed espionage and counter-espionage tactics. Fourth, although you were titled associate, your persuasive power assisted success as your liaisonship to nationwide illegit power brokers who broke bread with many legitimate power brokers. Fifth, in your responsive and developing network you intentionally low-keyed your own attribution of success across shadowy liaisons to the power brokers in the Mafia. Sixth, in the Mafia liaisons you brokered with little self-credit given, you scaffolded to engendering others' success through multiple operations within the Mafia, especially with Capo Trafficante and later with Balistrieri of Milwaukee. Seventh, your cached liaisons connected you and built trust in you. The trust in you was the glue that allowed you to become privy to Trafficante, Jr.'s engineering feats in Mafia circles. Eighth, you became a trusted associate apprentice as a made wiseguy-to-be, but in reality, it all points up to you being the made wiseguy without portfolio. Nine, this all being so, the prior eight steps, it was only a matter of time that your evidenced success and diplomacy with bosses such as Trafficante and Balistrieri allowed you access that only trusted made members of the Mafia family enjoyed. Tenth is, the evidence suggests if not validates that you gained the liberties of a Mafia made member. With some impasses, notwithstanding the lack of trust by Sabella, you as Donnie Brasco broke the red wall of the Mafia silence by your fifth and sixth year of infiltration—including your own insights into the fundamentals of intuition coupled with observations of what others couldn't see."

FBI AGENT JOE DOMINICK PISTONE: "The steps of negotiation, put that way, and my interactions with the Mafia bosses was never snug or preplanned. I managed to take each and every opportunity and act in an opportune manner to get the bosses to see the potential and make their own choices. Yes, I was aware of never taking ownership for their own mistakes by always, as we discussed earlier, allowing the bosses to take credit for what I suggested, if not analyzed for them. It was always their choices and their brilliance which kept me from being singed by their gains through risks taken."

COP DR DAN RUDOFOSSI: "My eleventh point is that doing what I would call 'verbal aikido' you deflected the strikes outward, drove them home and inward at the aggressors. Unlike the Kennedys, you managed to break bread with the colossal power brokers and unwritten elite via the Mafia powerbrokers without getting killed."

"Twelfth is you succeeded in a major coup when you landed the convictions and prosecution with stunning success singlehandedly. I know you had a team of attorneys, but without your intelligence and knowledge, they had no case to prosecute."

"So, my thirteenth point in your deep-cover operations is you achieving a quantum leap in an unformed inchoate field with no paradigm to lead you. To me, I bank my reputation on solidly stating you are not only a genius by evidence of your practical, emotional, and creative service, but as a service professional and police officer. I know of no other police or special agent that has shown the courage and tenacity in an honorable way and heroic tenacity to stay in a marathon for six years with stunning success as you have, and did. This is not flattery but a challenge to figure out more of your mindset and the why and how your genius can be translated into the lessons we can add to those learned thus far and we all can learn in our respective fields of criminal justice and science. Make sense as a forward on our mission?"

FBI AGENT JOE DOMINICK PISTONE: "Doc, I shared with you my honest thoughts and feelings. I like your poetic license, and as a psychologist your take on the reality of what I went through and did was not passive, I was not aggressive. I was doing my job as I had to do it. I lived and worked and became a gangster in the Bonanno family in not acting but being myself as Donnie Brasco. I never called myself a genius, so with that said, it is you making all these claims about my genius and heroism and not me! I am not going to deny what you say because you have solid points and building a case here. I can't disagree with as you are sketching out my six years from a psychological perspective and cop doc. I am with you on this."

COP DR DAN RUDOFOSSI: "I accept my responsibility if I may call you now in a collegial manner, Professor Joe Pistone. [Gesticulation of assent.] So, Professor Pistone, let me ask you to clarify for me and correct me if I am too left, or too right of center field, no pun intended.

"Well, when thinking back about the years spent with Lefty: Lefty was clearly filled and overlaid with *narcissistic defenses* (he was all about being a made guy and gangster no matter what he was into this identity where cheating, stealing, and even murder was secondary to accomplishing his status in the family). Lefty also had *addictive personality traits* as a gambler, where risk and excitement spurred him on to gamble in La Cosa Nostra. Yet he invested in you as Donnie Brasco. He invested fully in you and yet, as you put it, he could whack you if he felt you were not loyal or trespassing his honor code. As the penultimate classic wiseguy, he saw in you what Tony Mirra did, which was a potential street-level petty-theft guy to groom into a made man in the Bonanno family. In a way, if you think about it, you were the son he was grooming for the position within the Bonanno family. He took you under his tutelage."

FBI AGENT JOE DOMINICK PISTONE: "Yes, that is on the money. Lefty felt I was his protégé, so to speak. He believed I was cut out after a few experiences, some I disclosed earlier, where he observed me standing up in my way of doing things without leaving him unhinged, but not placating his wild notions as well. His smoking like a fiend in the car with the windows rolled up, and getting nasty suddenly due to jealousy and control issues with me. His checking to see if I was consistent in my work for him and testing my integrity, as sick as it was, to see if I was looking out for another capo or anyone who threatened our relationship and his being my lead in the family."

COP DR DAN RUDOFOSSI: "To complicate matters, as we left off earlier in our dialogues, Sonny Black Napolitano as capo realized he had to take you and Lefty under his umbrella. He defended you two from being pelted permanently after Capo Balistrieri found out in quiet rage that Conte was an FBI agent planted in his underground arboretum, or at least suspected this possibility was able to happen under Lefty's watch as a loyal made guy from the Bonanno family. In a stroke of nothing short of a miracle, Sabella as a captain in the syndicate decided to put Lefty on watch and spare you—since you were not a made wiseguy, you were not given a sit-down and carted away. That miracle as Donnie Brasco was one you in a way preempted and in your hyper-intuitive personality style dynamically and accurately foresaw as a potential trajectory if things went south as we say. Your hyper-intuitive preparation laid out an ingenious escape without any realizing how close you and Lefty by proxy came to death—ecologically-ethologically speaking. Existentially analyzing this situation, you remarkably saved not only your own life, but Lefty Ruggiero from the wrath of Balistrieri."

FBI AGENT JOE DOMINICK PISTONE: "Correct. That is an interesting way to look at it and process all that went down. But, yes, that accounts for that fiasco correctly. It worked, but the cover was blown with the other agent who got discovered. It was not blown off, but it had too many risk factors for me to be the one to initiate what then was credited by Lefty and yet, as you figured out, it was me who circumvented Lefty being whacked and me as his subordinate."

COP DR DAN RUDOFOSSI: "Another miracle was Sonny Black Napolitano decided at that point in time that the four captains that were his own competition had to be whacked, all at once. Sonny Black was to take out Sonny Red Indelicato, Big Trin Trincherra, Phil Lucky Giancarlo, and Tony Mirra, who also was very upset at your falling in with Lefty and in turn under the umbrella of Sonny Black Napolitano. Sonny Red's son Bruno escaped the hit and therefore you were up to bat as being made and becoming part of the crime Bonanno family formally at the point of an all-out perfect storm. You would have had to become the trigger man and then formally made as a Bonanno wiseguy with all the perks and bane as in henbane if anything was to go awry as it invariably will. But again, I see your ingenuity here as well to navigate not capitalize. Meaning in my mind's eye in synchronizing with yours, I perceive you did that verbal aikido again by staving off your own inclusion in a bloodbath and avoiding homiciding Bruno Indelicato. You did it arguably as a made man in all but portfolio and forcing your hand to commit murder. If you were forced to do a hit on Bruno with a pistol at your own head, you would be in the grizzly maze, but you gained a reprieve before that occurred. To me it was not intentional as avoidance, but rather once again circumnavigating away from being the guy who led the charge on the four captains but actually upstaged the massacre as best you could by not inflaming Sonny Black Napolitano, you allowed him as in aikido to make the move which would with his stunning anticlimax finding out you were shifting from the identity mode of Donnie Brasco and Donnie would shadow the identity mode of LEO Joseph Dominick Pistone."

FBI AGENT JOE DOMINICK PISTONE: "It was the perfect storm when you think about it. I anticipated the cascade of events to a degree, but not with certainty. I did know a storm was brewing and sensed the heads would roll. I tried to detour an all-out Mafia war of the family's internal structure. It was beyond my control, but you are right in saying I intuited, if you mean mentally, I had a picture beforehand of what would happen and in part it did. Not that I controlled or made it happen."

COP DR DAN RUDOFOSSI: "At the core of that perfect storm you were asked to pilot your crew. What a crew you had, the bosses thought they were in the lead and leading you, but in one sense you were guiding them as you piloted the ship as captain, without portfolio. With a slight trace of being the real strategist exemplar you are, you used verbal aikido to detour as much of the bloodbath. That potentiality was febrile and ready to explode. You held back from inflaming an already volatile ecology with ethological hypervigilance, and turf wars over territory."

"What I perceive is, you hid your intellect and your wisdom under your Donnie Brasco identity mode. Acting as if it was perchance—that you were unaware of the complexity undergirding what was brewing in the family feuds—you managed to lessen the toxic impact and explosive rage. The invariable eruption your mind's eye was tracking, in tune and sync with, compelled you toward taking cover and camouflage discussed earlier in our interviews. You again diminished the invariable harm without distinguishing yourself as the brain behind the syndicate machine."

FBI AGENT JOE DOMINICK PISTONE: "Yeah, that rage was evident with Balistrieri suddenly clamming up and reversal of his overt communication and welcoming nature after the realization of a breach in his syndicate. If you think about it, the fact Lefty was not whacked and I was left standing was a double reprieve and a miracle. As you suggest, I was aware of the dangers and moved as I was faced with the challenges not controlled, nor predictable, when the perfect storm came into port. Remember that Sonny Black Napolitano was itching to become the big boss in the Bonanno Mafia family. The obstacles for Lefty and I were the obstacles for Sonny Black Napolitano."

COP DR DAN RUDOFOSSI: "You had to create a believable fulcrum for Sonny Black Napolitano to be willing to wage civil war on the other captains that were organically in rebellion against him. As capos, these other three were agitators and ready to war on him, and by default you could easily have become the collateral hit by any one of them, or collusion by all three capos. By understanding and subtle wisdom conveyed, the three capos were three times Sonny Black Napolitano's power as they focused their plans to whack him for the sake of maintaining strict control within the Bonanno family. The truth is also elusive here because it was not only control for the sake of the Mafia family, but avarice and lust for power and blood thirst in their thwarted plan to assassinate Sonny Black, Lefty, and perhaps yourself as associate and deeply connected."

FBI AGENT JOE DOMINICK PISTONE: "It was ready to explode in a bloodbath for sure. If Sonny Black Napolitano had not taken action it would likely have been the reversal of misfortune. The one factor I had no control over was timing. But, as far as my anticipation of how things could unfold, as well as preparing for different possibilities and their consequent options, I looked ahead in my mind's eye and mapped out the potentialities, and went with the best possible trajectory."

COP DR DAN RUDOFOSSI: "Special Agent Pistone, if I am getting it right, and maybe I am getting it wrong, your major tactical obstacle was identifying how the canopy of shadows and doubts really would unfold. By not leaving clues and hints of Sonny Black's possible lethal plan, you really couldn't know how, when, and where the conflict would erupt. If Sonny Red Indelicato and other captains found out that Sonny Black Napolitano was planning a coup to counter the other gangsters' coup, the increasing likelihood of violence would ignite."

"You ensured subtly to cache your own thoughts and insight with responsibility without letting on your intuitive schema which was, if they got whiff of Sonny Black's Machiavellian power plays in their own counter thirst for power and bloodthirsty lust, Sonny would be whacked first, followed by Lefty, and no doubt yourself as a significant threat due your intelligence and street savvy in your established identity mode as Donnie Brasco. Blood thirst for Indelicato and gangsters was not a bad price for rolling the dice of caprice and wiles they were accustomed to. So, to clarify, if Sonny Black was whacked in the stone-cold death sentence, Lefty and you as his protégé did not stand a chance as collateral damage to the bosses in tandem as captains. This was not fact, it was not articulated, but you deduced this whole trajectory unfolding. Even more remarkable, Special Agent Pistone, was that you were not able to manipulate the situation, you had to subtly navigate the tempestuous nature of this internal murderous potential affair and use verbal aikido to avoid fatal collisions for you and the gangsters you were associated with."

FBI AGENT JOE DOMINICK PISTONE: "The way it went down was as I had thought it would, and in avoiding as best as I could without acting in concert was verbal aikido if you mean I moved and danced out of being hit directly and without affecting the moves they were planning in moving forward to an all-out war on Sonny Black Napolitano. He did the moves and strategy, but often bounced back and forth with listening to what he wanted to hear in a much calmer manner than say Lefty Ruggiero. The avoidance of those collisions was definitely in my mind and saved my life, and I would agree it saved Lefty and Sonny Black Napolitano rather than a shoot-out bloodbath which would take out civilians and others if it exploded into the streets. That dynamic was always on my mind as any effective and good detective or cop. Same with good special agents. It takes being and staying tough-minded. By not derailing, by acting too soon, or too strongly at a time too late, lives are saved. Laying out the safety buffers as best as you could to minimize harm is always in the back of your mind. Reality sets in."

COP DR DAN RUDOFOSSI: "So, here when you say staying 'tough-minded,' you mean by that all-encompassing term, is to be perceptive, in part as to the civilians to others being needlessly harmed. The paradox is that includes the wiseguys as well. Reading all the cues and sieving through to the selective importance of what is valuable, and discarding the mass of distractions, it takes once again discriminatory powers of selection in which some options and consequences are reduced and others opened wider. In this context you are quite aware of what you are strategizing, but you must present due to surviving as if you were unaware of what you were vigilant about to your associates and gangsters at the top. At the same time, without disclosing your nonverbal cues by being genuine in your gangster Donnie Brasco identity mode, your tough-mindedness is in part a very conscious control over leakage that could identify your intention and motivation."

"Meaning your tough-mindedness and discriminatory powers include equanimity from reacting and from being too passive. In this ecological-ethological niche of competing loyalties and territory, tolerating extreme ambiguity that is out of your actual control at that time in the spacing out of the Bonanno family hierarchy is demanded and yet hidden and equally silent."

FBI AGENT JOE DOMINICK PISTONE: "That is a key point, as equanimity and discrimination in judgment is called for in the discretion on the street and in my opinion administratively. That is the issue at the end of the rodeo and pony show. The fact that so many bosses have decided to judge the piece they never experienced and could never experience because they simply don't have what it takes to be a deep cover and infiltrate. I am not saying that we who do are better agents and cops. But we are better at what we do than they are and cannot do. That is a key piece of the ability to control and choose from a number of choices the best that works for you in the field. No one is going to take the bullet for you, or time dodging that bullet except for you. The nonverbal is always the most important because you are being observed and scanned to see if you are for real or a plant or impostor in the Mafia. If the boss, wiseguys, or the associates realize they have been duped, the sit-down means you are having your last meal ever. You are done for good."

COP DR DAN RUDOFOSSI: "In using verbal aikido, the tactical challenge you needed to overcome was achieved by using your own intuitive ingenuity. But it is clear the other layer was both an emotional and intellectual feat by accurately avoiding the deadly sit-down. You anticipated that the potentialities of hostile captains doing 'a sit-down' with Lefty and you when the smoke sifted through without a fire—the turning point would be smoking Lefty and you along the same end. I think to a degree Lt. Petrosino tragically was led on a similar sit-down with all its vainglory in Sicily unaware the capo di tutti was on to him and planned his execution after his last meal."

"The evidence inferred is that the other captains planned to ambush Sonny Black Napolitano, Lefty, and you. Strategically, the fact it did not go down as it ought to according to the other half of the New York syndicate is evidence you held a stunning victory by holding back the storm of overreacting too soon. Further, from an ecological-ethological analysis, the storm of mobster warfare was omniscient and ubiquitous, but yet didn't happen as anticipated by their side, but unfolded as your responsiveness by laying low in the bay of discontent within the Bonanno family lair. In conceptualizing the Bonanno internal powerplays, your ingenuity tactically from an intuitive existential anchor compelled you to lay low. I am considering you had no back-up to succeed as an agent. Realizing in your own real life-death pause how to avert the damage before it happened, you succeeded in conserving your life, Sonny Black Napolitano, and Lefty Ruggiero before they got massacred."

FBI AGENT JOE DOMINICK PISTONE: "Yeah, I mean the truth is, we had a potential civil war in the Bonanno family and extending to the other families, if not controlled. It is, as you say, a form of being able to figure out the differences and use discretion, which is my intuition sense. I did not form a written plan or make a chart that illustrated all these possibilities, but I did visualize and see the potential disaster if Sonny Black Napolitano or Lefty clashed with a sit-down with the other bosses first. Sonny Black and Lefty Ruggiero had the best opportunity to take action when they did and it worked. It was bloody and messy but it averted the all-out gangster war."

COP DR DAN RUDOFOSSI: "Finally, I'd like to take the knowledge and wisdom of understanding your strategy to a higher level. We can say your own navigational strategy worked for all four tactical arteries flowing with alacrity when Sonny Black Napolitano became the king of La Cosa Nostra in New York. Although perhaps it was the shortest of organized crime empires, it was a grandiloquent coup."

"By you presaging the unfolding of this civil war by your own *adaptive intuitive sensibility* by sketching the unique psychological dynamics of the Bonanno family with no navigational tools, in spite of the handicap of support, you piloted the fleet so to speak that was ultimately not your own to success. You winnowed through the Mafia maze ingeniously, without sinking or being sunk, as others who were less fortunate."

"Meaning from a soulful level as Louis Satchmo Armstrong would say with soulfulness amidst the dance of death, by not panicking, not divulging your exact insights to be sabotaged, and at the same time maintaining the integrity of being an FBI agent under fire internally as well as externally, on the cusp of civil war ready to erupt in the Bonanno family and associates."

"Special Agent Pistone, am I right on target when you rethink your own creative existential center and mindful tough-minded strategic carrying through of this very important dénouement to your narrative you wrote yourself and carried out to almost perfect effect? If I am not, please re-educate me and we can revisit this now?"

FBI AGENT JOE DOMINICK PISTONE: "I never heard my work summarized that way, but you have an unmistakable intuition for this deep-cover analysis yourself, that is worth thinking of Doc. But you break it down in ways I couldn't imagine and think of as you did in the way you did. But yeah, I would say my goal was to achieve intuitively by wrestling with the potentialities of the situations as they presented themselves to me. I had to do with steady evenness and not being pushed to doing anything I felt was too sudden, and I couldn't agree with. As I said, and you heard me very well and accurately, yes, that ability and stubbornness is tough-mindedness. It is deep inside me, and I can only be myself. I had to be myself and true to who I really am in doing my job as I set out to do, and did. Again, that ability is my tough-mindedness. Capish?"

COP DR DAN RUDOFOSSI: "Capito! In my analysis of the mettle that is the glint of your own impact and a reflection of your own self-awareness, the evidence stands in your corner as joining beneficent geniuses in history as my own clinical opinion and judgment of your level of productivity, originality, ingenuity, and perceptual acuity which is a hallmark of genius. I outlined in the beginning of this chapter for you to have read, when we both sit up and own your clarity of outcomes before they are played, you are and remain a genius, and you gave your best to the FBI, Special Agent Joe Pistone, I argued you did your best for those you even collared and that is to be deciphered as well. The evidence is overwhelming that it was your strategic thinking that overrode and redirected the too easily heated wipe-out toward making you a potential made wiseguy and potentially, had this gone a bit longer, an underboss to Sonny Black Napolitano. Your goal and even slipping, if only in fantasy for a few seconds, is not only a possible trajectory I agree with you would have been beyond remarkable, but the most likely one had the operation not been closed! It was also for your safety by the powers-that-be in my own interpretation of the reality that stings as much as the operation you masterfully handled for so many years. At the end of this interview, we can think if that works for you to do the existential analysis together on this respectfully and on a joint exploration. It is notwithstanding the issue of your mastery on another dimension that is intuitive, not academic, that is extraordinary and beyond rare, that is in the realm of understanding personality differences. For example, the crux of predicting when, where, and how to move forward, back, and, if need be, disappear in the fluid moments of brokering human relations and intelligence with effectiveness when one is not who one says he is. What comes to mind in this perspective, if anything?"

FBI AGENT JOE DOMINICK PISTONE: "Well that is a good question, Doc. When you're dealing with personalities that are so different, the first thing you gotta realize is each wiseguy is different. I was dealing with three major personalities here, besides all the others. Those three closest to me as you know were Toni Mirra, Lefty Ruggiero, and Sonny Black Napolitano. I had to cultivate each of the different personalities to my own advantage. You can't deal with Lefty Benjie Ruggiero as you deal with Tony Mirra. The difference between those two who were stone-cold killers was very different, and the way I learned to deal with Sonny Black Napolitano. Let me explain. Tony Mirra could be violently dangerous and volatile. He, as I shared earlier, could be likened to a violent animal when he got pissed off at virtually anything that was perceived as disrespectful. He could drop you in a heartbeat and leave you dead it if was to his advantage. Remember his advantage was a matter of what he perceived. In reality, it was to his advantage in some ways, and conversely to his disadvantage in other ways."

"If Lefty got angry, he in general was verbally angry. I mean, very verbally abusive and obnoxious and vile behavior, but not usually violent. By that I mean, after I got to know his sore points and nerves that were triggers, I could play them, rather than provoke him, to my advantage. As you pointed out, I did that as I understood his manner and style as sensitive on one hand, and hair-trigger rage over some issues and not others. Lefty would chain smoke and not care who he disrupted and bothered, including me. I appealed to him and he blew me off as he smoked away often with the window up. He also was a buff as a wiseguy. In his case, he was the classic dapper wiseguy who wouldn't miss a tag as a bad guy who followed and taught the rules. In that way he was a great teacher of the wiseguy's dos and don'ts."

"Tony Mirra was verbal, but could turn on a dime flip-over and be extremely violent. Deadly violent. He seemingly had little conscience for his fellow man and did not care if he walked up and whacked an associate or someone who had it coming to him for a violation of his rules as capo. Tony was explosive and couldn't fit in at all in a normal conversation in normal society. He knew Kuklinski and worked with him for a time, which gives you an idea of the quality of violence within his network."

"He was also not only irrational but also volatile and explosive at times. Tony and Lefty both were possessive and jealous, one could say, for controlling me and being my boss. Being a boss meant what was equal to a teacher in the gangster ways and means and that was always in dollars and cents brought in, not from upward to downward but from downward on the lower levels to the higher-level hierarchy up to the bosses at the top of each family."

"As I was saying, when you look at Sonny Black Napolitano, he never verbally abused anyone. But if he looked at you, it was enough. He was also a stone-cold killer as the others, but there was a difference. That is, if he had a difference of some opinion, and even disagreement that was passionate, he was a normal guy. I never felt threatened by disagreeing with Sonny Black; you could disagree with him. Sonny Black would talk to you and not ever lose control. In fact, he could articulate himself."

"The truth of Sonny Black Napolitano is he could fit into the normal world. Under the right environment and situation he would be a banker or teacher. Lefty and Mirra could not fit into the normal world. They were gangsters, born into this lifestyle and resonated with it."

"Sonny was the type of guy that you didn't mind spending time talking to about different topics which he was versed in at a level of intelligence that was communication with a purpose and meaning. He never verbally abused you, even as a wiseguy. I never witnessed him abuse anyone verbally. I learned all about pigeons he spoke about. He truly loved those pigeons. He spent quite a bit of money and time on his pigeons. He trained them and he cultivated a pride in keeping them and protecting them as beloved pets. He was a stone-cold killer, mind you, but he had a side that was very human. He could fit in to the normal world."

COP DR DAN RUDOFOSSI: "It seems to me you had to navigate not only your knowledge about each of the personalities that varied greatly, such as Tony Mirra's explosive anger issues and disorder nested in some anti-social personality character armor. Tony's narcissistic umbrella could bring death in a trigger-happy moment of real rageful violence if you didn't watch your boundaries in his instability. Lefty was more pedantic and paranoid in his personality structure with addictive personality features and in a way very histrionic in his core character armor. He was obsessive-compulsive and always needed to have his hands in everywhere. Lefty could flare up like a peacock in red-rage plumage when he felt insulted and disrespected, but could be understood to be more show than rage as long as you didn't push the boundaries too far. On the other hand, he would be more easily motivated to assist you as long as you danced the tarantella of gestures and gave him respect by biting your tongue in his outrageous self-indulgences from gambling, smoking, and the gamut of other luxuriating habits he had. If I remember correctly, when you held your ground and said you were not moving in where he wanted you under his crosswinds and thumbs to control you and he slowly accepted your stance, which was to be yourself and not give in to his pressuring you on issues of privacy even as an associate of his."

"Sonny Black Napolitano had a personality character armor that was more adaptive and pliant in realizing your own potential as Donnie Brasco. I imagine as your real personality never truly split, but your identity modes emerged, they had the full traces and the strength of your underlying ingenuity. He realized your genius as he was maneuvering into becoming the capo of the Bonanno family. He emerged as the king of the Bonanno family for the moment in his light, and your own as his potential made man. While that was all part of the business for the organized crime family boss, the other side of this development was the fact that you, in a very human way, became endeared as part of his own family. Like the original Joseph Bonanno"

"That is something I want to return to later when we work through a little of the emotional and existential residue, perhaps like gunpowder after a shooting that gets on the suit, tie, and gumshoes of even the best detective and dry-cleaner outfit, except we can keep it messy to a degree in educating our readers to the extent we disclose what is important to process and no more."

FBI AGENT JOE DOMINICK PISTONE: "Well, Doc, if he grew up in Minnesota, Sonny Black could have been a normal kid. He could have become a professional, and made a good impact on the world instead of becoming the gangster he did ultimately become."

"Sonny was a Brooklyn kid that grew up on the streets of Brooklyn which didn't give him that opportunity. So, yeah, Sonny Black Napolitano was very different than Lefty. He could fit in to the normal world and society with very different type of people. As I shared with you earlier today, Lefty Ruggiero, although different than Tony Mirra, was in some way just like him. Both Lefty and Tony could not fit into normal society. Because of their personality and character, they were not up to mingling in with different people that were not mafiosi. I'll be very frank with you, if Sonny Black grew up in a normal place in our city, he could have been a very different man with some real benefit to society, which is sad, but true."

"He was able to not only mingle with people, but he cared about his customers in his Italian restaurant and bar where he got to know his patrons and respond to each of them by name and personality."

"Of course, he was no pushover, and again he was a boss in the Bonanno family. Undoubtably, he had intelligence and finesse. It is sad, he could not get out of his lifestyle and join respectable society and civilization except by being a wiseguy. If he could, the truth is that he would still likely be here today. He would be doing something meaningful with his life and putting his ability to good use. You know it's sad he was born into the rut and life of the gangster he grew up in! Still, the facts are he was a gangster and lived and died that way as the rest of his good fellows. I gave him a way out but he chose to take the path he chooses. It's not cookie-cutter clear as those who live in the world of books and those who live under the shield but have hardly used it in reality on the tough rough-and-tumble streets. You know as you were a cop on the streets of Brooklyn in Bed-Stuy and Red Hook in the later 1980s."

COP DR DAN RUDOFOSSI: "I do know, and I, like you Joe, do feel the chagrin as a cop doc in the real world of knowing some 'bad guys' are kids who came from broken homes and broken walls where playtime meant fitting in with gangs and being tough enough to get the grade of street survival. Graduating to wiseguy culture, with the flashy cars and lifestyle without the umbrella of protection, one sinks into mediocrity and the race for one's place is merciless without guidance and someone to guide with a moral compass. On the other hand, some of these kids would be gangsters regardless of their background and born with tendencies that are antisocial and criminal in intent. The fact is, some of the best cops come from families with roots deep in organized and—not being funny—disorganized crimes. That is the lower-level petty crimes of number running and street lotteries. I may be wrong, but it seems that Sonny Black in his personality was obdurate in his loyalty to the culture of the wiseguy and specifics of his own crime family. His destiny defied the book stuff of Justice Hall, and also the fair play of a guy who could have thrown in the towel but instead decided the best part of honor was to surrender to the family he swore allegiance to. It cost him his life in the final analysis. No judgment and tragic pause for now. His end, being sad and tragic. I would like to respectfully return to this later with you." [Joe assents without much ado.]

136 Dialogue, Insight, and Discovery

"I would like to return to another reality here by trying to go deeper in figuring out the novelty of your adroit skill to have truly tackled and held down the complexities of organizing the mergers. The mergers, by dancing between intuitive sensibility and palpitating the arteries of the different family members and their personalities on a large scale as you weaved in and out of major crime figures, that you cached successfully from knowing your real identity as Donnie Brasco. That is on one level nerve-racking; as a street cop/investigator with you my sweat is pumped up on steroids of 100 gun runs. On the other, as a cop doc trying to capture the level of psychological ingenuity and dexterity emotionally and mentally to executively balance the tightrope and calibration of each encounter with wiseguys who could kill with a glance. No rehearsal and no performance, no scripts to look at, and no lines to finish your own narrative. It was creative exploration and heuristic movements as you shifted into your responsive tactics without losing touch as to your strategic goal. Even if you dissociated, you did so adaptively and functionally as long as you were in the saddle and that is what is so important to wrestle from the media-worthy hype, the sensational idealizations of you as player to actor roles, which is a fiction and need to append that fiction to you. In my clinical cop doc analysis, it was your inventiveness as to creating your own pathway and seeing your way through. Solo flight. You see my read on you, Special Agent Joseph Dominick Pistone?"

Envy via Sloppy Journalism

Sloppy journalism ranging from crass denial to attempts to defame Joe Pistone's motivation and to reduce his achievements as comparable to any detective work is harmful. Coloring deep shades of sleuthing as acting and not deftly the craft of Joe Pistone as ingenious artist, is envy at its worst. Metaphor underlies reality as palatable as color. The color of Joseph Pistone is ruddy and sanguine as aging wine; wine that is rare is cultivated, nice, and easy. Honesty, integrity, and real meaning of an appellation underscoring "genius" here incorporates exceptionally creative generativity. Joseph Dominick Pistone, FBI special agent as gangster, epitomizes what "genius" hewn does—active operational fluid adaptation. Exemplifying the Joseph Dominick Pistone I have come to know and intend for you to understand is his "being"—humble:

Humility is the generative linchpin of Special Agent Pistone's effective genius. Humility is crowned with

Fidelity to stay on course with doing what had to be done and not being derailed in his mission (mission-impossible as done);

Bravely navigating the three cultures he danced with (alluding to the three mistresses earlier) and his conserving his values as a law enforcement officer regardless of the tempests within "internal straits" and "external triangles" of individual differences between the Mafia families and within those unique Mafia family constellations.

Integrity to contend with "It-All": Joseph Dominick Pistone is finally a man, and as all men, he is no better or worse physiologically speaking. He has the integrity to be humble and remain above all who he is and was, the model for law enforcement officers and service the public has gained invaluable benefit from as a hero indeed.

FBI AGENT JOE DOMINICK PISTONE: "Doc, remember the merger was as follows, the Trafficantes and the Bonannos and the Balistrieris and the Bonannos and Columbos as at first Jilly. The verbal stuff never bothered me and remember in this puzzle I could push Lefty in directions I wanted him to go. He could be gauged by seeing how and where he would get upset. I could get him pissed off and know when he was ready to explode verbally. We were on the phone and I wanted him to tell me what was going on between the wars between the families and he called me a fucking prick and I said Lefty don't you ever call me that. I then hung up on him immediately. So, he calls back and finally I answer his call and he goes right back as his rants and raves raise in volume and intensity as he curses me again. I hang up again. He again calls nonstop, again he says don't you dare hang up on me again and is ready to start cursing again. I interrupt him and strongly tell him you can talk to me about whatever, but I tell you don't talk to me like that again or I will hang up on you again. So, then he finally starts to move from cursing me and with more calm and respect he starts to do what Lefty did with me. He starts to tell me what I am sure he never intended on telling me from the beginning. He includes me in on the real beef between the families and who is taking what and planning to do within each clique he was intimate with. I now encourage him and he is so pissed off at me, maybe them, and even himself that he gets to the point of telling me even more stuff. He then gave me so much intimate information he either would whack me and I knew he wouldn't or make me even more of a confidant. I was deeper in the loop and, as you put it earlier, that was not accidental and part of the overall strategy in achieving information as intel to use in the prosecution. You know it was like I was able to get him to act against his own nature to give me more and more of what was necessary to achieve my goal as an operative."

COP DR DAN RUDOFOSSI: "Yes, you used what we call paradoxical intention in existential therapy when we as docs get our patients to talk about things they would normatively censor and clam up on. In a deep unconscious way, you also got him to feel guilty as he knew he blew up on you wrongly and violently and what we would call an attempt for rapprochement which is a conciliation with a son figure which on some twisted level you served unconsciously for Lefty. It hints at his own father-son relationship and his need to fulfill that with you, albeit unconsciously. It finally also leaves us with the fact that he was entangled with you as his alter ego that allowed him to swell with pride when you were with him and aligned, which at any point of your separation from and with him triggered jealous pouting. It was a strange and strained relationship that, because it was also intermittent in his rage and hysterical outbursts, he was hooked in even deeper with you. Since he couldn't win with you, he kept on tackling with you hoping he could hook you into being his protégé even more and with full obedience as you were actually shaping his behavior and his emotional ties deeper into the proverbial Gordian knot; as he pulled in his attempt to control you, he became entangled deeper and deeper with you and obsessively compelled to gamble more and more on your guiding his cast of the die in dice. Make sense to you Professor Joe?"

Discernment: Integrity and Calculated Risk and Decisive Action

Psychologically speaking and spiritually relevant are Joe Pistone's multi-dimensional gifts to our intelligence community working on creating a model to identify with for both law enforcement and military sleuths and agents.

As a model agent mobilizing our war on terrorism, hardly abating or diminished, innovation on the human and down-to-earth ground warfare, sleuthing is needed more than ever as the edge to victory with integrity.

> Joseph Dominick Pistone eschews labels as do I, but calling "It" out as truth and expressing the very painful and traumatic leaps he leapt alone is critical. My explicit witnessing of complex trauma and complicated grief is the 'It' we need to gently, slowly, and meaningfully understand in a language that is sensible to Joe Pistone and Donnie Braco as an identity mode he lived and will always live. As navigator as all good cop docs and docs are, I operationalize and enlighten the darkness of heart with light. Light most poignant is not neon, but emanates within, and punctuates without!
>
> "It" is, not what "It" hides as "It is," but "It" is as "It" is hidden and needs to be identified in a safe haven for law enforcement officers. It is stunning to think, but this extends to wiseguys and it is no wonder that after the smoke settles, both older detectives and wiseguys meet in bars, cigar rooms, and piers and share what only both worlds can really understand in the final analysis.

FBI AGENT JOE DOMINICK PISTONE: "Exactly right as to how I psychologically survived and managed to work in my relationship with him. He, for example, would say I can't mention any names Donnie and you know that I already told you that. I would then say right, but are you talking about the first guy we were talking about, or the second guy we were talking about? You know how the wiseguys talk in riddles and circles so they can hide from any others eavesdropping what they are really talking about. He would then get upset and immediately say no, not at all, it's the other guy, the third guy we were talking about Donnie! I would then say to him, Lefty come on, I thought you were talking about the first guy not the third guy. I would say, you mean the second guy? He would say for fuck's sake no, Donnie, it's Dan let's say! You get it now?!? You know as we were talking about. You know it really is important to think of psychologically as knowing each of their personalities. Once you get into their personalities you learn how, when, and where to tweak each one to your own advantage."

COP DR DAN RUDOFOSSI: "You know Special Agent Joe Pistone and wiseguy Donnie Brasco, you are able to educate me as to the ability to paradoxically deal with dissociation adaptively, I call as you know adaptive functional dissociation. But you are an exception here as well. You function at a rare place of ownership and healthy resilience. [Shared laughter.] Your passion as to the realization of a genuine understanding with no malice and no undermining of the personalities each wiseguy had, but a reflection on yourself as an in-trench clinician is a metaphor you live by, if you let go with me for a moment, as you really analyzed their behavior, emotions, and cognitions on an unconscious dimension—at the center of their existence psychologically. I know and you know you are no clinical psychologist, but your depth and insight are beyond remarkable. Again I can only humbly acknowledge to you rare and impeccable as the stretch to creative ingenuity. If I am getting it right, and I may be wrong, your strategy was to get Balistrieri to connect with Lefty and Sonny and bridge the merger was shadow boxing by you remaining in the shadows as the welterweight knock-out champ. What I mean is, you even got Sabella on board not in spite of, but because they thought they had come up with the deal and were more likely to accept it. If your ego got in the way as in many other detectives and agents that can become what we call overly identified and invested in their identity modes as a wiseguy and claim what ought to be left to the wiseguys as their own. You were able to put your own ego aside as Donnie Brasco. In doing so, by not pursuing the prize, then paradoxically and with brilliant intention you were successful in releasing the wealth of intelligence that flowed with peaceful resolution and infiltration—point on!"

FBI AGENT JOE DOMINICK PISTONE: "Yeah, exactly. Remember, I made Sabella and Sonny think it was their idea. Initially, for that matter, I made Lefty and Sabella think it was their own idea to go to Milwaukee in the first place. The same thing with the marriage with the Trafficantes; I got Sonny to think that was their idea. You know, in thinking of this, one of the reasons I was successful in doing and being in the undercover job I was doing as Donnie Brasco was that I didn't judge the bad guy. My whole outlook was everybody makes choices. You made a choice to be a bad guy. I made a choice to be in law enforcement. I didn't make a choice to be a social worker in fixing people's home lives and managing resources and talent. I didn't decide to become a psychologist or psychiatrist and figure out the inner workings of your brain and mind as you Doc, for example. You worked past college another ten or so years to get licensed and that's not for me. I am not here to reform you as a wiseguy. I'm working here in an undercover capacity to gather information of your illegal activities that will stand up in court. That's my job right now. My job is not figuring you out as a psychologist or psychiatrist. I didn't make you a gangster. You made that choice. So, guess what? I don't feel bad about what I am doing. In an undercover capacity where you think I am Donnie Brasco and not an FBI agent, it's not my choice you're a gangster, it is your own choice."

COP DR DAN RUDOFOSSI: "Joe, not to interrupt you, but for a moment you chose and fulfilled your operation remarkably, but you yourself were, if we use Norman Mailer's term, thrown into the belly of the beast. It's like dancing on a tightrope as when you start to train a tiger, and even though you know a tiger is a tiger, you still can't help at some level deep inside admiring and even liking that tiger who could devour you in a heartbeat. Did you ever see *Life of Pi*?"

FBI AGENT JOE DOMINICK PISTONE: "Yeah, I did."

COP DR DAN RUDOFOSSI: "Do you remember how the author began to love the tiger as metaphor as real as its teeth and ferocity to see under it all its humanness under the umbrella of fate versus destiny by the Grace of G–d there go I, but for the Grace of G–d? At a certain point there was a reciprocity beyond a symbiotic relationship where it seemed some form of empathy emerged between the human and the tiger as the ferocious mirror within externalized in its graphic literal sense without. The reality, the tiger is like Sonny Black, who you shared was decent to a degree, but was a killer, as you put it, a stone-cold killer who had the other four captains whacked."

FBI AGENT JOE DOMINICK PISTONE: "Doc, the difference is this; the hatred and not that I experienced between the bosses I dealt with. Tony Mirra hated me with a passion and tried to get me killed. Lefty never tried to get me killed. Except after it came out I was an FBI agent, which he did not want to accept or believe. That is, after the trials he had changed his attitude. He was dead set on killing me! He had it out for me and to kill me with no doubts. Alright Doc, Sonny Black was different as to when he found out I was an agent. Alright, I guess, but don't know for certain, that if he had gotten the contract to get me by the bosses of the family, would he spare me?"

"Sonny Black's remarks to his girlfriend were very different than the others such as Tony Mirra and even Lefty Benjamin Ruggiero. Sonny's girlfriend spoke to us after he had disappeared and he said to her to tell me, "If you ever see Donnie, tell him that he was better than we were. Tell him that I loved him. Tell him he did a better job than we did."

"In other words, I did a better job at infiltrating them than they did at finding out who I really was. You see that is the thought processes of these three guys."

"Stone-cold killers as they all were. But when the day of reckoning came in, the reality after the operation closed down was all three of them were not the same. Mirra and then Lefty wanted to kill me, but not Sonny!"

"Now, I am not so sure Sonny wouldn't have if the opportunity was there to whack me. But he did not do anything to change his fate or mine. He did not go around spouting his hate and desire to kill me. He actually left me with a message of respecting what I did without taking it personally against me."

COP DR DAN RUDOFOSSI: "I'm talking to you, if I can as a cop doc. This is my thoughts, not yours. But although you never shared it with me, in my own intuition, you Joe Pistone have a heart of gold. Hear me with patience. Even though when you now talk about Lefty and Sonny, and even Tony Mirra as stone-cold killers and we go back to our original discussion, from a soulful sensibility, and as a clinician you strike me as being very decent and humane at your core by still caring and wondering what if they weren't gangsters by birth."

"My reasoning in part is that you are still you as a decent man, after all you've been through. Evident is that you can still connect to each of these very intense and, one can say, dangerous men as human beings. Their own humanity at very different levels is understood with a sanguine vista you can still appreciate."

"You clearly discern well and with me in educating me about the most important insight about you is your trusting me to share this authentically, as your level of toughness is reciprocal with your depth of character to really be able to extend past the work and still believe in the humanity of those you had to lock up or identify as victims of La Cosa Nostra. Sonny Black Napolitano as you've described him was in some ways a gentleman. In some ways he was on the fringe of becoming a decent guy. You shared with me your heartfelt feelings which now make even more sense as you spoke of Sonny Black Napolitano and you talking as two guys sharing the talk, walking the walk as you both did in the space of time you shared with him as timeless."

"The loss here is what we as psychologists/psychiatrists call disenfranchised and hidden loss. Perhaps even traumatic loss, which is all the healthier to express deep within our soulfulness as not being our fault in the lines drawn in fate. Lines with harsh contours in concrete forged in the jungle of the urban modern city."

"Why shouldn't that loss you experienced include sensitive souls even if born into tough worlds like La Cosa Nostra? The sacred worth of Sonny Black as a tragic man born into the world he was. You are not blaming him for being to a degree he was a captain in the Bonanno family with harsh judgment. As you pointed out, Sonny loved you, as you put it, as Donnie Brasco. Even when he knew you were Joseph Dominick Pistone, he respected you in some deep way as an agent of the FBI that was Donnie Brasco authentically as well. Authenticity for me as an existential analyst is redeeming, right here and right now."

"Perhaps, we can imagine without ever fully knowing but intuiting with empathy Sonny Black Napolitano's feelings remained as disenfranchised for him, as it was for you and me as you allowed me into this closed portal revisiting this in catharsis, in the here and now, as experienced all those years ago."

FBI AGENT JOE DOMINICK PISTONE: "Well, yeah, that makes sense when you put it in that perspective. Human being and my understanding of Sonny. After all, it was the neighborhood, the environment. You know what I am saying?"

"For Sonny, if he was born in Fargo, Minnesota, he may have been a working stiff. He could have been a business as a business owner, but he had the potential to do much better than what he actually turned out doing. While the other two guys, they would be wiseguys and whack people regardless. The drapes of their lives have been drawn. In that way he was tragic as his life could have been productive and I did enjoy our conversations as a normal type of guy, yeah even in that sense qualifiedly as a friend with strong boundaries I had in mind."

COP DR DAN RUDOFOSSI: "Yes, it is sad to hear about the tragic end of Sonny Black Napolitano for me with you. I can only imagine for you what it must feel like to recount when you think of the point of your departure from him as not only a wiseguy, but in some truthful way a tragic nice guy paradoxically as well."

"In other words, an aspect of humanity that even transcends the Donnie Brasco operation to the Donnie Brasco as a real guy who lived and breathed with Lefty, Tony, Balistrieri, Sabella, Trafficante, Big Trin Trincherra."

"Hey, but most of all it was very informative and meaningful in our dialogue that in your relationship with Sonny Black as a buddy, to the degree you could forge a relationship with him, his loss is a profound loss. I mean a meaningful connection that transcended the normal boundaries etched in stone and shielded by being an agent of the FBI for you and for him as a wiseguy, unlike you Joe, who could not switch off and find enlightenment without witness protection programs and bodyguard immunity from being whacked."

FBI AGENT JOE DOMINICK PISTONE: "Remember we discussed and you asked about Joe Messina. He was not a volatile guy that would fly off the handle. He was more like Sonny Black. He thought first and would not act on immediate hair-trigger anger to rage. He wouldn't lash out at you like Lefty, and worse as Tony Mirra would."

"Mirra would pull the trigger first. With Tony Mirra it was his own nephew that whacked him. If he was born in another context, he would wind up being the guy who was the bad guy, as that was who he was innately. He did not have the care of a normal person. Mirra, you can say, took to killing, as something he liked to do."

COP DR DAN RUDOFOSSI: [Moving on for now.] "What about the boss, Sabella?"

FBI AGENT JOE DOMINICK PISTONE: "Yeah, Mike Sabella was interesting as well. Different personality as well. Mike was a businessman. He was all about money and making money. You know the restaurant and day-to-day business of running his restaurant as day-to-day work was his focus and making money well was also important to him. But, hey Doc, you gotta remember, all these guys are killers."

"When we had our 'sit-down' they were normal. You know as sit-downs, he was normal. Mike Sabella was like Paul Castellano. He was a businessman. After talking a bit, he was more interested in doing business than being a Mafia venture as per the Mafia culture and dictates. It is very driven by the rules of the family."

COP DR DAN RUDOFOSSI: "The rules of the family as in 'this thing of ours' is as if it was a counterculture move to conquer the idea of being governed by the government. The Mafia is an ecology of violence, where trauma and loss circulate in a hub. Yet the Mafia knew and knows about certain boundaries which, as a psychologist, is also sensible and geared to survivability."

"As you wrote in your book on wiseguy culture, the dos and don'ts of the wiseguy culture has cult-like aspects to it such as rituals and mores which is almost the quality of addiction. Is that correct?"

FBI AGENT JOE DOMINICK PISTONE: "Yeah, exactly, and once you're in and once you're a 'made guy' you have power. That power and respect, you know, it's that they feed off of everyone. You know they are the mob guys and they get all the respect. This they keep feeding on. Power is like heroin, and some of these wiseguys are the junkies, feeding on 'junk'. The adrenaline rush with being among wiseguys is a rush as well."

COP DR DAN RUDOFOSSI: "You are dealing with an ecology of trauma and it is an adrenaline rush as you had to deal with the Mafia and almost being made, and being pulled from that is like in some ways the patrol cop who gets addicted to trauma because it is so hyperstimulating and expansive in his neural networks, and by keeping up with the constant stimulation and adrenaline rush has no time to pause about his/her losses. Eco-ethologically speaking, the impossible task you experienced and handled is overwhelming and given full discretion and yet the hammer of the lily-white man on the horse comes down hard and hits you if it's not perfect, which compounds the losses in the trauma when the rush of the streets subsides."

FBI AGENT JOE DOMINICK PISTON: "Yeah, exactly, it does make sense and that is when their expectations is not realistic. You are out there and working for six years on anything, and doing the best you can do. Its human nature, right, to call the six years a success; isn't that human nature, psychiatrically speaking, Doc? I mean, take it to the very end of the goal set in the operation, I mean Operation Donnie Brasco. Hey, that would have been the culmination of my work to take it to the end and be a made member of the Bonanno crime family. That is the culmination for being an undercover."

"Yeah, I don't mean it as braggadocios, but I had gone to the end of the operation when it was pulled. As I shared with you, one boss, Joe Messina, said don't trust Donnie Brasco, as he didn't know me long enough to give me that benefit of introduction as the third guy which is the Mafia tradition. Messina didn't give my hand to the big bosses such as Trafficante, but Lefty did as did Tony Mirra earlier, and later Sonny Black Napolitano who trusted me in the moves that put him to the top of the New York Bonanno family."

COP DR DAN RUDOFOSSI: "If I am getting it right, you were on the teetering edge of the acrobatic rope to be a made man in the Bonanno family. Sonny chose to do that. It is in a way his real self that did not give up his humanity in the messiness he was dealing with and respected you till the end. He held onto the humanity you perhaps brought to him uniquely. He was able to express with you and to you. No atheists in the foxhole. By confessing to his girlfriend, he forgave you. He left you with his genuine identity, not his wiseguy identity mode as well that was impressed that you kept your mental and emotional toughness. Although he was a stone-cold killer in practice, Sonny Black Napolitano, in the lost language of his self, was in the song of his life humane, as he let go and accepted his guilt without blaming you. He left you a gift in his farewell which was honest and tested true. If you accept it, the truth of his relationship with you was it was genuine. That said, like all relationships within its canopy, are very limitations and losses we all endure. Endings are never so nice and pleasant, but endings like this remain, as you put it well, unfinished business here of real loss and grieving."

FBI AGENT JOE DOMINICK PISTONE: "Yes, that is true. We did have a real relationship. Sonny was a complicated guy in that regard as a wiseguy who loved and, as I shared, had an affinity as an aficionado of his homing pigeons. But like all things and relationships, some end and this one ended after I did my best to get him to see why turning himself in and getting witness protection could have worked. It is what we make it, and I make it, as you put it, a loss, but in perspective as doing my job well and with that tough-mindedness."

COP DR DAN RUDOFOSSI: "The fact you also worked so hard and long at doing the merger you achieved with Trafficante and the Bonannos, the Balistrieris and Bonannos is all testament to your ability to your unique skill in forging relationships by truly gaining each member's trust by, as you educated me and all our readers, by being 'true to yourself.'"

FBI AGENT JOE DOMINICK PISTONE: "Yeah, the actual merger was with Trafficante and the Bonannos, and then the Balistrieris and Bonannos as the bridge between the different families all connected together. This is what I had in mind. Doing deep cover through the maze of each of their different personalities while ensuring I met their special needs for sure without losing my own need for boundaries was critical in the success of my approach."

"Absolutely, as you put it here. Yes, I was doing my job humanely. You're exactly right. As a 'human being.' As you point out, I did this under very difficult conditions and in very tough situations, and almost impossible challenges. It was doing my job and that's how I approached it. Tough-mindedness and being a human being."

Summary

In pausing, we will return to Special Agent Joe Pistone's unconscious noetic dimension in his being a human being, who held his ground in a way that was self-respecting without truncating others—he never demeaned any of the wiseguys in a personal way.

Being grounded as a uniquely decent and tough-minded cop, Joe Pistone, while semi-retired has done, does, and will go on doing what was, and is, right—as opposed to wrong.

One other side of Joe Pistone is a unique humility that we touched on in this chapter, placed in a highlight box within this chapter, and runs throughout our dialogue. Heuristically, as a cop doc filling in the spaces of a redemptive and respectful process of the therapeutic process, a window has been winnowed open. That snippet of a "sit-down" in telehealth by lassoing a fragment of a therapeutic session can only be done collaboratively. Perhaps in this chapter we have begun that process respectful of each other and responsive to one another and that is the mettle of therapy itself. In the next chapter and epilogue, we will continue in sketching in that draft of a session, or what may conceptualize as a fragment of a session.

In summing up this chapter, I will add that saluting Special Agent FBI, Joe D. Pistone is not a nice thing to do. It is the right thing to do!

I hope a smart future senator of New York State will put up a plaque for Joseph Pistone, or name the Brooklyn Queens Expressway Special Agent Joseph Dominick Pistone Pathway. It is time **Special Agent Pistone FBI Centurion Way** can one day never be fuhgeddaboutit by having it remind the law enforcement community that honesty, integrity, and courage count—not the belt parkway of fame and fortune, but of making a real difference in the safety and service Joe Pistone did and always will as his legendary work indubitably inspires us all.

My hope as a retired NYPD uniform member myself is that a leader within the NYPD will ensure Special Agent Pistone receives an honorary 1st Grade Detective Shield. Why? In my own hopeful psychological imagination as cop doc and professor, inspiration for promoting the finest and best as the crowning achievement to be granted in the world of law enforcement! Inspiration for new service officers in blue to follow—timelessly onward and forward—one at a time, as motivation that is crucial for students and practitioners alike.

"There is nothing new under the Sun," as I pointed out earlier, is attributable to King Solomon. The language we coin as novel, perhaps is more honestly coined as rediscovery of ourselves. Returning to the timeless and priceless values needing conservation is the myth of the hero, and his return: step in Special Agent Joseph Dominick Pistone. Joseph Campbell in his epic work on mythology of the hero (Campbell, 2008) reminds us that in academia education offers a journey of separation and return—perhaps endless and eternal of initiate to veteran and back to innocence.

Onward and forward to insight and process as we march on with Joseph Pistone's final chapter. In the last chapter, I explore heuristically as a cop doc filling in the spaces of a redemptive and respectful process of that snippet begun in this chapter of our "sit-down" as we arise and present in the space of a therapeutic session—as possibility played in the dénouement to follow.

Cop Doc Corner for Students Only—Debriefing

Genius is another abused, taunted, overused, tainted word by charlatans, street-culture cliques, and sensationalistic writers hardly earning the title of investigative journalist. The words "genius," "gifted," and "awesome" are bandied about in the media and entertainment as if they are bandanas worn like the color of the day.

Differences do count.

Being able to discern differences in self and others is the beginning of thought and discrimination for the better of all in a society that is plural and united. We have explored this idea boldly and humanely in this chapter with one of the most resilient and tough-minded agents that has been there, done it all, and has shared with all of us—including me as author—his true genius!

Let's return to discernment within the world of the COVID-19 pandemic. Stealth in the viral explosion matches stealth in distortions within the spheres of media outlets and quality differences in each circuitous route as reliable and valid. Validity in a spectrum from inept to dangerously inaccurate, from "point on" to "veridical." The critical skill of discrimination as the difference that equivocates between life and death. Subtle choices seemingly innocuous and almost predicated on caprice, such as ten seconds added to washing your hands after exposure to the COVID-19 virus, can be the tipping point as to survival or not! Perhaps taking medications within the first three days, or after the fourth day and fourth hour is the point in the continuum for living or dying. Other factors, largely ignored as confounds, may be critical, such as what are your medical-psychophysiological vulnerabilities, and what is your resiliency invulnerabilities?

The choosing between one set of procedures and another is weighted by wisdom and experience in discerning weighing in the best of multiple possibilities until one remains as the best. Understanding the etiology of the unknown viral invasion is crucial. Without understanding the etiology, one cannot move forward toward the ultimate intervention. The right choice demands responsibility matched by the wisdom to carry through on one selection of vaccine trial in distinction to another. Distinctions are the key to quality, effectiveness, and elegance. In a world of ignorance, all differences are forcibly erased.

As you and I look back into the creative dynamic of Joseph Pistone, it is important to notice that the hues in the color and creative design undergirding the structure of his education and ours on organized crime has been replete with all the variations possible, and yet there is always more to come.

We require pausing, and really clearing our lenses before leaping. After we pause, our realization is such ingenuity by Joseph Pistone was no simple investigation, nothing is at it seems it was, and much, as we have already seen, is deeper and more complex in the challenges faced by a single sleuth. As master sleuth, Joe Pistone used his ability to discern how to step forward when no map was available to coordinate his steps. After a real pause, absorbing this fact as truth, let's redirect to gain pragmatic insights to use and keep in mind.

Unbound will be the song sung in our last chapter: "Special" as Agent Joe Pistone's soulfulness pounded the asphalt jungles of the carmine Mafia wall of omertà. Joe was a cop's cop as well and remains so. We will touch on this mythology as well.

Special Agent Joe Pistone never had any obligation to silence! If he did, he would have been the FBI Mafia agent. He never crossed over that line and to those who have walked the beat and been plainclothes to detective, Joe's integrity and humility leaves an abundance of honor and respect that is way overdue!

Important Definitions and Concepts to Keep in Mind

Quantum psychic moment of trauma

The quantum psychic moment of trauma was formally introduced in 2007 with the publication of *Working with Traumatized Police Officer Patients* and revisited in *Using Five Police Personality Styles* (Rudofossi, 2007, 2009). It is crucial to keep in mind that this is a hypothetical construct which suggests that a breach in what has been afforded by an ecological niche toward proprioception in survival of officers, as one population dealing with severe and repetitive experiences of traumatic losses, experiences a novel and existentially altering experience in encountering the sudden and striking absence of affordances they have become acclimated to, assimilated toward, and accommodated with over a lifetime to this point.

It is a true or veridical and measurable construct that can only begin to be reconstructed by active listening to the narrative as disclosed in a free associative process, best characterized by a psychoanalytic process akin to "free association." It is far from limited by a psychoanalytic paradigm, but inclusive of an existential and logotherapeutic one. It is quantum as it breaches the expectations on a cognitive level, haptic tactual level of experience, and proprioception by disrupting the psychic experience of what the active participant has acclimated and adapted to within an ecological-ethological niche of survival in a world of traumatic loss. Being placed for the first time in an ecological-ethological niche where all that was afforded and prepared for is lost by the anomalous and abrupt maladaptation efforts to correct this anomaly is undone. The threat of death by being held until confirmed by a shoddy source that came through is an example for Special Agent Joseph Dominick Pistone. The lack of any preparation and experience for this life-threatening event is also life altering and the beginning of a remarkable introduction to the sensate perception of one's own transient nature of life. For clinical students and students of law, refer to the original theory in Rudofossi (2007, 2009), which includes the support by expert consensus and peer support with suggestions of intervention and monitoring for experimental and clinical experts.

Metaphorical map of eco-ethological existential equanimity

The map most of us are likely to use is not usually related to as a metaphor. Cartographers lay out coordinates with all kinds of directions as to where to go, what service areas to visit, and parenthetically what to avoid and not go near—as dangerous. Hayakawa (1991), the renowned linguist, US senator, and professor, asked us to think beyond the cartographer's map to a metaphor of the map we use in our mind and language formation.

Taking Hayakawa's ideas, Dr. Albert Ellis, the founder of rational emotive behavior therapy, utilized the Socratic method of asking questions, not settling on unfinished answers as solutions, and disputing non sequiturs in pressing his patients and colleagues to frame our responses to the world as rational as opposed to irrational. The result often is better subsequent health as distinguished from mental illness (Ellis & Joffe, 2019).

From a media ecological framework, Professor Neil Postman (1987) asked us to consider his conscientious objection to educate the very formally educated who at times fall off the Sisyphean precipice in believing he/she knows it all. His argument was episodic bits in an age where tsunamis are sandwiched between commercials for double-mint gum and subliminal messages of doubling pleasure leaves media consumers bemused and bewildered as we are befuddled as voyeurs of life with empty repeats of entertainment and amusement that keep us numb and unaware of real traumas and losses encountered. Professor Postman declared we are threatened by amusing ourselves to death, while the crushing movements of riots and upheaval destroy our freedoms. In answer to these morose trajectories that possibly threaten extinction of mindful expansion, cognitive science offers some hope. Discoveries of a fluid and dynamic cognitive map we all use to gain direction and movement that are dynamic and in flux are myths we may reflect and act upon. Joseph Campbell in the myth of the hero poignantly expressed that the metaphor is real and is not a reference to point to an analog of truth, as a chart a cartographer lays out.

Capturing Campbell's point is that the very heroic ability to distinguish the ability for movement in one's mental and cognitive universe of assimilation and accommodation almost always requires a different breach in expected outcomes and looking deep within to break new ground in the map one is setting for navigating outside of oneself. In our dialogues, Joe Pistone succeeded in deep-cover operations where nothing could be taken for granted. Joe navigated through traumatic losses abounding as we discovered in potentialities for success and mastery in equal measure. Adding to his metaphor as map within the rational analysis of the threats and life encounters he encountered heroically, he set a myth to live by as a special agent where opportunities to learn and build intelligence around becoming culturally competent always requires creating and recreating the map as metaphor in the foreground of attempting to balance extreme danger and rich gain of information and new ties forged with equanimity. His facility of tackling criminal enterprise is a cost-effective gambit.

Hayakawa adds that the symbolic language and hidden silence in the enquiry is akin to gaining peeks into unknown cultural problems for academic and scientific purposes as much as it is gained ground to enhance survivability when emerging perilous domains as organized criminal syndicates are wont to be and become. The evidence of the forging of subtle bridges and enterprise, while not directly laid out by Special Agent Pistone, was understood and intuited by his hyper-intuitive ingenuity and is left to be deciphered. We have just discovered a marking to explore in this book. Much more work needs to be done, but the foundation is present in what we may call and title a metaphorical map of eco-ethological existential equanimity.

Uncertainty principle and experimenter effect

Professor Dr. Werner Heisenberg discovered the uncertainty principle and applied it to the world of physics and nuclear fusion as an infant science, in which a margin of error based on human factors to ecological influences and observation must be acknowledged in the otherwise most meticulous methods used in scientific exploration (Heisenberg, 1952, 1971, 1989).

Through no fault of his own, Dr. Heisenberg was thrust into the mass-murdering world of Adolf Hitler and the forceful takeover of the democratic Weimar Republic by National Democratic Socialism. One of the less well-known contributions to science and most relevant to understanding deep-cover intelligence is the experimenter effect. The experimenter effect is when the research scientist conducting a controlled experiment, quasi-experimental research, or field experiment influences not only other participants, and is influenced by the experiment him/herself but, remarkably, impacts on the most physical inanimate aspects of the experiment as well. So, applying this finding of experimenter effect in the context of the uncertainty principle on a case of a patient in treatment with a clinician as primary care, such as a licensed physician, psychologists/psychiatrists, interprets into the inchoate and chaotic dynamics one cannot control for in the theater of field operations. Although unknown to the OSS as the predecessor of the CIA, in a twist of irony, a dynamic match leading to spy versus spy emerged within the third heartless hub of the Third Reich. A baseball player with an eidetic memory similar to

Joe D. Pistone's, named Moe Berg, was sent on a mission he accepted in which the goal would be to assassinate Dr. Werner Heisenberg (Becker, 1997; Dawidoff, 1995; Heisenberg, 1952, 1971, 1989).

Like Heisenberg, who was clearly an anomalous genius, Moe Berg, who had a genius IQ, repeat winner of *Jeopardy* and eccentric as an NYU and Columbia University Law School graduate, sought to confront Heisenberg in a moment of truth in Nazi Germany. In an intuitive hyper-sensitivity, he realized the hidden great saboteur of the Third Reich hijacked by Hitler and the National Socialist Democratic Party (NSDP), otherwise known from 1925 to 1945 as the Nazi party, was none other than Heisenberg. Professor Heisenberg in a way sabotaged the nuclear program he was forced into at first under protest to work on the first atom bomb and with wanton relish cached his intent to sabotage it. So, to clarify a complex situation, Moe Berg, the legendary baseball player, autodidact with an eidetic memory, Jewish American, was a spy engaged by the OSS to assassinate Heisenberg. Paused at the moment he and Heisenberg met. Let's now pause and add another crucial dynamic to this process.

In a different context, but paralleling applied scientific insight, Professor Dr. Freida Fromm Reichmann (1950), who was an analyst of a different sort—she was a psychologist-physician passionately attempting to solve mental health enigmas in the young science of psychoanalysis. In working on the issue of transference of earlier and unconscious conflicts into the present in all human beings, the clinician, if not made aware of his/her own conflict within the treatment milieu (ecological niche), and his/her human nature (ethological influences unconsciously brought to assessment and treatment), was discovered to impact unconsciously on the assessment, treatment, and ongoing experiment of analysis with her/his patient. In her classic work, Dr. Freida Fromm Reichman presents cases of intensive psychotherapy and the reality of counter-transference, including love and hate, that if unknown and not worked through is likely to transfer from earlier relationships with significant authority figures such as father, mother, to current relationships including, most significantly, the experimental nature of therapy between two participants.

Perhaps not so far from physics for Heisenberg and not so close to psychoanalysis for Dr. Reichmann to push away was the issue of how an experimenter in physics could impact on his experiment via ecological niches and more so how the nature of the experiment itself impacts on the experimenter's perceptions, intuitions, observations, measurement, and, most significantly, judgment (Heisenberg, 1952; Reichmann, 1950). In other words, Professor Heisenberg brilliantly educated researchers that experimenter effects ranged from impacting on the experiment and the ecological niche itself in multiple and complex nonlinear directions.

In transferring this useful understanding of applied interactions, often marginalized and largely silent, hints at the ingenuity discovered and perhaps reframed in our own psychological imagination. In her own remarkable analysis, Dr. Freida Fromm Reichmann married her own analysand, famed sociologist and psychologist-psychoanalyst Dr. Professor Erich Fromm (Fromm, 1957). In honestly disclosing the unexpected uncertainty principle and experimenter effect to Professor Dr. Sigmund Freud, her dilemma of being Erich's healer was in major conflict with the temptation to become Erich's lover—such an enigma prompted Dr. Freud to guide her to stop therapy and consider her love was potentially real. It was, and she married her mate.

Paralleling Dr. Reichmann was Heisenberg's hidden discovery in a parallel and quantum leap of scientific perspicuity wrestled with the experimenter effect on every empirical study in the field of physics in which the experimenter shaped and impacted on the subject or participant he/she studied and even more radical, the eco-ethological boundaries of psychophysics impacts on the existential meaning and vacuums that can frame a tense and conflictual relationship. Yet,

148 Dialogue, Insight, and Discovery

the key to this hypothetical construct is the ingenuity of Heisenberg's uncertainty principle and experimenter effect synergy in the synchronization of the moment when Berg, the baseball catcher in his identity mode as operational agent, saved the day rather than rued it. Bases were loaded for assassination, yet in an existential moment of choice to do Heisenberg in, or leave him in outfield, Berg paused. In the ever-contracting finite moment, he held back centripetal force to fire a slug by the slugger into Heisenberg. Counter-intuitively with use of his full power of discretion, he was compelled by centrifugal force to not shoot Professor Heisenberg. Why? It is clear Moe Berg picked up in a brief cryptic interaction Heisenberg's response to knowing he was being followed and in target that his adversary was I Claudius, not Nero. In a moment of probability tossing of the dice, his hyper-intuitive order overcame chaos and Moe Berg turned away. The tenacity to not act during an interaction is a master stroke in interactional synchrony. The brief meeting in the stitch of time yielded quantum results and the hit was caught by wisdom, as later the world would benefit from Heisenberg in untold ways toward controlling nuclear extreme warfare.

It is the principle of uncertainty understood in context that offers benefits yielded in the hidden lattice that staves off gambles more easily indulged in. All that glitters is not gold. All that appears orderly may be implicit sabotage, which in some ecological niches brings platinum results for all participants, even though at the time of choices taken it was unknown. As students of deep cover, you have witnessed Special Agent Joe Dominick Pistone staving off chaos with no explicit rules as markings until his genuine ability to tolerate the uncertainty principle and the multiple experimenter effects in constant flux within a six-year field experiment. Pistone's effective rules cast the dice in a mold that stitched the time of the syndicate from all-out bloodbaths into the halls of justice. His discernment in multiple experiments with bases loaded, with all its wiseguys uncontrollable and uncertainty margins of error were folded over with certainty at home base. It is remarkable to understand the catcher as spy who rolled the dice of probability and struck a home run once, or Dr. Reichmann twice. Although we cannot computationally ever know with certainty the veridical frequency, intensity, and duration of Special Agent Joseph Dominick Pistone's thrust into the world of the gangster and his ingenious intuitive moves and evasion of death and delivering death, let's allow our scientific minds to resonate with psychological imagination as to the punctuations of ingenuity with the few analyses we have peeked in on.

Conceptual and Writing Exercises for Student and Professor Only

1. A ladder to aspire toward our war on terror as a psychological war first and foremost begins with organized criminal enterprises. Unlike the Italian mafiosi, foreign enemies to the United States, United Kingdom, and European Union have waged war on the United States and allies. How does an agent move ahead and infiltrate a hostile and foreign nation to gather intelligence and in war-like conditions possibly assassinate a mass murderer? Read the text mentioned in this chapter, *The Catcher Was a Spy*, and write out the parallels you find with the insights you've gained and processed in this chapter.
2. In this chapter, Erich Fromm was mentioned as a classic analysand of Dr. Freida Fromm Reichmann and later became her husband and psychoanalyst of note. In his pivotal look underscoring conformity as an escape from freedom, he posits a sociological theory and psychological insight toward responsible dissent to being passive to conformity. Read your own copy of *Escape from Freedom* (Fromm, 1957), and seek out at least one similarity you can find in this chapter, or earlier chapters, depicting the culture, origin, or proliferation of organized crime thinking and dos and don'ts. In pausing and seeking your own critical

thinking skills to apply, now analyze why and how organized crime syndicates are often at odds with totalitarian governments, and write out two dissimilarities.
3. In most group formations and norm-setting processes, irrational thinking and dogmatic affirmations that overgeneralize findings, glorifying or idealizing any ethnic, social, or specialized group in distinction to another, hold dangers. Thinking dichotomously as groups, being inferior and superior are constructs that engender bias and increase the likelihood of violence. On the other hand, cultural groups including insulation serve to create cohesion and balance within each group's hierarchical structure that unfolds. Joe Pistone as Donnie Brasco knew and made it clear from the onset to consciously not turn off his spontaneity and self-discretion. It is crucial to not surrender one's own identity and it is here that Joe Pistone offers a crucial insight into the dynamic of survival and adaptation: Now you may want to go back and reread or peruse earlier chapters to find out and list Donnie Brasco's identity mode and his resistance to conforming to others' thinking blindly. Using at least two explicit examples, illustrate how Donnie Brasco resisted blindly stereotyping wiseguys, but rather intuitively and with burgeoning knowledge navigated using his newly developing metaphoric map.
4. In this chapter you will find the breakdown of how diplomatic negotiations were achieved by Special Agent Joseph D. Pistone in which his street savvies, mental toughness, and hyper-intuitive personality style all emerge in exacting a path of diplomacy within the treacherous and at times lecherous water of the crime syndicates, finding bridges to impasses and landing exits as needed. Chart out the listed achievements step by step and discuss in small groups the dangers suggested and explicitly provided. Now, in discussion, cull out at least one more additional danger you can suggest in your study group. What is to be done to redirect against that newly identified danger, if anything?
5. In this chapter you were offered a contextualized description of what was disenfranchised losses and multiple events that held potentially traumatic events for Special Agent Joe D. Pistone in the field of operations. List at least five different losses we touched on that are not part of acceptable cultural expressions of loss in law enforcement culture. Discuss how your own empathy for and with Special Agent Pistone can be expressed in a culturally competent manner that is respectful and includes active listening skills.
6. Is there at least one major loss among many for the Mafia family capos, made members, and associates you can choose and write about?
7. Is it really nature or nurture that creates an ecology of violence and ethological motivation to survive within the Mafia family that may be opened to intervention by relating to a law enforcement officer? Can you find a case of a statesman or -woman who came from a Mafia family and became a stalwart law enforcement officer and attributed his/her experience within a family milieu of organized crime as the fulcrum that motivated him/her to change and become a law enforcement, legal expert, or statesman?
8. Comb through this chapter and make a list of all the references to violence and threats of violence in the content and flow of disclosure of witnessed, threatened, and actual violence encountered by Special Agent Joe Pistone during Operation Donnie Brasco. Multiply that number by 3 and then by 2,190, which is 6 years [365 days × 6 years] to give you a rough and very conservative frequency of potentially traumatic events endured by FBI Special Agent Joseph Dominick Pistone. How can an agent possibly be renumerated for such overwhelming experiences of trauma and the cumulative impact it has had on his life, notwithstanding his intrinsic tendency for resilience and tough-mindedness? Your professor will lead the discussion and point out commonalities to consider and draw wisdom from with participation from all students.

References

Becker, E. (1997). *The denial of death*. New York: Simon & Schuster.
Campbell, J. (2008). *The hero with a thousand faces*. New York: New World Library.
Dawidoff, N. (1995). *The catcher was a spy: The mysterious life of Moe Berg*. New York: Random House.
Ellis, A., & Joffe, D. (2019). *Rational emotive behavior therapy*. Washington, DC: American Psychological Association.
Fromm, E. (1957). *The forgotten language: An introduction to the understanding of dreams, fairy tales, and myths*. New York: Grove Press.
Hayakawa, I. S. (1991). *Language in thought and action*. New York: Harper Collins.
Heisenberg, W. (1952). *Philosophic problems of nuclear science: Eight lectures*. New York: Faber and Faber.
Heisenberg, W. (1971). *Physics and beyond: Encounters and conversations*. New York: Harper & Row.
Heisenberg, W. (1989). *Encounters with Einstein*. Princeton, NJ: Princeton University Press.
Maslow, A. (1971). *The farther reaches of human nature*. New York: Viking.
Postman, N. (1987). *Amusing ourselves to death*. New York: Methuen.
Reichmann, F. F. (1950). *Principles of intensive psychotherapy*. Chicago: University of Chicago Press.
Rudofossi, D. M. (2007). *Working with traumatized police-officer patients: A clinician's guide to complex PTSD syndromes in public safety professionals*. New York: Routledge.
Rudofossi, D. M. (2009). *A cop doc's guide to public safety complex trauma syndrome: Using five police personality styles*. Amityville, NY: Baywood.
Rudofossi, D. M. (2012). *A street survival guide for public safety officers: The cop doc's strategies for surviving trauma, loss, and terrorism*. Boca Raton, FL: CRC Press.
Rudofossi, D. M. (2013). *A cop doc's guide to understanding terrorism as human evil: Healing from complex trauma syndromes for military, police, and public safety officers and their families*. Amityville, NY: Baywood.
Rudofossi, D. M. (2015). *Dealing with the mentally ill person on the street: An assessment and intervention guide for public safety professionals*. Springfield, IL: Charles C. Thomas.
Rudofossi, D. M. (2017). *Cop doc. The police psychologist's casebook—Narratives from police psychology*. New York: Routledge.
Rudofossi, D. M., & Ellis, R. R. (1999). *Differential police personality styles use of coping strategies, ego mechanisms of defense in adaptation to trauma and loss*. Symposium conducted at the meeting of the American Psychological Association, Boston, Massachusetts.

7
DISENFRANCHISED LOSSES AND COMPLEX PTSD—*ECO-ETHOLOGICAL EXISTENTIAL ANALYSIS*

Not all law enforcement and military agents are created equal. Some bureaucratic thinking follows the same way of dealing with radically shifting terrorists using the same old tactics and strategies that simply did not, do not, and will not, work. Einstein said that doing the same thing over and over again and expecting different results is insanity. Identifying with the victim mentality and on another hand conforming with that evil in reality is, in reality, one and the same attitude. How we may look at gangster Lucky Luciano, who when in a moment he was called to assist, defended the borders of the West Coast at war with fascism, and he did his "job" well. That is a fact. His motto with the US military was "loose lips sink ships."

Truth needs expression without fear. Not all silence is equal; not all dons have donned their character when civilization was threatened. Messes often created in bureaucratic triangles need solutions that are innovative. One step ahead of the bad guys means being aware of who those real bad guys are—in reality, indeed. Omertà is silence, but silence over what? Silence over an excerpt from a wiretap of La Cosa Nostra telephone conversation relating to the murder of William Jackson, as quoted in Peter Blatty's *The Exorcist* (1994):

JAMES TORELLO: "Jackson was hung on the meat hook. He was so heavy he bent it. He was on that thing three days before he croaked."
FRANK BUCCIERI: [Giggling] "Jackie, you should've seen the guy. Like an elephant, he was. And when Jimmy hit with that electric prod. [Excitedly] He was flopping around on that hook, Jackie. We tossed water on him to give the prod a better charge, and he's screaming."
As excerpted from *A Cop Doc's Guide to Understanding Terrorism as Human Evil: Healing from Complex Trauma Syndromes for Military, Police and Public Safety Officers and their Families* (Rudofossi, 2013, p. 48)

Introduction

This chapter sketches a series of losses as a hub that set complex PTSD and dissociation as adaptive functional dissociation in the experiences of Special Agent Joseph Dominick Pistone. Losses are significant, disenfranchised, and complex. Gordian knots existentially fit here in describing the experiences as spoken by the late Dr. Al Benner, cop doc, captain in the San

DOI: 10.4324/9781032202761-8

Francisco Police Department, and wingman in the United States Marine Corps. In more than one conversation with him, he put it well: "the police [Fed equivalent as well] administration does what it does without malevolence and conspiracy by placing the finest police folks in the line of fire without adequate protection from the aftermath and homecoming response to overload of traumatic loss." Dr. Benner left a legacy in which he too suffered the hits of multiple losses and kept on moving along with the most important antidote to the impact of such trauma which is resilience.

Special Agent Joseph Dominick Pistone as Donnie Brasco, not abstractly but on multiple levels, endured the harsh reality of constant threat and danger with different significant bosses of this thing of ours as in La Cosa Nostra. Each relationship held its "markings" and "knots" with light threads to platinum bonds he engaged his personal best in. That being the reality for Donnie Brasco, as he forged each connection and relationships over time and experience ranging from very threatening to very sybaritic ecological niches became reality for Joseph Pistone post Operation Donnie Brasco.

For Donnie Brasco, multiple potential experiences of loss interlinked with each potential trauma layered into the context of rapport with other member of La Cosa Nostra. Implicit and explicit rules, as noted earlier, created a maze to walk through. In some cases, these relationships become web-like designs not so easily unwoven from their own existential links, markings, and looped knots within each ecological niche. Not forgetting for a moment that for Joseph Pistone the FBI identity mode demanded adaptation with its own (ethological) survival motivation.

In a respectful collegial manner, Joseph Dominick Pistone was healthy and remains mentally healthy. His resilience and insight into how he remained remarkably healthy for having experienced the trauma he endured over six years of navigation within the Mafia is part of the picture. The other side, west of Eden, is that when celebrity and legendary status fades, it does not tarnish the losses and their re-emergence in many venues of leakage and disclosure. Among friends a transformation and reinvigoration of value that is more than linear emerges in the therapeutic dialogue to follow in respecting and valuing the identity mode of Donnie Brasco.

Joseph Dominick Pistone's exquisite losses as endured, and he still endures, are outlined unapologetically within this chapter. The purpose here is to point out that resilience does not mean one does not have memories and painful losses that bounce back into view after remaining hidden over stretches of time. It should be understood that those losses, while never gone, do not anchor the observing participant in the residue of painful perseveration of trauma as an unwitting victim (Rudofossi & Maloney, 2019).

Choice and responsibility are always extant.

Adaptive-Intuitive Resilient LEO Personality Style

In my other books and guides to complex PTSD, grief, and dissociative disorders in police and public safety populations, the adaptive-intuitive resilient officer/agent/combat soldier is very rare. It is almost non-existent in my clinical experience, that is as clinician and researcher, to discover an agent/officer with such resilience as Joe Pistone who did not receive appreciable treatment for complex PTSD (Rudofossi, 2007, 2009, 2012).

Special Agent Joe Pistone is the outlier in this N of 1. Notwithstanding, I am not inferring nor saying no defenses and traits that are conflictual and adverse are completely absent. Quite opposite of that posture is Joe Dominick Pistone's, and by proxy Donnie Brasco's, heroic, legendary, resilience toward traumatic and dissociative processes to survive.

Special Agent Joseph Pistone's ability to persevere and work through the level of losses is anomalous. While, for example, one can find lists of soldiers in combat, prisoner of war, and on special forces and operations with propensities and remarkable resilience, they are not of the same type and quality, nor quantity, as endured by Donnie Brasco. Joe Pistone had to live and prosper without a lapse in his cognitive, behavioral, and emotional self-presentation with others for years. Often daily conflicts based on his identity mode as Donnie Brasco, the wiseguy initiate, and Joe Pistone, the tenured FBI special agent, collided. In eco-ethological niches where worlds of values, thinking, and emotional collusions occurred, resilience becomes the outlier for intrinsic adaptiveness in his ability to heal from cumulative and traumatic losses. But that fact does not suffice in and of itself. In clinically moving into the exploration of complex losses and dissociative processes that emerge in the ecological niches of violence and trauma, gaining a handle on his own shield of the noetic dimension and resilience is well worth the while. In the following segments, Special Agent Joseph Dominick Pistone and Cop Doc Dan Rudofossi explore his psyche and resilience. Socratically, let's home in on some good questions to contemplate.

Questions to Guide You as Navigational Tools: Learning Objectives

1. In an attempt to gain a more realistic tabulation of the frequency of potentially traumatic events from narrative, try to estimate the duration and intensity of potential losses encountered by recounting the relationships forged that were severed when operation Donnie Brasco was abruptly closed down.
2. In understanding the discernment of Special Agent Pistone who invested in being Donnie Brasco for six years and dealt with the legal undulations post arrests, indictments, convictions, and trials, how much traumatic loss potentially was activated in identifying the various made wiseguys, associates, and others in La Cosa Nostra who knew him as Donnie Brasco?
3. Is there an innate inborn dimension that assists Special Agent Joe Dominick Pistone to sustain the identity mode of Donnie Brasco with balance and healthy resilience?
4. Does Special Agent Pistone's "adaptive functional dissociation" emerge as a personality style he came to the table with as adaptive resilient with hyper-intuitive traits which helped frame his success (Rudofossi, 1994, 1997, 2007, 2009; Rudofossi & Ellis, 1999)?
5. Remember that in most officers maladaptive dysfunctional dissociation becomes extant after leaving the trauma, addictions, and immersion, and retirement and aging has set in its process of regression and emergence of unworked-through trauma mazes. This is not manifest in the case of Joe Pistone. Was Donnie Brasco identity mode a result of Joe Pistone's natural resilience? Did his unique personality dynamics pique a healthier intuitive growth and spiritual empowerment rather than a maladaptive dysfunctional dissociation as in some of the best tough-minded detectives who suffer from severe complex PTSD and mood disorder?
6. In Special Agent Joseph D. Pistone's different identity modes, shifts among his identity modes, and adaptation, he gained in healthier means of working through by recounting his history and experiences to other agents. Is surviving, ethologically speaking, at one's best level, existentially speaking, experiencing life for all its worth without fear and anxiety possible for those who are not exceptional but quite the average service-oriented special agent, or police officer?

Returning to our final interview, Special Agent Joseph Dominick Pistone's mental acuity is atypical; it is not necessary for you to actively perceive in your own meta-cognitive understanding with effort. Some moments are more tearful than others. It is an old poor myth, perhaps best

154 Disenfranchised Losses and Complex PTSD

let out with turgidity, that emotions and passion have no place in academia and clinical work. Being real by allowing ventilation of passion to reason gives you, and me, motivation to add to our depth of emotional awareness, our own intellect, and increasing ability to glean intelligence from others. Perhaps the most successful and intelligent of special agents in the history of American law enforcement is Joe Dominick Pistone. It is a privilege to actively listen to the narrative to follow. Pausing for a moment, let's actively pay attention and listen as we take our last pause. Kindly become aware of one more task at hand to ferret out definitions as clues to understanding as follows.

Definitions to Be Aware Of

Alexithymia and adaptive functional dissociation
Distancing loss via screen memories
Endogenous wiring and antisocial behavior
Ghosting criminals, not being ghosted
Internalized witnessing
Noetic dimension and essential motivation
Oedipal strivings and crime
Responsibleness

Regardless of your education/training as you venture into this chapter as a criminal justice or law student, homeland security analyst, or a tenured agent or detective, please dare to imagine using your third ear, where losses become contextualized and valued—as gifts generously offered can be heard best with empathic ears. Get your note pads ready …

COP DR DAN RUDOFOSSI: "Special Agent Joe Dominick Pistone, I can so appreciate the elegance of your sleuthing in an age of J. E. Hoover's FBI. It was a time when agents were trusted as were officers in doing the right thing and getting a mission accomplished. It appears to me from our last dialogue that allowing discernment was bolstered by the key of trusting officers as well as agents well trained to do investigations of merit and worth. In that light there is much protest against policing in general and even in my view the outlandish defunding the police as a solution rather than reform within and without. Let me ask you in this context, what is your perspective on the recent events in policing?"

FBI AGENT JOSEPH DOMINICK PISTONE: "Doc, it is sickening to me. Agents have to be treated equally as perpetrators getting the same airtime and space!?! Including the psychologists/psychiatrists unlike yourself, how many of those who are judging and stereotyping police and overstepping police culture—without scrutinizing what we are all about? How come no one is asking us the questions to find answers we can give them?"

"It has come to the point where I can watch only so much of the news, as so much is sensationalism and negative stuff."

"You see an investigation going on and the media plays the agent as if they are equal in motivation and behavior as to the suspects they are investigating."

"Blind excusal of riotous behavior and violence against many innocent people is excused away. How does an officer who gets smashed in the face with a brick, gushing blood, get a flash in the snap polaroid exposure while some hoodlum ranting violence gets three minutes on national news coverage? Is that sensible at all? No, it's sick Dr. Dan. This is not civil rights. In the FBI we fought blood, sweat, and tears for civil rights for all American citizens. It is not one racial group over another, but learning to live in peace and civilly that is the crux of the issue. In dealing with criminal justice, one must be color blind as to the administration of justice."

COP DR DAN RUDOFOSSI: "I am with you Special Agent Joe Pistone! One clear message I hear from cops and special agents behind the politics and the easy pigeon-holing police as if we are one linear label is that as first responders, if we use the term Centurion, we are enjoined to lay our own life down for public safety, service, and civil liberties and rights, but with little rights and no right to counter in dissent and our own voice—something is critically wrong from a rational and humane perspective of justice and liberty."

FBI AGENT JOSEPH DOMINICK PISTONE: "Yes that's exactly it. Doc, let me tell you something, it's too sickening to watch anymore. As I see it, nowadays, legit law enforcement officers are attacked, and being treated like garbage."

"As if the police officers and special agents are equals to the perps who commit violent crimes. Look, police for the most part are doing their job legitimately and well. Underpaid for the risks and psychological impact they endure every day, they are then insulted and thrown on a garbage heap. Cops always had to deal with bad guys calling them the worst insults that are unearned."

"I am not saying all cops are squeaky clean. We all know those who are bad apples, but rotten apples exist in any group, occupation, and culture. But the vast majority are doing an impossible mission with minimum support. The funding for officers and their families is in the lower end of the middle class, which is evaporating. Now you see plastered all over this politician and pundit, shit man, the rat man saying, Defund the Police!"

"Who gets the free card to present officers as if we are all some low life that even kids need to worry about? It is not a black/white issue; the world is a lot larger than two colors. No good officer thinks in terms of black and white victims, nor perpetrators."

"I know you don't like the term, but, outside of the few crazies that get on the job, it is still that way, only a very few rare cops get on and commit murder, organized crime, and become hit men for the Mafia. By the public being hostile and the anti-police media coverage, I believe creates that ecology that drives these agents and cops to take their own lives, point-blank."

"The guy lifts out a fridge from a burglary and on the way out herniates his disc, now the officer is being sued because the rear-cuffs could have been done by front-cuffing him. If it wasn't so sad it would be comical? Capish?"

COP DR DAN RUDOFOSSI: [Uneasy laughter hardly audible in our shared ill-at-ease pain over such extreme prejudice and maladjusted racism against police.] "Exactly on point! Great line about the media pundits. You know my work on Centurioncide underscores attacking the individual and collective union of police and public safety officers and, as you know, the law enforcement culture we were part of as 'blue-blooded culture.'"

"Centurioncide captures the centripetal force to a hub of prejudgment and slander against officers and their loved ones who witness this humiliation of officers."

"Open assaults, property damage, and attacks on the people and communities we represent and live in add fuel to the fire of police trauma and loss. Targeting police as stereotypical Keystone Cops—or gangsters with shields."

"Stereotyping and ignoring individual differences are at the outer push to alienate officers by radical movements given credibility. This is a threat to science and society both."

"By immediately buying into blatant aspersions, illogical and ahistorical hysteria, a supercharge like the fictional Blob subsumes and transforms the mob."

"Conforming to half-truths that target police is the most dangerous move as 'might makes right in forcing change,' and 'legislating morality' as the linchpin of all fascist movements, it is centrifugal force to the periphery of society by marginalizing the most important service models."

"Joe, without letting our passion to support and keep the strength of police and policing intact, if I can suggest as a segue to shifting our interview into you as an individual, is it true that you spent your life in part fighting the excellent fight—against might makes right—from the ground up? In my estimation, and I can be wrong as the next fellow, you as an honorable special agent of the FBI kept it together, stayed 'with-it,' and weathered what would break apart most LEOs. You became a hero not as fabricated, but real as you are, Joe."

FBI AGENT JOSEPH DOMINICK PISTONE: "Hey, Doc, the reality is most will not ever have a clue of the real-deal work needed in doing deep cover. Most good cops, if not excellent officers, just don't have it in them to do the work I did, especially without blowing their cover. It's all about doing the job right. I did what I had to do. Just to say, this environment for police and special agents has changed so much, it is not as good for doing the necessary work to take down criminal enterprises. Centurioncide always existed but not like now, it is unparallel to any time save the late 60s and early 70s."

COP DR DAN RUDOFOSSI: "The journey you took was in the early 70s, which could make any human being and LEO shake. I am not talking about the LEO the lion. All joking aside, you emerged with a unique wisdom. I am seeking another gift unspoken and not to be forgotten in your lifetime, and beyond which I share with you as my friend and brother in blue, Special Agent Joe Pistone."

FBI AGENT JOSEPH DOMINICK PISTONE: "A funny point, which may not be that important, is the fact some of the wiseguys themselves really didn't believe I was a special agent of the FBI after the indictments and convictions came down. They couldn't believe that Donnie Brasco was a shadow of Joseph Dominick Pistone, Special Agent, FBI."

COP DR DAN RUDOFOSSI: "Redirecting for now, it appears when you did your deep cover what grabbed me was you rescued some wiseguys from themselves with no gratitude, and even less understanding on their part as individuals, but not all were inured as to your genuinely extending the SOS inflatable tube from their drowning on their own self-made sabotage."

FBI AGENT JOSEPH DOMINICK PISTONE: "It's hard to put it into words and explain Doc, by putting into psychological terms what is experienced here." [This difficulty in expressing loss and pain related to deep-cover work is exacerbated by the three worlds described as mistresses who all desired to monopolize and squelch Joe Pistone's feeling. The clarity of Centurioncide then is given clarity and release.] "Keep in mind the current anti-police sentiment pushes a lot of cops toward withdrawal and mental breakdowns because no one wants to push the envelope and be buried under exposing yourself to attacks from the front and back."

COP DR DAN RUDOFOSSI: "I connect with you. Officers have always worn some armor of invulnerability, but for most cops nowadays, it is a fear of allowing any vulnerability into the mix of police work, especially empathy and real connection with victims, witnesses, and even wiseguys."

"Constant loss unexpressed leaves the officer stuck in a world that views vulnerability as weakness. If it works, as we do our *Eco-Ethological Existential Analysis* of your experiences, we can return for some peek under the cover of your own conscious awareness of the existential unconscious insight that may be redeemable for you from your gifts you've shared graciously with me."

FBI AGENT JOSEPH DOMINICK PISTONE: "Well, the part that isn't that important but may be relevant here is that these wiseguys, although different in personality, were not all ruthless tyrants, but they all are capable of becoming stone-cold killers. That fact is never forgotten."

"Still, in the case of Sonny Black and to a degree, Lefty, they weren't without some compassion toward others."

Alexithymia and Adaptive Functional Dissociation

The outward lack of expressing certain emotions and feelings due to socialization and learning experiences is a core component of alexithymia and is also a defense with the use of identity mode variation within adaptive functional dissociation.

Alexithymia as resistance against expressing loss and pain related to deep-cover work is exacerbated by the three different worlds Joe Pistone lived in. Mistresses make sense in the context of adaptive functional dissociation and alexithymia as ways to distance oneself from the painful losses inflicted by living and adapting to eco-ethological niches of traumatic losses. Hardly allowed ventilation with others, the officer intentionally will use the gallows humor, the emotional and social distancing, and numbing via addictions the real feelings, including grief and loss, that are at the very human condition of grief. In the worlds of the wiseguy and police-oriented culture within eco-ethological niches, loss leaves one in a world that views vulnerability as weakness. Alexithymia (Levant, 1997, 2001) is gender based as being more common in males within macro-society; men act on, rather than express, loss, and avoid crying. Such emotional expression is considered unmasculine. In police culture in at least one large-scale study (Rudofossi, 1997) that was heuristic, quantitative, and clinical, evidence of alexithymia emerged that was endemic to police and public-safety culture regardless of race, culture, and gender differences.

Keep in mind that the current anti-police sentiment, which is understood as Centurioncide, has exacerbated emotional and mental withdrawal that is buried in an armor of invulnerability for most cops nowadays.

"A lot of these wiseguys, okay maybe not so much a lot of them, but at least some them, were not complete knuckle-draggers."

"In thinking about some of the gangsters, they sorted things out first and didn't just launch an attack on strangers or acquaintances they hardly knew."

"Sonny Black Napolitano had common sense. He was a real guy. You can say, Doc, under it all, I'd say that in a real life, he would have done better. If he had a fighting chance, he could have been an accountant, for example, rather than a gambling runner for the Bonanno family."

COP DR. DAN RUDOFOSSI: "It is no wonder that the eco-ethological niche in which you learned, lived in, and revisit so often influenced and shaped many adaptive functions including dissociation that worked in your varying identity modes. The alexithymia impacts on us all in some varying manner based on our proclivities toward dealing with loss and trauma events."

FBI AGENT JOSEPH DOMINICK PISTONE: "Sonny had common sense: He was a real guy under it all. In his dealings with people in the mob, and even more so outside the Mafia circles, he opened up his charity and benevolence to others most would scoff at and ignore in their time of need. In his restaurant he served his patrons with a sophistication and style of a real restaurateur."

"You know it makes me think, not for nothing, that under different circumstances, you know Sonny Black Napolitano, captain in the Bonanno crime family, would be Mr. Sonny Black Napolitano the normal all-around good guy and patriot."

"I'd say that in a real life, outside of the Mafia rubric, he would have done better."

"Hey, Doc, I wouldn't say he would be a bank president, but he would get along like everyone else. So, yeah, if he had the opportunity to really choose and not be part of this family and culture he was born into, he may have been very different as a real guy. He would be a decent guy and have a real family life, and contribute in many ways as a law-abiding and decent human being."

"But say, if you look at Tony Mirra, he had the calling of being a wiseguy and would not be anyone different at all; even with all the opportunity he could be afforded he would be violent and a stone-cold murderer. He wasn't wired to be normal."

"How could you be wired to be normal if you're told to kill a guy you know from when you're ten years old and you are ready to do it, and actually do it when you override your own decency to act that way. When your society tells you to do something you know is downright wrong and you do it, what is the hardwiring that allows you to do it? By society I mean the Mafia society."

"Not for nothing, this was not completely true of Sonny Black. Yeah, he was a murderer, but he maintained a connection to me and to others in his life in an appropriate way."

"But how could you be wired right if you could do it without any afterthought of murdering a friend and family member for years with no problem?" [Pause.]

COP DR DAN RUDOFOSSI: "I agree with your points and beyond the factual of nature and nurture as creating the complexity of the perfect gangster as in Sonny Black Napolitano." [Almost inaudible in tone.] "I heard when you suggested Sonny Black Napolitano could have been different and acted as a regular all-around American—a wish to be fulfilled if only in fleeting but important dreams. That wish speaks volumes as to the loss of Sonny, if only the time could be turned back. Hum ... What if he could have left being and even becoming the gangster he did become? The factual world cannot reverse itself, but in our imagination we are allowed such leverage, and that is the unconscious wish at its best, as reality sadly sets in its setting, leaving us all at times with the worst. Understanding and bringing these realities to mindful acceptance is our achievement at our best, if that makes sense for now?"

FBI AGENT JOSEPH DOMINICK PISTONE: "It makes real sense, as the entire Operation Donnie Brasco abruptly closed down without the timing I felt could have set a conclusion that was better. It was a success, agreed, but it could have been a little longer and the finishing touches would have been perfect. Well, near perfect."

COP DR DAN RUDOFOSSI: "Yes, near perfect. But the powers that be had enough and felt the risk to you was too much to toss the dice of chance on. I imagine that they were right in treasuring you as priceless and invaluable. I equally believe they ideally could have let go and trusted your skill and G–d-given ability would have led to stunning successes, even beyond the unparalleled successes you achieved up to that point in reality."

"Looking at your wise discernment, from another perceptual angle, aren't you really pointing out to our existential self-conscience that the Tony Mirras seemed to not only lack a real compassion for others, but real conscience. He was more deserving in a plain, simple, and tragic way to get what he reciprocally gave in karma to others in his final end. In that context, I wonder if you ever wonder as to why and how these associations emerge in the here and now and within the veiled context of losses being rediscovered?"

"Before you answer, for example, your association of Sonny Black, with all the wishful desire of Sonny being repositioned in a birth into a nice and normal world was balderdashed by reminding you and me that Tony Mirra committed monstrous murder of friends and innocent strangers without wincing, right after you shared with me the wishful desire under the fine points that Sonny could have had such a different life and even become your genuine friend, like brothers such as you and I?"

"The why becomes intelligible as a wish fulfillment hidden, since the end of that wish resulted in death that is unintelligible and painful to remember."

Distancing Loss via Screen Memories

Tony Mirra serves as a screen memory (although real and tangible); he achieved his just end in the moral ego defenses of Joe Pistone and me, and likely you as the reader after witnessing no remorse in his violence toward others. But within the wish to change who Sonny was, and how deep in Joe Pistone's wishes left unfulfilled, the loss and death of Sonny is censored from conscious awareness as well as from conscience acceptance because the fact Sonny Black was brutally homicided, his connection to Joe Pistone cannot be resolved without the psychoanalytic and existential motivation being exposed to conscious awareness and conscience sensibility. Parenthetically, what cannot fit in well with and for fulfillment of our deepest wishes, remains hidden under our own screen memories and defenses.

"It is no wonder the conscious mind buries and suppresses such painful losses under the defenses we are all so wont to make to function, and adaptive even if dissociatively under our blue shield of silence and toughness."

FBI AGENT JOSEPH DOMINICK PISTONE: "Hey, Doc, I wouldn't say Sonny Black would be a bank president, but maybe a bank midlevel manager, he would get along like everyone else living a normal life without all the high drama. His being whacked instead because he shook my hand, and supporting my entry into La Cosa Nostra, overriding Sabella, etc. I mean, if Sonny was given a college education away, far away from his lifestyle, and association with and to La Cosa Nostra, he would be alive today. Yes, I can say I wish that was possible, I guess."

COP DR DAN RUDOFOSSI: "I believe it is even therapeutic to do what you are doing right now. You are distancing yourself from, and what you did with Sonny Black and some others as well in terms of their death day and the ugliness witnessed. Wishes are good to express and not bury away as in omertà and the blue wall of silence. Kind of similar although motivations, conscious and conscience are quite different, maybe in some ways, unconsciously and unconsciencely they converge."

"Let me explain, what is called the 'noetic dimension.'"

Noetic Dimension: Essential Motivation

Dr. Viktor Frankl, who survived the atrocities of the Holocaust and the insidious rise of National Socialism, did not lose his humanity, and in his extraordinary record of his experiences and his lifelong work toward establishing logotherapy and existential analysis into a worldwide assessment and clinical treatment he remained true to his outlook. That outlook was

> not reducing the patient, witness, victim to any categorization but towards reestablishing the value of meaning, the attitudes associated with purpose toward finding meaning, and the resolve that no matter how extreme a condition one faces in life, one always has an irreducible choice and responsibleness toward self-initiative and meaning toward and shared with others. The irreducible experiences which include heroism and the tragic hits that traumatic losses deliver are made sensible and framed respectfully in this paradigm. It offers a sensibility rather than an oddness in one doing heroic work. In Joe Pistone's odyssey as Donnie Brasco, it is clear at this point how much of his priceless life and commitment to honorable ends was sacrificed to achieve what would assist the society we live in toward understanding and transcending for all the misadventures to tragic ends that organized crime portend.

"The noetic attempts to frame what is the unconscious center of our existence. It is so powerful because it is a human aspect of who we are, what is meaningful to us as individuals, and yet is worth sacrificing all we have, if not our own lives, for [Frankl, 1973, 1979, 2000; Graber, 2004]."

"For me, Agent Pistone, it is remarkable as to your efforts to save Sonny Black Napolitano. These guys, as bad as they were, had courage. In some ways it seems they held their position and ground, even as negative and harmful to themselves on one hand, that he hid from law enforcement and gave up to wiseguys who were to do him in, as you educated me about."

"So, yeah, if he had the opportunity to really choose and not be part of this family and culture he was born into, he may have been a very different person. He may have been a real guy. I mean he would be a decent guy with a real family life. Maybe he would even contribute in many ways as a law-abiding and decent human being."

FBI AGENT JOSEPH DOMINICK PISTONE: "I agree with what you're suggesting here about the unconscious as a motivator. I mean, as I said, and to repeat, Doc, if you look at Tony Mirra, he had the calling of being a wiseguy and would not be anyone different at all even with all the opportunity he could be afforded. I mean by wiseguy gangster, he would be violent, and a stone-cold murderer without a care about murdering whomever. He wasn't wired to be normal."

COP DR DAN RUDOFOSSI: "How interesting for us to pause, consider when you began talking about Sonny Black Napolitano, the moment the undeniable amiable affection if we can call it that respectfully emerged—it was key for you to qualify for both you and me his reality with a wish perhaps unconsciously for him having had the opportunity of a normal family life as some of his unique character really highlighted his difference from 'other gangsters' as being decent—'if only …' I never knew him myself, but knowing you and your thoughts about him brings a certain warmth and redemption without qualification as to his humanity in the tragic webbing of his fate and destiny as lived a day too fast, and a bag full of dollars too short. The sepulcher of Tony Mirra as the emerging cold-killing gangster by association also blotted out our staying with the losses Sonny Black Napolitano provokes under our screen memories." [Silence and pause for sadness to be processed is all the more meaningful in a cherished moment shared.]

FBI AGENT JOSEPH DOMINICK PISTONE: "I agree, but even looking at Tony Mirra as well, I often ask myself, how could you be wired to be normal if you're told to kill a guy you know from when you're ten years old—and you are ready to do it, and actually do it? How can a human being override his own sense of decency, and act that way? When your society tells you to do something you know is downright wrong, and you do it not because you don't know right from wrong, but because the boss says wrong is right when you're going the way of the hitman. So, guess what, you do it!"

"What is the hardwiring that allows you to do it?"

Endogenous Wiring and Antisocial Behavior

Dr. Samenow, Dr. Stone, and Dr. Hare have shown strong evidence that a biopsychosocial drive exists that provokes the criminal behavior in criminal personality-disordered individuals without normal censoring most persons have. In the prodigious work of Dr. Samenow on the criminal personality, he underscored the intransigent nature of those whose proclivities heighten the likelihood of commission of crimes. Some of his posits are that we miss the facts and try to find social, economic, and even political causes to not attribute guilt and responsibility for violence of all types leading to lawful interjection to stop criminal behavior. In the work of Dr. Hare we find instruments that help clinicians assess and intervene at times with imprisonment from serial thieves, robbers, rapists, and criminals. In Dr. Stone's work he uses a scaling of the human capacity to perpetrate acts of evil against other humans, which usually begins with animal cruelty. Dr. Stone empirically illustrates these gradations in sync with a lack of conscience toward the victims impacted on each rung of the ladder up. Although these three theorists and master clinicians are exquisite in diagnosis, all are adept and committed clinicians who offer real solutions including tough-love approaches and corrective consequences in assisting the patient to inmate in managing violence without obfuscating their own responsibility and hopeful gain of insight.

"That is my question Doc, to you. By society, I mean the Mafia society. Yeah, in a way your point is on the money. As it was not true of Sonny Black. Sonny maintained a connection to me. How could you be wired right if you could do it without any afterthought of murdering a friend and family member for years with no problem? Sonny could potentially do that, but he did not. Tony Mirra, no issue, as he was a killer through and through and he relished doing his job as he envisioned being a Mafia boss." [Pause.]

COP DR DAN RUDOFOSSI: "It appears although I shared some of the biopsychosocial theory about the endogenous-born antisocial personality-disordered criminal profile, nowadays we view this behavior as a complex interaction of 'nature and nurture' that leads to criminal behavior, but the monstrous murder of friends, family members, and innocent strangers without wincing is uniquely the psychopathic variation which is rare even among those who have antisocial personality disorder."

FBI AGENT JOSEPH DOMINICK PISTONE: "I met some of those pure psychopathic type of gangsters like at Pat's when I was made to wait till being vouched for or be whacked and put in a body bag. It's interesting again, but remember I shared with you that the film *Donnie Brasco* had Al Pacino go for a sit-down and ride to his death as payback for having me shake Sabella and others' hands. It was not Benjie Ruggiero, Lefty was interdicted before he was whacked. He also was in major denial that I was who I was, a deep-cover special agent of the FBI. The part that comes to mind is very significant and a farewell of sorts to me. It was Sonny Black Napolitano, not Lefty saying to his wife, but in reality it was Sonny Black who told his girlfriend the bartender that when he was going for a sit-down, he knew it was a likely hit on himself. He said if it was to be anyone who was an FBI special agent who gained his trust, he was glad it was me. As I said, it was as it was. I did my job and that is it."

COP DR DAN RUDOFOSSI: "The deep-cover operative all police and special agents dream of as glorious as the purple heart a hundred times over, but in your heart of hearts it is not with any weakness but tremendous courage and faith that you had to do what you did. It is, I guess, and it was as you redefine and interpret that stunning achievement with the marking of having lost a real gumba as much as losing Donnie Brasco after the curtains of the operation were abruptly closed."

FBI AGENT JOSEPH DOMINICK PISTONE: "He left behind the tokens that were very important to him as to his being a catholic and his faith. But that message to me did mean something important to Sonny Black Napolitano for me to understand. I believe he knew his card was up and they were going to likely whack him. He was traditional and felt as part of La Cosa Nostra it was something he had to take as a true made member of the Bonanno family. He had made it big and only very temporarily, the minute the FBI disclosed my identity and started to make deals, his days were numbered as a vendetta for his mistake of letting an FBI agent into the closed world of the Mafia."

COP DR DAN RUDOFOSSI: "Respectfully, as a cop doc, I would like to suggest Sonny Black Napolitano was gifting you with what we sometimes understand as a transitional gift with his cross and saints left as tokens of his faith; all this and the message made his murder, as tragic as it was, have some meaning, even as he was taken away in the car to his death. In dying words truth is spoken and Sonny Black spoke his truth to you through his lover he was leaving last before his life was shot short. Sonny Black Napolitano was glad it was you; he cherished and valued the gift of his bond with you as genuine. This message becomes then the noetic bridge in him to you. That is the legacy shared in both your identity and Donnie Brasco as revealed to Sonny Black Napolitano as FBI Agent Joe D. Pistone. The message by his girlfriend became the epiphany of a non-physical bridge, deliverable to you and perhaps redemptive to you as well in your private sensibility. Sonny Black Napolitano reached becoming the capo di tutti and you become made wiseguy if but for a moment in time."

"To the veracity of our own existential analysis, Sonny Black transcended the plight he was in and gifted you with a reality no one else could bestow as a wiseguy. Sonny Black, knowing he was going to die, respected the fact you honestly did as you had to do. He respected you as honorable and as a deep-cover operative doing his job, as he had to do his in his own world of the gangster, we bemoan but understand as far as our rational mind can stretch in stunned sadness."

"Still, in the honor among wiseguys and within that culture, he exonerated you from guilt in his denouement message and that is agape, if one wants to label such a sad and tragic redemption in the face of cruelty and fate less than it has the right to be, proud. The synchrony and achievement are not to be unsung and unheard. That is, the transitional object cannot be reduced to becoming an object to wither and waste away. You succeeded in bridging a gap and cultural miasma to the untouchable unknown world of the gangster. Sonny Black knew he was going for a ride and with no return ticket. Sonny knew full well at that point of leaving his girlfriend that you were both Joe Pistone and Donnie Brasco. Sonny Black knew you as you were, are, and will always be—he respected and affectionately as a member of his family said goodbye!"

"Sonny Black revisited and internally witnessed by you is priceless as his words become a transitional bridge now taken inside your soulful self. You earned respect even among those you had to infiltrate as an honorable and gentle law-enforcement officer and human being. You and I can take this truth and set it free at Quantico, 26 Federal Plaza, and One Police Plaza. As a scientist and clinician, I am gifted to also say as a colleague and dear friend to have framed this truth we can both take to the bank of courage, virtue, and service." [Silence for a few moments.]

FBI AGENT JOSEPH DOMINICK PISTONE: "I would agree with that analysis Doc, as being a unique truth not so evident as a crime scene but as important to it. Sonny did ensure I would know he reached out to tell me he was glad it was me that was the undercover and he held no hard feelings against me. It makes sense to value that bridge between us and the fact Sonny respected Donnie Brasco as the real me as well in doing my job as best as I could. I was real, as you and I established, and that was very important to me, that I never acted. I lived and did my job as best as I could and I got the job done well. I am taking in and thinking now of that bridging the gaps with Sonny. This is good, thank you Doc, it was done with respect and insight."

COP DR DAN RUDOFOSSI: "You're very welcome, Special Agent Joe Pistone. In fact, when I speak of you, I always respect and include your other identity mode, Donnie Brasco. I understand and fully support this was no acting. Living both identity modes, oscillated in your return to normal society where Donnie is the shadow that follows you, as we all have shadows in the light of day; if not, denial creates ghosting you, instead of you actively and purposively ghosting the past."

> ### Ghosting Criminals, not being Ghosted
>
> The ecological survival (ethological) niche here is providing the unique skill to hide in open society and in closed societies without being noticed as a participant observer. It is the unique skillfulness of fitting in without creating undulating waves of notice, paranoia, agitation, or resistance while doing any investigation. You stay visible but your real identity mode is as hidden as an invisible ghost. After the operation, not denying nor obfuscating the cat-and-mouse operation is crucial to not letting its residue of trauma, loss, and dissociation as maladaptive and dysfunctional to set in and obsessively ruminate and agitate oneself.

"I know you know what I mean without details here. But at no time were you acting or playing out a role. It is true Sonny Black is left as a murdered mafioso so to speak. It is with his insight in the worst of moments that your identity as Donnie Brasco stung, as he had forged his trust in the shadow identity that now is resigned to that identity. But you have put it well, you always were and are dominantly Joe Dominick Pistone in all your complexities, including the enormous sacrifices you did masterfully for all."

"Your modes of identity emerged in the defenses that shaped and shape all your ingenuity as a superb agent doing deep cover, having down-deep cover, and always able to draw on the remarkable depth of your deep cover."

"As a cop doc, Special Agent Joe P., I look for evidence as artful science. We can play forward and see the truth of your infiltration as beneficial to Sonny, as paradoxically he connected with you in life and beyond as his message conveys."

"This is my point for you: in my gaining an education by you, my input is much smaller, I imagine, than what I have taken from you. I hopefully have gained enough wisdom to impart to our readers with your input and wisdom the proper lessons needed to learn here, from our joint dialogues as education. As, of course, this is not our last communication, but our last interview, before closing the chapters of this casebook for students, I will return one last time to Sonny Black, but for now, if you will, kindly indulge me with answering my next question about the beginnings of the operation."

FBI AGENT JOSEPH DOMINICK PISTONE: "You mean Operation Donnie Brasco, Doc?" [I affirm, Joe affirms it works for him.]

COP DR DAN RUDOFOSSI: "You were around 35 years of age when you began Operation Donnie Brasco. That happened after doing a very successful tour of duty as an intelligence officer in the US Navy?" [Joseph confirms.] "Could you go back and share with me the experiences of induction to becoming the shadow boxer of Joseph Pistone as Donnie Brasco from a psychological perspective. What that means for me, is to understand your own thoughts and feelings in your own words as to becoming Donnie Brasco, with any additions we have not covered as of yet. To allow yourself to associate to whatever comes to mind."

FBI AGENT JOSEPH DOMINICK PISTONE: "Well, I mean, I went through the academy in the FBI under Mr. J. Edgar Hoover. If you imagine, there was no academy like the one at Quantico today. Our training was done at both the Old Post Office and at the Department of Justice for defensive training. Our firearms training was different as you would go to the Marine barracks at Quantico. Once I had a week in Washington DC, and with having to go down to the United States Marine Corp barracks, you needed to get housing as priority one. Certain apartments were vetted for. At that time in the 70s, you had to pay for apartments yourself and there was no housing that was given to you open acceptance. Since you had to pay for your apartment, which you also had to share for a number of long weeks, it was all on you to motivate yourself. I mean, you had no entitlement to be given all you needed, but you had to show that self-motivated initiative. There was no silver spoon. Nobody who would hand deliver anything; you had to live and breathe in that apartment for 14 weeks."

"Remember, in 1972 they opened the academy and everyone was housed at the FBI Academy for the first time."

"When I came on as a probationary special agent, you had to find living quarters in Washington DC and dress in suit and ties."

"There was no babying you, and everyone was subject to the same rules across the board. No favoritism, but initiative, drive, and motivation were your handle, and not your supervisors or instructors. The rules were, if you broke the rules once, the consequences were swift and fair."

"We all knew the rules of the bureau. Even when no major rules were broken, then a week censured; under the bricks; or a week without pay; or you being transferred somewhere were all possible punishments, or some combination as well. You knew those rules and hey, it didn't matter who you were. All of us were subject to these rules, and abiding by our training as in the NYPD you were told to do such and such, and you did it. Simple as that and clear, as that instruction kept everyone on the same page and on track."

"In class you might come in and as you silently look around, that one day, there was an empty seat. We all knew what that meant. What it meant was clear to all of us. Simple, but effectively done; if you failed an exam, you were gone. There was no such thing as a second, third, or fourth chance to go on after you failed. Being done was done, and that kept the FBI a major and effective law enforcement bureau!"

"You had to rough it out and carve out your own reputation without being distracted and without expectations of being entitled to anything you did not earn. We all felt and knew that was unfair to your mates, and their sense and expectation of fairness. No one was catered to. No preference for any reason, same was true of demerit. We all had the ability to gain entry into the FBI academy. Finishing would be a different story."

"That was it for all of us and no resentment. The message was straight and on point, either you got what it takes to become an FBI special agent or not."

"Those who didn't have what it took were not bad, or losers in our eyes. But they were just not good choices. They did not have the right balance and motivation for becoming an FBI agent. Being elite as a law enforcement officer was achieving excellence and integrity to do what one was expected to do in service and sacrifice for what each of us was called for."

"Look at what is going on today. In comparison with the old days the agents who violate the rules of the FBI would be fired or suspended. They would be gone, period."

"In my experience and perspective this is unfortunate. Unfortunately, if an FBI special agent did what some of these agents do today, they would be gone immediately. Their shield gone; it would not be returned after the wrongdoing."

"In the days I worked as an agent, an ASAC [Assistant Special Agent in Charge] did something wrong. That is one time and one day he acted outside of the rules set for him as a special agent of the FBI."

"Our director, Mr. J. Edgar Hoover, brought him down to a street agent. The ASAC accepted his penalty from our director, and that was that. He knew he broke the rules, and it was an automatic demotion."

"Hey, Doc, we are not like IBM suits, who are motivated by money and the bottom line, it is all about profit and business. Integrity, fidelity, and bravery was truly where the FBI was, and is still at in my estimation."

"But for me the lack of emphasis on service and integrity and allowance of too much leeway is not a good direction. For me more than all of the issues internally, as in all law enforcement agencies and offices, a more sickening occurrence is occurring nowadays. It's sickening nowadays when a working agent is branded no different than a perp, that is, when things go awry. In the history of effective law enforcement, one needs to be judged by one's peers. Nowadays a lot of judgment is done by pundits who have read books about policing but have not been police. I guess we are back to what you call Centurioncide."

COP DR DAN RUDOFOSSI: "As you know, Special Agent Pistone, Centurioncide is the systemic attack on police and public safety officers which include all federal-level law enforcement agents! It is the lack of respect and dehumanization of all officers whether a five-man police department or a 51,000 department."

"What comes to mind without censoring any thought or association?"

FBI AGENT JOSEPH DOMINICK PISTONE: "A great example of leadership is Mayor Giuliani and Commissioner Bernard Kereck, who battled terror at its worst during September 2001 with leadership at its very best. Leadership at its worst is currently baiting and diminishing law enforcement officers and our Commander in Chief, as assaults and outright violence against law enforcement is at its lowest level of disrespect. Not only disrespecting and demeaning police, but the citizens and communities served, as crime and murder has skyrocketed. Trumpeting alarms with any situation that is not perfect among police performance is never the purview of civilians and for good reason. One needs to be judged by a jury of one's peers. As far as I can see, the anti-police groups cannot come close to understanding the dynamics involved in doing real police work properly."

COP DR DAN RUDOFOSSI: "Yes, in Centurioncide, as I have conceptualized it for seven years, police are judged by people with no credibility in even being remotely culturally competent as they never performed a rescue, service, or intervention where blood, guts, and vomit littered their shirts and outfits. When being told we are heroes, most of us by habit say with a shrug and smile, no worries, I was doing my job, glad to see you're feeling better.

But having said that, let's leave Centurioncide for a future book and platform to usher in all future conversations with communities and educators to remedy a bias and racism that is international and virulent against the very Centurions that lay their lives down for all as for us, all lives matter!"

FBI AGENT JOSEPH DOMINICK PISTONE: "Doc, right on the money here and very well said. I know about your work and educating many others about the enormous toll on law enforcement by the hatred now made legit by a gangster much worse and without the rules of the wiseguys, these dumb-guys and -gals are by design domestic terrorists, as asserted."

"Centurioncide is the term that is going to become part of the American language. It expresses what we have to deal with as human beings—law enforcement officers. Thanks."

COP DR DAN RUDOFOSSI: "You lived it more than I could imagine. I am also glad we are on the same page here. Our front page for the future will be Centurioncide."

"If we could, I would like to redirect to J. E. Hoover, who clearly was one tough boss. I only know the biased history and cannot know him in a personal and professional way as you lived this epic time with him as your boss. I understand from our conversations that J. E. Hoover had a flare-up nose for anything that was fugazy, that is, in the rules and codes of law enforcement."

"Remarkably, you forged a workable and respectful relationship that enabled his ability to truly trust you and support you as one of his best, regardless of his skeptical mind."

"Redirecting focus, and thinking backward to forward, it appears that you had to innovate yourself when you started living at 92nd and 3rd Avenue. You had to in essence shadow your real identity as Joseph Dominick Pistone into Donnie Brasco. Your entry into organized crime with Jilly from the Columbo family was as an orphaned petty jewel thief wiggling his way into the New York organized crime family network. It baffles my mind that J. Edgar Hoover, who has been portrayed and undermined in so many ways as a caricature, an almost dehumanized founder of the FBI as rigid, narrow, and a dictator. Please educate me here."

FBI AGENT JOSEPH DOMINICK PISTONE: "J. E. Hoover was much more than that of course. But more telling is the reality that he was one tough boss who took no nonsense as his approach."

"Mr. Hoover's pursuit of gangsters of any ilk was always matched by his more than obsessive nature to keep his own agents straight and on point. We had to be meticulous in operations and administration. But he knew how to lead and let you do your job with trust and discretion once you were into doing the right thing."

COP DR DAN RUDOFOSSI: "Interesting, as you give me some facts from narrow fictions to think about. If I am getting it right, Mr. Hoover stretched his trust to an elastic grasp when it came to you. That must have been no easy feat, I am sure for him as much as you."

"Meaning it was all uncharted territory. I may be wrong, please correct me if I need correction here. Anything that comes to mind Special Agent Joe Pistone, if you could, please share with me as freely as you can?"

FBI AGENT JOSEPH DOMINICK PISTONE: "I'm going to tell you things as they come to my mind. This has to do with becoming a special agent as they are remembered." [Dr Dan gesticulates a strong, yes, without blurting out a loud, 'Yes' to this gift.]

"Well, with being an undercover, I remember getting an apartment at Ruppert Towers at 92 and 3rd Avenue in the city of New York. You know Ruppert Towers used to be the old brewery. They renovated the area and made the brewery into apartment buildings."

"You see, once I infiltrated the Mafia, most of the guys had places around Knickerbocker Village. So, once I got Lefty Ruggiero and Tony Mirra to trust me and they felt I was good with them, they looked at me and said, hey, Donnie, why don't you move down here with us. We can get you in by Knickerbocker Village and you don't have to go all the way uptown. It's no sweat. Move close to us and we will be near each other. Right next to each. You'll have no worries. Hey, Donnie since we know the renovators and management and they owe us, it's a shoe-in for you to move in. But I refused. My intuition was to say no. Doc, I'm not telling you this to show I am smarter than the other agents who were trying to infiltrate other groups and would jump all over this offer. But not me. Let me tell you my reasoning. First, why would I want to be with them, they are gangsters, for 48 hours a day. If I could, why would I move from being near them to living with them for 24 hours a day, if I can help it? You get my point? It seems simple, but this was no easy choice, although I took a risk with that hard line, it was necessary to me to do upfront. A line in the sand of Operation Donnie Brasco, I put in the sand between them and me."

COP DR DAN RUDOFOSSI: "I think I get your very important point, you wanted to assert your own sense of autonomy in what is usually forbidden in La Cosa Nostra. By doing what you did as the line in the sand. Because once you are down their line of scrutiny, you being to live with them all the time, the message is clear, they own you! You made your own name and style for yourself. You let down important boundaries as Donnie Brasco. If I got it right, you wanted to assert your autonomy and style if we look at it within the family as Donnie Brasco, not Donnie doormat and servant?"

FBI AGENT JOSEPH DOMINICK PISTONE: "Yeah. Let me give you more context here. You know, I said to Lefty and Mirra, 'Hey, I like it up there, uptown works for me.' They were up there, and they visited. I said, 'You seen my pad yourselves. I don't see any need that would compel me to move near you guys.'"

"Remember Doc, another undercover would jump at the chance. He/she could say I am riding with them, and I can see their every move directly. This is a brilliant opportunity to get intelligence on them. But by not following them, I made them know I was my own man here. You see my point, Doc?"

COP DR DAN RUDOFOSSI: "I think I do, as there would be no mystique, no character, no ingenuity, and what we have truly identified as tough-mindedness, which is at the core of the real Joe Pistone and parallels into Donnie Brasco."

"If I can put it well enough, Donnie Brasco from the onset was the shadow of the real you, and not vice versa. What I mean is, the real you was maintained in your identity mode where survival in your own ecological niche was laid out by you—quite intentionally."

"By you keeping your own sense of what needed to be done in advance, you could develop Donnie Brasco as the shadow of Joe Pistone, and not Joe Pistone as the shadow of a make-believe Donnie. Put another way, if you went along with the program being cast for you to act in, you knew they would be writing the script for your real identity. The consequence would be, the danger is you would be more vulnerable to becoming a true shadow of a wiseguy by satisfying their needs alone—they would never respect you as they were destined to. That would be burying the real you under the covers of their operational use of you. By you firmly saying no, and asserting yourself as if you were born Donnie Brasco, Joseph Pistone the agent was only known to you and in the shadow of their gangster world, psychologically."

"In other words, on another level, if you were born into the Colombo or Bonanno family you would act as you did. It was superb and convincing adaptation. Being tough-minded and sticking to your plan as it evolved, your choices strategically stopped detection by defection to the other side of courage by not conforming: Your undercover survival and adaptation was asserting your own existential and psychological-physical space that you intentionally set the boundaries at first base that you intuited and knew would lead to the home base."

"What followed, if I got it right, is the ecological sensibility with [ethological] survival suitability made an impression on Lefty and Mirra as competing bosses for your loyalty. You did this in a transcendental, unconscious way, as much as a conscious style of becoming Donnie Brasco. Am I being sensible, or totally off in my analysis?"

FBI AGENT JOSEPH DOMINICK PISTONE: "Exactly. Your analysis is on point Doc! Because, if I would have moved then to where Lefty and Mirra wanted me, I would be their shadow, and not Donnie as worthwhile as a potential wiseguy to apprentice into the fold. I kept being the real me. Doing undercover required my being mentally tough. Yeah, and faith in a higher authority to watch over me."

"Hey, Doc, remember that situation when I was held in Patsy's bar. If I stayed, once you're beat, meaning you don't do what is necessary to make an impression that is fitting in the world of the gangster not law enforcement, you are tagged. So, even though you never meant it, you're done. Let me explain that expression."

"To the extent of a physical confrontation, when Frankie was holding me by gunpoint in the bar, Frankie was confirming I was who I said I was, or even claimed to be. I was trustworthy because my contact I established, remembered to vouch for me. Remember, in this situation I was under the gun for a while. After they cleared me, I tell Jilly, and without hesitation, 'Jilly, hey, no disrespect, I can't be with this guy anymore.'"

"When I did that move with Jilly, it made me into another person, that is not Donnie a rag type of guy who will giggle when he is disrespected, but the way it transformed was Donnie is a tough-minded future member of the family, he is not a rag and not a push-over. Getting my point, this too was a move to establish my identity in the family as Donnie who is able to discriminate what is acceptable, what is not, and who is acceptable and who is not."

"I had to let Jilly know this is not for me anymore. Think about it this way, in the context you brought up, that this guy held me inside the bar backroom to whack me, and roll me up in a rug if I couldn't prove who I was. I made it out alive because I was vouched for by a known member of the Mafia. It worked out by the grace of God."

"But for me it went too far. I had to clock the guy Frank on the way out as a point of me making my own integrity and personality clear right from the start. It sent the message to all the wiseguys that I was a tough-minded associate. I was to be trusted by not accepting being roughed up, and punked out. It also laid it clear to all that I was straight up. It would be a warning to others to not insinuate that I was a snitch or a rat. It made my personality as Donnie Brasco more defined by doing what a real wiseguy in training and gaining intel would do. I had a choice to make and to define me. I did just that. I had deliberately set out to achieve a certain boundary for Donnie Brasco as a real future member of the family."

COP DR DAN RUDOFOSSI: "So, you were able to not only just survive as Donnie Brasco. You were able to figure it out under a mental and emotional marathon for Joe Pistone, Special Agent, Federal Bureau of Investigation. There were no rules, no regulations, and no books, nor even folklore. No traditional patrol or investigative guides to maneuver as you did."

"You charted out what you had to do, without any map. Clocking Frankie, when you were held by Jilly when you were newer to the Mafia scene, and beginning and challenged was tough stuff! It was as you said necessary to step up to the plate of the wiseguy world and not lose that opportunity to lay down the markings that would help you foster respect and command presence as a future wiseguy."

FBI AGENT JOSEPH DOMINICK PISTONE: "It is as in the apartment being aware of what is required on the spot when you are confronted with situations that demand your immediate attention. Ignoring a disrespect and marginalizing of your own self-worth is tantamount to being labeled a loser for the rest of your time within the wiseguy world."

COP DR DAN RUDOFOSSI: "Having understood your motivation better, the part that chilled me is when you dealt with Tony Mirra belittling the stranger on the phone with his Midwest family in Canarsie and bullying him to get off the phone or be whacked in a heartbeat. It is just one example of how this challenge and day-to-day risks increased. I am sure many we will never know as it would be an encyclopedic work and an elephant's memory to recall each potentially traumatic event accurately. My point is that the frequency and intensities of potential traumatic events was exponential when we try to gain an estimate."

FBI AGENT JOSEPH DOMINICK PISTONE: "You know, a lot of this stuff became second nature to me. You were a street cop in Bed-Stuy, Fort Greene, and Redhook when it was homicide ally. It becomes bred in you. Your neighborhood as to where you grew up and developed is major in getting street smarts. It's something you can't teach, it's there. You learned it when you were a young guy and so did I. You can't teach that street smarts nor the inborn intuitive sense. It is, in my opinion and experience, a gift, so to speak, or the opposite in some situations, perhaps sometimes it is a little or a lot of both. There are basketball players for example, and then there is a Michael Jordan."

[We both laugh as to the truth of this reality!]

"It's hard to define, but it's not brain surgery as to whether you have it, or you don't." [We both laugh lightheartedly, but get ready to tackle the fact that even as agreed on, being born talented and sometimes the opposite, analyzing the complexity is no easy task.]

COP DR DAN RUDOFOSSI: "Yes, you're right, it's not brain surgery. As you describe the ecological niche as I would call the neighborhood. That is, 'how' you grew up, and 'where' you had grown up ecologically framing it right; 'when' you grew up, and as important is 'why' you chose, for example, the FBI while others in the streets chose crime, conning others, and the dead ends."

"The cultural niche you are in homes in on survival for you as a street kid, toward becoming a street-smart teen, and yet is only part of the full picture."

"I agree, it's not rocket science, nor brain science. The fact you have alacrity in agility and facility to move around and home in on just when is the right timing, where is the right place, how to gain confidence in confidence men, and decisive effect in coordinating the pieces, is a lot more than throwing dice or the luck of the draw! Still, brain science and perceptual psychological science can enlighten our exploration of resilience in dealing with traumatic losses."

FBI AGENT JOSEPH DOMINICK PISTONE: "I guess when you look at it that way, it is brain science that frames the hardwiring for me and for others who do not have what it takes in being undercover as not having that basic hardwiring to do this mission."

"I have said to you many times, Doc, it is not that those other officers are lesser cops or agents, but only a certain type of agent or detective can really become undercover and do their job well. It makes good sense to include that in our discussion as well. You need the mental toughness and, as you said, to be a human being to carry the mission out to its end. You can learn a lot but not the basic hardwiring and ability which must be there in the first place, or in the last place—it is not."

COP DR DAN RUDOFOSSI: "Speaking of tough-mindedness, Special Agent Joseph Dominick Pistone, what you did in reality and for how long you did deep cover for six years plus, would knock the sails out of most agents and tenured detectives at the pace and intensity of your actual infiltration."

"Let's take a brief look together, if that works for you. I would like to do with you what I have at times done with other officer patients, and in your case try to gain a more realistic perspective of the number of traumatic events you experienced. Kindly let me know if this concept works for you?"

FBI AGENT JOSEPH DOMINICK PISTONE: "Yeah, go ahead Doc, I am all ears. Go for it. I'll let you know if it makes sense to me."

COP DR DAN RUDOFOSSI: "So, if we look at your infiltration into the Bonanno family over a six-year stretch without shrinking from the truth. You lived, breathed, walked, and talked Donnie Brasco for what comes out to roughly 2,190 days."

"So, 2,190 days, mind you, all days are different than each other, and without much breathing space for a break, on and off the job of being a gangster in the Mafia—you were still married, and with kids. You were always aware you were at core a special agent of the FBI."

"You in reality had to deal with three wives, or mistresses as you and I estimated. Each one was vying and vetting for you, in three different directions."

"Let's pause and think about it honestly, at least four times a day at minimum, even on the best of days, some threat existed to your life and limb, your heart and soul. Am I right?" [Assent as yes.]

"This being so, your inner vulnerability, where you knew well the danger and risk involved each moment you were amidst the lions, tigers, and bears on land, and the saltwater crocodiles and bull sharks in the creeks along the FDR, BQE, and Belt Parkway kept your cortisol flow and lactic acid demands conscious and unconsciously on marathon identity mode as a split between being FBI special agent deep cover and wiseguy Donnie Brasco identity mode. The calculations, at a conservative frequency, to say nothing for intensity of emotional and mental trauma, was 8,760 times at minimum. Let me explain my trajectory as a quantitative analysis for us to grasp."

"With 365 days in a year, and 4 times at a conservative minimum of jumpstarts to alerts in your sympathetic nervous system for fight or flight (flight becoming almost impossible) we come to 1,460 events a year. For six years, we have a rough and likely grossly minimized frequency of 8,760 potentially traumatic events over six years."

"We are not even attempting to assess post-Donnie Brasco moments where we both know you were accosted, stalked, and tracked—unsuccessfully, thank G–d! If you and I realize that in the digest of my guide, I use as a guide not a bible, nor a map, but as a tool in my skill as a clinician and cop doc, and for officer patients to survive mentally, emotionally, and soulfully (Rudofossi, 2007, 2009, 2013), your experiences are stunning! I, with your help, am trying to simply sketch in the rawest MASH-like assessment what was truly a mental, emotional, and psychological-psychiatric marathon run for six years without stop, save you breathing in 'gulps and gasps of air,' and yet you are as resilient as any outstanding officer has been and will be."

FBI AGENT JOSEPH DOMINICK PISTONE: "Put that way, I never thought of what I did and do in that way. It does make sense as you put it for sure. Your quantitative analysis does set the record straight in giving a picture of what life was like as a special agent in a mission to accomplish. I mean the number of events as you said that may be viewed as traumatic is way beyond the usual."

COP DR DAN RUDOFOSSI: "Before we go on here in our interview, it is important for me to grasp the fact that you know I bear witness with you in our assessment as a whole as to the enormity of the knapsack you carried for all of us as Special Agent Pistone. I have admittedly caught and captured some new ways of looking at and understanding your experiences as Donnie Brasco and Joe Pistone alike."

"On the other hand, to set the record straight, as a cop doc privileged to gain your trust, I have no intention of flattering you or extolling you as a superman. But in slowing down the speed of gravity and getting you to realize the remarkable gifts you've been blessed with on one hand, and on the other hand what you've given so freely to society in being and becoming the human being you are and will always be, it is worth all the effort to stand on the point that you are still you. Notwithstanding that point, you did what is possible, and clearly as an outlier have placed your mark in psychological history for other agents and police to navigate without decompensating and imploding. You also, from a noetic dimension, absorbed much traumatic loss no one agent/officer should be exposed to. Finally, you did mission-impossible-successfully!"

FBI AGENT JOSEPH DOMINICK PISTONE: "You know, talking about all the trauma and adrenaline rushes and those numbers it's hard sometimes to express the feelings about the experiences in psychological terms. Sometimes it's just hard to put into words and explain to anyone what I experienced was, Doc."

"Like I said, a lot of the guys, they are not complete knuckle-draggers. We spoke about Sonny. We, as you know, had spent a lot of time together. Sonny was the type of boss that thought things out with common sense, and, again, in another life he would have been able to blend into society. If he only would have been born into a normal family, he would have been fine with normal people. I mean, as I said, Sonny, had to think things out in a common-sense way, he would ask questions and really listen to your point of view. He could be a guy you could actually talk with and chew the fat with."

"In distinguishing Sonny Black from Tony Mirra, Tony was a thug. Tony was not going to be anything else but a thug. Tony wasn't dumb, but he was not hard- or softwired to be normal. That's a fact, although I am not a psychologist/psychiatrist like you Doc, that's clear as day that he was born the way he was."

"A lot of these guys who are hitmen and the muscle in the families are not wired normally. Look, how could you be wired normally? For example, when someone you knew as a friend from ten years old is whacked, just like that."

"I mean, think about this, you know this guy from when you were both kids, and through the passage of time and life experiences you are suddenly and out of the blue ordered to kill him. You are given no reason but just a strict order, take him out. At that point you don't even pause. You do exactly as you're ordered to do. So, you kill and do exactly what you are told to do without even hesitating."

"So, because you were ordered to do the hit, you do the hit on your childhood buddy? You do it without question for the good of your own society? Yeah, I know the wiseguys were born into that culture. But that is the Mafia society. I mean, is that society itself normal?"

"You know Doc, as a psychiatrist/psychologist, in your own point of view, I always wondered to myself, if you could be the interviewee for a moment here in my place. I have a question that tugs at me. Hey, those guys with 14 or 15 hits under their belt as a Mafia hitman, well, are they considered to be serial killers by you as a forensic and cop doc shrink? Maybe their being a hitman in the Mafia culture and crime syndicate makes them just an average wiseguy?"

COP DR DAN RUDOFOSSI: "That is an incredibly good question. This question is one that asks of psychologists and psychiatrists a key question that is direct and astute. That question, if I got it right, is that a hitman who does serial killing as a hitman in the Mafia has a lot in common with the horrific serial killer. The Boston Strangler, while motivated by disturbing and psychotic ideas and in his case a dissociative identity disorder [Rudofossi, 2022], is markedly different from a hitman/hitwoman in the criminal syndicate. Let me offer my opinion. The hitman who surreptitiously kills victims under stealth of their malevolent thinking is usually doing it because they are paid, but the hitman usually, but not necessarily, has a higher level of preplanning and meditation than a serial killer with psychosis. The question is comparative and, in my judgment, answered on a case-by-case individual level of assessment and diagnosis. The hitman in general acts with a higher level of malevolence (*malum in se*) in comparison to the capacity for evil of a serial killer who is psychotic or insane from a legal perspective. In my opinion and clinical judgment, Albert DeSalvo's criminal record, while replete with psychosis and a schizotypal personality disorder and dissociative identity disorder, is nonetheless perpetrated under the jurisprudence of the insanity defense and invariably has a high level of the capacity for human evil [Rudofossi, 2022]. Juxtapose this with Albert Anastasia, who was a violent and murderous gangster of the Genovese crime family, killing people directly and via others with a higher level of serial killing and culpability, notwithstanding he is diagnosable tentatively with antisocial personality disorder and psychopathic personality features. In sum, your hypothesis is in sync with mine in a classic sense and intuitively as well—hitmen and murderous gangsters that murder numerous victims (including those with criminal records themselves) are serial killers by definition. Finally, serial killers also have unique individual differences—all inexcusable and recused 'stone-cold killers' from innocence by saying I was just following orders of disorders—using your inimitable language, Special Agent J. D. Pistone."

"Your question is very worthy of being answered with more detail. I have asked myself and debated that question in my earlier book, *A Cop Doc's Guide to Understanding Terrorism as Human Evil: Healing from Complex Trauma Syndromes for Military, Police and Public Safety Officers and their Families* [Rudofossi, 2013]."

"Let me point out that others who specialize and are expert in this area of psychopathic personality are doctors Stanton Samenow, Michael Stone, Reid Meloy, Robert Hare, and Dave Grossman, who are in agreement that 'hitmen,' as we understand them, have an intrinsic quality and personality trait that is antisocial, and in some cases psychopathic on a spectrum of dimensions from pure evil to lesser capacities for evil [Hare, 1999; Grossman 1996, 2013; Meloy, 1988, 2001; Samenow, 2001, 2012; Stone, 2017; Stone & Brucato, 2019]."

"I would concur with my esteemed colleagues and say yes! Technically, while some clinicians and researchers would disagree, that is by emphasizing psychopathic to terrorist activity as being largely cultural and psychosocial in its etiology, or root cause, I strongly disagree."

"In order to assess this properly, we need to look at case-by-case examples to get all the particulars and dynamics. But when we add the biopsychosocial dimension and existential center, the ability to ignore the basic human response to distress and fear in other humans takes an incapacity to not have the hardwiring that sets off alarms and acting out with extreme violence and aggression regardless of motivation. I will add to my colleagues' point of view that terrorists and serial killers, including hitman, are not likely to rehabilitate—I would not want to risk their ever being let loose on the public to commit violence on such an enormous level again."

"Looked at another way is, suppose the fellow the hitman is torturing, or outright killing, would normally be halted by some stop-gap on actually doing what is fantasized or imagined."

"For most humans we have inhibitions with strong alerts in the brain. Existentially we say to ourselves, this could be your son/daughter, your brother/sister, your dad/mom. Don't do it!"

"From a neurological perspective, the limbic system threshold and normal level that triggers alarms in the biological neurological circuitry is turned off and out or criss-crossed via inhibition. It is the same with the addictive component in the hardwiring of what is located in what is called the mesolimbic system [Hare, 1999, 2011; Grossman, 1996, 2013; Meloy, 1988, 2001; Samenow, 2001, 2012; Stone, 2017; Stone & Brucato, 2019]."

"Some patients who do not receive enough stimulation in what most of us consider all too much in their activities will seek out more and deeper thrills. The thrill seeking is to counter the boredom within biophysiologically. They seek out never-ending sources to rush in and gain stimulation equivalent to a rush of dopamine from external sources. It is due to lacking such stimulation in their own brain neuronal circuitry and function. Add to that the research that shows the antisocial personality traits associated with lack of empathy have reduced interconnections between the ventromedial and mesocortical prefrontal cortex which trigger that alarm for emotional processing of empathy, as well as guilt, or what we can say is processed as and one's conscience. The experience of guilt via learning and modeling and the amygdala of the limbic area of the brain which balances anxiety and fear responses and the ventromedial prefrontal cortex have a poor neurocircuitry, to say nothing of the neurons that are responsible for health and mental illness being dysfunctional [Hare, 1999, 2011; Grossman, 1996, 2013; Meloy, 1988, 2001; Rudofossi, 2007; Samenow, 2001, 2012; Stone, 2017; Stone & Brucato, 2019]."

"So, returning to the original question you posed as intimation is so on point, are these hitmen serial killers: from a forensic psychological perspective the answer is yes."

"The hardwiring is off and derailed. The other question for criminal justice is how much culpability can be attributed to biological tendencies in distinction to choosing responsibly? I will say, as you intimate, and I agree the position that hitmen and -women with multiple homicides on their belt are serial killers. Among hitmen, I don't know definitively, but an important scientific study can be developed as a research question worth investigating: what are the variations in traits and personality features that can lead to classifying different types and severity along a dimensional continuum?"

"For now, it appears 'hitmen' have an endogenous tendency to be overtly violent. It is the opportunity that ecological niches of organized crime families can legitimately pique their own sense of legitimacy to reward the more antisocial behavior within that culture. To the brasher psychopathic killer who serves the needs of his organized crime family, the reward of instrumental and intermittent conditioning may enhance such derivatives of destructive drives including the blood thirst of killing for such mentally and behaviorally disturbed perpetrators."

FBI AGENT JOSEPH DOMINICK PISTONE: "That gives a definite answer, that yeah, these guys are hardwired in an off-balanced way. I want to add another piece to this puzzle."

"In my experience, my view, that is, my experience for six years of living with and being a wiseguy, I don't think the organized crime family is necessarily a culture. I don't think the Mafia is a culture from an anthropological perspective. It's a deviancy and abnormal to be a gangster, it is a different world, but it is not a formal culture like others."

COP DR DAN RUDOFOSSI: "I agree with you. I don't think deviancy is a culture anthropologically speaking. It is a poor myth and even more so a broken one."

"A culture needs to promote its continuity. By operationally defining culture itself, mafiosi fail by not sustaining a family network toward survival and transgenerational transmission. In confusing culture from individuals cohering to crime as cohesion to the connected view of generation to generation where mores, totems, and taboos act against its own generative value, by maximizing traumatic loss and risk of death. Culture implicitly needs to support survival and stable continuity of its most valued traits, behaviors, and emotions for maximizing internal cohesion. Interfamilial feuds and intrafamilial conflict can exist in cultures and often is a highlight, but the variability is too extreme. On the other hand, traditions do survive among its members and perpetuate the life of successors; it is more in effigy than in perpetuity as tragically flawed. If I got it right, the subculture of Mafia families maintains control of their Mafia family by the threat of violence and murder as the steady shadow where one's survival is ensured tentatively and quite anxiously. Survival in such an ecological niche is too precarious for perpetuating a culture. Ethologically, survival without a permanent structure and tradition that preserves itself and its members with maximum stability is bound to self-implode and destroy itself. So, in a loose way, Mafia families can be coined a cultural entity by a far stretch, but it is much better to speak of as paracultural. From a clinical perspective, I am hard pressed to categorize the Mafia as a culture that can withstand the durability, survival assurance, and integrity of allopatric specialization and sensitivity toward its own members."

FBI AGENT JOSEPH DOMINICK PISTONE: "Doc, from a purely academic view, and even practical sense, your point to my point makes perfect sense. An interesting fact I noticed was that in looking at the Mafia as not being a proper culture, per se, a truth is that everyone in that Mafia family is not a member of La Cosa Nostra."

"Let me explain. For example, not every blood relative is part of the Mafia family, even though they are all closely related. Take Lefty Ruggiero, whose sister was a nun, and she lived a very different and gentle lifestyle, although she never abandoned her wayward brother."

"Then take Sonny Black Napolitano, who had a cousin he was fond of. His cousin did car washes, and was he a straight guy, you know what I mean?" [Rhetorically asked.]

"Hey, his cousin, that is Sonny Black's cousin, may not have been totally pure, but he was a hard-working regular guy. A real entrepreneur. He was not a killer; he was not involved with the organized crime component. Yet he was able to run a legit business on his own with an attitude where he could look like a wiseguy to be, but he was a regular guy. You understand me?" [Gesturing in the affirmative, I listen intently.]

"A guy as you mentioned that worked with Tony Mirra was Richard Kuklinski, the Iceman, as he was called. The guy was a hitman and hardwired to kill. He was that type described a psychopath. For one thing, he was mentally disordered with the killings he did. I mean the type of slayings like hanging the guy from his back until he was dead, because he cut ahead of him in a bar while he was waiting to use the bathroom. He fed his victims to rats in hidden caves, sometimes it took days for death to set in. This behavior was extreme sadism behind his acts of murder. He had a twisted mind. He's a serial killer and fits the exact summary you gave for a serial killer and hitman. I rest my case and the evidence on that fact. That is no cultural link, it is cold-blooded murder, and he is the stone-cold murderer."

COP DR DAN RUDOFOSSI: "When you think of the vista of your expansive experience within the Mafia, do you think there are qualifying aspects to our looking at hitmen as serial killers, since this is workable research and a clinical question I think worth looking at by serious students of criminology, forensic psychologists and psychiatrists, attorneys, and forensic examiners?"

FBI AGENT JOSEPH DOMINICK PISTONE: "These other guys like Lefty and Tony Mirra were not insane. But they were not fully balanced as normal people were. They each had different personalities. Tony was very violent and the murdering type. In the murdering business, Lefty was a murderer and serial murderer too."

"But, still, when you look at it, certainly relatives of the Mafia members, and even relatives of the capos as bosses may have had no part of the Mafia's business—such as murder, or even illegal activities. Take a guy like Tony Mirra. He, as I shared with you, was a real gangster and cold-blooded killer. But, still and all, when I was hanging out with him, his mother was elderly, and he would stop to take out his mother. He was gentle in talking with her and that part of his humanity remained. So, you know, the complexity of some of these guys and their personalities and the minds of these guys are not easy to figure out. Even though I think your outlook is very helpful, as you've said, each case is a different one, without whitewashing the murderer behind the mask."

"Doc, you take a guy like Sonny Black Napolitano, and without getting into any detail here, he always worried about his kid and how he was doing. He even asked me to look out for him if anything happened to him. That shows you he was more than just a stone-cold killer, although make no mistake, he could kill someone he perceived as a threat. He was a killer and also by definition, even my own and yours with me, a serial killer, but in some way he maintained his place for being more decent than the others who lost their entire humanity. That is significant, you know. I am saying they have different levels of being cold-stone killers in my view, but they all fall within that net if we are honest about it. As I said, the gangster world and their rules of dos and don'ts is very different than the world of the law enforcement professionals, and both differ from the normal world around both other world views."

COP DR DAN RUDOFOSSI: "I think your dénouement to this piece was a rich and important component to your credit to bring up and explore as we both have exhausted the cultural question of the Mafia, the questions of the different families and the dimensionality of being and becoming a serial killer as a hitman is a degree not looked at before. We broke this wall open, and I agree it is one that a new generation of researchers and clinicians can delve into. Joe D. Pistone, special agent that you are and will always be, if I can ask you about Sonny Black with no details about his kid, if I am getting it right, it seems like he had a heart that worked well with many relationships, even beyond his kid, and even asking you as a trusted associate he truly respected in a brotherly way. For example, his love of his girlfriend, his kid, and even his pigeons as his pet birds. Extending his ability toward empathy, he did care genuinely for his patrons of all hues and casts of humanity in his restaurant, am I correct?"

FBI AGENT JOSEPH DOMINICK PISTONE: "Yeah, well, that's true. He had this dark side, but he was always worrying about his kid, his girlfriend, and others. But that was deep inside as well. You know, he worried how would his kid do in the world if he was whacked. Yeah, Sonny cared about people in his life and had deeper relationships, and a heart you can say in that regard. As I shared with you Doc, Sonny did respect our relationship as genuine as a guy who was a Mafia boss could!"

"He was clearly the boss, my boss as Donnie Brasco, but he at times confided in me in a brotherly way."

COP DR DAN RUDOFOSSI: "The significant truth that transcends our dialogue for now, and this book, is that here for the first time, it is apparent that affection went both ways. In my view as a cop doc, a wonderful empathy and genuine aspect of what makes you the tough-minded special agent deep cover you are includes being the gentleman with a great heart of courage and human decency that you are above board and cover too." [Silence, and processing our dialogue and insight we move to another relationship Donnie Brasco forged over years in the Bonanno family.] "How was the relationship with Lefty like? From your perspective, as far as a boss, how did you experience the real Benjamin Ruggiero aka Lefty?"

FBI AGENT JOSEPH DOMINICK PISTONE: "Lefty was a real wiseguy buff. He would get jealous of my relationship with Sonny Black. I think Lefty kind of looked at me as possibly a father-son relationship."

"As Lefty's son was a junkie, the age difference between Sonny and me was more like a father and son. In Lefty's mind, I think he saw me as a son he didn't really have. His son was the prodigal son. A junkie always in pursuit of addiction and never really there for his dad."

"Remember, I didn't bring my intelligence down to that level of the street to just infiltrate the Mafia. I was not going to become a common street thug for anyone's sake."

"In other words, I didn't dumb myself down to make myself out to be and act like a street thug. I think that was something that Lefty caught on to and understood my stance to be of value. A value that overstepped the regular wiseguy wannabe and left me as the real deal in his eyes."

"Lefty looked at me as a street-smart guy. But not a street-smart guy without brains, but one who was able to be of value. Value to him on some level, not only in the Mafia, but as a good son."

"He had some connection to me, and his desire to take me under his wings, that kept him focused on me. He caught on that in some ways he could groom me into becoming his ideal son, and then make me into a made man, a wiseguy in the Mafia family he belonged to, where we would be together as a father and son relationship. Then he had feelings of jealousy for my relationship with Sonny Black Napolitano as well. Lefty was very possessive of me as his apprentice."

COP DR DAN RUDOFOSSI: "You had to carve out your relationship with Lefty. He held you almost in a clingy way. But in a way, once again with all you had to manage in becoming a wiseguy, you had to transition and deal with Sonny Black as capo without giving the devil his due. Unlike Charles Daniel, who made immortal with a fiddle and a bow, you couldn't be Daniel Webster, but you had to manage two made men and in hierarchy among the other bosses as Sabella, Trafficante, Trincherra. I even forget, any of those bosses could bring death on any associate just for the asking if they whimsically felt an itch for vendetta—even if it was a fiction." [Agent Joe Pistone affirms.]

"For me, it seemed like Lefty's thinking that he was in full control with the Milwaukee deal. You moved just right to get the doors of perdition open as it readied to swing close—hard and fast with the Milwaukee pitch. Your executive thinking of all the players at once again helped you deal with Frankie Balistrieri separately and distinctly without anyone getting whacked. Of course, including you, but also distancing yourself from the limelight and sandpile, which was again nothing short of ingenious major executive thinking and strategy."

FBI AGENT JOSEPH DOMINICK PISTONE: "As I mentioned before, you had to satisfy all these people and their demands which were all different. That's not to say, for example, keeping Lefty happy was easy. It was not easy, and plenty of tolerance of his selfish behavior was a staple of me dealing with a prodigal father in a way, although I know he deeply respected me and wanted me to follow in his footsteps as well. But I knew how to read his temper rising, his hot temper could mean he could become violent, but knowing how to maneuver with him was not as dangerous as Tony Mirra for example."

"Remember, Doc, dealing with Lefty was a tightrope. But I knew he felt in some way I was like a son to him. That's exactly why whenever Sonny would tell me stuff, I didn't run to share it with him. I would cut out Lefty. The reason why I cut Lefty out of the real scoop was I knew that if Lefty found out about any conversations I had with Sonny alone, that would throw him off. I mean let's make no mistake about it, that would throw Lefty off into a real frenzy."

COP DOC DAN RUDOFOSSI: "Because of jealousy over competing for your attention as if he was another dad, trying to steal his precious son from him?"

Oedipal Strivings and Crime

It appears that with Sonny Red Indelicato and his son who had disappeared, and in a way was the ever-missing son on the run, Bruno was saved from certain death when the preemptive hit was done by Lefty and Sonny Black in their coup of the Bonanno family. Lefty Ruggiero similarly perhaps shielded and grappled with Donnie Brasco as a real son, rather than his addict son that was more of a prodigal and distant son to him. Sonny Black Napolitano also had an oedipal attachment with Donnie Brasco, but along the lines of a brother, which in different formations of compromise unconsciously can lead to a similar desire to care for the brother who one may compete with, but also, in guilt over having existentially harmed him, desire to do the very opposite and protect and embrace him. This unconscious constellation is hypothetical and not evidenced with empirical evidence, but moves the observer far into the reaches of the unconscious and the compromises underlying the surface with an in-depth look at motivation. What are irrational jealousies and competition in Mafia captains are made sensible within the context of unconscious strivings where murder is a fantasy, and resolution by its opposite of protection and inclusion is the outcome. That perhaps explains the elusive aspect of the love and hate spectrum in the Donnie Brasco dénouement with Sonny Black Napolitano and Lefty Benjamin Ruggiero and their respective brother and son relationships idealized and compromised as their formation and attempted resolution of their oedipal conflict. As Dr. Brenner reminded me in clinical supervision many times, including my own training analysis, the unconscious is ubiquitous and emerges in all conflict until its underpinnings become known (Brenner, 1974, 1982).

FBI AGENT JOSEPH DOMINICK PISTONE: "Jealousy was real for Lefty; I knew he felt like I was betraying him. You know, this is why I had to put him in about any conversation I had with Sonny. I had to do so delicately. I finessed the conversation. I had to tell him about my conversation with Sonny. That would throw Lefty off track. But remember, I had to ensure he, meaning Lefty, did not backtrack and then discuss what I told him again with Sonny. You follow what I am saying?"

COP DR DAN RUDOFOSSI: "I think I do. It's all about a chain of command and trust. Your direct boss is your boss, and not your boss's boss. So if you overstep your authority and go to the top-level boss first, you've disrespected the rules of the hierarchal command and shot yourself in the proverbial foot. Correct?"

FBI AGENT JOSEPH DOMINICK PISTONE: "Yes. Remember, it's like Sonny who then will come back to me and say to me, 'Donnie, why did you tell Lefty what we just discussed privately in our conversation?' But underlying all this is, Sonny felt I was closer to him, and Lefty pulling in the other direction felt I was closest to him and owed him my real allegiance first!"

COP DR DAN RUDOFOSSI: "The dance, if I am getting it right, is you are thrust into a triangle of sorts where you are forced to hold back from one mistress, from what you just did with the other one. That is in order to protect that mistress from getting jealous. So diplomacy and tact as to which potential misstep can detonate an explosion of jealous rage from Lefty. You navigated extraordinarily well with Lefty. But if Sonny hears you surrendered any confidence, that is, as a given trust between you and Sonny given privately, you just betrayed the future capo, if not capo di tutti, Sonny Black Napolitano. So, between Sonny and Lefty, you navigated yet another ongoing mafioso grizzly maze."

"For our analysis, if we pause and redirect, this maze of fatal potentialities is a sequence of multiple layers of stress and strain where traumatic loss and death surround survival ethology in an ecological niche you had to tightrope through more than once a day and in many memorable moments consigned to the unconscious depths, but still quite potent and dormant for now."

FBI AGENT JOSEPH DOMINICK PISTONE: "Hey, I like that metaphor a lot. It is as you suggest. You know it was like a six-year tightrope walk when you think about it. It's like the Flying Wallenda high tightrope act of pyramid making in the sky. Walking across Niagara Falls, the great Blondin Jean Francois Gravlet. The highwire act of crossing Niagara Falls. I didn't fall, but it is interesting to think how close and how many times I was tested and got through." [Laughs with genuine relief at expostulating the reality of surviving it all. Me too, vicariously allowing myself to imagine how tough-minded, ingenious, and at the same diplomatically savvy he had to be.]

COP DR DAN RUDOFOSSI: "The Wallenda family, which included even his own progeny dying in the line of duty, reminds me, and I imagine you, of the miracle in the pause. A long pause that you crossed as the Rubicon for you and other agents we pray will make it as you did in the future trails, trials, and travails they are invariably to face. Special Agent Joe Pistone, what a great metaphor that you've come up with to describe your own six-year tightrope balancing feat. But in your own humility, I will emphasize you were no seven-person team, you were solo, and uno in the field of operations and in your identity mode as Donnie Brasco. Existentially, it was not only six years of infiltration, but the novel alterations through repetition of many times doing impossible tightrope feats defying gravity and the laws of entropy where a catastrophic end was glanced at multiple times and in varied ways with you remaining calm and diplomatic. Was it true, as we discussed informally at times, a spiritual faith you had that held this all together as noetic glue?"

FBI AGENT JOSEPH DOMINICK PISTONE: "Thanks for saying that, Doc. Yeah, I have an aspect of faith in everything I do. In my strong belief in my heart and soul, hey, you don't survive without faith! I have faith in everything I do. You don't survive without having some real faith. That is my own belief here. I give no apology for my belief. Having some belief that we as humans have our Higher Authority, and that unseen Almighty looked out after me. It is what carried me and still does and lays deeply inside of me. That was my belief, as I said, my faith in our Higher Authority carried me. My philosophy then during Operation Donnie Brasco was, whatever is going to happen, is going to happen. I'm going to do what I am going to do. I'm going to do my job! I know I am being looked out for. You can't make it any simpler or any more complicated than that. It is my belief. I am firmly being taken care of by our Higher Authority. That expression you used and quote from Churchill makes a lot of sense to me, there go I, but for the Grace of G–d, go I."

COP DR DAN R: "You know, Special Agent Joe Pistone, I lost a friend of mine recently. I had the privilege to hang tight with in Texas, Abilene, where we presented as keynote speakers on trauma over a decade and a half ago and when we both won awards at the Viktor Frankl International Conference in Texas, Dr. Steve Southwick. He was a renowned clinician and researcher at the National Center for PTSD in Clinical Neuroscience and Yale University Medical School. Part of his lifelong work was understanding how some POWs, combat veterans, and folks who are born or develop pernicious diseases stay resilient and live life purposely after the heaviest trauma. No doubt you are extraordinarily resilient. Dr Steve Southwick and I had met two plus decades ago as we both had used and explored with our respective populations and patients in the police and military world using logotherapy and existential analysis. As you know, I modified my approach and made some integrations with other modalities, including in our own dialogues and exploration for this book. It is to Dr. Viktor Frankl that I resonated most with from a realistic perspective in developing an approach to help officers on the ground dealing with heavy casualties of traumatic loss, dissociative disorders, and grief. One of many books he gifted patients suffering from trauma and loss is captured in his masterpiece, *Man's Search for Meaning* [Frankl, 1973, 1979, 2000; Graber, 2004]. The survival of this extraordinary man as an outstanding psychologist-psychiatrist is often mistaken with readers believing he did not advocate pursuing meaning, but rather naturally allowing meaning to ensue within our attitudes and purpose we found in our daily challenges and life situations. In other words, by allowing meaning to ensue rather than pursuing an ideal concept, Frankl suggests to do good with, and on behalf, and for others as service, most of us can invariably embrace. In doing so, an attitude of service leads to finding meaning even in the most extreme situations, including traumata we experience. It is within our faith that transcends the most disturbing of life conditions that we all face one day, including our own mortality, that one succors life and meaning. In making one's goal of seeking meaning into a directive that must be done, paradoxically the goal is lost. By allowing attitudes, goals, and creative expression to emerge when one finds experiences that allow purpose to form, even in the bellicose turgidity of the Mafia ecological niches, paradoxically the richest meaning emerges, as does motivation to embrace life, in the most extreme sundry tests we are put through in our life's journey. Our ability to choose life and hold onto faith and leaps in faith, resiliency towards trauma ensues. Does Frankl, Southwick, and my own attitude make sense to you in relation to your own experiences as you experience living on the tightrope of life and death for six years?"

FBI AGENT JOSEPH DOMINICK PISTONE: "It makes all the sense in the world to me! It is exactly my philosophy as I lived it. I never pursued fame, or harming anyone. I did my job with integrity and as best as I could as an FBI special agent. I was assigned a task to do, and I did it well." "It was my tightrope walk I took and walked as well. But every step of the way, the fact that G–d helped me is ever present and within me. I am here today and have survived well because of my ability to believe in a power that transcends myself and my own will as faith! In fact, I endorse and, in my experience, agree with you, Dr. Southwick, and Dr. Frankl that I never pursued meaning directly, but I like that concept of letting it ensue. Like my mental toughness, my resilience and my faith were within me. Hardwired and, I think as you may say, softwired as well."

COP DR DAN RUDOFOSSI: "I am honored to hear and confirm that fact. As Frankl often said, 'Destiny is not fate, as we are born to. It is our choice and responsibility within the bounds of freedom that meaning is all the clearer.'"

FBI AGENT JOSEPH DOMINICK PISTONE: "Destiny is laid out as hardwired in my view. But faith is faith and one's personal ballast and compass in any storm. Doing the right thing and pursuing truth and justice as law enforcement officers, it is never perfect. I like your point you always bring out, which is that life itself and being a special agent is almost always messy. I believe in G–d. I didn't bow to any man, whether on the white horse galloping in, or the black horse crashing in on the party. I remained true to my beliefs and believe in G–d. I don't pontificate and preach, but I try to do the best I can do in my life as my major goal and fulfillment. Capish?"

COP DR DAN RUDOFOSSI: "Capito, Special Agent Joe Pistone. Thank you kindly. Speaking about your own personal faith is key in understanding the real you, and your challenges and strengths for prosperity. It seems we are converging on the perspective you hold sacred and that has carried you all along the odyssey as FBI agent and Donnie Brasco as shadow and cover in your real life experiences—existentially speaking of situations—eco-ethologically ripe with traumata minefields. In wrapping up our interviews, is there anything you would like to take pause and reflect on with me again, or share anew?"

FBI AGENT JOSEPH DOMINICK PISTONE: [Pause.] "You know, I don't know if we discussed this or not, and I'm unsure if this goes along with your thought process. But I never just came out and told him about what happened with the Milwaukee situation. You know what I am referring to Doc?" [Expressing 'Yeah, I know' by gesticulating. Special Agent, Joe Pistone continues.] "Because I knew if things could and did in reality go south, I didn't want to be blamed 100 percent. So, I engineered it so it was their own decision-making process. By 'their' decision, I mean Lefty Ruggiero and Mike Sabella's decision-making. It was not prefabricated, but more again of being myself and thinking through beforehand the possibilities of a deal going poorly, that if I was to have taken credit for, I was going to be the easy scapegoat. Let me go back and give you some background here with Milwaukee. First, the Bureau [FBI] broached the deal I had in mind with suggesting I work with my fellow undercover doing his operation there to infiltrate the local syndicate directly interjecting and insinuating myself with him. You know, my first point was now directly dealing with the world of the FBI. I asked my FBI boss, 'who is the undercover agent here?' I stood my ground and I let them know it was me who had to make these decisions in the field and complicating Donnie Brasco as a wiseguy initiate who was breaking some significant ground was also doing operations by taking care of my own safety and integrity at the same time. Remember when I told you much earlier to your interviewing me I said, in doing deep cover a very important reality is the fact as to who is going to look after you as a deep cover is the most important plate to cover. I told you, remember that answer is, without doubt, very clear."

"You are your own best caretaker and nobody else! While team cover and assistance are all necessary, one reality to share from our interviews is this: anyone even thinking of becoming a deep-cover special agent as an LEO is to truly understand without procrastination that you need to be your own best friend and ensure you know how to keep yourself alive, safe, and gaining the advantage on your enemies."

"If I didn't know the undercover agent, I was not going to risk my life needlessly. I was not going to risk the operation, as Donnie Brasco was not only the operation, he was me! At that point, I wasn't sure Lefty Ruggiero and Mike Sabella were 1,000 percent in with Balistrieri as well. You see, of course I knew the undercover agent. So, I told Lefty as follows, 'Hey I got a call from a guy who I knew ten years ago,' and that's it, and no further comment from me. I made a bridge not a moat and that was that."

"So I plant that seed in Lefty's brain that a guy I knew ten years ago, I guy that I thieved with ten years ago, got in touch with me again suddenly. I repeated a few times to Lefty in different ways and times that I knew this guy ten years ago. The seed was laid, a seed again was sprouting when repeating to Lefty to share with the bosses in Milwaukee that the guy called me again. I told Lefty in a subtle way that the guy I knew as a gangster type that seemed okay, without vouching directly that he told me, 'Donnie, hey, I got a pretty good business going here,' and that's it."

"The next time I told him where this guy is and he says, 'Yeah, it's a business, but it's a business that is mob controlled. I can't do the business out there, or they'll blow me up if I try to move in on their share.' So, he tells me, 'Hey Donnie what does this guy got?' I say, 'the guy told me he's got a business like I said. He also let me know it seems to be a pretty good business out there.' Well, Lefty's ears perked up. I say, 'Lefty, yeah, it's good business that's what I can tell you from what he told me and that's all he told me.' I said no more after this time to Lefty. When Lefty asks me what I think he should do, I tell Lefty, 'To be totally frank, I don't know what to say and tell you what to do, Boss.' By this time, Lefty is now getting hooked into his own style of curiosity and ambition as a gambler and wiseguy."

"Lefty now probes me more, and I know he's interested in angling in once again. Lefty then persists as I knew he would! Lefty asks me again and again, 'Hey, Donnie, what's the actual business deal that he's in? How is he making money?' I say he is in the vending business. Lefty being the way he is, persists, 'Donnie, let me ask you a question, does this guy got any money himself to expand the business?' I say, 'Lefty, I don't know. I can call him and find out, that is if you want me to find out, Boss.'"

"Doc, I know we spoke about this earlier in general, but here in our finishing the interviews I want to make sure I make a point. Remember, I am getting specific with the details here and the inner working, as I knew Lefty well enough and how to get his curiosity and interest to get deeper and more involved himself, but without me pushing it, I let him pursue the making of the deal. Guess what? Lefty did it. I intentionally stretched it over a month's time, and, hey, it ensued."

"Let me give you some information to fill the gaps. During this time, I tell him, 'Hey, Lefty, this goodfellow does have some trucks, he's got some vending machines as well, I mean I saw the machines and trucks myself. Lefty,' I say, 'he's even got an office for himself. Pretty neat package deal.' I draw the ecology here for Lefty sketching the visuals: 'Lefty the guy operates out of his own office,' I say, 'but the problem is he can't put his machines anywhere to make a real dime. The problem for this guy who calls me to get you in on his deal has one major block, Lefty. The problem is that the family out there will blow him up! That family boss is La Cosa Nostra family run by the capo Balistrieri.'"

"Lefty now is fully captivated and drawn to the gamble addictively. Lefty says to me, 'Does he have money, any real money, you know of Donnie?'"

"I say, 'I don't know Lefty. But if you want I will work hard on finding out if the guy has any real money to talk about, you know.' After giving some time to elapse, I tell Lefty on the QT, 'Lefty to answer your question, yeah, well, he says he has money.'"

"Lefty says, 'Donnie, how much money does he have invested in this business?'"

"I say, 'Lefty, I didn't ask him exactly.'"

"Lefty says to me, 'Donnie, well find out how much money he has? Is it $100,000 at least?' I say, 'Lefty, yeah, he says he got 100,000 in the bank.'"

"Finally, Lefty tells me, 'Well you go out there for us, Donnie. I want you to check up and see if he really has $100,000 in his bank account, is he for real, or is he a fugazy?'"

"So, I go out to Milwaukee and when I come back, I say, 'Lefty, he has an office, its real nice, and he has at least two trucks I saw myself. Plus, he has a number of vending machines.'"

"Lefty then says to me, 'Oh yeah, well Donnie, let's bring this to our boss, captain Mike Sabella.' Lefty and I talk a bit and then we both go to the capo, Mike Sabella. I stay on the side intentionally to avoid being looped in to my 'bosses' making 'decisions.'"

"Mike and Lefty discuss the business end. Mike says to Lefty, not me mind you, 'Okay, Benjie Ruggiero, you've got my permission.' Captain Sabella says, 'Hey you, Lefty, bring Donnie with you. Both of you, go out to Milwaukee and I want you to see what's going on together. See if we can work this into a business deal that will bring us some money upward.'"

"By this time the deal is being done. Lefty and I go out there to check out the business for Captain Mike Sabella. We give him the low-down on the deal. We come back and I planted the seeds and watched the seedlings get planted and backed off after the story that Conte [deep cover in Milwaukee] was associated with the Bonannos for the past ten years. I still did not own and push the deal formally. Now it was firmly Lefty that introduced the deal to Captain Sabella and he now forged this deal within the Bonanno family and between the Bonanno family and Balistrieri."

"So, the deal and triangle here was set up, but remember, as we discussed earlier, I had done my setting the firm support for the deal in my own style as a deep cover. I never pushed the deal but allowed Lefty and then Mike to take the full credit. Therefore, as in your analysis, the full strategizing for the actual deal which was a life saver for me later being blamed, and Lefty was taken with a bit of clemency and not as a vendetta and certain death. It was not accidental, and yet I did not fully plan it all out from the beginning. This is what I mean when I say, I knew how to work 'It' well. You know what I mean, and does this offer you any more to share with your students and me?"

COP DR DAN RUDOFOSSI: "Yes, in many ways the intuitive and executive part of your brain was working out different possibilities as trajectories and the paths each would take. Each complexity was pre-empted intuitively and ingeniously without getting caught under the guillotine. I think another noetic finding here to hold onto is the fact you've brought me to witness what you've internally witnessed here for your own growth and insight, as we discussed earlier. But you shed more light in detail, and even more so from a psychological perspective for us to hold on to."

"Let me summarize, and correct me if I am wrong. First, you were truly setting up with all your inquisitive and survival skill to master your ecological niche at home base and expanding your territorial imperative by having the alpha members of the family unit own their own dance. You choreographed the dance, which you did not set up forthright, which would lead to you being fully blamed, but if I am getting it right, ingeniously set up all the right coordinates from the onset so they could move their pieces in the right moves which did happen. However, you removed yourself from getting webbed if it backfired."

FBI AGENT JOSEPH DOMINICK PISTONE: "Yeah, you got it right down to the wire here. I didn't know exactly how it would settle in the end. But yes, the main point was, I set up the pieces and the right moves that they could use. It was their own decision to move forward, to back up, to stay still, or to leap ahead: Whatever each boss decided to do was their own choice, not mine. This difference, of ensuring each boss made his own decision, was my layout. The board was arranged to strategic advantage. So Milwaukee for me was a strategy where all the right moves set up the right keys and locks for each boss to reject or to grab hold of and leap forward. Look, Doc, I did the same thing in the way I set up the situation in Florida. It was not me, but Trafficante, that took all the opportunities as they were set up for him to go for. The risks and the dime being dropped on the nightclub and the variables I couldn't control still did not deter me, and I was taking multiple risks, as you said potentially traumatic events, but the deal being achieved was felt as real good tactics."

COP DR DAN RUDOFOSSI: "Tactically brilliant, strategically ingenious in design. You laid each foundation uniquely adapting to the needs of that particular family through not just targeting the capo's ecological niche and the needs and resources they had as possibilities, but you grasped each capo's ethological motivation to survive and gamble on major profits by getting into the capos' heads and, I may add, their tendencies psychologically speaking. If I try to analyze this with you, the most telling is your keen ability to responsively hook into each capo's personality by knowing each individual's difference as major movers and shakers. The evidence is you were successful in never getting whacked and also ensuring the bosses you were close to never got whacked. Secondarily, their deals from Balistrieri and Trafficante as major capo di tuttis took leaps due to your prompts. The deals made are exquisite and, if I am getting it right, were bridges that were formed as firsts ever, that is even in the Mafia family circle meetings."

FBI AGENT JOSEPH DOMINICK PISTONE: "It was like rolling that roulette in the casino, and although you don't control the final point of that roll, I believe you have better than the odds when time and use just the right spin. You see, I would say to Lefty, 'Hey Lefty, you kept pushing me to set up this deal with you and to go down and scout out this operation in Milwaukee. I am a good soldier, an associate in the Bonanno family, but remember this is your idea Lefty, your move, it's not mine.' I also repeated to Lefty that 'I told you it has been ten years since I was thieving with this guy, and it is totally your decision as to whether we move forward or not, it's not my decision Lefty.'"

"In doing this I motivated Lefty very differently than Trafficante and Balistrieri for that matter. But I insulated myself as much as I could from ever being the decisionmaker, or deal breaker. In essence, I ensured each boss knew, and I mean emphasized, that I was not telling him, one way or another, what to do—but he was always making this as his own decision. That was especially so at my direct boss's leverage such as Lefty, and for that matter Captain Mike Sabella. Doc, this is not the full picture because, if you remember, I did this and it was true of Sonny Black. Each did what he did. But I was able to set up the situation to see if he would do what could be done, that is potentially. In the final analysis, it was them that got it done, not me. Using another example, Sonny was there and made the decision in Florida. Sonny Black had nothing to do with the Milwaukee situation. Lefty and Mike Sabella were the ones who made all decisions in the Milwaukee situation. But the main point is, with Florida I did the same thing as with Milwaukee with Lefty and Sabella in dealing with Trafficante, as it worked in a different niche with Sonny Black Napolitano and Trafficante in Florida. The major danger in Milwaukee, don't forget, also was the danger of the sit-down and getting whacked in New York. Sabella was pissed about the fall-out with Balistrieri pushing away and the silent treatment after such a warm and gracious welcome in Milwaukee. If you remember, Lefty was likely up to bat and getting ready to be whacked. Miraculously it was decided not to whack Lefty Ruggiero. This was because the big capo Balistrieri did not want to ventilate unfinished business, an error in his judgment. It was a huge mistake to let Special Agent Conte in in the first place, leaving egg on Balistrieri's face. In saving face, so to speak, Lefty was spared, along with Sabella, being whacked."

COP DR DAN RUDOFOSSI: "It was their piece of reality and you were the facilitator and cultivated their reality by moving 'It' along within the ambiance of their unique ecological niche and ethological layout for survival to thrive in the best of potential and fertile ground for homicide or generativity. No accident, you coaxed, presented the potentialities as if he set it up, in a nice and easy architectural layout. You trained and teased out each capo looking at your layout—but taking what was your own design, as their own blueprint. I'm not finished. Because the difference in this interview is we have realized you perceived the layout perceptually way before they did. What you did worked in stimulating a merger. Your actualizing that merger averted a bloodbath. What I think is missed here in your genuine humility is not only discovery of your genius, but that you helped the FBI realize a network that could be mapped out in intelligence gathering and operational decisive identification as to each crime family when Operation Donnie Brasco closed down. This was achieved with foresight that is visualized and thought of at some deeper level by you. That leaves me with yet another insight into your intelligence. Somehow visually seeing and perceiving the events with veracity before they actually fell into place, your accuracy was much better than we can just say was chance and luck. Your mind perceived this with ingenuity way beyond the norm, which indicates your strategic identification of the problem and solving ability as again being ingenious. In the context of the quantitative analysis in regard to trauma events looked at another way, it is clear that you endured and set course on what was and is a true mental and emotional marathon."

"More so, you not only anticipated strategically what could have gone wrong by protecting yourself, but your efficacy of the operation itself with accuracy was on point at the same time. The unheard aspect of your existential center of awesome police work is no points were known beforehand in your architectural vision with multiple minefields to navigate through!"

FBI AGENT JOSEPH DOMINICK PISTONE: "Remember Doc, if I had just gone in there and vouched for this guy with Lefty and then with Sabella and they found out Conte was deep cover in the FBI or perceived as a rat, I would have been gone after that with a whack job as not doing my homework and vouching for a deep cover who compromised the Bonanno family. That is, as you point out, I am not putting it in the mafioso bosses realizing I was an FBI special agent, I am saying as a wiseguy associate I would be taken out."

COP DR DAN RUDOFOSSI: "What happened to Sonny Black as captain and heir to the Bonanno family in New York could have happened to you earlier if you didn't realize and insulate yourself ingeniously from being vulnerable to a contract. In your intervention you deftly kept dancing in the shadows. By allowing yourself to stay in the wings, the bosses were allowed to pirouette into the limelight you helped choreograph, but did not dance in by allowing the visible and noticeable engineers to remain in charge. This adaptive function helped you in dissociating as Donnie Brasco through each move as a detonation minefield. If any Mafia soldier to boss detonated in their own error, each error could lead to death. Each choice they made, and you realized, was loaded as potentially a minefield you were sweeping through with no metal detector and no back-up."

FBI AGENT JOSEPH DOMINICK PISTONE: "Yeah, exactly Doc Dan. Remember when we started, I shared with you I did undercover work as I was good at it. It was natural for me. It does not mean any officer that does not do this type of work is less a cop, investigator, or detective. I brought in the Bonannos and I laid the groundwork."

"In repeating and giving a message to those who enter into doing the work I did, it is key to remember, only one person who saves your life in this business. That is yourself."

"The Navy Seals or NYPD Street Crime were not with you when the bad guys had a trigger-happy finger and getting ready to play 'pull the trigger.' It was me and the bad guys period. Nobody was there to ride in on that white horse and save you. When you were doing the eco-ethological analysis, you brought me to pay a lot of attention to forgotten trauma, but you also for me, you helped me by putting 'It' into a healthier and still real perspective, also understanding things from a psychological and psychiatric perspective makes sense. I appreciate your insights and clinical interpretations which I resonate with. I agree that it was a minefield of trauma. Six years of work in which my own tough-mindedness by the Grace of G–d helped me go as I did intact, and thinking about your point, it was far from over when Donnie Brasco was closed down."

COP DR DAN RUDOFOSSI: "Special Agent Joe Pistone, you brought out aspects of your work and profession that are unique to our dialogue. The gifts you have delivered, I pray I have interpreted correctly, respectfully, and with good judgment are on point, on point with blue blood which is our culture and our shield of honor and humility! Clinically and as a cop doc you enriched and made me wiser in what Dr. Ferenczi called active analysis, which is when the shrink is shrunk a bit, and the patient is expanded a bit as well in mutual and collaborative work."

"The dome of narrative and interpretation shields either one of us from getting carried away. I am assured with our reality and dialogue that some future agent or detective will gain some useful intelligence. Your life will inspire some young adult to travel onto the path of law enforcement. My hope, I know yours as well, is this book will awaken chiefs, bureau and administrative directors of law enforcement, as to the enormity of tasks asked of one agent as in your case, that require the highest moral, emotional, and intellectual integrity and sacrifice. Your name and reputation as Special Agent Joseph Dominick Pistone and Donnie Brasco is one of honor and respect for others and self!"

"You did not relinquish the most important credo of our profession—protect and defend by uncovering those who organize and cohere around criminal activity. The truest reflection of the inner core you shared with me is you, as do I and many brother and sister officers, salute the Highest Authority in the soulfulness each of us does as public service and safety officers. You've done what few dare to do, and did it in the greatest deep-cover operation! My sergeant's shield is made sterling in the radiance of your FBI special agent's shield. The luster will not fade and neither will you as faith springs eternal, as does the courage and ingenuity of your inspiration for daring to dream the impossible dream that was done under your watch. I thank you for the honor of trusting me with your insights and your deeper psyche and soulfulness that helped stitch our discovered insights and responsibility to share this with others for inspiration for their own aspirations as the torch of justice tempered with compassion."

FBI AGENT JOSEPH DOMINICK PISTONE: "After all this time and over the years that I have spoken with you Doc, I must say you captured my thoughts, feelings, and mindset perfectly. Dr. Dan, I relate to you as one of my brothers in blue, as a cop, and cop doc. Doc, I thank you for your own integrity and words, including reviewing chapter by chapter with me and gaining my thumbs up on each page as it turned into print, we shared in our journey."

Summary

In this final interview with Special Agent Joe Pistone, I cannot do full justice to the remarkable gentleman and law enforcement officer he truly is. While I am privileged and honored to share with all readers Joe Pistone as an East and West Coast police legend, truth be told his story has been told by himself in the wonderful books he has written for public knowledge and consumption. As Special Agent Pistone, the author and trainer, he certainly does not need me or any doc to scaffold his ideas about his lassoing wiseguys responsible for murder, corruption, and entanglement with organized trafficking of multiple illegal venues to justice, including corrupt officers as rare as dodo birds but still in need of being stopped and taken off the street.

Paradoxically, at the end of this book you have the story of the human being and soulful warrior with the glint of genius and the armor of integrity to absorb for life and law enforcement and in living well. In reading and rereading this book, please keep in mind that the weight of Special Agent Pistone's unconscious noetic dimension was forged but anchored in the pressing push and pull of desire. But his compromise and novel solutions defy gravity as a tightrope walker that awoke dancing in a new unexplored and uncharted space.

Finally, in the epilogue, which is where an author can indulge in poetic license and to playfully expand the boundaries with psychological imagination, I will do some serious layout of my concept of Centurioncide and within the elasticity of deep cover. I will return and offer suggestions to ensure the real and deeply genuine Joe Dominick Pistone is to remain vitalizing and in perpetuity a wise sage and leader to all of us who have entered into the portals of law enforcement and great detective work, for deep cover, infiltration, espionage, and counterespionage are all the purview and domain of detective sleuthing and I know of none better by admission than Joseph Dominick Pistone, Special Agent aka Donnie Brasco of the Federal Bureau of Investigation, United States Department of Justice.

Cop Doc Corner for Students Only—Witness to Noetic Dimensionality

Now the end is near, but experiencing Joe Pistone and Donnie Brasco was and can remain by rereading and being witness to a remarkable journey of a true-blue American hero. My witnessing and Socratic exploration scaffolded into Joe's achievement of "internal-witnessing" as ongoing and timeless in scope and depth.

As in all human interactions, leaving through the momentum of moments etched in "blood, sweat and tears" as the real Winston Churchill called his mission, includes growth not just for the interviewee if done well by the author who is taken on a journey as much psychologically speaking but anthropologically speaking (Churchill, 1941; Rudofossi, 2007, 2009). Achieving what I call "internal witnessing" is owning our collaborative insights and makes writing this book all the more worthwhile. I have grown in my own personal and professional inspiration by having spoken to and getting to know the genuine gentleman behind the titles and identity modes.

In doing an *Eco-Ethological Existential Analysis*, tragic optimism is a motivator that can only be heard and identified in an empathic manner. By highlighting identity modes in both verbal and non-verbal expressions as unconscious adaptations to survival, a healthier normalcy is delivered to the law enforcement officer that would otherwise remain hidden and disenfranchised from his own internalized witnessing of courage, challenge, and overcoming the harshest tests. This living witnessing of complex trauma understood and redirected to a position internalized as self-valuing memories can be life-affirming if not lifesaving. That is, in the ongoing surge of public safety officers struggling with depression, maladaptive dysfunctional dissociative disorders, trauma, grief, aggression, and addictions, the compromise formations modified in an *Eco-Ethological Existential Analysis* framework are quite effective (Brenner, 1974, 1976, 1982). Psychological defenses and victories are provoked in fields of trauma. At times inability to emerge the victor helps all of us redirect to our insight to a responsible compromise to the noetic dimension. The noetic as the dimension where we attempt to overcome the worst situations with courage and faith mustered from the dust of wear and tear worked into mortar shells after the victor and vanquished have left the battlefields of street encounters. The average police officer who has walked the beat is no robot, no automaton, but a very human being who has seen it all and experienced it all within their first three years of pounding the asphalt foliage from green to blue. In spite of attempts to white- and blackwash through the walls and bricks of urban war zones where the hues of humanity unlike any other species show their personal best and worst, officers maintain for the most part dignity and integrity in service. In battles fought after the war is over, waves of questions emerge. Urban war zones is not us versus them, but is a melee of the vagaries, the travails, and trials each officer must place on her/his Corfram shoes and Sam Browne belts with double loops for the victims, the witnesses, and the perpetrators (Cox, 2000; Rudofossi, 2015; Messing & Rudofossi, 2019; Rudofossi & Ellis, 1999).

The field of operations is as wide as the world and as constricted as a beat representing all of the human conflicts and emotions for each officer to tackle. In a world that has become full of division and artifices that reify the human being who dons the shield as I wore it with thousands of others, most fade away after duty in choir practice to addiction, depression, and, sadly, aggression. In conclusion, often officers and agents fade away by turning against themselves, not others, and rather than in the public arena they have served, it is in the private world of insensibility and retreat from life as most know it. With responsible outreach and insight, it is in society's respect, valuing, and treasuring the heroes we know and have known to shield all of us from the uglier and meaner sides of the street that we owe gratitude, and to that I hope you will honor the service and ingenuity of Special Agent Joseph Dominick Pistone as much as I have grown to know and appreciate his unique markings on us all, and hopefully the next special agent doing deep cover and the guy or gal who could have turned into a hood but instead turned away and left the shadows behind in the dust of the dark shadows for light of justice tempered with mercy.

Important Definitions and Concepts to Keep in Mind

Responsibleness

Responsibleness is a concept Dr. Viktor Frankl introduced into the clinical nomenclature and the domain of existential analysis. The term and concept are largely used in doing therapy and intervention with patients engaging in existential analysis and logotherapy. The term responsibleness is side by side with the concept of liberty and liberation. In the Franklian approach to dealing with mental and behavioral disorders, it is imperative that the patient accepts and even invites in his/her journey to restoring health after bouts with addiction, depression, and aggression a sense of being responsible, in part, for his own emotional disturbance. Unlike cognitive behavioral and psychoanalytic treatment, in logotherapy and existential analysis the clinician will ferret out with the patient's honesty and collaboration the areas where a lack of an acceptance and over-indulgence in guilt and too much responsibility for the ills of the world, others and self has contributed to dysfunctional and aberrant behavior and emotional illness.

Internal witnessing

Internal witnessing is when the patient is able in an *Ecological-Ethological Existential Analysis* developed by Dr. Rudofossi to rely on his own integration of traumatic, grief-stricken, complex bereavement, and dissociative processes the reality of working through the guilt, addictive, aggressive, angst and anxiety disorders, and depressive-manic responses to trauma experiences without self and other downing and irrational dysfunctional coping techniques and withdrawal. It is the ability for the patient/client to internalize the reality of situations' tragic and sad outcomes without the concomitant mental fatigue, chagrin, and psyche-ache. The reversal to acceptance of a healthier outcome is the patient's success in internalizing the therapeutic insights for self-growth and development from clinician to patient whereby the patient has now narrated and integrated internally the courage, integrity, and challenges in enduring repetitive traumatic losses, for example as did Special Agent Joe D. Pistone.

The lessening to redirection of empowerment and motivation to move forward and not be stuck in maladaptive and self-destructive modalities without excessive guilt, anxiety, complex trauma, grief, and dissociative disorders is the achievement of internal witnessing.

Cop Doc Corner for Students Only—Debriefing

Dancing in the shadows where light and darkness shift and illuminate truth ever so deftly and powerfully in silent thrusts, Special Agent Joe Pistone understood the difference between knowing in distinction to believing, as critical to genius in soul, as much as in mind, and actions that followed. Analysis existentially is not done routinely as it is here.

The process of recounting one's story is not always therapy, but becomes therapeutic when an agent is able to learn even one key point from a licensed cop doc psychologist who sought and found resilience in Joe Pistone. Without doubt, Sir Joe Pistone was, and remains, a hero. As Joe put it humbly, "mental toughness" aided him in his successes.

In this book we expanded and set up scaffolds and bridges around Joe Pistone's metaphor of mental toughness and in doing so educating all of us. True and time-tested genius—for all of law enforcement, whether deep cover or not—is what Joe realized in action, not dreams alone. Since I learn from all my patients, students and colleagues, and mentors, I thank Joe Pistone for all he shared with me. There is much more to be said, but as in all journeys, we have come to our end point as we move onward and forward.

Let's be honest with this situation, without blaming the parties involved but discerning without doubt that Special Agent Pistone's integrity as Joe Pistone remains to this day. He is the incomparably good guy here—and the wiseguys, "not for nothing" as we are wont to say as LEOs, are invariably the gangsters. As Joe educates all of us in his professor identity mode, he is a great educator, and he educated all of us that not all wiseguys are created equal. Some gangsters are more humane and decent than we can imagine, although tragically flawed; redemption is not a human limitation but one that is noetic and transcends the divide.

We can all humbly be taught by Professor Joe Pistone that some wiseguys are hidden good guys if they only had the opportunity to learn a different way to be loyal to what counts, as real civic virtue, critical thinking, and standing true to all values supporting decency to all—save the terrorists and such anomalous destroyers of humanity.

The tarantella of guys wise in crime and pirouettes who have hung their Borsellino brim hats on one side of the brick wall as the white starched shirts of special agents waltzing the Viennese waltz move forward and synchronizes in a courteous salute, adieu! Joe Pistone remains my brother in blue; our blue-blood brotherhood and sisterhood never fades into the anonymity of shadows and fog. We have chosen to actively listen to our calling which transcends nature and nurture into the noetic dimension we have traversed, but could never shrink nor reduce in the moments we all share with life and living in the service of others. There go I, but for the Grace of G–d, providing me with the gift and blessing of a friendship and brotherhood that is timeless and priceless in its perpetuity!

Conceptual and Writing Exercises for Student and Professor Only

1. Another interesting and clinically remarkable outcome for me to share with those of you who are in the streets as LEOs and civilians in the field of exposure to trauma is that Special Agent Joe Pistone is an adaptive resilient intuitive LEO (Rudofossi, 2009). After obtaining the original work in personology by the author, what can you find yourself in listening actively to the narrative in this chapter and revisiting earlier ones that highlights this personality style of legendary FBI deep-cover operative Joseph Dominick Pistone?
2. What is the key to the emotional survival of Special Agent Joseph D. Pistone in the face of the reality that he was and will always remain Donnie Brasco, not as an acting role but as a true identity born of the genius he was and remains for us to understand better in looking at deep cover as real operations necessary in a world of increasing organized crime?
3. Evidence of Agent Pistone's adaptive resilient intuition is his creative adaptation to margins in narrow gaps, as he negotiated compromise in his conscious and unconscious formations,

he was faced with was no accident. Being alive and well is no easy feat. He rose with the ugly, nefarious betrayal, and triple-crosses he overcame. Agent Joe Pistone's "noetic dimension of soulful faith" was vitalized by his "mental toughness" and subsequently his emotional resilience. List three factors you can find which underscore the process of his noetic dimension and mental toughness using his biography or this chapter.
4. Is the myth of the fading warrior hero enervated or vitalized when Joe Dominick Pistone rose upon leaving the battlefield he faced as a special agent of the Federal Bureau of Investigation? Pick up one of the books written by Joe D. Pistone and summarize his own words as to coping with his repetitive losses and completing his mission. Juxtapose the insights you've gained in this book and especially this chapter as to the psychological impact of his traumatic experiences.
5. In estimating the enormity of challenges faced on a daily basis by Joe Pistone, without going by the myth of "I'm okay, trauma flows off of me like a Duckbill," how can a proper estimate of sacrifice be made for Special Agent Joe Pistone? Discuss the ramifications of redressing the issue of care in assessment of those on the front line of infiltration into organized crime syndicates.
6. What solutions are possible to inoculate agents to withstand trauma, grief and bereavement, and dissociation at the end of the process of infiltration and the judicial process?

References

Blatty, W. P. (1994). *The exorcist.* New York: Harper Torch.
Brenner, C. (1974). *An elementary textbook of psychoanalysis.* New York: Anchor.
Brenner, C. (1976). *Psychoanalytic technique and intra-psychic conflict.* New Haven, CT: International University Press.
Brenner, C. (1982). *The mind in conflict.* New York: International University Press.
Cox, G. (2000). *Complicated grieving and bereavement: Understanding and treating people experiencing loss.* Amityville, NY: Baywood.
Churchill, S. W. (1941). *Blood, sweat and tears.* London: Putnam.
Frankl, V. (1973). *Man's search for meaning. An introduction to logotherapy.* New York: Torchstone.
Frankl, V. (1979). *The unheard cry for meaning: Psychotherapy and humanism.* New York: Simon and Schuster.
Frankl, V. (2000). *Man's search for ultimate meaning.* Cambridge, MA: Perseus.
Graber, A. V. (2004). *Viktor Frankl's logotherapy.* Lima, OH: Wyndham Hall.
Grossman, D. (1996). *On killing: The psychological cost of learning to kill in war and society.* New York: Little, Brown.
Grossman, D. (2013). *On combat: The psychology and physiology of deadly conflict in war and peace.* New York: Hachette.
Hare, R. D. (1999). *Without conscience: The disturbing world of the psychopaths among us.* New York: Guilford.
Levant, R. (1997). *Men and emotions: A psychoeducational approach.* The Assessment and treatment of Psychological Disorders Video Series (Video and Viewers Guide). New York: Newbridge Communications.
Levant, R. (2001). Desperately seeking language: Understanding, assessing and treating normative male alexithymia. In G. R. Brooks & G. Good (Eds.), *The new handbook of counseling and psychotherapy for men,* Vol. 1 (pp. 424–443). San Francisco: Jossey-Bass.
Meloy, J. R. (1988). *The psychopathic mind: Origin, dynamics and treatment.* Lanham, MD: Aronson, Jason.
Meloy, J. R. (2001). *The mark of Cain: Psychoanalytic insight and the psychopath.* Hillsdale, NJ: Analytic.
Messing, P., & Rudofossi, D. (2019). The unbearable wetness of being. Opinion/editorial in *American Police Beat Magazine,* pp. 26–27.
Rudofossi, D. M. (1994). The effects of repetitive trauma in adulthood and dissociation. Talk given at the NY Society for the Study of Multiple Personality and Dissociation, Columbia University, New York.

Rudofossi, D. M. (1997). *The impact of trauma and loss on affective differential profiles of police officers.* Bell Harbor, MI: Bell and Howell.

Rudofossi, D. M. (2007). *Working with traumatized police-officer patients: A clinician's guide to complex PTSD syndromes in public safety professionals.* New York and London: Routledge.

Rudofossi, D. M. (2009). *A cop doc's guide to public safety complex trauma syndrome: Using five police personality styles.* New York & London: Routledge.

Rudofossi, D. M. (2012). *A street survival guide for public safety officers: The cop doc's strategies for surviving trauma, loss, and terrorism.* Boca Raton, FL: CRC Press.

Rudofossi, D. M. (2013). *A cop doc's guide to understanding terrorism as human evil: Healing from complex trauma syndromes for military, police, and public safety officers and their families.* New York and London: Routledge.

Rudofossi, D. M. (2015). *Dealing with the mentally ill person on the street: An assessment and intervention guide for public safety professionals.* Springfield, IL: Charles C. Thomas.

Rudofossi, D. M. (2022). *Narratives from forensic psychology: A case book.* San Diego, CA: Cognella Custom Preliminary Edition.

Rudofossi, D. M., & Ellis, R. R. (1999). *Differential police personality styles use of coping strategies, ego mechanisms of defense in adaptation to trauma and loss.* Symposium conducted at the meeting of the American Psychological Association, Boston, Massachusetts.

Rudofossi, D., & Maloney, M. (2019). *Aboriginal trail: Trials, travail, and triumph using psychology with Aborigine police.* Amherst, NY: Teneo Press.

Samenow, E. S. (2001). *Before it's too late: Why some kids get into trouble—and what parents can do about it.* New York: Three Rivers.

Samenow, E. S. (2012). *Inside the criminal mind.* New York: Random House-Crown.

Stone, M. (2017). *The anatomy of evil.* New York: Prometheus.

Stone, M., & Brucato, G. (2019). *The new evil: Understanding the emergence of modern violent crime.* New York: Prometheus.

EPILOGUE—FUTURE OF NO ILLUSIONS

Centurioncide (Complex Traumatic Loss and Dissociation)

> "The individual who is not anchored in God can offer no resistance on his own resources to the physical and moral blandishments of the world. For this he needs the evidence of inner, transcendent [authentic religious] experience which alone can protect him from the otherwise inevitable submersion in the mass."
>
> (Jung, 1955)

An epilogue is the one place where an author is allowed what is called poetic license. I am ever appreciative that in this casebook on Special Agent Joseph Pistone's life, legend, and psychology taken in moments shared together that a bridge was forged. It is here I will share a bit of heart and soul without losing track that we have a casebook as text and it is worthy of science and historic value. Unapologetically, all we have in the end as student to professor, and as author to term project writer as an undergraduate, is the humanity and soulful gifts we leave for prosperity, and to our own posterity.

The gifts of Joseph Dominick Pistone as a special agent and as pioneer have been laid down before this book. This casebook shares a different window of the psychological and psychiatric vistas of the hazards and cyclones of doing deep cover. It also opens the possibilities and windows of the multiple gains in doing police work, detective work, and being a deep-cover operative without exaggeration. It is also only a window into the work necessary for clinicians and researchers in the domain of trauma, grief, and dissociative processes to better understand the consequences of such endeavors in police operations. In my minority opinion, it is a good word of caution in a movement to exercise not only discretion but discernment between the very slippery Sisyphean slope of solipsism and egotism and true science as heuristic and non-advocacy, but respectful and gradual observation, classification, and nosology, to interventions of an ambulatory nature to lasting assessment and treatment modalities.

Responsibleness

I have written this casebook in a time of what I have called Centurioncide. In my view, a conflict between ideas that have kept freedom of choices, intellectual freedom, and freedom of speech sacred is under siege with theories without critique being mantras and blueprints

DOI: 10.4324/9781032202761-9

pronounced as truth with a religiosity that is not religion, nor based on any millennium-long religion but quite the opposite, based on academic criticism, revisionist thinking, and under the rubric of post-modernism. It is, in my very adamant and yet gentle voice, important to pay dear attention to the accumulated wisdom of the classical thinkers in the sciences (no science is soft or hard, or social or physical, save the labels we artificially attach and stain them with). Science and the method of science is equidistant and a way of understanding the world around us we as human beings would like to understand better and with great caution choose to improve. In doing so, a call unheard nowadays is caution to remember and keep ever present the ability of fads, waves of enthusiasm, and attached passion to drown out reason, discipline, and the reality of history as incontrovertible and veritas fact from fancy. It is more than bombastic to wash away contemporary history from its context, culture, and structure of society with the caveat we are all individuals with differences to be respected. It is in this peace of limitations, respect, and responsibleness I have written this casebook. It is only with the generosity of time and review chapter by chapter and its modifications that it is in print and in your hand. In the responsibleness of Joseph Dominick Pistone to assert, affirm, and stand for his own center of being and becoming who he was to become as Donnie Brasco and Joe D. Pistone, he did not follow a protocol or rote commands, but his own choices matched with responsibleness. In bringing to you his wisdom I have steered away from pleasing you, him, me, or anyone but save conserving the lessons and wisdom culled from moments of significant courage, determination, and unwavering integrity. Owning our choices with genteel toughness is crucial. Tough-mindedness as a scientist is learned.

Soulfulness

Passion and the adrenaline rushes that stir addiction, depression, and dissociation within the walls of trauma and chains of the mind succumb to the depths of soulfulness stirring under the deepest of covers—soulfulness evidenced here, from ground-up, onward and forward as Special Agent Joseph Pistone's deep cover punctuated the science and art of camouflage and sleuthing without detection. His success in infiltration without deflection into becoming pulled into the temptation of the other side is yet another near miracle of faith and commitment. The other side is the double of the other side we all have as in the Destrudo and Thanatos that pressure us to defeat and surrender to coercion, and defeat of the indefatigable human spirit we can say without unnecessary censoring is soulfulness. All the unheard, unnoticed, and unsung dimensions of intellect and soulfulness could have remained buried in a wall of trauma, dissociation, and grief, but in this regard my own soulfulness called to create this book, as yet a miracle I am ever grateful for, by the grace of an ineluctable, non-reducible aspect within each one of us that reflects the noetic dimensions and the unconscious transcendent conscience within a calling each person can hear in their own journey tapping into their own invisible source.

It is in this quest that you can appreciate Joe D. Pistone and Donnie Brasco as history, without distorting his odyssey, as I frankly stitched together with the greatest of generosity by a hero for us all. Preserving values in historic memory worth conserving in the finest and best, for all people, at all times, is what matters most of all!

The "heart of all matters is what matters" and is the one blessing we can all count on as human beings! Officers have their own voice as do all other human beings. Special agents need to be heard one at a time, and it is here that I will ask you to pause as I address a very critical bridge as a cop doc that Joe Dominick Pistone and I have crossed together and I will summarize in the next few pages as Centurioncide is laid out in its essence.

A Criminal Lack of Justice: Centurioncide

Officers Dissenting and Expressing their Own Unique Voice—One at a Time

When officers voice dissent toward an elected official they feel aggrieved by—as a result of being threatened or globally judged—each voice, individually and collectively, has been too often squelched.

A prime example is in NYC at the funeral of two slain officers, one of Chinese American heritage and one Hispanic American, shot because their assassin ad hominem decided to Centurioncide Officer Ramos and Officer Liu because they were pigs needing to be slaughtered. Their immediate families, including Officer Liu's fiancée and Officer Ramos's indigent population in an impoverished area where he was a minister as well as police officer, grieved with his immediate children and wife his brutal death. Reports of officers not standing at solemn attention to the mayor of NYC was taken as a command discipline, although many officers felt the mayor had irresponsibly blamed officers for racism they had no part in; that occurred in another geographic domain.

A private and solemn respect to a fallen fellow officer by active and retired officers is a healthy way of expressing one's beliefs as to the failures of the system. Whether one swore to protect other citizens as a police officer, a doctor, professor, or a citizen, it is one's inalienable right to express dissent civilly when one believes one is wronged and, in reality, one is treated as an invisible member of any society. As I wrote in *Terrorism as Human Evil*, when 98 percent of psychologists and physicians identify themselves as of one political persuasion, it is certainly force, not power, that exists in such a skewed misrepresentation of leaning to the left or right of the podium (Rudofossi, 2013).

Force corrupts and absolute correct enforcement of politics makes for bad mental and physical health. When colleagues begin to speak up in rational and passionate dissent, perhaps a healing and real process of dialogue will ensure real growth and movement toward progress. Such progress may include conservation of values and traditions worth saving, such as individual expression of dissent and markedly divergent views from the majority. This is true in the police and public safety professions as well, where one's own private sensibility cannot be flushed away in rants. It is crucial for calm to redirect one's attention with intention to heal, not force legislation against those that serve.

Legislation is one means of forceful control. Some journalists and their tabloids are another means of revictimizing survivors of cumulative and complex trauma and loss in a spiral where ventilation and expression are stymied in conformity. Such as the example given where posthumously Officer Ramos and Officer Liu were given detective status.

In all prejudgments a critically harmful selective bias exists that indicts, judges, and prosecutes all involved without viewing the evidence before vehement declarations of guilt—or innocence for that matter. This is a cornerstone of democracy, a republic, and a plural society, by uncritically accepting a view that in desiring to appease all segments of society, we are most likely to appease none. In rants that splinter a plural view into a linear perspective, vistas are closed as are the rights of differences to abound in a free society. Since all human beings are at times irrational, biased, and uncritically accepting of their own views, attempts to legislate morality and silence stultify critical sobriety by allowing only certain questions to be asked. The result is invariably one-sided judgments, mischaracterizations, and opinionated dogma as active listening and growth are deadened.

In the United States we have a representative government for all people and supported by the franchise for all groups and religions in which no one race, religion, or creed is dominant. Yet, it is almost incredulous that a society that is democratic and based on the constitution has the most forceful executives overstepping the constitutional safeguards when convenient to do so and disavowing the debt and protection owed to police who have been targeted for assassination. An example unique to Centurioncide is political force that pushes aside conscience for what is unconscionable, and conveniently indicts an officer acquitted by a jury of his peers because his invisibleness is in sync with his invincibility myth—a poor and maladaptive myth that takes all freedoms except for the very officers who lay their life on the line for all others, save themselves.

Lately, police officers who are caught in tragic enforcement situations have immediately, and without judicious review, been adjudged to be wrongful and labeled as racist, fascist, and incompetent, more often than not. Some of these labels are defamatory and inflammatory in hate and violence, spurring mass demonstrations where other minorities have been overstepped. Further, constitutional safeguards marginalized by elected officials who have used their official position to defy protection against double indemnity and due process for officers is allowed. In doing so, in a very tangible way as community representatives for all constituents, some public officers have disregarded the fact that officers are also represented at a lower rung, perhaps but in a status quite vulnerable and, as it stands now, unprotected.

It would be unconscionable for delegates of police officers' unions to remain silent on this systemic disregard of life lost when two officers in the NYPD were killed in December of 2014, those two being Detectives Ramos and Liu, who were murdered for wearing the uniform of service and for doing just that, serving others so well.

Third, when a tragic outcome occurs, as when the Gardner death occurred, even when an individual officer expresses genuine remorse to the family of the grieved, irascible demagogues irresponsibly label all officers and that specific officer as being maliciously intent on murder. This creates hidden and disenfranchised loss and trauma—cumulative complex traumatic losses for the officer and their family that are supported by an ethos of intolerance and severe damage that is immeasurable in its malice and impact.

Instead of responsible leadership, the grief of officers and the extended fraternity and sorority is left disenfranchised. Grief is worsened by irresponsible rhetoric that at base is biased and hostile.

However, in being fair minded, while all human beings, including politicians, are allowed errors in thinking and in judgment, egregious bias needs to be publicly and earnestly declared a mistake.

Addressing this in good conscience goes beyond platitudes and may start redressing the damages psychologically impacting officers and their elected representatives in a culturally competent manner.

This is especially so when those in responsible leadership roles do not position their own stances on peaceful resolution by endorsing the very constitution that has given them the privilege of representing all constituents in their communities, including police and public safety personnel. Accepting legal judgments by one's peers as the foundation of representative government is the entire franchise hard won over years of conflict in this country for all citizens. Justice will never please all members of society and, although far from perfect, it is harmful to globally judge police by superhuman standards of performance no human should be held accountable for.

On a larger scale, because someone is not elected or re-elected, for example, chaos would take over if the losing group in a pluralistic society waged hateful and divisive rhetoric targeting individuals.

Implied or direct misanthropic attacks on an entire police and public safety department affect all officers, with the risk of consequent trauma. When an officer is scapegoated beyond the law, all sworn officers properly upholding the power of law against forceful violations of freedom vicariously suffer inequity and damages. Such implied slander, libel, and pejoration is the heartless impact of traumatic loss I have called Centurioncide.

The Dilemma of Double-speak and Inequity as Psychological Damage

The dilemma of officers silenced when sworn to uphold the constitution is that as public officials the need to express dissent is viable with the qualification as private citizens expressing their views. Perceived unlawful directives need to be allowed ventilation and dissent as individuals, and collectively by unions representing officers.

Yet an inequity exists if an officer who expresses their own views publicly faces the full force of censure and official discipline. Police are not simply automata, and are also educated nowadays. Officers have many different views as citizens who understand the hypocrisy and double standards when the double-speak of the politician exercising the most blatant violations and acting irresponsibly is left unchallenged by the media power elite.

After one death, I watched for hours as the tears rolled and drums in cadence played as a daughter of a friend who was a detective asked why a man would kill this officer? What did he do to get killed? The rain broke for a moment of light. His family spoke of their losses in an unfettered way as officers by the thousands stood by respectfully.

Respect with empathy and compassion is a trait of most officers I know. I said sadly and tragically he was mentally ill and evil, as humans can be when they blind their own conscience.

As I looked at my friend's daughter's innocence, and her telling question, I remembered how many officers have come to me crying behind closed doors. Many of these full-back and powerful officers were silently hiding and suffering from the assaults on body and mind they suffered.

The officer's questions are in their hearts and souls and silent as the whistling wind hardly heard—as this young teen, they also dare not ask what they think in their private despair. That compelling question is what did these officers do to deserve this violence and betrayal by the public they serve? Why don't the elected officials and directives acknowledge their ultimate sacrifices for all of society and all lives?

It is almost unconscionable and elitist to assert the police use force rather than service and to add disenfranchised grief to misery and trauma to be blind to the losses accumulating on real street cops and investigators, from police officer to chiefs of patrol. My family is minority as Jewish European American; I have never once worried if we were in need of fighting racism and brutality by my peers. I never experienced that ugly face, save a few unsavory rare incidents, in 30 years. I knew and know that my brother and sister officers as my colleagues, no different than my peer clinician psychologist/psychiatrists, have a few incompetent and iatrogenic colleagues, but most are trustworthy and empathic decent professionals.

It is crucial to voice that fact assertively and affirmatively to gain competence with police as well as clinicians, although the hope of this chapter is that both can see the joint utility of such an odd and viable union is not so distant and certainly not the outlier.

Voicing Dissent: The Sounds of Silence

The union leadership that is, again, one chosen by the vast majority of officers needs to stand by their own members or lose credibility, as do so many politicians today. Union leaders, in defending the officers' integrity and right to be protected from bodily and, I would add, psychological harm, represent the very officers killed in cold blood. To denounce the voices of such real leadership shows an ignorant and elitist stance of authority by force against the voice of reason that is always dialectical and represents more than one view.

The question is, who is behind forceful attacks on legitimate police union leaders, those who advocate for acknowledging the terrorism that has gone against officers and their families without minimizing the need for refinement and improvement in policing as a legitimate endeavor? Why is silent passive and non-violent dissent, as espoused by leaders such as Mahatma Ghandi, William F. Buckley, Jr., Gore Vidal, Dr. Martin Luther King, Jr., and the writers of our constitution, including the first amendment civil rights leaders, being the focus of such virile and coercive attacks?

In mental health it is crucial to allow a voice of dissent which is peaceful and healthily passionate by the union leadership representing the voice of the officers and first-line supervisors in police and public safety, in this example of the city of New York, to be expressed, hopefully heard, and acted on by people of all races and religions who stand by the sacred dimension of civil liberty, society, and justice for all.

The outcome of some politicians' sloppy ignorant aspersions, that are not only elitist and do not represent the majority of people but are also extremely harmful to the psychological well-being of the victims (including some small, but militant, groupings of community leaders that are responsible for creating an ecology of fear, withdrawal, hostility, and violence), is likely to increase by also suggesting that officers are all of one aggressive and hostile ilk when, in reality, they have been the recipients of such aggression. Defunding the police, casting police as one singular body of closed-minded oppressive automatons and enemies of freedom, is hating speech and catalysts for violence, that is, Centurioncide.

However, this is not universal. On Sunday January 11, 2015 the French prime minister, Manuel Valls, declared, "We are all Charlie, we are all police, we are all Jews of France." Dissent is key for a political realism that is inclusive and embraces police, including special agents as citizens, including the right to have different opinions in a democracy that is based in part on the French Revolution that led to the American Revolution. Intellectual freedom includes unpopular and even contrary views. Morality cannot be legislated and when attempts to do so have become law, all freedoms have been sealed into doomed homogeneity.

The fifth problem is not only are officers not respected as part of the community, but also labeled by a radical schism from outside the community as pigs, racists, or outsiders. While no politician or activist of sound mind would label any officer in such a slanderous manner, it is no doubt the jingoism and xenophobia of elitist groups that did inflame the vulnerability of historically vulnerable populations and cultures, including public safety officers, and those served in minority areas to an us-versus-them mindset.

It is to the credit of the highest standards of comportment and integrity in the training and quality of police officers and first-line supervisors who are basically rendered victims who have no voice as of yet in attempting to open up dialogue, even if somewhat expressive, have been for the moment pushed aside! By excluding the very members of society that serve with such disservice, vicarious and direct psychological trauma is applied.

Blaming the victim has been studied by many sociologists and only diminishes what reciprocal and respectful dialogue can begin to heal and solve by real apology and by rectifying years of systemic abuse caused to police and public safety officers as a community and, most importantly, individually.

Solutions in Real Leadership and Leaders Stepping Up to Centurioncide

It is true that community leaders who can share with officers the grief and identify with the victims of terrorism, domestic or foreign, are the keys that open the lock for which communication and connection are essential. Leaders need to be acknowledged and addressed as individuals within eco-ethological niches that can support and work with truly pluralistic populations and, in doing so, become culturally competent with police and public safety populations. Grief expressed by community leaders is a conduit to healing when done with full and unadulterated condemnation of murder in cold blood in place of excuses.

Assassin Ismaayl Brinsley was terrorist ad hominem in his own distortions. He posted his clarion of hateful force against police after hearing how evil all police, aka pigs, were. His message on social media, "they took one of ours ... let's take two of theirs." While writing this article on the mislabeling of officers as if all are one amorphous and ignorant group, the NYPD family as a larger culture experienced a chilling murder of two citizens in cold blood and rampant violence. Ismaayl, a psychotic individual who had specifically set out to kill and wrote, "I'm putting wings on pigs today," was full of violent rage. Catalyzing the emotional contagion of blame and loose speech by those in elected positions and known saboteurs who rabble rouse, Ismaayl fulfilled his purpose in life. That purpose was to kill and hate with a vengeance, which to some is reducible to being called "social justice." This does not imply that racism does not exist, and by each and every group and culture, as do bias and corruption in police departments—as in education, as in politics, as in the judicial system, and polling system: one would be equally ignorant to say so! But it is not acceptable to label a man, who in acting as an officer with a personality style that is hyper-excited or -vigilant in performance of his duties, with the incendiary label of "racist" or a "pig." If anyone were to say this to any other professional in any context that was public and use this term as an elected public official for political or riotous gains, they would be subject to harassment charges and official misconduct for using their office to legislate pejoration and judgment without due process as provided by law.

As to implicit racism against any group as a whole, being labeled racist is anathema to collective reason and is motivated most likely by projection of one's own unconscious and unresolved intra-psychic conflicts with unresolved identity problems, including racial and cultural identity (Brenner, 1974, 1982). As Professor Dr. Charles Brenner keenly reminded me in my clinical training, an anti-war activist who violently attacks a soldier is unaware that his unconscious militancy caches his rage under a peaceful banner in the most egregious actions of social injustice.

Social injustice is unconsciously motivated by inadequacy in self-identity through reaction formation, or presenting the opposite of what one feels, such as hatred toward self, by projecting this onto all others, in the name of pacificism; killing soldiers and police is such an evil (Brenner, 1974, 1982).

I would add that on a mass contagion of hysteria and unconscious feelings of inadequacy, the Orwellian message in a world where unconscious rage is salved with social justice by violent riotous behavior that favors one group as elite and all others as subordinate nowadays is a new norm we must distance ourselves from to keep sane in an increasingly insane world.

As the French prime minister, quoted earlier, stated in relation to a tragic murder, police, Jews, Christians, and journalists who express their views deserve the respect of being called leaders, and we may have a lot to learn from them as examples of civic responses to complex situations. The "pigs" who were to wear wings were police officers who were both minority officers and, indeed, were members of the very communities they were characterized and stereotyped by their assassin as being separatist, elitist, and alienated from, fueled by what he felt was the racially motivated death by police officers, namely the truly tragic deaths of Gardner and Brown, which have been viewed as caused by excited delirium syndrome. As the assassin psychotically acted out his own rage against them in cold blood, Ismaayl is not an outlier, but old news and quite dull-drum as a murderer looking for a cause to murder for and with.

Stop, pause, and redirect for a moment and consider the self-proclaimed social justice guru of the Symbionese Liberation Army (SLA), Field Marshal Donald DeFreeze, who killed Oakland

Schools Superintendent Marcus Foster with dum-dum bullets laced with cyanide. Dr Marcus Foster happened to be one of the pioneer Black American educators who embraced all students and parents in need of social support and community outreach. His murder with dum-dum bullets with cyanide, and the extreme cruelty in kidnapping Patricia Hearst, was said to be social justice. Whose justice is socialized in divisive and hateful chasms that echo in narcissistic cocoons. Such chambers of horrors are where real justice is forgotten and hidden, hiding under pyres of loss awaiting our own redemption as mental health practitioners and community leaders who ought to become more wont toward abjuring being led as pawns and activists, not scientist-practitioners who are empathic to all citizens in need, including the Centurions on our front lawn.

As an elected official it is reasonable that one must clearly separate with qualifications what is one's personal opinion and one's use of authority to focus on individual issues of predilection. Otherwise abuse of authority in office and not elected representation becomes the staple of government over citizens as objects, rather than participant citizens. Communities represent many different cultures and values, including individual differences in opinions in the United States, not just a single view or culture. In gaining cultural competence it is crucial to understand the power of being a community representative, elected or not, and to exercise justice as color blind, as the great American leader Dr. Martin Luther King would write about in his tome on justice as the mantle of conscience (King, 2011).

Us versus Them in Black-White Dichotomies: Far-Left to Far-Right Fringes—Mirrors and Echoes

Milgram's classic work on obedience to authority underscored blind adherence to executives without critical discussion and dissent, where cult leaders who have led many to the fountains of euphoria and Kool-Aid laced with poison as utopia have cast all kinds of labels on the dissenting voice. Reverend Jim Jones, in the guise of civil rights, removed any real vestige of such in a biased and linear way and chose one group of disenfranchised people of color and allowed any excess to occur as long as the leadership and community condoned him as leader. Another infamous group was the Manson Family of white supremacists. Both groups of the far left and right meet in the middle where atrocities happen. Understanding history is crucial to not repeat the same mistakes again and again as George Santayana proclaimed many moons ago.

Questions Emerge with No Easy Answers: Cop Doc to Therapist's Third Ear

How do we begin healing a population of warriors who are lawful and serve to protect and defend the very freedoms we call our rights? In order to make it tangible, the majority of the free world depends most of all on a service that is a power rising to the occasion of fighting for the freedoms we all take for granted. Those freedoms are fought for in blood, sweat, and tears, as the power of the service of public safety that ranges from security all the way up in skill and training to police and special units. The point is to clearly and effectively identify terrorism as human evil (Greenstone, 2005, 2015; Grossman, 1996, 2013; Mcknight, 2012; Rudofossi, 1997, 2007, 2013; Stone, 2017; Stone & Brucato, 2019). Those who defend liberty are not ever terrorists, but those who force their will on others by the force of their authority without consultation have an increasing edge to their swords of tyranny. This epilogue includes Centurioncide because this so impacted our conversations, but is parenthetical to the entire book and yet part of its core as solution to a prevailing hidden problem as identified.

Boundaries of Empathy and Clarity for Officers as Open Doors and Shaded Windows

Clinicians seeking cultural competence in dealing with police and public safety personnel who are sworn officers in a free society understand the open-door policy is secured when the window is shaded with safety and security for freedom of expression, ventilating grief and feeling validated as distinct and valued officers. Yes, boundaries are critically important, and understanding these boundaries is crucial to asserting a real impact with real officers.

Officers who do the grunt work and deal with the messy and unclean violence the street encounters cause to hearts and souls face encounters on the real fields of freedom trammeled in pools of officers' sweat and blood, with hardly room for pause. Being an empathic therapist who can nod in agreement and listen with a third ear to the tears dropping in silence needing expression to you is crucial and important.

I know this very well, as I am not only a therapist, but also a retired street cop and police sergeant, as were the two officers who parked on Myrtle and Tompkins Avenue, on the very patrol sector 20 years earlier in the confines of the 79th Precinct. As they were assassinated in cold blood by a murderer who, due to mental illness and the capacity for human evil, carried out a biased crime—although it is not listed as biased because the law enforcement officer is not protected as the last hidden minority. Again, Centurioncide offers a center to extend and define the bias so rampant that has proliferated on police and public safety communities worldwide.

Assault or homicide against officers is largely disenfranchised. The word disenfranchised is a very misused word in psychology, and even used by known terrorists, as one can read in my book, *Terrorism as Human Evil* (Rudofossi, 2013). The franchise of all citizens is to be free of violence and harm in their life, professionally and personally. All lives matter, including blue lives, must be included in a discussion of police and community relations that promise hope, compromise, and resolution for all citizens.

Do we know any other professional so apt to be targeted and assaulted as a police officer? When one in four officers is a subject of assault this is not an individual problem or clinically rare case, but one that is a social problem and needs to be dealt with socially by those in power, as the franchise can be lost. In calling for community activism it is crucial that violence to officers on a physical and emotional level be addressed. This also needs to involve civic leaders, not demagogues in politically active positions, to responsibly care and respond to their needs. In working on unity and any community-relations approach, a dialogue must be had that opens up the facts of trauma and losses suffered by officers.

When politicians blatantly use their office to divide and conquer, rather than respect the very laws that have protected them and their legitimacy, it is no wonder officers are left feeling disenfranchised. Legal battles will result and the justice in a democratic society will be judiciously divided and persuasively argued, but needs to happen in order for the police and public safety officers to feel a sense of security and balance.

By Acknowledging Centurioncide, a Start for Healing and Rapprochement is Ignited

In this age, some politicians feel free to furiously showcase their own biases against all police without identifying that, tragically, people with physical and mental health illness will invariably die in police, medical, or firefighters' custody; instead of catalyzing solutions to lessen this tragedy and identify problems, stereotypes and stigma coexist without critical thinking. Blaming the rescuer is not a viable answer. Polarization of communities and police can be changed by unifying the individual officers with the individuals who make up the community, one step at a time.

Solutions Exist: But Problems need Solutions calling for Community-by-Community Responses

The need for cultural competence with officers by clinicians and academic leaders alike makes it crucial to discard worn and archaic myths as not only dysfunctional, but also in need of revision. Community relations are a bidirectional street where officers can feel validated and not labeled and threatened with a forceful order of being politically correct which has nothing to do with real science and more to do with para-intellectual double-speak.

Trust is the basic component of any alliance, and following through with tangible and consistent support is crucial, otherwise politicians will be seen in the eyes of the troops as not being real and caring statesmen. To become real is to become humane and to listen to the individual officer's traumatic losses beyond the veil of the deep and historic culture of the anti-blue line divided by black and white militant dichotomies to the left and right of the fault line. We are all vulnerable as human beings, and this makes us objects of division, rather than open to the mutual healing and repair so crucial to mental health and wellness.

In being a cop doc, it is crucial not to appease and stand by when human capacity toward evil is inflamed and to jump on conformity without reflecting on, stopping, pausing, and redirecting to realistic solutions. Statesmen and stateswomen can embrace this message of cultural competence in applications for real-life encounters with real police. As clinicians or students and educators, we have active listening as our best negotiator for "Our Freedom" (Rudofossi, 2009):

> **O**h, how blessed in freedom's martial tune which is willing for liberties bellow rung,
> **U**nderpinning our sacrifice—which is never free,
> **R**epublic—suffering tears and losses—regain meaning each time we say 'tis of thee …
> **F**ire will not burn out our spirit and water will not drown our plight,
> **R**elinquish our freedom sooner give up our sight,
> **E**qual to our own responsive call: Mercy tempers your chalice with justice's pearls,
> **E**ver present to guard our hard-won dreams and ideals thundering in Emerald drums,
> **D**are to say yes with bowed heads to the Ultimate meaning and stance,
> **O**ffer our heart and soul, clasped hands to our real founder invisible and eternal in awe,

May G–d balance the scales we chose to embrace—justice and liberty as Eternity's Grace! No, police are not ignorant, brutal pigs, and they are not saints or demons—police in the United States are individuals who have been called to service and each is an individual with their own personality and style. One commonality with military service personnel is that each officer/soldier serves by keeping us all safe and well, not by being different from the public, but through promoting trust, safety, and service. Police come from the public pool of citizens and ought to be given the share of their responsibility with the support and empathy from the communities they serve.

First responders pay not only with their lives but with their overall mental health. At an elementary level, the community asks of police, firefighters, and EMTs to put their own safety mentally and physically aside as they serve in some areas that are extremely hostile environments (Greenstone, 2005, 2015; Grossman, 1996, 2013; Mcknight, 2012; Rudofossi, 1997, 2007, 2013; Stone, 2017; Stone & Brucato, 2019).

In classic form, a colleague and friend of mine from Texas, Dr. Greenstone, has laid out practical and deeper levels of hostage negotiations along the lines of the founder, Dr. Harvey Schlossberg, in the harsh ecological and ethological niches of Fort Worth, Texas. In compensating officers of Hostage Negotiations Units, we are now dealing with officers being delegitimized by the very instigators of what Dr. Greenstone explains as Stockholm Syndrome (Greenstone, 2005, 2015) that is happening to officers as well.

It is with passion and a commitment to being therapeutic to drive home the unique value and special qualities officers possess and employ in serving the interests of public safety and individual rights that must be safeguarded.

Framing justice overrides the intolerance of injustice and mendacity, which not only rhymes with audacity, but is its doormat.

Centurioncide is a pandemic when the very first line of responders are undermined and defeated by the columns within the society they have born from. The side of communism and fascism has shown tragic results when either are lauded as truths. Doing police work, as doing science and health interventions, is sloppy and messy as human beings are fallible and imperfect. That is not to say the ideal of doing excellent and committed work is to be overhauled and cast aside, but it is to say that reality is critical in understanding that police and first responders are not saints and not demons, but are called in during crisis to do the artful imposition of both.

Resilience over Centurioncide: Special Agent Pistone's Veracity over Mendacity

Joe galloped over the mendacity with veracity as we push backward and review the lessons offered in this book; he has read each chapter and the fluid rush of the refined straits to rivulets and gulfs where he shared himself honestly and without fanfare.

Special Agent Joe Pistone will always be a legend in the world of blue. Let's not allow a great hero, Special Agent Joe D. Pistone as a heroic pioneer and genius in his domain, to be left aside without real understanding and applause while he is with us! So would some tabloid commentator be minimizing his intellectual and soulful prowess to luck? Genius is more than an IQ and EQ tabulation—genius is the punctuation one impresses on reality's juncture. Unseen and hidden in plain sight and allowed expression and understanding for use in the consumers of its own product and field is the test of its substance and durability. Joe Pistone's life as special agent, instructor, author, and investigator has made the right make-up of genius as his cup. I sipped from this cup because I can lift a scent of light from the shades that darken the world.

Smelling out Fiction: Omertà, Hitman, and Mafioso are More than Operatic Sopranos

Being able to smell out fact from fiction and leave broken plates to illumine our paths once ground down and refined into lessons learned is a key to paving any road. The unknown is now better known in the psychology of the deep cover.

On the other hand, convenient self-righteous summaries that minimize Donnie Brasco to undigestible bits of misinformation don't fit reality, such as stating Joe Pistone was a great actor.

Wiseguys, as viewed by millions, offer some inner path of darkness to redemption in all of us. They too have their own stories to tell, and mostly unknown and unheard, in the relationships Special Agent Joe Pistone shared while he closed down the families, redeemed their humanity in their differences and traits. Differing in the complexion of their reflective hues and relationships with Joe is enlightening for the next deep-cover operative and detective as much as the clinician who also is challenged with formidable inroads to treatment via rehabilitation.

As a street cop, I would never trade in some of the best years of my life assisting other folks who were salty, peppery, and black, white, yellow, and red and much more—most never had their voices heard, but in our interactions and lessons learned on both sides of the inner fences we created, others will once again re-create, and some new officers will discover.

The open mind and society owe the one allegiance Joe Pistone teaches so well. The diligence of saying in his dialogue the same commitment to expression in mental toughness he taught me and, hopefully, you: no human being is a record needing to repeat himself on the stylus of someone else's recorder and player. He lived what Sinatra sung, he did it his way. He was the first to say it's not the only way, but it was my way on the highway of freedom of expression, speech, and intellect. Organized crime included omertà: silencing the expression of dialectic for one theory in the race to victor the vanquished can only result in the closing of the human mind and psyche. It is no wonder that Joe Pistone opened the doors to dissembling the closed society of organized crime. Humanity is certainly a worthy participant in the animal and plant kingdom; perhaps without hubris it appears we are dominant. With understanding, we may earn our way without stepping on so many shrubs, rabbit holes, or snails.

To honor Special Agent Joe Pistone as a hero with a thousand faces of heroism is to add justice to his extraordinary life. To do so is to realize explicitly that the gift one is born with is not as important as the intrinsic gift to cultivate and harness with passion that very gift until it is fruitful and flowers. The shield is not a barrack of national socialisms, or isms period, where one is stuck rolling up the Sisyphean wheel in the grasp of an eternal Pyrrhic victory where each morning repeats the same Orwellian task once again reified as endless futility.

In this regard, the weary cop doc and agent that Joe and I present give young men and women the possibility of their future within the wells dug deep in the pillars of tradition and values as virtue, where liberal traditions and freedoms are conserved in the dialectical process of both.

If there is still a doubt of Special Agent Joseph Dominick Pistone's integrity and moral compass, turn back the pages, please reread this book, until the message is clear. The message hinted at in this book, is that most cops—let me pause—I mean even tenacious street cops, couldn't come near to achieving what Joe Pistone did achieve. Dream and make your own markings on the path of your own life by understanding you only compete with yourself to be the best you can be personally. In seeing what could be done by Agent Pistone, imagine what good you could do as the officer you are in your own unique way; no one can replicate anyone else and it is by understanding yourself first that you can understand others.

Finally, honor is not a goal for Joe Pistone, but it was, is, and remains my goal for him. The point is that when good men and women are silent about evil, people who intentionally perpetrate evil in turn invigorate revolting evil in perpetuity. In synchrony, we all need heroes and models to fight what is revolting in humanity and in doing so emulate the best of the finest in becoming our own personal best! Joe stood up to it all and to this we owe him honor, well-called!

In turn, if good men and women who are skilled as students and practitioners in psychology, criminology, psychiatry, and law do not bring attention to the possibility, hope, and optimism in tragic moments of what is possible in extraordinary heroism, then our modeling health and good behavior is lost in moral depravity. For what is best in being human beings is sown amidst violence, poverty of conscience, and depravity of morality. Thirst for compassion is parched in hunger when no heroes exist. The dim fire of soulfulness fades into obscure shrill gasps for hope. In an age without heroes, the youth that aspire toward good in most of us and society as a whole are wont to find models to scaffold off the ledge of ignorance and violence. Service with integrity and bravery is a fire escape. Many fires exist worldwide. Discretion, not reduction of critical thinking and discernment, can liberate the new special agents and cop docs to pursue the roads they must navigate in proscribing limitations of bold and brave tackling of terrorism and crushing oppression based on religion, race, and culture. Your own ability to think is the culmination of a wave with unlimited quantum possibilities, rather than the field of delimited prescriptions where police are reduced to political suasions rather than poesis and persuasion.

Let me bring this point to life as my own experience as a young 25-year-old police rookie. I responded to an elderly man grabbing hold of memories as he urinated on himself and pleaded from the fiftieth floor in public housing to help him up, and to not have EMS bring him to a nursing home. If I betrayed his trust as a veteran, that he would do himself in at some point later was a true threat. He looked into my eyes and let me know this truth and dare to respect him and not reduce him into an old man needing to be remanded to a nursing home, undignified and unheard.

I remember having the untoward task of convincing this 88-year-old gentleman that life, even when not as vivid as before, is still worth clinging to and with human dignity.

He said what can an 88-year-old invalid do but coil into a ball and hope to be left unharried in his own world? Leave him alone, or else. Well, I sat with him in the urine-stenched hall of his untended apartment in the city projects. I told this gentleman that Sophocles had the same dilemma as he did now. I let him know Socrates settled his account in Ancient Greece successfully. I said as I recall, when Sophocles the playwright was being readied to be whisked into a forced home for invalids, he retained his right to a trial in the Polis of Athens. Sophocles gently took out his hand-written *Oedipus at Colonus*. He firmly said to his judges, "if you think the author of this work who is truly incontinent at times, cannot control his urine at times, must be placed in forced institutional care, then I will do as told. But first hear my account by reading my book." They did! As we all know, Sophocles kept his freedom with some help from his friends. He went on to write three versions of Oedipus that we have to this day. Oedipus was the linchpin of many debates from the Forum to Vienna cafes as Freud modified his own ingenuity on the oldest yarn. (The purpose of sharing this experience is to relate to you as the reader that I wish I could claim I was a saintly police officer, that I knew exactly what to say from some patrol guide order, but I didn't! I wanted desperately to help this senior gentleman while being a third of his age.)

I think at that time I pondered in my own existential unconscious-conscience that if I was graced to be 88 years old, I hoped to have my own mind—as he did. Another wish was that I could articulate grief as well as he did. A third wish was that, on another level, I felt helpless and pained with him empathically. Selfishly, I also pondered, I hoped someone would care for me too, and convince me not to give up on life, as I did with him if I reached his Rubicon and would help encourage me to cross it. In that hot August day, we both made it down the stairs, as he did not like elevators, with help from my police partner, and he choose life and social services assistance. I know nothing further from his life and future. I impacted on this moment in his life and he left me with memories that I choose to embrace with purpose and shared lessons in respecting him—case in point which I am sure you understand and get. The soulfulness of a regular street cop, EMT, ER nurse, and doc and cop doc is largely unheard and unnoticed; I hope with his small segment of experience it is noticed as a speck in a larger sea.

Pauses that call us to reflect and mediate on an agent committed to justice. The deadly and darker lions are not lacking in education, experience, and wisdom, but denying some are ingenious is a deadly den one may fall into. Sadly, the history of humanity does not evidence that the humanization of brutality is parallel and linear with the gathering of degrees. But the degree of justice has always aligned with **f**idelity, **b**ravery, and **i**ntegrity. The archway to wisdom calls for empathy, compassion, and wisdom to jettison the bulwark of integrity with courage. That not all FBI agents, as not all police officers, of any hue and background, are equal and even decent is a very painful truth for all of us as LEOs to acknowledge when the shield becomes used to proffer favor and interest, rather than justice and integrity to serve the people as "sheepdogs" as Professor Lt Colonel Grossman calls us in our united call for duty! Humility is the crown of the special agent and police investigator who discerns with discretion used wisely. It is in the reflection of what is visible in deeds by an invisible, but ever-present source of all our good, as Creator, that any ghosts in the machine of politics with the audacity to correct the worthiest of callings for diminutive returns of lifeless black and white tones is vapid and colorless regardless of claims.

Pith in the moments of life is worthy in all its color, its messy and not correctible collages, but experiences which is what life itself is all about. Not for our time only, but timelessly asserting lessons learned here. No illusions exist in what we do by living up to our vow of loyalty to uphold as sacred service of Centurions. All shields may need polishing, but it is one that covers all citizens, whether undercover or not. The shield serves all the varieties of human experience and life well worth preserving, as the tradition of the Centurions that cover us one and all, now and forever!

Again, thank you for your sacrifice for all of us, Special Agent Joseph Dominick Pistone! Agent Pistone experienced potentially being stung many times in his identity mode as Donnie Brasco; sipping *atropa belladonna* in the shade of many nights alone, and with no back-up, Joe remained straight and on point. This survival anomaly must include the psychological and spiritual peace to bring it forward, with meaning and purpose. Outside of sensationalism, miraculously, only a bitter taste was left, but not terminal bitterness. For anyone who knows the temptations of the streets and the violence of the hood, this is not a miracle, but multiple miracles in multiple contexts. To me, that is the life preserver, and the preservation to wish and embrace that despair is the prison we make in our own minds. All lives matter, but blue blood is truly the coronation of the sacrifice outside of me, myself, and I in an age of entitlement and blind narcissism. You prove that molds can be broken in extraordinary, inspiring ways! In your case, Special Agent Joseph Dominick Pistone, you stood by JFK's admonition, "Ask not what your country can do for you, but what you can do for your country."

We all salute you Special Agent Joseph D. Pistone! As you've said, and I repeat with your own added passion and reason: **There go I, but for the Grace of G–d, go I…**

References

Brenner, C. (1974). *An elementary textbook of psychoanalysis*. New York: Anchor.
Brenner, C. (1982). *The mind in conflict*. New York: International University Press.
Greenstone, J. L. (2005). *The elements of police hostage and crisis negotiations: Critical incidents and how to respond to them*. Boca Raton, FL: Routledge.
Greenstone, J. L. (2015). *Emotional first aid: A field guide to crisis intervention and psychological survival*. Duluth, MN: Whole Persons Associates.
Grossman, D. (1996). *On killing: The psychological cost of learning to kill in war and society*. New York: Little, Brown.
Grossman, D. (2013). *On combat: The psychology and physiology of deadly conflict in war and peace*. New York: Hachette.
Jung, C. G. (1955). *Modern man in search of soul*. San Diego, CA: Harcourt Brace.
King, M. L. (2011). *The trumpet of conscience*. New York: Beacon Press.
Mcknight, D. (2012). *Streets of Mogadishu: Leadership at its best, political correctness at its worst*. Rockledge, FL: Freedom Press.
Rudofossi, D. M. (1997). *The impact of trauma and loss on affective differential profiles of police officers*. Bell Harbor, MI: Bell and Howell.
Rudofossi, D. M. (2007). *Working with traumatized police-officer patients: A clinician's guide to complex PTSD syndromes in public safety professionals*. New York and London: Routledge.

Rudofossi, D. M. (2009). *A cop doc's guide to public safety complex trauma syndromes: Using five police personality styles.* New York and London: Routledge.

Rudofossi, D. M. (2013). *A cop doc's guide to understanding terrorism as human evil: Healing from complex trauma syndromes for military, police, and public safety officers and their families.* New York and London: Routledge.

Stone, M. (2017). *The anatomy of evil.* New York: Prometheus Books.

Stone, M., & Brucato, G. (2019). *The new evil: Understanding the emergence of modern violent crime.* New York: Prometheus.

Valls, Manuel (French Prime Minister) as quoted from Associated Press, Sunday January 11, 2015.

INDEX

abnormal psychology 51
abysmal low frustration tolerance 117–118
accommodation 146
accountability 113
active analysis 101, 116–117, 184
active learning 11
active listening 11, 19, 20, 29, 39–40, 42, 126
adaptation 2, 4, 6–7, 13–14, 36–37, 82, 96–97, 124–125; boundaries as 78–81; problems of 27–28
adaptive functional dissociation 12–13, 16, 33–34, 47, 53, 59, 96, 110, 138–139; and alexithymia 157; process 122
adaptive functioning 35, 85
adaptive-intuitive resilient LEO personality style 151–152
adaptive intuitive sensibility 132
adaptive necessities 85
addictive personality traits 112, 118, 128
administrators 41–42; judgements 124
adrenaline rushes 171, 192
agape 162
agendas 42
aggression 117–118
aging process 111
alexithymia, and adaptive functional dissociation 157
alienists 51
altruism 97
Anastasia, A. 172
angles of ethological affordances 81, 96–97
anomaly 11–12
anthropomorphic assessment 124
anti-police biased ecology 38–39
antisocial behavior, and endogenous wiring 161
ant-lion, the 74–75
apathy 18
Arendt, H. 85

assimilation 38, 146
assistance, deferring 33
authenticity 93, 140

balance of power 127
becoming 85
becoming real 82–88
behaviors, limiting 100
being 85
being-yourself 29, 38
beliefs, standing up for 108–109
belonging 90
Benedict, R. 16
Benner, A. 151–152
Berg, M. 147, 148
blind adherence 198
blood loyalty 2
blue blood 15, 155
Boas, F. 5, 16, 41, 46
Bonanno crime family 31, 32; marriage of families 57–63, 136–139, 142–143, 183
bonds, developing 64–65
book smarts 24, 27–29, 33, 41–42, 46, 47
Bornstein, H. M. 97–98
bosses 90–91
Boston Strangler 171–172
boundaries 5, 30; acceptance of 98; as adaptations 78–81; camouflage as 25–26; concentric circles 72, 78; definition 74; learning 80; in Mafia culture 72, 73, 76–78; as milestones 78–81; multi-cultural 73–75; permeability 85; punctuating 6; respecting 44; setting 2, 166–168
Brasco, Donnie, legend 4
Brenner, C. 13, 20–21, 50, 82, 90, 91, 177, 197
Brinsley, I. 197
bull's-eye focuses 123

calculated risk 137–138
camouflage 24; as boundary 25–26; definition 25; ecological-ethological niches and 25–26; mimicking 25–26; survival and 25–26
Campbell, J. 5, 88, 146
casebook 1–2
causality 10
censoring 96
Centurioncide 14, 155, 156, 165–166, 191–192, 193–204; acknowledging 199; and empathy 199; healing 198–199; and leadership 194, 196, 196–198; officers expressing dissent 193–195; pandemic 201; political force 194; psychological damage 195; resilience over 201; scapegoating 194–195; solutions 196–198, 200–201; and voicing dissent 195–196
Centurions 155, 204
chain of command 91
chimpanzees 29
choices 139
clinical case supervision 50
closet narcissism 50
commitment 16
community leaders 196–197
community relations 200
compassion 157, 195, 202
compassionate mercy identity mode 34–35
compromise formations 13, 20–21, 50
compromises 5, 13, 185
conflict 5, 68
conformity 97
conscience, lack of 161
constitutional safeguards, overstepping 194
control 183
cop docs 11, 12, 20, 37, 39, 42, 200
counter-transference 66
courage 16, 39, 162
creativity 24, 59, 104, 114, 138
crime, and oedipal strivings 177
criminal behavior, and endogenous wiring 161
Cuban Missile Crisis 126–127
cues, reading 131
cult leaders 198
cultural-anthropologic paradigm 5
cultural belonging 90
cultural changes, law enforcement 12
cultural competence 146, 200
cultural context 72
cultural differences 41
cultural niches 169
cultural rules, continuum of 72
cultural sensitivity 26
culture, outliers of 89–90

Dades, T. 108
danger 10
darkness, allure of 13
Darley, M. J. 97
death, danger of 10

death threats 4
decency, overriding 88–89
decision-making 41, 180–184
decisive action 137–138
deep cover 9; definition 10–11, 20; false myth about 66; hypothetical constructs 10
deep-cover operatives, micro-culture 1–2
deep-cover survival 13–14
defenses 50
DeFreeze, D. 197–198
de-individuation 77–78, 79, 97
democracy 193
DeSalvo, A. 171–172
destiny 179
Destrudo 13, 20–21, 90, 118, 192
developmental path 5
deviancy 77
dialogue 19
dignity 203
diplomacy 32, 58, 59, 63, 76, 115, 177
discernment 120–121, 122–125, 137–138, 148, 158
discipline 80–81
disconnect 39
discretion 131
discrimination 120, 122–123, 124, 131
disequilibrium 36
disloyalty 73
dissent, voicing, and Centurioncide 195–196
dissociation 29, 34
dissociative functioning 85
distancing 159
domestic world 82, 83–84
Donnie Brasco (film) 37–38, 110, 161
Donnie Brasco identity mode 32, 37, 38, 50, 51, 54, 72–73, 82–88, 90, 92–93, 97, 129, 151, 164–169, 204
doppelgänger, the 51, 92, 101, 104, 105
double identity mode 51
doubles 92, 110
double-speak, as psychological damage 195
dress codes 33
drives 13, 90
drive theory 13
dynamic equilibrium 101, 104
dysfunctional identity 36

Eco-Ethological Existential Analytic, adaptive functional dissociation 96
eco-ethological existential equanimity 145–146
eco-ethological niches 13, 25–26, 31, 38, 47, 50, 96, 125, 152, 157
Ecological-Ethological Existential Analysis 4, 5, 11, 27, 35–36, 43–44, 47, 87, 156, 187
ecological milieu 50
ecological niches 51, 59, 82, 84
education 103
Einstein, A. 90
Ellis, A. 145
emotional flexibility 24

emotional intelligence 2, 24, 46, 59
emotional leakage 25
emotional motivation 2
emotional overload 82
emotional transference 65–66
emotion, states of 24
emotive behavior therapy 145
empathy 111, 195, 199, 203
empowerment 187
encounter 53–55, 69
endogenous wiring, and antisocial behavior 161
endurance 184
envy 136
equanimity 131
equilibrium 101–102, 104
Eros 13, 20–21, 90
essential motivation 159–160
ethics 37
ethological accommodation 96
ethological affordances, angles of 81, 96–97
ethological intelligence 24
ethological motivation 2, 28, 29, 73
evidence 164
exhibitionistic narcissism 50
existential analysis 50, 126, 133, 137, 162, 187
existential awareness 64
existential center 92
existential perspective 89
existential struggles 12
existential unconscious-conscience 203
experience, sharing 39–40
experimenter effect 146–148
expert practitioners, humility and respect of 39–43
exposure, threat of 14

family hierarchy 2
family life 82, 83–84
FBI 34, 51, 79–81, 126, 180
FBI academy 164–165
fears, confronting 101
Ferenczi, S. 101, 116–117, 184
fiction, smelling out 201–204
first responders 33, 34, 155, 200
fitting in 2, 29, 32, 64, 97, 105, 164, 168
force, corrupting influence 193
forensic psychological perspective, killers 171–174
Foster, M., murder of 198
Frankl, V. 16, 50, 92, 101, 102, 159–160, 179, 187
free-association 82–83, 145
Freud, S. 13, 20–21, 50, 90, 147, 203
Fromm, E. 147
frustration tolerance 103–104, 117–118
functional dissociation 138–139

gangster identity mode 54, 110, 122
gangster's world, encounter in the 53
Gemini Bar-Club 57
gestalt 122
ghosting 164

gifting 162
Gilmartin, M. 14
goals 28
Goleman, D. 2
Goodall, J. 30, 31
Gotti, John 96
Gravano, Sammy the Bull 90, 95
Greenstone, J. L. 200
grief 194
Grossman, D. 90, 172, 203
guardedness 14–15
guilt 173, 187

habits, learning new 124–125
Haeckel, E. 114–115, 117
Hammarskjold, D. 76, 77
Hare, R. D. 161, 172
hatred 139
Hayakawa, I. S. 145, 146
healing 15
Heidegger, M. 85
Heisenberg, W. 146–148
heroism 160
hero, victory of the 88
heuristic approach 104
heuristic exploration 100–101, 116
high frustration tolerance 103–104, 117–118
Hippocratic Oath 16
homework 32
homicided 15
honor 162, 202
Hoover, J.E. 12, 54–55, 79, 92, 126, 165, 166
hostage negotiations 89
human dignity 203
humanity 141
human nature 142, 147
humility 81, 116, 136, 178, 203–204
hyper-intuitive 61–62, 148
hyper-intuitive personality style 126, 128–129
hypervigilance 14–15, 16, 122
hypothetical constructs, deep cover 10

IAB [Internal Affairs Bureau] 2, 45
identity: hidden 54; innovation 59; integrity of own 105; maintaining own 39; reclaiming 113
identity innovation 5
identity modes 13, 24, 26, 29–32, 34–35, 36, 37, 38, 39, 51, 101; compassionate mercy 34–35; conflict 152; crossing into 105; definition 51–52; distinct 54; Donnie Brasco 32, 37, 38, 50, 51, 54, 72–73, 82–88, 90, 92–93, 97, 129, 151, 164–169, 204; double 51; gangster 54, 110, 122; LEO warrior 34; living 123; loyalty to 72–73; rescue 110; shifting 106–107; special agent 79–80; take down and collar 34
idiographic assimilation 96
illegitimate force, disempowering 44–45
immersion 33, 37
indefatigable human spirit 16

Indelicato, Bruno 63–64, 92–93, 177
Indelicato, Sonny Red 177
individual differences 11, 88–89
individuation 79, 97, 97–98
inequity, as psychological damage 195
infiltration 2, 27, 28–29, 31, 32, 36, 37–38, 62, 75, 83, 103, 166
infiltration propensities 103–104, 117–118
informants 16; assessment 41–42
information, paradigms 12
ingenuity 4, 31, 37, 58, 105–106, 107–108, 109, 114, 121, 129, 138
initiation rites 24
inner view, hidden 84–85
integrity 14, 26, 107, 109, 123, 137–138, 202
intelligence 24, 27–28, 29, 33, 41, 46, 47, 59, 87–89, 91; circle of 114–115
Internal Affairs 2, 45
internalized witnessing 187
intuition 112
intuitive sensibility 26–27, 87, 182
Italian American culture 104

jealousy 176–178
jingoism 196
journalism, sloppy 136
Jung, G. C. 50
justice 203

Kernberg, O. 50
killers 88–90, 94, 111, 133–135, 139–140, 157, 161; forensic psychological perspective 171–174; psychopaths 174
killing 63–65, 74, 88–90, 92–93
King, Martin Luther 198
knowledge 101
Kuklinski, Richard 64, 174

labeling 46
Laing, R. D. 77, 79
Latané, B. 97
law enforcement: cultural changes 12; media portrayal 38; rules 80–81
law enforcement paradigm 102
leadership, and Centurioncide 194, 196, 196–198
leakage 66
legislation 193
legislators, judgements 124
LEO warrior identity mode 34
Likert scale 72
limitations 100
loneliness 60
loss 11; difficulty in expressing 156; distancing via screen memories 159; multiple potential experiences of 151; unexpressed 156
loyalty: Mafia 16, 17–18; police 15; walls of 2

McKnight, D. 90
macro-society 157

made man, the 38, 82–85, 93, 94, 142
Mafia and Mafia culture: boundaries in 72, 73, 76–78; chain of command 177; codes and customs 37; control 174; as deviancy 173–174; ecological niches 51, 84; ecology of violence 141; explicit rules 73; family 6, 25–26; family hierarchy 2, 78–79; family relatives 174–175; killing 63–65, 74, 78, 88–90; morals 37; multi-cultural boundaries 73–75; new habits 124–125; Omertà 16, 17–18, 73, 78, 202; punishments 73; rules 2, 72, 141; upward flow of money 125; upward movement 125
Mafia liaisons 127
maladaptive dysfunctional dissociation 33, 36, 53
map 124, 145–146
markings 76, 77, 78, 84–85, 95, 100, 151
Maslow, A. 125
Mead, M. 5, 16, 41
meaning, finding 160, 179
meaningful connection 141
media ecological framework 145–146
media, the 126; perspective on policing 154–155; sloppy journalism 136
Meloy, R. 172
memory 61, 151
mental health 151; and voicing dissent 196
mental toughness 4, 28, 38, 42, 53, 56, 66, 76, 88, 97, 97–98, 106–107, 108, 109, 110, 111, 112–114, 121, 169, 202
Messina, Joe 141, 142
metaphor, use of 106
micro-culture, deep-cover operatives 1–2
Milgram, S. 198
Milwaukee situation 180–184
mimicking 25–26, 97
mindfulness 1–2, 15
mindset 23, 63, 82
Mirra, Tony 29, 31, 63, 84, 85–86, 88, 89, 90, 94, 111, 128, 142, 158–159, 169, 171; personality traits 133–134, 134, 135, 139, 141, 160–161, 174–175
misinformation 96
mobbing 26
moral compass 92, 111, 124, 202
moral integrity 97
mortality, dealing with 85
motivation 13, 47, 62, 187; deeper aspect of 55–57; emotional 2; essential 159–160; ethological 2, 28, 29, 73; underlying 93
multiple personality disorder 37, 51
multiple worlds 13
Murder Inc 57
myths 93

Napolitano, Sonny Black 5, 15, 29, 60, 63–64, 65, 87, 88, 89, 90, 91, 94–95, 113, 142, 159, 160, 161, 171, 174, 176, 183; denouement message 162–164; family relatives 175; oedipal attachment

with Donnie Brasco 177; personality traits 134–135, 139–141, 157–158, 175; power plays 128–135
narcissism 50, 128
navigational coordinates 111
negotiation 127
neighborhood, the 169
noetic dimension 45, 50, 69, 106, 110, 159–160, 171, 185, 186–187
noetic-values 12, 21

oedipal strivings, and crime 177
Omertà 2, 16, 17–18, 73, 78, 202
ontogenetic charismatic genius 117
ontogeny 115, 117
operational definitions 4
Operation Donnie Brasco: beginnings 164–169; closed down 158, 162, 183
Operation Underworld 126
original deviancy, capitulation to 117
oscillating equilibrium 104
outcomes 104
outliers 4, 11–12

pacificism 90
paradigms 12
paradoxical intention 101, 137
participant observers 41
patience 103
patriotic shadows 126
performance 4
Perlin, M. 101, 110
personality dynamics 50, 133–135, 139–141, 143, 157–158, 160–161, 174–176
personality, establishing 82–88, 90
personality style 126
personology 89–91
phenotypic development 12
phylogenic development 12, 114–115, 117
Pistone, Joe 59; achievement 11, 15, 58, 62, 84, 110, 127–129, 162, 169, 183–184, 192, 201, 202; active listening and learning 11; adaptive functional dissociation 12–13; adaptive-intuitive resilient LEO personality style 151–152; anomaly 12; background 55–56, 164; becoming Donnie Brasco 164–169; books 9; boundary setting 166–168; casebook 1; contract on Bruno 63–64, 92–93; creative genius 59; creativity 114; developmental path 5; diplomacy 59; discernment 148, 158; emotional intelligence 46; FBI training 79–81; frustration tolerance 103–104; hyper-intuitive 61–62; identity innovation 5; indefatigable human spirit 16; ingenuity 4, 58, 105–106, 107–108, 114, 121, 129; initiation rites 24; as inspiration 184–185; integrity 202; intelligence 27–28, 91, 176; intuition 112; intuitive sensibility 26–27, 87, 182; journey 88, 192; life journey 9; living arrangement stand 82–83, 166–167; marriage of families 57–63, 136–139, 142–143, 183; memory 61; mental toughness 4, 53, 88, 97–98, 111, 112–114, 121, 126, 131, 167, 202; Milwaukee situation 180–184; mindset 63; moral compass 202; motivation 55–57; naval career 55–56, 56–57, 112; navigates Sonny Black's power plays 128–135; navigational strategy 132–133; as outlier 4; outliers 12; outlook 139; perspective on policing 154–156; philosophy 179; problem solving 180–184; religious faith 91–92, 178; resilience 201; sacrifice 204; Schindler comparison 106–108, 109; sense of duty 56; strategy 124; training 23–24; traumatic events experienced 170; *Unfinished Business* 112; use of mobbing 26; vision 5, 53–68; *The Way of the Wiseguy* 32; wife's accident 68; wisdom 105–106, 115
police: funding 155; loyalty in 15
police officers, reductionistic caricatures of 28, 48
police work 36
policing, JP's perspective on 154–156
political correctness 90
political force 194
Postman, N. 145–146
potentialities, maze of fatal 178
potentiality 125
power 141
power relationship 96
pragmatic intelligence 59
predators 14
prejudgments 193
primate behavior 30–32
problem identification 42
problem solving 180–184
Procrustean method, the 73–74
projections 93
projective identification 50
protect and defend credo 185
protection, lattice of 113
psychoanalysis 50
psychological costs 2
psychological damage, inequity as 195
psychological imagination 11–12, 12–13
psychological mindedness 12–13
psychological-physical space 167
psychological survival 138
psychologists/psychiatrists, role 37, 50
psychopathology 51
psychopaths 174
PTSD 36, 151

Quantico, Virginia 79–80
quantum intra-psychic moment of trauma, the 45, 61, 69, 145
questions 3–6

racism 197
rapport skills 104
rats 2

reality 39, 87
reality-based knowledge 96
reality checks 74
recognition skills 104
reductionistic caricatures, of police officers 28, 48
regressed toward the mean 109, 117
Reichmann, F. F. 147
Reik, T. 55
relationships, developing 64–65
religious faith 91–92, 178, 179–180
representative government 193–194
rescue identity mode 110
researcher credibility 6–7
resilience 10, 138, 151, 178–179, 201
respect 141, 195
responsibility 44; diffusion of 97
responsibleness 187, 191–192
risk, calculated 137–138
risks 126
role playing 27, 28–29, 66
Rudofossi, D.M. 6–7, 9, 145, 187, 203
Ruggiero, Benjamin Lefty 60, 61, 62, 63, 65, 84, 87, 90, 91, 94, 96, 105, 112–113, 118, 122–123, 128–131, 132, 136–138, 142, 175–178; Milwaukee situation 180–184; personality traits 133, 134, 135, 161, 174
rules: danger of violating 32; Mafia 2, 72, 141
rules of engagement 85–86

Sabella, Mike 60, 62, 113, 141, 159, 180–184
sacrifice 204
Samenow, E. S. 161
Samenow, S. 172
Santayana, G. 198
Sapir, E. 41
Sapir–Whorf hypothesis 41
scaffolding 109, 127
scarring 14
Schindler, O. 106–108, 109
schizos-phrenos 77
Schlossberg, H. 200
science 192
screen images 93
screen memories, distancing loss via 159
security, need for 51
self-destructive modalities 187
self-reliance 180–184
self-worth 169
sense of duty 56
sensitivity 77–78, 97
serial killers 171–172
shadows 87–88, 89, 92, 93, 126, 164, 166, 167
Sicilian culture 78
sit-downs 63–64, 69, 78, 98, 141
sixth sense 54
sloppy journalism 136
social distance model 97
social injustice 197
societal obligation 44–45

Socrates 203
Socratic method 89–90, 145
Solevetchik, J. 50Southwick, S. 178–179
special agent identity mode 79–80
special ops 66
specificity 77–78, 97–98
split personality 37, 92–93
spontaneity 103
standard operating procedures 33, 35, 47–48
statesmanship 63
static equilibrium 102, 104
Sternberg, R. 114
Stockholm Syndrome 85, 200
Stone, M. 161, 172
strategy 124, 132–133
street smarts 27–29, 33, 46, 54, 57, 106–107, 176
strengths 85
stress, multiple layers of 178
stress relief 43
success: distinguishing 120; prediction of 103
support group 92
support, lack of 10, 60, 66–67
survival 2, 6–7; camouflage and 25–26
Symbionese Liberation Army 197–198
symbiotic relationships 139

take down and collar identity mode 34
teamwork 29
tenacity 5
terror attacks 90
Thanatos 90, 192
therapeutic intervention, undercover work as 111
therapeutic jurisprudence 101, 110
third ear 53, 55, 62, 91
threat, of violence 23, 174; constant 151
three mistresses, the 66–68, 68, 74, 82, 91, 157, 170
tightrope walking metaphor 91, 178
timing 103
tokens 162
tough-mindedness 12–13, 83, 89, 126, 131, 167, 192
toughness 24
Trafficante, Santo, Jr. 127
Trafficante, Santos 58, 62, 142
training 23–24, 39–40, 66
transcendental unconscious, the 102
transference 65–66, 147
transitioning 24
trauma 11, 15, 19; cumulative 35–36, 45, 194; dramatized versions 47; ecology of 142; emotional weight 35; finding meaning 179; frequency of events 169; hidden 194; minefield of 184; number of events experienced 170; potential 151; quantum psychic moments 45, 61, 69, 145; tsunami of 47
traumatic loss 145, 146
treatment milieu 147
trust 16, 83, 113, 127, 142, 154, 164, 177, 203

uncertainty principle 146, 148
unconscious, the 93, 96, 160
undercover agents: assessment 40; operational world 31
undercover investigative work 10–11
undercover work, as therapeutic intervention 111
unpredictability 32

Valachi, J. M. 90, 95
Valls, M. 196, 197
verbal aikido 127, 129, 131
victims 94
violence: ecology of 141; threat of 23, 174

vision 5
vulnerability 170; insulating self from 180–184

walls, setting up 2
Wambaugh, J., *The Blue Knight* 36
weakness 65
Whorf, B.L. 41
wisdom 101, 102, 103–104, 105–106, 110, 115, 125, 203
wish fulfillment 159
world views 87; colliding 53–55
World War II 126

xenophobia 196

Printed in the United States
by Baker & Taylor Publisher Services